J.K. LASSER'S™

INVESTOR'S
TAX
GUIDE

Look for these and other titles from J.K. Lasser™—Practical Guides for All Your Financial Needs.

J.K. Lasser's Pick Winning Stocks by Edward F. Mrkvika Jr.

J.K. Lasser's Invest Online by LauraMaery Gold and Dan Post

J.K. Lasser's Year-Round Tax Strategies by David S. De Jong and Ann Gray Jakabin

J.K. Lasser's Taxes Made Easy for Your Home-Based Business by Gary W. Carter

J.K. Lasser's Finance and Tax for Your Family Business by Barbara Weltman

J.K. Lasser's Pick Winning Mutual Funds by Jerry Tweddell with Jack Pierce

J.K. Lasser's Your Winning Retirement Plan by Henry K. Hebeler

J.K. Lasser's Winning With Your 401(K) by Grace Weinstein

J.K. Lasser's Winning With Your 403(b) by Pam Horowitz

J.K. Lasser's Strategic Investing After 50 by Julie Jason

J.K. Lasser's Winning Financial Strategies for Women by Rhonda Ecker and Denise Gustin-Piazza

J.K. Lasser's Online Taxes by Barbara Weltman

J.K. Lasser's Pick Stocks Like Warren Buffett by Warren Boroson

J.K. Lasser's The New Tax Law Simplified

J.K. Lasser's New Rules for Retirement and Tax by Paul Westbrook

J.K. Lasser's New Rules for Small Business Taxes by Barbara Weltman

J.K. LASSER'S™

INVESTOR'S TAX GUIDE

Elaine Floyd, CFP™

John Wiley & Sons, Inc.

Published by John Wiley & Sons, Inc.
Published simultaneously in Canada.

This publication is designed to provide accurate and authoritative information in regard to the subject matter covered. It is sold with the understanding that the publisher is not engaged in rendering professional services. If professional advice or other expert assistance is required, the services of a competent professional person should be sought.

Library of Congress Cataloging-in-Publication Data:

Floyd, Elaine, 1946–
    J.K. Lasser's investor's tax guide / by Elaine Floyd.
        p. cm. -- (J.K. Lasser--practical guides for all your financial needs)
    Includes index.
    ISBN 0-471-09285-1 (pbk. : alk. paper)
        1. Investments--Taxation--Law and legislation--United States. I. Title. II. Series.

    KF6415.Z9 F58 2001
    343.7305'246--dc21   2001046850

Printed in the United States of America.
10 9 8 7 6 5 4 3 2 1

About the Author

Elaine Floyd, CFP™, is a financial writer who specializes in all areas of personal finance including investments, tax planning, retirement planning, college planning, estate planning, and insurance. A former financial consultant with a major investment firm, she writes books, articles, and online courses designed to educate, motivate, and inform. She is the coauthor (with Bambi Holzer, Senior Vice President—Investments, A.G. Edwards) of *Getting Yours: It's Not Too Late to Have the Wealth You Want, Set for Life: Financial Peace for People over 50*, and *Retire Rich: The Baby Boomer's Guide to a Secure Future* (all published by Wiley). In addition, she has collaborated with a number of other top financial consultants to produce books and articles on investing and personal finance. She lives in Bellingham, Washington.

Contents

Introduction

In May 2001, Congress passed sweeping tax legislation known as the Economic Growth and Tax Relief Reconciliation Act of 2001. While the capital gains tax was left unchanged, virtually every other area of an investor's financial life was tinkered with, including tax brackets, retirement saving, college saving, and estate planning. And because many of the rules are designed to be phased in (or out) over the next ten years, understanding the new legislation involves more than spending an evening with a tax guide and memorizing the rules that apply to you. Now, you not only must know what will be happening and when rule-wise, you also must know where *you* will be when those rules go into effect.

For example, the estate tax exemption equivalent (the amount you can leave to heirs estate tax free) will rise over the next decade; in 2010 the estate tax disappears altogether — but for one year only unless Congress acts again, which it probably will. In the old days, you could visit your attorney, put an estate plan in place, and pretty much count on current laws being in effect when you died. Now, it is impossible to know what laws will be in effect when you die, making planning extremely difficult. Because of the many complexities in the law, one pundit has claimed that no one actually read the tax bill before it was passed.

Following is a summary of key aspects of the new legislation. While it is suggested that you be mindful of the various phase-in dates, we do not recommend that you memorize the rules and consider them cast in stone. Many analysts have predicted that Congress will continue to tweak the tax code in the years ahead, and many of these rules may fly out the window before they are enacted. Our advice to investors is to have a firm grasp of your tax situation for two years at a time — the current year and the following year. This is so you can time your strategies for optimal tax impact. Beyond that, any rules you see here or anywhere else are up for grabs.

Rebate Checks

Most taxpayers got a gift from Uncle Sam last year in the form of an "advance payment" — $300 for single individuals and $600 for couples — to account for a new 10 percent bracket that went into effect January 1, 2001.

Tax Rates

Starting July 1, 2001, all marginal tax rates were reduced by one percentage point: the 28 percent bracket became the 27 percent bracket, the 31 percent bracket became the 30 percent bracket, and so on. (See Chapter 1 for details). These new brackets remain in effect through 2003. In 2004 they go down by one percentage point again and stay there through 2005. In 2006 they go down again and stay there permanently. The tax planning implications of these bracket reductions are clear: if you can defer income, do it. A thousand dollars in ordinary income will lose $386 to federal taxes this year if you are currently in the 38.6% tax bracket; wait till 2006 and you'll lose just $350.

Phase-outs Being Phased Out

Currently, if your adjusted gross income (AGI) is over a certain amount ($132,950 in 2001), you must reduce your tax deductions according to a specific formula (see Chapter 1). These phase-out rules will gradually be eliminated, but don't hold your breath. The phasing out of the phase-outs doesn't even start until 2006.

Child Tax Credit

Here's one break you can take advantage of immediately if you have kids and your income is not too high. Effective 2001, the child credit rises from $500 to $600 and remains in effect through 2004. In 2005 it rises to $700 and stays in effect through 2008; in 2009 it rises to $800, and in 2010 it rises to $1,000 and stays in effect permanently (?). The credit gets reduced by $50 for each $1,000 that your income exceeds $75,000 if single or $110,000 if married, We won't comment on the tax planning implications of this one. (Have more kids? Wait to have kids? Realize by this dollar amount attached to children that the tax credit doesn't begin to cover the cost of raising them and forget the whole idea of having a family?). Adoptive parents also get a break: the maximum credit for adoption expenses will rise from $5,000 to $10,000 in 2002.

Marriage Penalty Relief

Right now, it's generally cheaper for two people to file as single individuals than as a married couple filing jointly, assuming nothing else changes but the ring on the finger. The tax bill gradually erases this inequity by increasing the basic standard deduction for a married couple to twice that of a single individual and expanding the 15 percent tax bracket. However, the phase-in does not even start until 2005 and will not be complete until 2009. Anyone for a long engagement?

Education Incentives

One of the most important changes in the tax law was the increase in the contribution limit to education IRAs from $500 to $2,000. Also, starting in 2002 distributions from Section 529 plans are now *tax free* (not taxed at the child's rate as before) if they are used for qualified education expenses. These and several other provisions represent significant tax breaks for college savers. See Chapter 8 for full details.

Retirement Plan Contribution Limits Increased

Finally, Congress has done something about the meager $2,000 IRA contribution limit that was set in 1981 and never adjusted for inflation. Starting in 2002, the IRA contribution limit increases to $3,000; in 2005 it goes up to $4,000, and in 2008 to $5,000. Also, the new rules have a catch-up provision that allows people over 50 to contribute an additional $500 in years 2002 through 2005 and $1,000 in 2006. The rules concerning income limits for IRA deductibility or Roth IRA eligibility did not change. See Chapter 7 for details. The contribution limits for 401(k) plans also go up: In 2002 the limit is $11,000; in 2003 $12,000; in 2004 $13,000; in 2005 $14,000; and in 2006 $15,000. After 2006 future increases will be indexed to inflation. There is also a 401(k) catch-up provision for people over 50, who may contribute an additional $1,000 in 2002; $2,000 in 2003; $3,000 in 2004; $4,000 in 2005; and $5,000 in 2006. After 2006 the catch-up limit will be indexed to inflation in $500 increments. Please note that these are federal limits; individual employers may impose lower limits.

Estate Taxes Go Down, Then Out . . . Then Back In 2011

The most complicated part of the tax bill deals with the federal estate tax. Under current law, an individual may leave up to $675,000 (called the *exemption equivalent*) without any gift or estate tax due. Amounts over the exemption equivalent are taxed at progressive rates ranging up to 55 percent. The new legislation increases the exemption equivalent and reduces the highest estate and gift tax rate over the next decade. In 2010 the estate tax is repealed. However, because Congress was prohibited from enacting legislation extending more than ten years out, the estate tax is due to be reinstated in 2011. Questions on estate planners' minds are: 1) Will the estate tax indeed be repealed in 2010 or will Congress enact legislation between now and then to repeal the repeal? 2) If the estate tax is repealed in 2010, will Congress extend the repeal so it does not "sunset" in 2011? In other words, do we or don't we need to worry about estate taxes? Try to stay alive until we find out the answer.

As the legislation stands now, the exemption equivalent and highest gift and estate tax rate for years 2002 through 2011 are as follows:

CALENDAR YEAR	ESTATE AND GST TAX TRANSFER EXEMPTION	HIGHEST ESTATE AND GIFT TAX RATES
2002	$1,000,000	50%
2003	$1,000,000	49%
2004	$1,500,000	48%
2005	$1,500,000	47%
2006	$2,000,000	46%
2007	$2,000,000	45%
2008	$2,000,000	45%
2009	$3,500,000	45%
2010	N/A (taxes repealed)	35% (gift taxes only)
2011	$1,000,000	55%

Prior to the passage of the Economic Growth and Tax Relief Reconciliation Act of 2001, taxpayers looked forward to the stamp of certainty our legislators could finally put on provisions that had for months been the subject of speculation. However, the provisions as passed are hardly conducive to a clear understanding of the law. In addition to the ten-year time frame over which the rules take effect, there is now an ever greater possibility that the tax code will change again and again due to the haste with which this legislation was passed.

Come to think of it, it's important for investors to know that new laws are being enacted all the time, usually without the fanfare that accompanied the Economic Growth and Tax Relief Reconciliation Act of 2001. Changes that do not affect the majority of the populace but that *do* affect investors are constantly being introduced in Congress and quietly passed into law. As a tax-conscious investor, one of the best moves you can make is to stay on top of new legislation and either make your opinion known to your legislator prior to passage, or at the very least, be aware of new laws as they are passed and incorporate the information into your tax and investing strategies.

Tax Rules Every Investor Needs to Know

CHAPTER 1

Understanding Taxes and Investing

It's not what you make, it's what you keep that counts.

Sometime between January and April of every year, investors discover the real truth in this Wall Street adage. This is when they sit down with their calculators, computers, or accountants and tally up their investment activity for the year for the purpose of preparing their annual tax returns. The more successful they were, the more they must share with their silent partner, Uncle Sam. And if they had a bit of bad luck? Well, Uncle helps by taking some of the sting out of their losses, too.

What can be so disconcerting about this annual ritual is that the tax bill is often a huge surprise. Somewhere buried in the back of most investors' minds are the general rules concerning taxes and investing. The awareness of how *their* investment activity will be taxed, however, does not come to the forefront until they stand face to face with a blank form 1040 and the dreaded schedule D. All throughout the year, when they were shouting buy and sell orders to their broker or happily clicking away on the Internet, they were focused on the market and the securities at hand, not on some arcane tax rules. It is not until they gather all their confirmation slips together and either dump them on their accountant's desk or begin the painful process of logging every purchase and sale onto schedule D that the reality hits them: They should have been paying more attention to taxes all year long.

Not only might some of their investment decisions have been different ("Gee, if I'd held that stock one more week, my profits would have been taxed at the lower long-term capital gains rate"), but they also might have set aside some of their profits in a special "tax kitty" so that they would not have to scramble for cash at tax time. Or if they had not thought about taxes at the time they were firing off buy or sell orders throughout the year, they might at least have taken a moment between Christmas and New Year's to match up gains and losses and enter any year-end orders that could benefit them taxwise. But no. The custom in our country is to think about taxes as little as possible, and usually this means only in connection with tax *preparation*. Tax *planning* has not really caught on yet, except for people who have advisors who insist on it.

Even less frenetic investors—people who invest in mutual funds and bonds they plan to hold to maturity—often find surprises at tax time. Sometime in January they get these strange-looking 1099 forms with weird numbers on them ("Honey, do you remember getting a check from XYZ Mutual Fund for $938?"). Soon enough they find out that these numbers represent investment income that is taxable to them *even if they reinvested it back into the fund!* And *even if the fund lost money for the year!* They also find out that the Internal Revenue Service (IRS) is getting a copy of the same form and will be looking for that exact number to appear somewhere on their tax return. There will be more on this Chapter 4, along with some tips that can help you avoid such taxing situations in the future.

Investors cannot really be blamed for being in the dark about taxes throughout the year. Your final tax bill depends on how a lot of things shake out—things you cannot know about with complete certainty until the tax year is over. Admittedly, this makes tax planning difficult. For example, you cannot know for sure what your tax bracket will be until you have calculated your taxable income for the year. And you cannot know that until you have added up all income from all sources—including investment income you may not even have earned yet—and subtracted the various exemptions and deductions. Even tried-and-true guidelines may not always apply depending on what has been happening in your investment account. For example, if you have a short-term gain on a stock, there may be no need to hold it more than a year if you also have a short-term loss you can match it against. We will be talking more about matching gains and losses in Chapter 2. Although tax planning can be a bit like trying to hit a moving target, the key is to (1) know the rules, (2) know your personal tax situation, and (3) take your best shot at minimizing taxes while maximizing investment returns. This book will help you do that.

We will grant you that reading about tax laws is not the most fun way to pass the time. Did you know that as of June 2000, the U.S. Treasury had issued almost 20,000 pages of regulations containing more than 8 million words? Fortunately, you do not need to read all these words to understand what you need to know to be a tax-savvy investor. By reading this book through, you can brush up on the main tax rules affecting investors even if you do not try to memorize all the rules at once. Just learn the key principles that apply to the type of investing you generally do. Then when you are faced with a particular situation ("Let's see, was the holding period for long-term gains exactly one year or more than one year?"), you can go to the appropriate section and look it up.

Understanding Your Marginal Tax Rate

The most important piece of information to keep in mind as you evaluate investment opportunities throughout the year is your *marginal tax rate*. This is also called your *tax bracket*. This can be a bit tricky because as we have already noted, you cannot know for sure what your tax bracket will be until you know what your taxable income will be for the year. However, the brackets are rather broad, so unless your income is quite variable or you get a large, unexpected bonus at the end of the year, it is not too difficult to estimate at the beginning of the year what your bracket will be for the year. If you are close to the next bracket, just be aware of both brackets and that depending on how your year goes, you could fall into either bracket.

What Your Tax Bracket Means

A basic feature of our progressive income tax system is that a person's income is taxed at different rates. In 2001 (starting July 1, 2001) through 2003, the first chunk is taxed at the 10-percent rate. The second chunk is taxed at the 15-percent rate. The next four chunks are taxed at the 27-, 30-, 35-, and 38.6-percent rates, respectively. (The top four rates are scheduled to drop by 1 percent in 2004 through 2005 and by another 1 percent in 2006 and thereafter.) The exact amounts of these chunks depend on your filing status. We will talk more about this and get to the exact calculation of the tax brackets in a moment.

Your marginal tax rate, or tax bracket, refers to the highest rate at which your last chunk of income is taxed. The assumption is that any investment decision you may be considering would affect your last dollar of income; all the rest of your income presumably would remain the same. Thus, if you are in the 27-percent tax bracket and you are considering selling a stock on which you have a $2,000 short-term gain, you would calculate the tax on this particular transaction by multiplying 0.27 by $2,000. If you had no other offsetting transactions during the year (more on this in Chapter 2), you would want to be sure to set aside sufficient funds to pay the taxes on your profit.

The other thing your marginal tax rate is useful for is in comparing various strategies. For example, let us say you are considering contributing $5,000 to a retirement account that offers a full tax deduction. You can find out how much you will save in taxes by multiplying your tax bracket by the $5,000. If your bracket is 27 percent, you will reduce your tax bill by $1,350 ($5,000 × 0.27 = $1,350). This means that you are really out of pocket only $3,650 ($5,000 − $1,350 = $3,650). The tax savings will come back to you either through higher take-home pay (if you adjust your withholding at work), a bigger refund when you file your tax return, or if you owe, a smaller check you have to write to the government in April.

The reason it is so important to keep your tax bracket in mind when you invest is that the actual tax impact of an investment transaction—that is, the act of receiving a check from the government (or writing one)—is usually separated in time from the transaction itself. You could sell a stock in January of 2002 and not pay tax on the gain until April of 2003—a full 15 months later! The good part about this is that you have use of the money during this time. The bad part is that without careful planning, you could spend it all and find yourself short of funds when the tax is due. Whenever you are contemplating any investment transaction, just get into the habit of calculating the after-tax result by multiplying your profit times your tax bracket regardless of when or how the tax dollars actually will change hands.

How To Find Your Tax Bracket

The tax rate schedule is based on *taxable income*—that is, the number found on line 39 of your 1040 form. Note that it is not based on your *total income* (line 22) or even your *adjusted gross income* (line 32). Taxable income is derived by taking your total income—including your regular wages and your taxable investment income—and subtracting a whole bunch of deductions, including the $2,900 personal exemption you and your dependents each get just for being alive. This is why it is nearly impossible to determine your tax bracket by estimating your annual salary and looking it up on the tax table. For one, you may be ignoring all the investment income you hope to receive during the year. For another, you may overestimate your tax bracket because you will not have taken into account all the deductions that reduce your income for tax purposes.

The best place to start is by looking at your latest tax return. Go to line 39, look up the number, and refer to the tax-rate schedule to get an idea of what bracket you are in. The reason it is only an idea at this point is that you are looking at last year's income and this year's tax-rate schedule. However, at least you are working with a closer number than if you simply took your gross salary and looked it up on the schedule. Next, consider whether your income will be higher or lower this year than last. Look at the sources of your income. Is it mostly wages or salary? If so, do you expect any significant raises or bonuses, or will your salary stay about the same? Did you have a lot of investment income last year? How much of it is likely to be repeated this year? If most of your investment income was from capital gains, it may be hard to determine early in the year what your results will be for the full year. Do not let this keep you from tax planning, however. You may not have many firm numbers to work with at first, but as the year shapes up, you will be able to get a better handle on your tax situation.

Throughout this book we will be giving examples of the after-tax consequences of investment strategies using a representative tax bracket. Be sure to substitute your own bracket, if different, so that you can relate the information to your own situation. Table 1.1 shows the 2001 tax-rate schedule.

TABLE 1.1   2001 Tax Rate Schedule (Effective July 1, 2001)

TAXABLE INCOME ($)	MARGINAL TAX RATE (%)
Single	
0 to 6,000	10.0
6,000 to 27,050	15.0
27,050 to 65,550	27.0
65,550 to 136,750	30.0
136,750 to 297,350	35.0
Over 297,350	38.6
Head of Household	
0 to 10,000	10.0
10,000 to 36,250	15.0
36,250 to 93,650	27.0
93,650 to 151,650	30.0
151,650 to 297,350	35.0
Over 297,350	38.6
Married Filing Jointly and Qualifying Widow(er)s	
0 to 12,000	10.0
12,000 to 45,200	15.0
45,200 to 109,250	27.0
109,250 to 166,500	30.0
166,500 to 297,350	35.0
Over 297,350	38.6
Married Filing Separately	
0 to 10,000	10.0
10,000 to 22,600	15.0
22,600 to 54,625	27.0
54,625 to 83,250	30.0
83,250 to 148,675	35.0
Over 148,675	38.6

Understanding Your Filing Status

If you are like most people, you assume that your filing status as a taxpayer is pretty easy to determine. You are either married or single, right? Or you are single and supporting a child or two, in which case you proudly call yourself head of the household. Like everything taxwise, however, filing status is not as simple as it may appear. A marriage certificate or the absence thereof does not necessarily dictate how you will file. If you have been through any transitions during the year (marriage, separation, divorce, widowhood), you understandably may be confused about how to file. And if you are contemplating any changes in marital status in the future, you may want to look at the tax implications of such a move (in addition to the usual emotional considerations, of course). Taxes rarely dictate *whether* a person should get married or divorced, but they may suggest *when*.

The five choices you have in filing status are

Single

Married filing jointly

Married filing separately

Head of household

Qualifying widow(er) with dependent child

Here are some guidelines.

If You Are Single as of the Last Day of the Year

If you are unmarried as of the last day of the year, you would file a tax return as a *single individual*. Exceptions occur if you are widowed or support dependents as head of household (see the following).

If You Are Married as of the Last Day of the Year

If you are married as of the last day of the year, for tax purposes, you are considered married for the whole year. This means that if you exchange vows shortly before midnight on New Year's Eve, you can file a joint tax return with your spouse just as if you had been married at the beginning of the year. Your official filing status would be *married filing jointly*. You may not file as a single taxpayer, even if it would result in lower taxes.

You may, however, elect *married filing separately* if that would result in a lower tax. Usually it does not. If this is your first year of marriage and you are not sure how to file, it is easy enough to calculate the tax both ways and choose the one that is most advantageous. It is worth noting that if you are married and file separately, you may not be able to take advantage of certain benefits, such as the Roth IRA conversion privilege (more on this in Chapter 7). It also limits your net capital loss deduction to $1,500 instead of the usual $3,000 that everyone else gets (more on this in Chapter 2).

One reason to file a separate return is if you do not trust your spouse and think that he or she may be trying to pull some funny stuff with the IRS; however, the IRS recently has liberalized its innocent spouse rules, so you have less to worry about if you unwittingly sign a fraudulent return.

The vast majority of married people file joint returns. If you are contemplating a wedding and cannot decide whether to get married this year or next, calculate the tax both ways—as a married couple filing jointly and as each of you filing single returns. On second thought, maybe you should not do this. You may decide not to get married. Congress included some so-called marriage penalty relief provisions in the Economic Growth and Tax Relief Reconciliation Act of 2001, but they do not go fully into force until 2009. Anyone for a long engagement?

If You Are Unmarried and Maintain a Household for One or More Dependents

If you are unmarried on the last day of the year and pay over half the cost of maintaining the principal home for yourself and another relative who both lives with you at least half the year and qualifies as a dependent, you may file as *head of household*. This will give you a higher standard deduction and a lower tax-rate schedule than if you were to file as a single individual. If you are still legally married but your spouse has not lived in the home during the last six months of the year due to special circumstances such as education or military duty, you also may elect the head of household filing status as long as you paid more than half the cost to maintain the home for a child or stepchild.

If Your Spouse Died during the Year and You Did Not Remarry

If your spouse died during the year, you are considered married for the whole year. If you did not remarry before the end of the year, you can file a joint return for yourself and your deceased spouse. If you maintain a home for qualifying dependents, you may use *qualifying widow(er) with dependent child* as your filing status for two years following the year of the death of your spouse. (For example, if your spouse dies in 2002, you may use the qualifying widow(er) status in 2003 and 2004.) After that, you may switch to head of household filing status as long as you maintain a home for a dependent child.

If Your Spouse Died during the Year and You Did Remarry

If your spouse died during the year and you remarried before the last day of the year, you may file a *joint return* with your new spouse. Your deceased spouse's filing status is married filing separately for that year.

If You Are Divorced

If you are legally divorced from your spouse on the last day of the year, you are considered unmarried. You may file as a *single* individual or, if you maintain a home for a qualified dependent, as *head of household*.

If You Are Separated but Not Divorced

If you are living apart from your spouse but not have not made your separation legal through a divorce or separate maintenance decree, you are considered married for tax filing purposes. You may file a joint return with your spouse or separate returns as married individuals. An exception to this is if you paid more than half the cost of maintaining a home for a child and your spouse was not there for six months of the year, in which case you may file as head of household (see previous section on head of household).

NOTE

If you get divorced for the sole purpose of filing as single individuals and at the time of the divorce you intended to remarry in the next tax year, the divorce does not count for tax filing purposes. You and your spouse must file as married individuals.

If You Are Confused

Separation and divorce bring with them a whole slew of tax rules about who can claim the kids as dependents, what to do about alimony and child support, and more. If you have your wits about you, download a copy of IRS Publication 504, "Divorced or Separated Individuals," from the IRS Web site (www.irs.gov) and study up. If not, get a good divorce lawyer who also understands taxes.

We bring you this information about filing status so that you will know what you need to do if your situation ever changes. We do not mean to suggest that you should make crucial life decisions concerning marriage and divorce based on the tax code. While tax planning is important, filing status is one of those aspects you have little control over—in other words, your marital status should determine your filing status, not the other way around. So let us get on to some of the things you *can* control.

Kinds of Income

The following subsections discuss the various kinds of income.

Earned Income versus Unearned Income

The tax code differentiates between *earned income* and *unearned income*. Earned income is the kind you have to work for. It includes wages, salary, tips, bonuses, and the like. Unearned income is income you did not have to work for. It includes interest, dividends, capital gains, and other investment income. (Apparently the IRS does not think that all those hours you spend studying stock reports and mutual fund prospectuses count as work.) You can tell which kind of income you have received by the way it is reported (unless it is not reported, in which case you are responsible for reporting it yourself). Earned income is reported on W-2 forms. Investment income is usually reported on 1099 forms. Other types of income include rental income, pension and annuity income, and Social Security benefits. Our focus in this book will be on investment income.

The distinction between earned and unearned income comes into play especially with regard to children. Those little dependents that cost you a fortune to raise but save you a few bucks in taxes every year are allowed to have a certain amount of each type of income without having to file a tax return. However, if they are under age 14 and their unearned income exceeds a certain amount, the excess is taxed at the parents' rate. This is to prevent parents from putting all their assets in their children's names to avoid paying income tax. More will be said about the "kiddie tax" in Chapter 8.

Ordinary Income versus Capital Gains

For investors, the distinction between *ordinary income* and *capital gains* is crucial. Ordinary income includes interest and dividends. It is reported on schedule B and taxed at your highest marginal tax rate. Capital gains are the net profits you receive when you sell securities for more than you paid. Capital gains (and losses) are reported on schedule D and have lots rules that govern how they are taxed. Acquainting you with these rules—some of which are new —and suggesting ways to apply these rules to your investment strategies are two of the main purposes of this book. Managing capital gains and losses through the timely purchase and sale of securities is one way that you can lower your tax bill without substantially cutting into your investment returns. It is tricky but worth it. There will be more on this in Chapter 2 and throughout the rest of the book.

Taxable Income versus Tax-Free Income

The interest you earn on savings accounts and on corporate and government bonds is fully taxable at your highest federal income tax rate. In contrast, the interest on municipal bonds is federally tax-free (also called *tax-exempt*). Although you must report municipal bond interest on your tax return, you do not have to pay tax on it. The IRS really does not care how much tax-exempt interest you receive unless you are also receiving Social Security benefits. In that case, part of your tax-exempt interest is used in the formula to determine whether or not you must pay tax on your Social Security benefits (more on this in Chapter 10). Thus, if you earn tax-exempt interest, just enter it on line 8b of your tax return and delight in the fact that it does not go into the column that ultimately will determine your final tax bill.

Because municipal bond (muni) interest is tax-free, it is usually lower than the yield you would receive on an equivalent taxable bond. However, once you figure taxes into the equation, the muni yields end up being higher for investors in high tax brackets. For example, at the time of this writing, 30-year Treasury bonds are yielding 5.36 percent, whereas AAA municipal bonds are yielding 4.93 percent (this happens to be an unusually narrow spread; usually there is a wider differential, suggesting that munis may be a great buy right now). For an investor in the 30-percent federal tax bracket, the 4.93-percent muni is equivalent to a 7.04-percent taxable bond. We will talk more about how to compare taxable and tax-free yields for your tax bracket in Chapter 3.

Return of Capital

For tax purposes, *return of capital* really is not income at all. However, you should be aware of it because some investments generate income that your broker may tell you is somehow "not taxable." The reason it is not taxable is that it is your own money coming back to you. Investment income is only taxable when it is new money earned on top of the amount you invested. Bond interest is a perfect example of this. If you invest $10,000 in a taxable bond and receive interest of $800 per year, the $800 is taxable. When you get your original $10,000 back when the bond matures, it is not taxable because it is your own money; you paid income tax on it a long time ago when you first earned it (unless you inherited it or received it via some other nontaxable means). Some investments, instead of paying back your $10,000 all at once on some predetermined date in the future, pay you back over time. Thus, in addition to the interest, you get a little of your $10,000 back every year. This can make it seem like you have got an extraordinary investment: higher income than usual and part of it is not taxable to boot! The problem is that with these investments you cannot look forward to getting your original investment back at some point in the future because when that time comes, you already will have received everything you are going to get. Investments that offer return of capital are not necessarily bad or good; they need to be evaluated on their own merits. The important thing for investors to understand is what return of capital means. It is simply your own money coming back, not a way to pull the wool over the eyes of the IRS. You generally must reduce your cost basis by the amount of the nontaxable distribution when calculating your gain or loss after sale. There will be more on this in Chapter 2.

Tax-Deferred Income

Certain types of investments and certain types of accounts allow you to earn income that is not taxable in the year it is received. Instead, the investment earnings build up tax-deferred, and income is taxed as it is withdrawn. A traditional individual retirement account (IRA) is an example of this type of account. Let us say that you invest $2,000 a year in a traditional IRA that earns an average of 8 percent per year. At the end of 20 years, you will have $91,524 in the account. Of this, $40,000 represents your own contributions ($2,000 × 20), and $51,524 represents investment earnings on which you have paid no tax. If this is a deductible IRA, which means you deducted from your taxable income each year's $2,000 contribution, the entire $91,524 eventually will be taxable. The amount of tax you will pay will depend on how much you withdraw each year and what your tax bracket is at that time. Thus, if you take out, say, $5,000 in one year, you will report the $5,000 on line 15 of your tax return and add it to your other taxable income for that year.

If it is a nondeductible IRA (such as a Roth IRA), meaning you already paid taxes on the $40,000, only the investment earnings—the $51,524—will be taxable, and only as you withdraw it. Taking money out of a nondeductible IRA is a bit tricky: Part of each withdrawal is considered taxable, and part is nontaxable; the proportion is determined by the ratio of investment earnings to nondeductible contributions of the entire account. Thus, in this example, 43 percent of your $5,000 withdrawal would be nontaxable ($40,000/$91,524 = 0.43), and 57 percent would be taxable. We will cover retirement plans and IRAs in Chapter 7.

Tax-deferred annuities are private investments (not government-sanctioned retirement plans) that operate in a similar manner. The basis for the tax deferral is a life insurance component that is part of, but not the primary characteristic of, these contracts. Life insurance has long enjoyed tax-advantaged status, which means that investment earnings in a life insurance contract build up free from current tax. Withdrawals may be taxed differently depending on the terms of the contract. In some cases, it is last in, first out (LIFO), which means that the first withdrawals you take are presumed to be investment earnings (not your original capital) and therefore taxable. In other cases, a portion of each withdrawal is deemed return of capital and therefore not taxable, and a portion is deemed investment earnings and therefore added to your other taxable income for the year and taxed at ordinary income tax rates.

Total Income

By the time you enter the amounts of all your taxable income on lines 7 through 21 of your tax form, you will be ready to add it all up and enter the total on line 22 (Figure 1.1). This, for tax purposes, is considered your *total income*. For example, wages go on line 7, interest income goes on line 8, dividends go on line 9, and so on. Your net capital gain (or loss) goes on line 13. The simplicity of this one number sitting on its own line belies the hours of frustration you (or your accountant) may have gone through sorting out all your stock transactions in the process of filling out schedule D, but there it sits, a testament to your success (or not) as an investor last year. If it is a big number, you can feel pleased that you did so well. Enjoy the feeling, because when you get to the second page of the tax return, you will find out what all that success cost you. If it is a negative number in parentheses, now is the time to find a little joy in what must have been a bad year because it will help you reduce your total income for tax purposes.

Once you have determined your *total income* and entered the amount on line 22, the fun part begins. This is where you get to hack away at your income by subtracting various exemptions and deductions to get your *taxable income* as low as possible. Your taxable income—which you will get to eventually on line 39 on page 2—is the amount that determines how much tax you owe. It is what you arrive at after you have subtracted all the deductions you are legally entitled to. However, before you get to taxable income, there is an interim step you have to go through: calculating your *adjusted gross income* (AGI).

Adjusted Gross Income

If you look at the tax form (see Figure 1.1), you will see that exemptions and deductions are taken in two phases. The first phase takes you from total income

Form **1040** Department of the Treasury—Internal Revenue Service
U.S. Individual Income Tax Return **2001** (99) IRS Use Only—Do not write or staple in this space.

For the year Jan. 1–Dec. 31, 2001, or other tax year beginning , 2001, ending , 20 OMB No. 1545-0074

Label (See instructions on page 19.)
Use the IRS label. Otherwise, please print or type.
LABEL HERE

Your first name and initial | Last name | **Your social security number**
If a joint return, spouse's first name and initial | Last name | **Spouse's social security number**
Home address (number and street). If you have a P.O. box, see page 19. | Apt. no.
City, town or post office, state, and ZIP code. If you have a foreign address, see page 19.

▲ **Important!** ▲ You **must** enter your SSN(s) above.

Presidential Election Campaign (See page 19.)
Note. Checking "Yes" will not change your tax or reduce your refund.
Do you, or your spouse if filing a joint return, want $3 to go to this fund? . . . ▶ You ☐Yes ☐No Spouse ☐Yes ☐No

Filing Status — Check only one box.
1 ☐ Single
2 ☐ Married filing joint return (even if only one had income)
3 ☐ Married filing separate return. Enter spouse's social security no. above and full name here. ▶
4 ☐ Head of household (with qualifying person). (See page 19.) If the qualifying person is a child but not your dependent, enter this child's name here. ▶
5 ☐ Qualifying widow(er) with dependent child (year spouse died ▶). (See page 19.)

Exemptions
6a ☐ **Yourself.** If your parent (or someone else) can claim you as a dependent on his or her tax return, **do not** check box 6a
b ☐ **Spouse**
c **Dependents:**

(1) First name Last name	(2) Dependent's social security number	(3) Dependent's relationship to you	(4)✓ if qualifying child for child tax credit (see page 20)
			☐
			☐
			☐
			☐
			☐
			☐

If more than six dependents, see page 20.
d Total number of exemptions claimed

No. of boxes checked on 6a and 6b ____
No. of your children on 6c who:
• lived with you ____
• did not live with you due to divorce or separation (see page 20) ____
Dependents on 6c not entered above ____
Add numbers entered on lines above ▶ ☐

Income
Attach Forms W-2 and W-2G here. Also attach Form(s) 1099-R if tax was withheld.
If you did not get a W-2, see page 21.
Enclose, but do not attach, any payment. Also, please use Form 1040-V.

7 Wages, salaries, tips, etc. Attach Form(s) W-2 — 7
8a **Taxable** interest. Attach Schedule B if required — 8a
b **Tax-exempt** interest. **Do not** include on line 8a — 8b
9 Ordinary dividends. Attach Schedule B if required — 9
10 Taxable refunds, credits, or offsets of state and local income taxes (see page 22) — 10
11 Alimony received — 11
12 Business income or (loss). Attach Schedule C or C-EZ — 12
13 Capital gain or (loss). Attach Schedule D if required. If not required, check here ▶ ☐ — 13
14 Other gains or (losses). Attach Form 4797 — 14
15a Total IRA distributions 15a — b Taxable amount (see page 23) — 15b
16a Total pensions and annuities 16a — b Taxable amount (see page 23) — 16b
17 Rental real estate, royalties, partnerships, S corporations, trusts, etc. Attach Schedule E — 17
18 Farm income or (loss). Attach Schedule F — 18
19 Unemployment compensation — 19
20a Social security benefits 20a — b Taxable amount (see page 25) — 20b
21 Other income. List type and amount (see page 25) — 21
22 Add the amounts in the far right column for lines 7 through 21. This is your **total income** ▶ — 22

Adjusted Gross Income
23 IRA deduction (see page 27) — 23
24 Student loan interest deduction (see page 27) — 24
25 Archer MSA deduction. Attach Form 8853 — 25
26 Moving expenses. Attach Form 3903 — 26
27 One-half of self-employment tax. Attach Schedule SE — 27
28 Self-employed health insurance deduction (see page 29) — 28
29 Self-employed SEP, SIMPLE, and qualified plans — 29
30 Penalty on early withdrawal of savings — 30
31a Alimony paid b Recipient's SSN ▶ — 31a
32 Add lines 23 through 31a — 32
33 Subtract line 32 from line 22. This is your **adjusted gross income** ▶ — 33

For Disclosure, Privacy Act, and Paperwork Reduction Act Notice, see page 56. Cat. No. 11320B Form **1040** (2001)

FIGURE 1.1 IRS form 1040

(line 22) to adjusted gross income (line 33). The second phase takes you from adjusted gross income to taxable income (line 39). The adjustments that get you from total income to adjusted gross income are very specific and consist of the following:

IRA deduction

Student loan interest deduction

Form 1040 (2001)   Page **2**

Tax and Credits	34	Amount from line 33 (adjusted gross income)	34
	35a	Check if: ☐ **You** were 65 or older, ☐ Blind; ☐ **Spouse** was 65 or older, ☐ Blind. Add the number of boxes checked above and enter the total here . . . . ▶ **35a**	
Standard Deduction for—	b	If you are married filing separately and your spouse itemizes deductions, or you were a dual-status alien, see page 31 and check here . . . . ▶ **35b** ☐	
● People who checked any box on line 35a or 35b or who can be claimed as a dependent, see page 31.	36	**Itemized deductions** (from Schedule A) **or** your **standard deduction** (see left margin) .	36
	37	Subtract line 36 from line 34	37
	38	If line 34 is $99,725 or less, multiply $2,900 by the total number of exemptions claimed on line 6d. If line 34 is over $99,725, see the worksheet on page 32	38
	39	**Taxable income.** Subtract line 38 from line 37. If line 38 is more than line 37, enter -0-	39
● All others: Single, $4,550	40	**Tax** (see page 32). Check if any tax is from **a** ☐ Form(s) 8814 **b** ☐ Form 4972 . . .	40
	41	Alternative minimum tax. Attach Form 6251	41
Head of household, $6,650	42	Add lines 40 and 41 . . . . ▶	42
	43	Foreign tax credit. Attach Form 1116 if required	43	
Married filing jointly or Qualifying widow(er), $7,600	44	Credit for child and dependent care expenses. Attach Form 2441	44	
	45	Credit for the elderly or the disabled. Attach Schedule R . .	45	
	46	Education credits. Attach Form 8863	46	
Married filing separately, $3,800	47	Child tax credit (see page 36)	47	
	48	Adoption credit. Attach Form 8839	48	
	49	Credits from: **a** ☐ Form 3800 **b** ☐ Form 8396 **c** ☐ Form 8801 **d** ☐ Form (specify)_____	49	
	50	Rate reduction credit. See the worksheet on page 38	50	
	51	Add lines 43 through 50. These are your **total credits**	51
	52	Subtract line 51 from line 42. If line 51 is more than line 42, enter -0- . . . . . . ▶	52
Other Taxes	53	Self-employment tax. Attach Schedule SE	53
	54	Social security and Medicare tax on tip income not reported to employer. Attach Form 4137 . .	54
	55	Tax on qualified plans, including IRAs, and other tax-favored accounts. Attach Form 5329 if required .	55
	56	Advance earned income credit payments from Form(s) W-2	56
	57	Household employment taxes. Attach Schedule H	57
	58	Add lines 52 through 57. This is your **total tax** . . . . ▶	58
Payments	59	Federal income tax withheld from Forms W-2 and 1099 . .	59	
	60	2001 estimated tax payments and amount applied from 2000 return	60	
If you have a qualifying child, attach Schedule EIC.	61a	**Earned income credit (EIC)**	61a	
	b	Nontaxable earned income . . **61b**		
	62	Excess social security and RRTA tax withheld (see page 50)	62	
	63	Additional child tax credit. Attach Form 8812	63	
	64	Amount paid with request for extension to file (see page 50)	64	
	65	Other payments. Check if from **a** ☐ Form 2439 **b** ☐ Form 4136	65	
	66	Add lines 59, 60, 61a, and 62 through 65. These are your **total payments** . . . . . ▶	66
Refund	67	If line 66 is more than line 58, subtract line 58 from line 66. This is the amount you **overpaid** . ▶	67
Direct deposit? See page 50 and fill in 68b, 68c, and 68d.	68a	Amount of line 67 you want **refunded to you** . . . . ▶	68a
	▶ b	Routing number [ ] ▶ c Type: ☐ Checking ☐ Savings	
	▶ d	Account number [ ]	
	69	Amount of line 67 you want **applied to your 2002 estimated tax** ▶	69	
Amount You Owe	70	**Amount you owe.** Subtract line 66 from line 58. For details on how to pay, see page 51 ▶	70
	71	Estimated tax penalty. Also include on line 70	71	
Third Party Designee		Do you want to allow another person to discuss this return with the IRS (see page 52)? ☐ **Yes.** Complete the following. ☐ **No**	
		Designee's name ▶ Phone no. ▶ ( ) Personal identification number (PIN) ▶	
Sign Here Joint return? See page 19. Keep a copy for your records.		Under penalties of perjury, I declare that I have examined this return and accompanying schedules and statements, and to the best of my knowledge and belief, they are true, correct, and complete. Declaration of preparer (other than taxpayer) is based on all information of which preparer has any knowledge.	
		Your signature Date Your occupation Daytime phone number ( )	
		Spouse's signature. If a joint return, **both** must sign. Date Spouse's occupation	
Paid Preparer's Use Only		Preparer's signature ▶ Date Check if self-employed ☐ Preparer's SSN or PTIN	
		Firm's name (or yours if self-employed), address, and ZIP code ▶ EIN Phone no. ( )	

Form **1040** (2001)

FIGURE 1.1   IRS form 1040 *(Continued)*

Medical savings account deduction

Moving expenses

One-half of self-employment tax

Self-employed health insurance deduction

Self-employed SEP, SIMPLE, and qualified plans

Penalty on early withdrawal of savings

Alimony paid

Some of these adjustments are not related to investing and therefore will not be covered in this book. Anything relating to IRAs or retirement plans will be covered in Chapter 7. The most important thing to understand at this point is that your adjusted gross income, or AGI, is a very important number. After your tax bracket, it is the second most important number to keep in mind when tax planning because it determines whether you can take advantage of certain benefits and strategies.

A relatively recent addition to our tax code are what are called *phaseouts*, also called the "stealth tax" by cynics who think they should be repealed. By implementing phaseouts, Congress gave us certain goodies with one hand and then took them away with the other. For example, the Roth IRA is considered by many to be the premiere IRA, offering tax-free withdrawals and no minimum distribution requirements at age 70½. Are you eligible to contribute to a Roth IRA? You will have to check your AGI to see. If it is over $110,000 (single taxpayers) or $160,000 (married filing jointly), you are out of luck. Your AGI puts you over the limit for Roth eligibility. If your AGI is between $95,000 and $110,000 (single) or between $150,000 and $160,000 (married filing jointly), you can make a partial contribution.

Throughout this book we will be referring to income limits that determine eligibility for certain tax breaks. In most cases we will be referring to your AGI (in certain cases your AGI must be *modified* further and therefore is referred to as MAGI). You will get more out of the information in this book if you have your AGI handy so that you will know at a glance if you qualify for the particular deduction or tax credit under discussion.

Taxable Income

From your adjusted gross income, you will subtract two more important deductions to arrive at your taxable income: your itemized (or standard) deduction and your personal exemptions.

Itemized (or Standard) Deductions

On line 36 you will enter the total amount of itemized deductions carried over from schedule A. These include the following:

Medical or dental expenses that exceed 7.5 percent of your AGI

Taxes—state and local income taxes paid, real estate taxes, personal property taxes

Interest paid—mortgage interest and points, investment interest (special rules apply; more on this in Chapter 10)

Gifts to charity

Casualty and theft losses

Unreimbursed job expenses such as travel and union dues that exceed 2 percent of your AGI

Miscellaneous deductions such as tax preparation fees

If the total of these itemized deductions does not equal the standard deduction amount, you can forget about schedule A and simply enter the standard deduction for your filing status, as shown in Table 1.2.

TABLE 1.2 Standard Deductions

IF YOU ARE UNDER 65 AND FILING AS	YOUR STANDARD DEDUCTION IN 2001 IS
• Single	• $4,550
• Married filing jointly	• $7,600
• Married filing separately	• $3,800
• Head of household	• $6,650
If you are over 65 and filing as	
• Single	• $5,650
• Married filing jointly	• $8,500
• Married filing separately	• $4,700
• Head of household	• $7,750

Note: If you are married filing separately and if your spouse itemizes deductions, you may not take the standard deduction.

It can be easy to overlook deductions that legitimately may help you reduce your taxes. We will be covering tax-deductible investment-related expenses in Chapter 10. For more information on miscellaneous deductions (including expenses that are definitely *not* deductible), see IRS Publication 529, "Miscellaneous Deductions."

Watch for phaseouts. Itemized deductions currently are affected by phaseouts. If your AGI is over $132,950 in 2001 (single or joint), you must reduce the amount of itemized deductions you are allowed. Keep this in mind if you are affected by these phaseouts because they require a whole shift in your approach to tax planning. Deductions you thought were sacrosanct may no longer do you any good. However, you can look for some relief later on. The Economic Growth and Tax Relief Reconciliation Act of 2001 provided for the gradual phaseout of the itemized-deduction phaseout, reducing it by one-third in 2006 and 2007 and by two-thirds in 2008 and 2009. The overall limitation is eliminated in 2010.

Personal Exemption

The personal exemption is the amount you get to subtract for yourself (and your spouse, if filing jointly) just for breathing. This amount was $2,900 per person in 2001. In addition, you get to take exemptions for each of your dependents, also in the amount of $2,900 per person. If you have a pretty straightforward family situation, determining the number of dependents is easy: Just count the kids. However, if your situation is at all complicated, with stepchildren and custody arrangements, grandparents depending on you for support, lazy cousins or brothers-in-law, or a child who was born or died during the year, you may not be sure how many dependents you can claim. You can get the full rundown in IRS Publication 501, "Exemptions, Standard Deduction, and Filing Information," but here are some guidelines for common situations.

Basically, the idea is that everybody gets to be claimed as an exemption on somebody's tax return. However, nobody can be claimed as an exemption on more than one tax return. People who support themselves can claim their own personal exemptions, along with their spouse if married. People who are supporting others can claim the people they are supporting as dependent exemptions. Where it gets tricky is when a dependent also has income of his or her own or when someone else is contributing to the dependent's support, such as the noncustodial parent. In these rather murky situations, who gets to claim the dependent as an exemption?

The IRS offers five tests to determine whether or not you can claim someone as a dependent. These are:

Member of household or relationship test. The person must either live with you as a member of your household or be a close relative, such as a child, parent, sister or brother, aunt or uncle, or in-law. A cousin does not count as a relative but may be claimed as a dependent if he or she lived with you as a member of your household.

Citizen or resident test. The person must be a U.S. citizen or resident or a resident of Canada or Mexico.

Joint return test. In order to be claimed as a dependent, the person must not file a joint return with a spouse, even if he or she met all the other dependency tests. For example, if your daughter is married and files a joint return with her husband, she may not be claimed as a dependent even if she lived with you for most of the year and you provided more than half of her support.

Gross income test. Generally, you cannot take an exemption for a dependent if that person had a gross income of $2,900 or more for 2001. However, this test does not apply if it is your child who is under age 19 at the end of the year or under age 24 and a student.

Support test. You must provide more than half of a person's total support during the calendar year.

The support test is the key test and the most complicated one to figure out. According to the IRS, the way to determine whether you have provided more than half of another person's support is by comparing the amount you contributed with the entire amount of support the person received from all sources, including his or her own funds. Sounds easy enough. But there are five pages of small print in Publication 501 explaining what this all means, including two pages dealing exclusively with divorced or separated parents. If you have any question as to whether or not you can claim someone as a dependent, study the rules carefully.

The personal exemption is also currently subject to phaseouts. If your AGI is over $132,950 (single) or $199,450 (married filing jointly), the amount of the personal exemption ($2,900 in 2001) starts being reduced until it disappears for AGIs over $255,450 (single) and $331,950 (married filing jointly). This phaseout is also being eliminated gradually by The Economic Growth and Tax Relief Reconciliation Act of 2001. However, the first reduction does not occur until 2006, same as the gradual elimination of the itemized-deduction phaseout described earlier.

Tax Credits

After you have subtracted all your allowable deductions and entered the amount of your taxable income on line 39, you turn to the tax tables to find out how much tax you owe for your filing status. You put this number on line 40. Then the fun really begins (maybe). If you qualify for any tax credits, you get to subtract these amounts directly off your tax bill. Tax deductions merely reduce your taxable income; the amount of tax you save is some fraction of that as determined by your tax bracket. Tax credits, on the other hand, reduce your tax bill dollar for dollar.

The only problem is that many investors do not qualify for tax credits. Still, you should see which ones you are eligible for and take whatever you can. In Chapter 8 we will be talking about education tax credits in connection with college planning.

Other Taxes

Just when you thought you were finished, you find a section in the middle of page 2 of your tax form called "Other Taxes." Fortunately, this does not apply to most people. The big one here is self-employment tax, which you already know about if you own a business and file schedule C. Likewise, if you took an early IRA distribution, you knew you were not going to get away without paying the 10-percent early-withdrawal penalty (unless you got around it by qualifying for one of the exceptions discussed in Chapter 7).

Total Tax

On line 57, you will enter your *total tax*. This is the number you come up with after you have added up all your total income, subtracted adjustments to arrive at your adjusted gross income, subtracted exemptions and deductions to arrive at your taxable income, looked up the amount of tax you owe, subtracted any credits you qualify for, and added any other taxes you may have to pay. (This all sounds so easy, doesn't it?) Of course, the thing you are dying to know is if you have to write a check to the government or can expect to get one from it. To find out, you subtract your tax payments for the year, including any amounts withheld as shown on your W-2 or 1099 forms, as well as any estimated tax payments you may have made during the tax year.

However, before you do that, take a moment to pause and reflect on the number that sits on line 57 of your tax return—your total tax. It is easy to get distracted by tax withholding, figuring if you get a refund from the IRS, you are getting a break on your taxes. I have even heard people say that they do not pay any income tax because they get a refund every year. Clearly, this is misguided thinking. Still, it is easy to think that as long as you are getting a refund, you have your tax situation under control and are minimizing taxes as much as possible. No. All it means is that you are overpaying the government.

To find out if you are minimizing taxes as much as possible, you need to examine your tax return in connection with some of the guidelines you will read about in this book to see if you really are taking advantage of tax-saving opportunities, especially with regard to your investments.

Taxes and Investing

Taxes add another dimension to your investing. They should never be considered to the exclusion of everything else but rather in conjunction with all the other factors that go into your investment decisions. For example, one of the most difficult dilemmas for stock investors is whether to hold a stock long enough to qualify for the lower long-term capital gains rates and risk seeing the stock go down before the year is up or sell it now and capture a short-term gain even if it means paying the tax at a higher rate. Unfortunately, no book can help you answer this question. All you can do is understand the tax ramifications of the various investment decisions and factor them into your analysis.

The rest of this book covers tax rules as they relate to investing in stocks, bonds, mutual funds, and real estate, as well as to some of the strategies and goals you may be working on, such as saving for retirement or college. Even if you have a professional prepare your taxes, it is important to understand the basic tax rules because your accountant probably will not be around when you are trading online at 11:00 P.M. and wondering about the tax impact of selling 100 shares of AOL. So get ready for some complicated stuff, and happy investing!

CHAPTER 2

Investing in Stocks

There's a rite of passage every first-time stock investor goes through when forced to grasp the impact of the preceding year's trading activity in the process of preparing taxes. It is something like having your life flash before your eyes. Only this time you are looking at it through a different lens. You are looking at it in review and coming to grips with the wisdom or folly of each and every investment decision. "How could I have bought that stupid stock?" you may wonder. "Why did I sell that one so soon?" you may say to yourself. Reviewing your trades can be a very humbling experience. It also can help you become a better stock investor.

If you are not sure how you ended up for the year, the process of logging your trades and matching gains and losses will make your success (or failure) abundantly clear. Summing everything up at the end of the year forces you to look at your portfolio in totality rather than focusing on individual trades. If you take the opportunity to learn from it, it will help you become a better investor, perhaps paying more attention to diversification and how to correlate your stock picks so that your portfolio works more like an orchestra than a bunch of individual instruments each playing its own tune.

If you have been gloating about one extraordinary stock pick, you may be forced to see that your one big success was canceled out by lots of little losers you conveniently forgot about. Conversely, you may find that despite what seemed like a bad year, you did not do as badly as you thought. It can be easy to sweep last year's trading activity under the rug and look forward to a new year, but the Internal Revenue Service (IRS) forces you to take one last look at what you did. Trust us, you will be a better person because of it.

This is not why the IRS makes you do this, of course. Uncle Sam wants you to add up all your gains so that he can take his share of your trading profits. And this is the other epiphany new investors have when their first year of trading is over: *They have to pay taxes on the money they made!* It is this realization that turns emotions on their head. Instead of feeling good about your investing success, you are now feeling bad because you owe so much in taxes. Instead of feeling bad about your losses, you find some comfort in the fact that your taxes will be a bit lower than they otherwise would have been.

Once your thinking shifts from how you did as an investor to how your investments are affected by taxes, you are ready for the next big leap in your investor education. Instead of finding out after the fact what the taxes will be on trading activity that occurred during the preceding year, you will think about the tax consequence of every investment decision *before you make it*. This is crucial to increasing your after-tax returns. Many investors focus on reducing trading costs as a way to enhance their investment returns, but with federal taxes taking a bite as big as 39.1 percent of your profits (more, when you factor in state taxes), taxes are what you really should be focusing on. There are so many ways to structure your trading activity to minimize taxes that there simply is no reason not to do it. Yes, it takes a little extra effort. All throughout the year, you must be mindful of all your stock positions—when you bought them and the price you paid—rather than focusing only on the transaction at hand. However, this too will make you a better investor. For example, if it were not for the tax breaks that come with short-term losses, some investors would never dump their "dog" stocks. Paying attention to taxes helps you avoid common investor mistakes, such as falling in love with a bad stock or selling your profitable ones too soon.

NOTE

Seldom do investors have just one trade for the year. It is the way your gains and losses net out at the end of the year that matters. This means that it is vital to coordinate all your investment activity throughout the year.

Capital Gains and Losses

For tax purposes, a stock is considered a capital asset, subject to special rules concerning capital gains and losses. First we will cover the basic rules, and then we will go into the ways these rules can be applied to your investing strategy.

Long-term capital gains are taxed at favorable tax rates: 20 percent for investors in the 27-percent tax bracket or higher or 10 percent for investors in the 15-percent tax bracket or lower. To qualify for a long-term capital gain, a stock must be held at least one year and a day. For example, if you invested $5,000 in XYZ on November 1, 2001, sold it on November 2, 2002, and received net proceeds of $7,000, your gain is the difference between $7,000 and $5,000, or $2,000. If you are in the

27-percent tax bracket *and you have no other trades for the year*, you would owe taxes at the 20-percent long-term capital gains rate, or $400 ($2,000 × 0.20).

Short-term capital gains are taxed at your highest marginal tax rate. A gain is short term if the stock was held one year or less. For example, if you invested $5,000 in XYZ on November 1, 2001, sold it on November 1, 2002, and received net proceeds of $7,000, because you held the stock exactly one year (not more than one year), your $2,000 gain is taxed at your highest marginal tax rate. If you are in the 27-percent tax bracket, you will owe $540 in taxes ($2000 × 0.27).

Capital gains may be offset by capital losses before calculating the tax. This is the part that really can save taxes as long as you are not too proud to dump your losers. By moving up your investment day of reckoning from April 14 to December 29 or so (anytime before the last business day of the year), you can assess your portfolio for gains and losses and execute transactions that will help your tax situation. If you already have taken some gains during the year and also have some unrealized losses on the books, you can sell the losing stocks to help offset the gains.

Here is how the matching process works:

> **NOTE**
> Your holding period begins the day after you bought the stock and ends on the day you sold it. For example, if you bought a stock on April 30, 2001 and sold it on April 30, 2002, the gain or loss would be short term because the holding period actually began May 1, 2001, the day after purchase. The holding period is based on trade date, not settlement date.

> **NOTE**
> It goes without saying that your gains and losses must be realized to affect your taxes. You must sell the stock and establish the long- or short-term gain or loss before the end of the year in order for it to be included in your capital gains tax calculation for the year.

STEP 1   Short-term gains are matched against short-term losses to determine the net short-term gain or loss.

STEP 1   Example 1

In addition to the $2,000 short-term gain on XYZ noted previously, you also have a short-term loss on ABC of $1,000. To determine your net short-term gain, subtract the loss from the gain:

$2,000   (short-term gain on XYZ)
−1,000   (short-term loss on ABC)
$1,000   (net short-term gain)

If you had no other transactions, your $1,000 net short-term gain would be added to your other income and taxed at your highest marginal tax rate. If you were in the 27-percent tax bracket, you would pay $270 in taxes, giving you a net after-tax gain of $730.

STEP 1   Example 2

In addition to the $2,000 short-term gain on XYZ, you have a $4,000 short-term loss on QRS. Now you have a net short-term loss of $2,000

$4,000   (short-term loss on QRS)
−2,000   (short-term gain on XYZ)
$2,000   (net short-term loss)

NOTE

$3,000 in capital losses is the most you can deduct against other income in one year. If your loss in this example had been $4,000, you would deduct $3,000 from other income and carry the remaining $1,000 loss over to the next year.

If you had no other transactions for the year, your $2,000 net short-term loss would be deducted from your other income, resulting in lower tax. For example, if you were in the 27-percent tax bracket, your $2,000 short-term loss would save you $540 in taxes ($2,000 × 0.27 = $540), making your after-tax loss just $1,460. This is what we mean when we say Uncle Sam shares some of your pain if you lose money on stocks.

If you also had some long-term gains or losses, you would not figure the tax yet but would go on to step 2.

STEP 2   Long-term gains are matched against long-term losses to determine the net long-term gain or loss.

STEP 2   Example 1

In addition to your $2,000 long-term gain on XYZ, you also have a $1,000 long-term loss on JKL. In this case, your net long-term gain is $1,000.

$2,000   (long-term gain on XYZ)
−$1,000   (long-term loss on JKL)
$1,000   (net long-term gain)

If you had no other transactions, you would multiply your net long-term gain by your capital gains tax rate (20 or 10 percent) and add this amount to your tax bill. If you were in the 27-percent tax bracket or higher, you would owe $200 in tax ($1,000 × 0.20 = $200), making your after-tax gain $800 ($1,000 × $200 = $800).

STEP 2   Example 2

In addition to your $2,000 long-term gain on XYZ, you also have a $5,000 long-term loss on MNO. Now you have a net long-term loss of $3,000.

$5,000   (long-term loss on MNO)
−$2,000   (long-term gain on XYZ)
$3,000   (net long-term loss)

If you had no other transactions, you would be able to deduct this amount from your other income and save taxes at your marginal tax rate. For the 27-percent tax bracket, this $3,000 net long-term loss would save you $810 in taxes, making your after-tax loss $2,190.

If you also had a net short-term gain or loss from step 1, you would go on to step 3.

STEP 3   The net *short-term* gain or loss is matched against the net *long-term* gain or loss to determine the net long- or short-term gain or loss.

STEP 3   Example 1

Short-term gain and long-term gain. You have a net short-term gain of $1,000 from step 1 and a $1,000 net long-term gain from step 2.

$1,000 (net short-term gain)
$1,000 (net long-term gain)

Since these are both gains, they are not used to offset each other. In addition, since they are taxed at different rates, they are not added together. The $1,000 short-term gain is taxed at your highest marginal tax rate, whereas the $1,000 long-term gain is taxed at either 20 or 10 percent.

STEP 3   Example 2

Long-term loss and short-term gain. You have a net short-term gain of $1,000 from step 1 and a net long-term loss of $3,000 from step 2. Netting these out would give you a net long-term loss of $2,000.

$3,000   (net long-term loss)
−$1,000   (net short-term gain)
$2,000   (net net long-term loss)

You would use this loss to offset other income. To find out how much tax you would save, multiply $2,000 times your tax bracket.

STEP 3   Example 3

Short-term loss and long-term gain. You have a $2,000 net short-term loss from step 1 and a $1,000 net long-term gain from step 2. In this case, you have a net short-term loss of $1,000.

   $2,000   (net short-term loss)
−$1,000   (net long-term gain)
   $1,000   (net net short-term loss)

You would use this $1,000 short-term loss to offset other income.

STEP 3   Example 4

Short-term loss and long-term loss. You have a $2,000 net short-term loss from step 1 and a $3,000 net long-term loss from step 2. You would deduct $2,000 of the short-term loss and $1,000 of the long-term loss from other income (total $3,000) and carry forward the remaining $2,000 long-term loss to next year. When applying losses against other income, you must use up the short-term loss first. If you have more than $3,000 in short-term losses as well as some long-term gains, you retain the character of each loss when carrying it forward; next year you would apply the short-term loss first to other gains or, if losses again exceed gains, to other income.

To sum up the tax effect of all this netting:

If the net result is a short-term gain, it is taxed at your highest marginal tax rate.

If the net result is a long-term gain, it is taxed at 20 percent if you are in the 27-percent tax bracket or higher or 10 percent if you are in the 15-percent tax bracket or lower.

If the net result is a loss of $3,000 or less, it is deductible against other income. (*Exception:* If you are married and file a separate return, your deduction limit is $1,500.)

If the net result is a loss of more than $3,000, you may deduct $3,000 against other income and carry the balance forward to next year. At that time, you can use the loss carried forward to offset next year's gains. If losses again exceed gains, you may deduct up to $3,000 of other income. Any unused losses may continue to be carried forward until they are exhausted.

Investment Implications of Capital Gains Tax Rules

It may take you awhile to get the hang of all these capital gains tax rules. It can help therefore to remember the one key guideline that serves all investors most of the time: *Make your losses short term (one year or less) and your gains long term (more than one year).*

The reasoning behind this is simple: Short-term losses are better than long-term losses because they can offset short-term gains, which ordinarily are taxed at your highest marginal tax rate. Long-term gains are better than short-term gains because they are taxed at the lower capital gains rate of 20 or 10 percent.

For this reason, you will not always want to wait until the end of the year to find out where you stand taxwise. By then, you may have missed an opportunity to take a short-term capital loss. For example, let us say that you invested $5,000 in XYZ on October 1, 2001. On October 1, 2002, your investment is worth $4,000, giving you a short-term paper loss of $1,000. If you sell now, you can realize the loss and use it to offset other short-term gains realized this year. However, if you wait until the end of the year to sell (assuming that the price has not changed), the loss will be long term. Then you would have to use it to offset long-term gains, which receive favorable tax treatment anyway. To really stay on top of your tax game, you must pay attention to each stock purchase date and review the position before the one-year anniversary. If you have a loss, consider selling on or before the year is up. If you have a gain, consider holding on until after you have held the stock at least one year and a day.

Exception to the Rule: You Already Have Short-Term Losses

This said, you must keep your entire portfolio and all this netting in mind because depending on what's going on in your portfolio, this key guideline may not apply to you. For example, if you are carrying over a short-term loss from a previous year—or if you have already realized some short-term losses this year —you can freely take short-term gains to the extent of your short-term losses. In this case, it does not do any good to hold out for long-term capital gains because the lower tax rate will not apply: You will net out your short-term gains with your short-term losses and escape the tax anyway.

Defer the Tax on Profitable Stocks by Not Selling

If holding a stock for more than one year is good because you are taxed at lower capital gains rates, *not selling* the stock is even better because you will not be taxed this year at all. Your open positions are not subject to the gain/loss netting game but rather are ignored until you finally close out the position. If you are contemplating selling a profitable stock, consider not only the capital gains tax but also whether it will push you into a higher tax bracket or make you subject to one of the phaseouts for the standard deduction or personal exemption.

As noted in Chapter 1, if your adjusted gross income (AGI) is over $132,950 in 2001, you are allowed fewer itemized deductions and personal exemptions. If taking a gain would make you subject to these phaseouts, the transaction will cost you more than just the capital gains tax. This may give you an even greater incentive to hold onto the stock. Of course, you could owe one heck of a capital gains tax by the time you finally sell. Or if you wait too long and the stock tanks, your gain could turn into a loss—which brings us to our next rule.

When Making Investment Decisions, Balance Both Investment and Tax Considerations

The key to maximizing after-tax returns is to make good investment decisions that also are tax-savvy. Usually this means basing your buy/sell decisions primarily on investment considerations, with taxes playing a lesser role. Think about it: If your short-term gain evaporates while you are waiting for it to turn long term, you will not feel so happy about claiming the loss on your tax return; you will be kicking yourself for not having nailed down the gain. On the other hand, there will be times when a transaction designed strictly for tax purposes is the right thing to do. The bottom line: When making a decision for investment purposes, always think about the taxes, and when initiating a transaction based on tax considerations, always think about the investment ramifications. Do whatever you think will give you the highest after-tax return.

Five-Year Rule

In 1997, Congress passed a law designed to encourage people to hold their stocks at least five years. Starting in tax year 2001, if you are in the 15-percent tax bracket or lower, your capital gains tax on assets held longer than five years is 8 percent instead of the usual 10 percent. If you are in one of the higher tax brackets, your five-year capital gains tax is 18 percent instead of 20 percent.

There is just one catch. For the 15 percent or lower tax bracket people, the lower rate applies to securities that have been held five years as of January 2, 2001 or later (meaning they could have been purchased as long ago as December 31, 1995). For everyone else, the five-year holding period starts on January 2, 2001. This means that you will not qualify for the 18-percent capital gains rate until 2006 and only on securities purchased after January 2, 2001.

So what about all those stocks you have owned for years and plan to own for many more years? How do you get the tax break on them if you had to have purchased them on January 2, 2001 or later? Well, Congress gave you a little break. You can do what's called a *deemed sale,* which involves paying the regular capital gains tax on gains achieved up until January 2, 2001 and then starting your holding period anew. If you hold the stocks until 2006, your next batch of gains will be taxed at the 18-percent rate. One of the best parts about this is that you do not need to make this decision until you file your 2001 tax return, which gives you until April 2002 (or October 2002 with extensions) to decide. The thing you do *not* want to do is elect the deemed sale if you think you will be selling the securities before 2006. This would mean paying taxes before you need to and getting no additional benefit. And you may not do a deemed sale on securities in which you have a loss, no matter how attractive that idea sounds.

Since paying taxes before their time is anathema to most of us, the decision to do a deemed sale is not to be taken lightly. If you have a large gain in a stock, you could be out of pocket a lot of tax money, and all you get in return is 2 percentage points knocked off part of the taxes you would pay anyway.

Example

You invested $10,000 in a stock in January 1990. On January 2, 2001, your holdings were worth $70,000, for a $60,000 unrealized gain. If you do a deemed sale, you will owe $12,000 in capital gains taxes at the 20 percent rate ($60,000 × 0.20 = $12,000). The tax will be due by April 15, 2002 (remember, even if you file for an extension, you still have to pay your taxes by the April filing deadline).

Now fast forward to 2006. Let us say that your holdings are now worth $100,000 and you decide to sell. Your taxable gain is the difference between the current market value ($100,000) and the new basis that was established when you did the deemed sale on January 2, 2001 ($60,000), or $40,000. You would owe tax on the $40,000 at the five-year capital gains rate of 18 percent, or $4,800. Altogether, you would have paid a total of $16,800 in taxes ($12,000 + $4,800 = $16,800) versus $20,000 if you had not done the deemed sale, for a difference of $3,600 ($20,000 − $16,800 = $3,600). Based on these calculations, it would appear that doing the deemed sale was a good idea because it saved you $3,600 in taxes.

However, you have to think about what you might have done with that $12,000 had you not forked it over to the government five years ago. If you had not done the deemed sale and instead invested the $12,000 at just 6 percent, you would have earned more than the $3,600 tax differential. In this example, it clearly would have been better to hang onto the stock and pay tax on the entire gain at the 20-percent rate rather than paying part of the tax early in an effort to save 2 percent on subsequent gains. However, every situation is different, and you must run the numbers for your own case. Generally, experts recommend doing the deemed sale only if you have a small gain as of January 2, 2001. It will not cost you much in taxes, and it will start the holding period for the five-year gain rate should you decide to keep the stock that long.

In any case, keep in mind that going forward, any stock you buy now will qualify for the five-year capital gains rate of either 8 or 18 percent, depending on your bracket, as long as you hold it more than five years. This could be a real boon for retirement planning. If you expect to be in the 15-percent tax bracket when you retire, you could defer (by not selling) and then significantly reduce the amount of capital gains tax you will pay on appreciated securities. It also has implications for college saving: Give appreciated stock to your teenage son, and let him pay the capital gains tax at the 8-percent rate. We will talk more about income shifting and family planning in Chapter 8.

Understanding Your Cost Basis

NOTE

In the interest of simplicity, we are omitting commissions in the examples throughout this book. You should not do this, however, when reporting your transactions. Otherwise, you will pay too much in taxes.

As we have seen, capital gains taxes are based on the difference between your sales proceeds and your cost basis. Both these numbers must be readily at hand to figure your capital gains tax accurately. The sales proceeds are seldom in question. When your brokerage firm sells a stock, it tells the IRS what your sales proceeds were by issuing form 1099. The IRS will then be looking for the transaction to appear on your tax return.

If you do not want to pay capital gains tax on the entire sales proceeds, you will need to subtract your cost basis to determine your net gain (or loss). This, of course, means that you have to *know* your cost basis. This will not be a problem if you keep good records and if the transaction was relatively straightforward, such as selling 100 shares of stock that you bought last year. Just be sure to include brokerage commissions on both sides of the transaction to determine your net gain or loss.

Example

You bought 100 shares of XYZ at $60 per share and paid $30 in brokerage commissions for a total investment of $6,030. You sold it six months later for $70 per share and received net sales proceeds of $6,970 after paying another $30 in brokerage commissions. Your net gain is $940 ($6,970 − $6,030 = $940), not $1,000. As long as you record the total dollar amounts of your transactions (rather than the price per share), you will have no trouble with cost basis—assuming you keep the records, of course.

Where cost basis can cause tax nightmares is where you (1) bought the stock a long time ago and did not keep your brokerage statements, (2) received the stock by gift or inheritance and have no idea what cost basis you should use, (3) acquired stock at lots of different prices and on many different dates, or (4) sold only a portion of your holdings. Let's look at each of these situations in more detail.

You Bought the Stock a Long Time Ago and Lost the Paperwork

You can try calling your broker and asking for a copy of your statement, but if you really did buy the stock a long time ago, you may not even know whom to call given all the mergers and changes that have taken place in the brokerage industry. If you know the date of purchase, you can go to www.bigcharts.com and look up the historical price, which is adjusted automatically for stock splits. If bigcharts.com does not go back that far, you can try calling the company. If it does not have historical pricing information, you can go to the library and look up the stock tables on microfilm. When determining your cost basis this way, you are supposed to use an average of the high and low trading prices of the day. Of course, the newspaper price will not be adjusted for subsequent stock splits. For this, you can call your current broker, who should have access to historical split information.

What if you cannot remember when you bought the stock? You could try taking your best guess based on whatever records you do have and be prepared to justify your rationale to the IRS if audited. Worst-case scenario: You will have to use a cost basis of zero and pay capital gains tax on the entire net proceeds. Let this be a warning to anyone who tends to dump all their records every few years. Statements establishing cost basis must be kept until the position is closed out, even if it takes decades and you are not the one to do it. This brings us to the next scenario.

You Received the Stock by Gift or Inheritance

What if you did not buy the stock yourself but rather received it by gift or inheritance? You should know whether the donor was alive or dead when you received the stock, because it will have a bearing on your basis.

GIFT

So your favorite aunt has decided to give away some of her stuff before she dies, and you are the lucky recipient of 100 shares of American Electric Power. Since you are not exactly a utility kind of investor, you would like to sell the shares and buy something more aggressive. How do you calculate the gain? Well, lucky for you, your aunt kept good records and knows exactly how much she paid for the stock. On a gift, your cost basis and holding period are the same as the

---

Example

You inherit 100 shares of AEP from your aunt. You sell the shares at $49 and receive proceeds of $4,900. Your aunt tells you she bought the stock 30 years ago at $27 and has statements confirming her investment of $2,700. Your net long-term gain is $2,200 ($4,900 − $2,700 = $2,200).

donor's cost basis and holding period. Just subtract the amount your aunt paid from the amount of sales proceeds you received, and this is your taxable gain.

The exception is if you sell for a loss. In this case, your basis is *either* the fair market value of the stock on the day you received it *or* your aunt's original cost basis, whichever is *lower*.

Example

You receive the 100 shares of AEP when it is worth $25 per share. Two years later the stock is trading at $20; you sell your shares and receive net proceeds of $2,000. To determine your net loss, you would subtract your sales proceeds from fair market value on the date you received the gift because that is the lower basis: $2,500 − $2,000 = $500 net long-term loss.

If you sell the shares somewhere between your aunt's cost basis and fair market value on the date your inherited them, you would report no gain or loss.

Example

You inherit the 100 shares of stock AEP when it is worth $49 per share. Two years later the stock is trading at $30, and you sell your shares. Since the $30 sales price is between your aunt's cost ($27) and the fair market value on the date you inherited it ($49), you would report neither a gain nor loss on the sale.

INHERITANCE

What if your aunt died before she got around to gifting the stock to you and left it to you in her will instead? Ah, now you get to enjoy a step-up in basis. On inheritances, your cost basis is the fair market value of the stock on the day you inherit it (or six months later if that valuation is chosen by the executor). Thus, if you sell the stock on the same day you inherit it, your cost basis is the same as your sales proceeds, and your net gain is zero. If you sell the stock at a later time, you will calculate your gain (or loss) by subtracting the stepped-up basis (the fair market value on the day you inherited the stock) from your sales proceeds.

As part of the Economic Growth and Tax Relief Reconciliation Act of 2001, this step-up in basis on inherited securities is being eliminated in 2010. This means that if your aunt dies in 2010 and you inherit the stock, you would calculate your basis as if it were a gift, as noted earlier. In other words, you would assume your aunt's cost basis. Let us hope that she left good records because she will not be around to tell you what she paid for the stock. Whereas it used to be advantageous for a person to wait until after death before giving away stock

> ### Example
>
> You inherit 100 shares of AEP from your aunt when the stock is trading at $49 per share, giving you a basis of $4,900 (remember, it does not matter what your aunt paid for the stock because it is an inheritance, not a gift). Six months later you sell it for $53 per share and receive proceeds of $5,300. Your net gain is your sales proceeds of $5,300 minus your basis of $4,900, or $400. Even though you held the stock for less than 1 year and a day, your gain is classified as long term. Why? This is just the rule: Inheritances are always presumed to be long term, regardless of how long you or the donor held the stock.

so that the recipient could receive a step-up in basis, this advantage will disappear in 2010. Then it will make no difference whether the donor is alive or dead when the stock changes hands—at least as far as cost basis is concerned. (Please note: This elimination of the step up in basis in 2010 is part of the repeal of the estate tax and may change between now and then. Please see Chapter 8 for more information on the estate tax.)

You Acquired the Stock at Lots of Different Prices and on Many Different Dates

Let us say that you have been accumulating Microsoft stock over the years. You purchased several 100-share lots, all at different prices, and acquired even more shares from the company as a result of stock splits. How do you calculate your basis on your total holdings? It should be easy if you have your records. All you do is add up the total dollar amount of your investments. Although it may be nice to know that a two-for-one stock split causes your basis to drop by half on a per-share basis (100 shares purchased at $60 each becomes 200 shares purchased at $30 each), you really do not need to keep track of your per-share basis as long as you know the dollar amount of your investment.

> ### Example
>
> You buy two 100-share lots of Microsoft, investing $7,000 and $8,000, respectively, or a total of $15,000. After each 100-share stock purchase, the stock splits two for one. The effect of each split was to double the 100-share purchase as well as the holdings you already had, giving you a total of 600 shares. If the stock is trading at $70 per share, your holdings are worth $42,000. If you sell all 600 shares, your gain is $27,000 ($42,000 − $15,000 = $27,000). You need not worry about the per-share basis as long as you know the total dollar amount of your investment.

You Sold Only a Portion of Your Holdings

Here is where this basis business gets really complicated. If you sell only a portion of your holdings, how do you know what the basis is for the shares you sold? For example, if you sell 300 shares of Microsoft and keep the other 300, how do you know which 300 shares you sold, and how do you determine the cost basis of those shares?

Unless you specify otherwise, the IRS will presume that you sold the first shares you acquired. This is called *first in, first out* (FIFO). You may not average your cost; this method is reserved only for mutual fund sales (see Chapter 4).

Example

You bought your first 100 shares of Microsoft at $70 per share. When it subsequently split two for one, your cost basis for these 200 shares dropped to $35 ($70 ÷ 2). Then you bought another 100 shares at $80. When the stock split two for one again, you received 300 shares. Thus 200 of those shares went with your first purchase and reduced your cost basis of these now 400 shares from $35 to $17.50. The other 100 shares reduced your cost basis on your latest purchase from $80 to $40. Thus you now have a total of 600 shares. Of these, 400 have a cost basis of $17.50 and 200 have a cost basis of $40. If you sell 300 shares, they will be presumed to be part of the 400 earliest acquired shares having a cost basis of $17.50.

As you can see, the problem with letting the IRS decide which shares you sold is that often this will result in a higher tax. If the stock price has been climbing steadily, your basis will be lower for the first shares you acquired than for the last. If you are interested in taking the smallest taxable gain possible, you may want to sell shares acquired at the highest price. You can do this through *specific identification*—that is, telling your broker *at the time you place the trade* which shares you are selling.

Note that you may not wait until your accountant is filling out schedule D after the trading year is over to decide which shares you sold. To identify which shares you are selling, simply tell your broker at the time you place the order that you wish to sell the shares you bought on such and such a date at such and such a price. Make sure the broker sends you written confirmation of these instructions. Without it, there will be no way to confirm that you identified which shares you wanted to sell. If you are delivering a stock certificate for the shares you are selling (as opposed to selling shares held in street name in your brokerage account), record the certificate number and any other identification that they bear before you turn in the certificate so that you can prove which securities you sold. Although specific identification may be a little more trouble than letting the IRS apply its FIFO method, it can make a significant difference in the amount of capital gains tax you pay on securities accumulated over a period of time. It may even allow you take a loss instead of a gain. Get into the habit of identifying securities as part of your tax-savvy investing program. And always make sure that you get written confirmation from your broker. This is one of those administrative details some brokers let fall between the cracks, but you must have it as part of your tax documentation.

The Wash Sale Rule

Once investors figured out how beneficial losses could be for saving taxes, it did not take them long to hit on the idea of selling a stock for a loss and then buying it back again right away if they thought it was still a good investment. No can do, the IRS said. This would look too much like you were selling the stock for tax purposes only and that your real intention was to keep the stock as an investment. Thus the IRS implemented the *wash sale rule,* which says that if you sell a stock for a loss and buy the same stock back within 30 days of selling it, you cannot deduct the loss. In addition, to catch those sneaky people who might think about doubling up on their shares in anticipation of selling their holdings, the wash sale period covers 61 days, running from 30 days before to 30 days after the date of sale.

Example

You buy 100 shares of Dell at $50 on March 1, 2002. On June 1, 2002, the stock is trading at $45, and you sell all your shares for a $500 short-term loss. On June 29, 2002, you buy 100 shares of Dell at $48. This violates the wash sale rule because you bought the same stock back within 30 days of the sale. You are not allowed to deduct the $500 loss.

Buying Fewer Shares

If you buy fewer shares in a wash sale than the number of shares sold, only a proportionate part of the loss is disallowed.

Example

If you had bought only 50 shares of Dell on June 29, 2002, you could have deducted half your $500 loss, or $250.

Substantially Identical Securities

The wash sale rule prohibits you from buying back *substantially identical securities* within the 61-day wash sale period. What constitutes substantially identical securities? Well, obviously, buying back the exact same stock as in the Dell example violates the wash sale rule. However, you may buy shares in IBM or another computer stock because even though the companies are in the same industry, the securities are not considered substantially identical. Buying a call option on the same stock you sold *would* violate the wash sale rule because an option and its underlying stock tend to move together. The bottom line is that if you are not substantially changing your investment position, the tax loss is not allowed under the wash sale rule.

Adjusted Basis

If you are denied a tax loss because you repurchased identical securities under the wash sale rule, you can add the amount of the disallowed loss to your basis in the new securities. This essentially postpones the benefit of your loss rather than eliminating it entirely.

Example

You buy 100 shares of Dell for $5,000 on March 1, 2002. On June 1, 2002, you sell all your shares for $4,500, for a $500 short-term loss. On June 29, 2002, you buy 100 shares of Dell for $4,800. This violates the wash sale rule. Although your $500 short-term loss is disallowed, you may add $500 to your cost basis on the new shares, adjusting your basis from $4,800 to $5,300. If you sell the stock a month later for $5,500, your gain would be $200 ($5,500 − $5,300 = $200), not $700.

Adjusted Holding Period

The holding period is also adjusted when a loss is disallowed under the wash sale rule. The holding period for the new stock goes back to the purchase date for the old stock. This makes it impossible to convert a long-term loss into a short-term loss. However, if you end up selling the stock for a gain, it may enable your gain to go long term sooner than it otherwise would have.

Example

Since the 100 shares of Dell purchased on June 29, 2001 violated the wash sale rule, your holding period goes back to the date of original purchase, or March 1, 2001. If you sell the stock on March 2, 2002 or earlier, your gain or loss is short term. If you sell it on March 2, 2002 or later, it is long term.

Losses Only

If you sell your position for a *gain* and then buy back the same stock, the wash sale rule does not apply.

> **Example**
>
> You buy 100 shares of Dell for $5,000 on March 1, 2001. On June 1, 2002, you sell all your shares for $5,500, for a $500 short-term gain. On June 29, 2002, you buy 100 shares of Dell for $4,800. This does not violate the wash sale rule. You must report the gain, and your basis and holding period on the new purchase are not adjusted.

Gifts and Inheritances Exempt

Stock received through gift or inheritance is exempt from wash sale rules.

Partial Sales Okay

If you buy 100 shares of stock on June 1 and sell 50 shares for a loss on June 10, you are not violating the wash sale rule even though you are retaining part of your position. The wash sale rule is not designed to prevent people from taking a bona fide loss in the process of reducing their position. It is designed to prevent you from sustaining a loss for tax purposes and then recovering your full position within a few days.

Matching Rules

As we have noted, if you buy replacement stock under the wash sale rule, you must adjust your basis and holding period. For this reason, you must be able to identify the securities that represent the replacement stock. This is not always so easy to do when you have multiple transactions. To keep things straight, you must analyze your transactions in chronological order.

> **Example**
>
> You buy 100 shares of Dell on March 1, 2002. On June 1, 2002, you sell your shares for a $500 short-term loss. On June 29, 2002, you buy 100 shares of Dell. On June 30, 2002, you buy 100 more shares of Dell. Only the shares purchased on June 29 would have their basis and holding period adjusted. The shares purchased on June 30 would not be affected by the wash sale rule.

Related-Party Rule

Do not even think about having your spouse buy the replacement stock that you cannot buy under the wash sale rule. This would violate the related-party rule, which prohibits you from deducting a loss on a sale of securities to a relative such as a spouse, parent, or child. The same goes for a corporation or other entity that you control.

Example

You buy 100 shares of Dell on July 1, 2001 and sell them for a short-term loss on August 15, 2001. On August 22, 2001, your spouse buys 100 shares of Dell. The loss would be disallowed under the wash sale rule because the stock was replaced within 30 days of the sale by a family member.

Avoiding the Wash Sale Rule

Sometimes tax-related investment decisions can help save you from yourself. In other words, you may be better off just selling your losers and getting them out of your portfolio rather than trying to keep the position and somehow get around the wash sale rule. If you are so attached to a stock that you cannot bear to let even 30 days go by without holding the position, well, maybe you are just too attached to it. There are several other ways you can take advantage of a stock's potential—if not directly, then indirectly. By establishing a loss for tax purposes and then reinvesting the proceeds in similar but not substantially identical securities, you can take advantage of at least some of the attributes of the stock you are selling.

Buy a different stock in the same industry. Industry sectors often move in unison. This is called *sector rotation,* and it can last anywhere from a few days to several months or longer. If your sector has been in the doldrums (hence the reason for your loss) and you are afraid it will pick up before you have a chance to buy your stock back, just buy another stock in the same industry. This preserves your investment play without violating the wash sale rule.

Buy a mutual fund. Find a mutual fund that invests in your sector and holds a large position in the stock you like. Exchange-traded funds (ETFs) are as easy to trade as stocks and offer the added benefit of diversification (more on mutual funds in Chapter 4).

Buy the preferred stock. Preferred stock in the same company is not considered substantially identical to common stock unless it is convertible into common stock and trades at prices that do not vary much from the conversion ratio. This may defeat the purpose because preferred stocks are different animals from common stocks (higher yields, lower volatility, and lower growth potential), but if you love the company so much that you cannot bear not to be invested in it, this may be the way to go.

Wait 30 days before doing anything. You could think of the 30-day restriction as a kind of cooling off period during which you pause and reflect on the wisdom of jumping back into the same stock on which you just took a loss. Perhaps your love affair with the stock will cool, and you will be ready to move on to something else.

Double up. If you simply cannot bear to go even one day without owning your beloved stock, then prove your commitment by doubling up. If you have a loss that you would like to take for tax purposes, buy an equal number of shares, wait 31 days, and sell the position purchased at the higher price. Of course, if the stock tanks, you will be magnifying your losses, but hey, at least you will own the stock. If you plan to do this, pay attention to the calendar. To take the loss this tax year, you will have to double up at least 31 days before the last trading day of the year.

Dividends

Capital gains taxes certainly represent the most complicated aspect of taxation on stock trades. Before we get into some even more complicated stuff on short sales and options contracts, let us take a break and talk about dividends. Dividends are easy to understand because they are taxed as ordinary income, and there is not a lot you can do to manipulate your portfolio to reduce the taxes on them, except buy stock in companies that do not pay them. Oh, you can sell a dividend-paying stock before the ex-dividend date to ensure that you will not receive the next dividend, but it is hardly worth the bother and commission costs, especially since, theoretically at least, the stock price just before the ex-dividend date already includes the dividend. (*Ex-dividend* means "without the dividend." Anyone who buys a stock on the ex-dividend date will not receive the next dividend. For this reason, stock prices generally drop by the amount of the dividend the day they go ex.) Selling a stock before the ex-dividend date might enable you to convert ordinary income to capital gains, but it may not be worth it once you factor in trading costs and the effect on the rest of your portfolio. Here we go again making something complicated out of something that is supposed to be simple. Let us back up.

Dividends are distributions of money or stock paid to you by a corporation in which you own shares. Most dividends are paid in cash and reported to the IRS on form 1099-DIV. When you fill out your tax return, you report dividend income on line 9 of your form 1040, and it is added to your other ordinary income for the year. See how simple it is?

When a Dividend Is Not a Dividend

Some mutual funds pay dividends that include capital gains distributions. These are not the simple kinds of dividends we are talking about here. We will talk more about mutual funds in Chapter 4.

Reinvested Dividends

Some companies let you reinvest your dividends into more shares of stock. You still must pay income tax on these dividends each year, even though you are not taking the money in cash. What is more, you must pay tax on the little service fee the company deducts from your dividends to do this for you. Of even greater significance is the fact that each time a dividend is reinvested, it is like a mini-stock purchase that you must keep track of so that you will know your basis when you eventually sell your stock. With each dividend reinvestment, you acquire a few more shares whose cost basis is equal to the fair market value of the stock on the day the dividend was reinvested. Do this over a period of years, and you will have many small lots of stock purchased at different prices. If you sell all the stock at once, you need not worry about your per-share cost basis for each ministock purchase. All you have to do to determine your capital gain is add together the amount of your original investment plus the total of all the dividends you have received (and paid taxes on) over the years. Subtract this grand total from your sales proceeds, and this is the amount subject to capital gains taxes (either long or short term depending on your holding period). If you sell only a portion of your shares—well, all I can say is, I would not want to be your accountant. Figuring out the basis for each of your many shares of stock is not impossible, just tedious. Without the paperwork, it *is* impossible. Recall our earlier discussion on FIFO versus specific identification. If you do not specify which shares you are selling, the IRS will presume that you are selling the shares acquired first. As long as you have records showing the date and price of each stock purchase and reinvested dividend, you can determine your basis and go on to calculate your capital gain or loss.

Purchasing Stock at a Discount

Some dividend reinvestment plans allow you to invest additional cash and buy stock at a discount. If you do this, you must report as dividend income the difference between the cash you invest and the fair market value of the stock on the dividend payment date.

Stock Dividends

Some companies issue stock dividends in lieu of cash. For example, you might receive an extra 10 shares of stock as a "freebie" stock dividend. How you treat this for tax purposes depends on whether the stock dividend was declared taxable or tax-free.

TAXABLE STOCK DIVIDENDS

Taxable stock dividends are not taxed as ordinary income, as they would be if they were paid in cash. Instead, they are treated as if you had reinvested them, as discussed earlier. Your basis is the fair market value of the stock on the day of the distribution, and your holding period begins on that date.

Example

You bought 100 shares of XYZ at $45 on March 1, 1998. On October 1, 2001, when the stock is trading at $50, you receive a taxable stock dividend in the amount of 10 shares. Your basis and holding period on the original 100 shares do not change. Your basis on the new shares is $500 (10 ($50). Your holding period for these 10 shares begins on the date you received them, or October 1, 2001.

TAX-FREE STOCK DIVIDENDS

Tax-free stock dividends are treated a little differently. Instead of creating a new lot of stock with its own basis and holding period, a tax-free dividend (which includes stock received through splits) attaches itself to your original investment, adjusting the basis by the amount of the distribution and assuming the same holding period.

Example

You bought 100 shares of XYZ at $45 on March 1, 1998. On October 1, 2001, when the stock is trading at $50, you receive a *tax-free* stock dividend in the amount of 10 shares. In this case, your basis on the original investment is adjusted. Add the value of the stock dividend ($500) to your original basis ($4,500), giving you an adjusted basis of $5,000. To determine your per-share basis, divide this amount by your new number of shares: $5,000 ÷ 110 = $45.45.

The most important thing to keep in mind about dividends is that cash dividends are taxed as ordinary income and stock dividends—even those deemed tax-free—are taxed as capital gains. Capital gains income usually is preferable to ordinary income because, as we have discussed, if the security is held long term, it is taxed at a lower rate. Also, it is not subject to the $3,000 limit for deducting capital losses. In other words, given the choice, tax-savvy investors usually take every opportunity to earn capital gains income, eschewing ordinary income whenever possible.

Once again, however, we caution you against letting taxes rule your investment decisions to the exclusion of investment considerations. Dividend-paying stocks tend to be more conservative than non-dividend-paying stocks, involving larger, more established companies. They tend to be less volatile, and many companies have a record of raising their dividends every year, making them excellent investments for retirement income. Dividend-paying stocks, however, are not just for conservative investors. Some people think that growth companies that reinvest all their profits do not always use the money wisely. These investors would rather receive cash dividends and reinvest the money themselves, even if it means paying ordinary income tax on the dividends.

Short Sales

When you sell a stock short, you are selling shares you do not own in the hope of buying them back later at a lower price. You are making a bet that the stock will go down. If it does, you will have a capital gain based on the difference between the amount you received when you shorted the stock and the amount you paid to buy it back.

Example

You think XYZ will go down in price. You sell short 100 shares and receive proceeds of $4,000. Six months later the stock is trading at $30. You cover your short by buying 100 shares at $30, or $3,000. Your short-term gain is $1,000 ($4,000 − $3,000 = $1,000).

Since every stock transaction involves both a buyer and a seller, someone will be looking to receive those shares of stock you sold short. In the typical short sale, your broker will borrow the shares on your behalf and deliver them to the buyer. Now you are on the hook to the broker and will at some point have to replace those borrowed shares by buying them on the open market. When this happens, you are officially closing out the position ("covering your short") and establishing your gain or loss for tax purposes. In the meantime, your broker will charge you interest on the loan of stock as well as any dividends the buyer is entitled to receive while the short position is open (these may be deductible as an investment expense; see the section on writing off investment expenses at the end of this chapter).

A loss on a short sale is not deductible until the position is closed and the shares are delivered to the broker. This seems obvious. Just as a gain or loss on a long position is not established until the position is closed out by selling the stock, a gain or loss on a short position is not established until the position is closed out by buying or delivering the stock.

Example

You short 100 shares of XYZ in November 2001 when the stock is trading at $50. By December 31, the stock is at $60, but you do not cover your short until January 2, 2002. You would report the short-term loss on your 2002 tax return.

Short selling is done in a margin account. If the stock goes against you, you will be on the hook for a greater sum of money, increasing your interest costs and, of course, your potential capital loss. Your losses theoretically are unlimited on a short sale. This is why investors generally do not keep short positions open too long if the stock is going against them. Vigilance is a requirement of the game, as is the willingness to cut your losses sooner than you otherwise might if you were long the stock and had all the time in the world for the stock to turn around.

Your holding period on a short sale is the period of time you actually own the stock before delivering it to the lender. Since your broker likely will snatch the stock the instant it hits the account after you enter a buy order to cover your short, your gain or loss on the typical short sale will be (very) short term. However, there may be instances when you have a long-term gain or loss on a short sale. This can happen when you short stock you already own.

It may seem odd that anyone would short stock they already own, but it does happen. People used to short stock they already owned in an attempt to lock in their profit this year and defer the tax to another year or convert short-term gains into long-term gains. This was called *shorting against the box,* and it was perfectly legal before 1997. Now such a transaction is called a *constructive sale* and eliminates the very tax benefits the strategy was trying to achieve. If you short a stock that you already own and on which you have a profit, you must

Example

In February 2001 you buy 100 shares of ABC at $10 per share, investing $1,000 (100 × $10). In November 2001, when the stock is selling at $50, you execute a short sale of 100 shares (100 × $50 = $5,000). In February 2002, you deliver your shares to close the short sale. The tax law treats the short sale as a constructive sale of an appreciated financial position. You must report the $4,000 gain in 2001, the year of the short sale, not in 2002, when you delivered the securities. To shift tax reporting to 2002, you would have had to close the short sale by the January 30, 2002 and obtain similar stock, which you would have had to hold for at least 60 days after the closing of the short sale.

report the transaction in the year the short sale occurs, not when the position is closed and the securities are delivered (which means you might as well just sell the stock). However, there is an exception. If you deliver the securities before the end of January (technically, before the thirtieth day of the next year) and continue to hold *substantially identical securities* for at least 60 more days, you can report the short sale in the year of the delivery of the replacement stock —in other words, you can defer it to the following year. Note that you must both deliver the securities *and* hold them for 60 more days. Obviously, this means that you must acquire an equal number of substantially identical securities (using the same definition as for the wash sale rule) so that you can deliver one batch and hold the other.

If you have owned the stock more than a year at the time you put on the short position, your gain or loss will be long term—as long as you do not try any funny stuff like buying more stock and using it to cover your short instead of delivering the shares you have held long term. In order to qualify for a long-term gain on a short sale, you must meet three conditions: (1) You must have owned the stock more than a year at the time you enter into the short sale, (2) you may not acquire any shares of that stock while the short position is open, and (3) you must use your long-term shares to close the short sale.

Example

You buy 100 shares of XYZ in March 2000 for $5,000. In April 2001 the position is worth $6,000. You sell the stock short and establish a long-term gain of $1,000 ($6,000 − $5,000 = $1,000). You cover the short in October 2001 by delivering your shares. You do not enter any orders to buy XYZ during April to October while the short position was open. You may report this transaction as a long-term capital gain.

You may not realize a short-term loss on a short sale if you held substantially identical securities long term. This is to keep you from taking a loss without substantially changing your position.

Example

You inherited 200 shares of QRS from your aunt in 1998. In July 2001, you fear for the market but do not want to sell your aunt's beloved shares, so you short the stock at $40. In November 2001, the stock is at $50, and you cover your short, taking a $2,000 loss (200 × $10 = $2,000). You may not claim this as a short-term loss on your tax return because you held the same stock for more than a year when you initiated the short sale.

Worthless Securities

A stock that goes to zero is a short seller's dream. It is the best outcome you could possibly hope for. Although there may be no official announcement by the company that the shares are worthless, you cannot keep the position open forever and defer the taxes on your gain. You are required to report the gain in the year it became known that the shares were substantially worthless. Lucky for you, you will not have to cough up any cash to cover the short—just the taxes.

Although some of the rules for short sales can get complicated, most of them were instituted to prevent people from trying funny stuff with short sales in an attempt to defer gains to another year or convert short-term gains into long-term gains or long-term losses into short-term losses. Do not let these complicated rules make you crazy. Just use your common sense. If you are selling short for investment reasons—because you think a stock will go down—the rules are clear and easy to understand. If you are laying on complicated short/long positions in an attempt to evade taxes or get around the wash sale rule, you should know that somebody else probably has tried it already, and there is probably a rule prohibiting it. Even the IRS is not clear about some of the rules; for more vague information on short sale tax rules, see IRS Publication 550, "Investment Income and Expenses." The bottom line: Devote your time and energy to finding good investments, not trying to dodge taxes that are yours to pay.

Options Contracts

Puts and calls are contracts that confer either the right or obligation to either buy or sell shares of stock. One contract controls 100 shares of stock. A *call option* is associated with the purchase of the stock. A *put option* is associated with the sale. There are four things you can do with options.

1. You can *buy* a *call* option and acquire the *right to buy* the stock.
2. You can *sell* a *call* option and assume the *obligation to sell* the stock if it is *called away from you* by the buyer of the option.
3. You can *buy* a *put* option and acquire the *right to sell* the stock.
4. You can *sell* a *put* option and assume the *obligation to buy* the stock if it is *put to you* by the buyer of the put.

Let us look at the investment and tax consequences of each of these transactions.

Buy a Call Option

If you *buy* a *call* option, you acquire the right to *buy* 100 shares of stock at a specific price by a certain date. There are three things you can do with an option after you buy it: (1) sell it for a gain or loss, (2) exercise it and buy the stock, or (3) watch it expire worthless. The holding period on options is generally less than a year, but some option contracts cover longer time periods; in such cases, your holding period can be either short or long term, as with any capital asset.

Let us look at the tax and investment consequences of each form of disposition.

SELL THE OPTION

In this case, you will incur a gain or loss based on the difference between the amount invested and the net sales proceeds, as with any capital asset. This is very straightforward.

Example

In January, when stock XYZ is trading at $52, you buy one XYZ May 50 call option for $500. (The price is quoted as $5; since it controls 100 shares, you add two zeroes to the quote to determine your purchase price.) This call option contract gives you the right to buy 100 shares of stock XYZ at $50 anytime before the third Friday in May. The 50 is called the *strike price.* May is the *expiration month*; all option contracts expire on the third Friday of their expiration month. Let us say that on April 15 the stock is trading at $60 and the option is worth $12. If you sell the option for $1,200, your short-term capital gain would be $700 ($1,200 − $500 = $700).

EXERCISE THE OPTION AND BUY THE STOCK

In this case, the cost of the option contract is added to your basis in the stock to determine your gain or loss. Once you exercise the option, you have an open position in 100 shares of stock, just as if you had acquired stock through any other means. Your gain or loss is realized when you sell the stock. Your holding period may be either short or long term depending on how long you hold the stock after purchasing it.

Example

Using the same circumstances as earlier, you decide to exercise your option and buy 100 shares of stock XYZ at $50. Your basis in the stock is $5,500: $5,000 for the stock (100 × $50) plus the $500 premium you paid for the option. If you turn around and sell the shares immediately on the open market at $60, you will realize a short-term capital gain of $500 ($6,000 − $5,500 = $500).

WATCH THE OPTION EXPIRE WORTHLESS

This is not what you were aiming to do when you originally bought the option, but if the stock is trading under the strike price on the expiration date, your option indeed will be worthless. When reporting the transaction, the date of the "sale" would be the option expiration date, and your net loss would be the full cost of the option. Your holding period likely would be short term, beginning on the date you bought the option and ending on the expiration date.

The preceding examples show what happens when you buy an option contract. Next, we'll cover what happens when you sell an option—specifically a call option.

Sell a Call Option

If you sell a call option, you are assuming the obligation to sell 100 shares of the underlying stock if it is called away from you by the option holder. In this case, you are on the other side of the transaction just discussed. You would receive the option premium paid to you by the buyer and wait for one of several things to happen. You could (1) cover your position by buying back the same option contract, (2) let the option be exercised, or (3) let the option expire worthless. Let us look at each of these forms of disposition.

COVER YOUR POSITION

This works similar to a short sale. You sell the option contract in the hope of buying it back later at a lower price. In this case, your gain or loss is determined in the usual way: by subtracting your investment cost from your sales proceeds.

Example

On January 1, 2001, when stock XYZ is trading at $52, you sell one XYZ May 50 call and receive proceeds of $500. On April 1, 2001, the stock is trading at $60, and the option is trading at $12. You are worried that the stock will keep going up and be called away from you at $50. You cover your position by buying back the option. It costs you $1,200. Your short-term loss is $700 ($1,200 − $500 = $700).

LET THE OPTION BE EXERCISED

If you have not closed out your position before the expiration date, and if the stock is trading above the strike price on that date, the holder of the call will exercise the option and buy the stock from you at the strike price. If you already own the stock, you will simply turn over your shares and receive proceeds equal to the strike price. If you do not own the shares, you will need to buy them on the open market and turn around and sell them at the strike price. Naturally, this will create a loss because the option holder would not exercise the option unless the stock were trading above the strike price at expiration.

In any case, you will have a sale to report on your taxes. When reporting it, the option premium you received is added to your sales proceeds. Your net gain or loss depends on your basis in the stock. If you already owned the stock at the time you sold the option (this is called *covered call writing*), your gain or loss may be long or short term depending on when you acquired the stock. If you did not own the stock at the time you sold the call (this is called *naked call writing*), you would have a short-term loss because you would have held the shares for only an instant before they were delivered to the option holder.

Example

Using the same circumstances as earlier, let us say that instead of covering your position, you do nothing. On the third Friday in May, the stock is trading at $60. The option holder exercises the option and buys the stock from you at $50. You receive $5,000 for the stock; if you add the $500 option premium you already received, you would report net sales proceeds of $5,500. The amount of gain or loss would depend on your basis in the stock. If you had bought the stock two years ago and paid $3,000, you would have a long-term capital gain of $2,500 ($5,500 − $3,000 = $2,500). If you were forced to buy the stock on the open market at $60 in order to deliver it at $50 on the expiration date, your short-term loss would be $500 ($6,000 cost − $5,500 sales proceeds = $500 short-term loss).

LET THE OPTION EXPIRE WORTHLESS

This is the happiest outcome of all for call writers. Collect the option premium and hope the stock is trading under the strike price on the exercise date so that it will not be called away from you. You would report a short-term gain in the year the option expires. Your sales proceeds are equal to the option premium you received; your basis is zero.

Example

On October 1, 2001, you sell one XYZ February 50 call and receive proceeds of $500. On the third Friday in February 2002, the stock is trading under $50, and the option expires worthless. You would report a $500 short-term gain on your 2002 tax return.

So far we have covered the investment and tax implications of call options from both the buyer's and the seller's perspectives. Put options are the mirror image of call options. The tax implications are virtually the same, whereas the investment implications are the exact opposite. When you buy a *call* option, you want the stock to go up. When you buy a *put* option, you want the stock to go down. When you sell a *call* option, you want the stock to stay the same or go lower. When you sell a *put* option, you want the stock to stay the same or go higher. Let us look at the strategies involving puts.

Buy a Put Option

When you buy a put option, you acquire the right to sell 100 shares of the stock at the strike price by the expiration date. This is a bearish strategy and is an alternative to short selling. If a stock is trading at $50 and you think it will go down, you could buy a put option giving you the right to sell the stock at $50. If the stock goes to $40, you could exercise your option by buying the stock on the open market at $40 and then turning around and selling it at $50. You also could simply sell your put. The methods of disposition for puts are the same as for calls. You can (1) sell the put, (2) exercise the put and sell the stock, or (3) watch the put expire worthless.

SELL THE PUT

The tax consequences are exactly the same as for calls. This is very straightforward. Determine your gain or loss by subtracting your cost of the put from your sales proceeds. Of course, the investment considerations are just the opposite. What will make a call rise in value is if the underlying stock rises in value. What makes a put rise in value is if the stock falls. Do *not* get these mixed up.

Example

You think stock XYZ, currently trading at $50, will fall in value. You buy an October 45 put for $300. (This is called an *out-of-the-money* option because at present it is not profitable to exercise; no one would want to buy stock XYZ at its current price of $50 and turn around and sell it for $45. In this case you are betting that XYZ will be trading below $45 at expiration; if it is not, you lose your entire $300 option premium. Both calls and puts can be either in the money or out of the money depending on whether or not they are currently profitable to exercise.) Let us say you are right, and XYZ drops to $40. In July, your put is worth $800, so you sell it. You will report a short-term gain of $500 on your tax return ($800 − $300 = $500).

EXERCISE THE PUT

You exercise a put by selling the stock. Remember, a put gives you the right (but not the obligation) to sell the stock at the strike price on or before the expiration date. When you exercise a put, you add the put premium to your sales proceeds. Your gain or loss depends on your basis in the shares. Your holding period is short or long term depending on how long you held the shares.

Example

Put buying is often used as a hedge when your real interest is in owning the stock. The put serves as a kind of insurance policy against a dramatic price drop. Let us say that in January you buy 100 shares of XYZ at $47. You are worried about a price drop, so you also buy an October 45 put for $300. This makes your total investment $5,000 ($4,700 for the stock and $300 for the option). On the third Friday in October, XYZ is trading at $40, so you exercise your option and sell the stock for $4,500. Your short-term loss is $500 ($5,000 − $4,500).

You also could buy and exercise a put on stock you have held long term. In this case, you would add the option premium to your basis in the stock, and your gain or loss would be long term. If you buy a put on stock that you have held one year or less, the purchase of the put may be treated as a short sale; the exercise or expiration of the put is considered the closing of the short sale.

WATCH IT EXPIRE WORTHLESS

If the stock is trading above the strike price at expiration, you would not exercise the option; you would let it expire worthless and consider the option premium you paid the cost of hedging your bets.

Example

Using the preceding example, let us say that XYZ is trading at $50 at expiration. A put option giving you the right to sell at $45 obviously is not worth anything, so you let the option expire worthless and take comfort in the fact that your stock, which you are still holding, is going up. You add the $300 option premium to your basis in the stock and report a short- or long-term gain or loss whenever you finally sell the stock. Of course, you could have bought the put without owning the stock. In such a case, you are out the full cost of the option premium and would report it as a short-term capital loss in the year the option expires.

Sell a Put Option

The last option strategy we will cover is put selling. When you sell a put you assume the obligation to buy the underlying stock at the strike price if it is "put" to you. You are on the opposite side of the transaction from the put buyer, who bought the right to sell the stock at the strike price. If he or she decides to exercise the put, you are obligated to buy the stock from him or her. There are three things that can happen, depending on how the stock moves. You may (1) close out your position by buying the put back, (2) be forced to buy the stock if the option is exercised and the stock is "put" to you, or (3) let the put expire worthless. The tax implications are fairly obvious, but let us quickly review them, along with the investment implications of selling puts.

CLOSE OUT YOUR POSITION

Again, the tax implications are obvious and straightforward. If you sell a put and then close out the position by buying it back, your gain or loss is determined by subtracting your cost from your sales proceeds. Unlike calls, puts go up in price when the underlying stock goes down. Thus, if you sell a put and the stock goes down, you will have to buy it back at a higher price, creating a short-term loss. Conversely, if the stock goes up, the put will fall in value, and you can buy it back at a lower price. Buying puts is a bearish strategy. Selling puts is a neutral or bullish strategy.

Example

You think XYZ, currently trading at $50, will stay the same or go higher. You sell an October 45 put and receive the option premium of $300. Oops, it turns out that you are wrong, and XYZ falls to $40. If you do not close out your position, you will be forced to buy the stock at $45—not an attractive proposition when the stock is trading at $40. The put, of course, has risen in value and is now worth $800. You close out your position by buying the put for $800. Your short-term loss is $500 ($800 − $300 = $500).

LET THE OPTION BE EXERCISED

If you are still short the put at expiration (that is, you have not closed out your position by buying the put), and if the stock is trading below the strike price, you will be forced to buy the stock at the strike price. For tax purposes, you will subtract your put premium from the cost of the stock to determine your basis. You will report a short- or long-term gain or loss whenever you sell the stock.

Example

Using the preceding example, instead of closing out your position, you let your option be exercised. As required, you buy 100 shares of XYZ at $45. Your basis in the stock is $4,800 ($4,500 for the stock and $300 for the option premium). You sell the stock 13 months later at $55. Your long-term gain is $700 ($5,500 − $4,800 = $700).

YOU WATCH THE OPTION EXPIRE WORTHLESS

This is really what put writers want to happen. They want to collect the option premium without having to either buy back the put or buy the stock. You would report the full option premium as a short-term capital gain in the year the option expires.

> **Example**
>
> In September 2001, you sell an XYZ February 45 put and receive the option premium of $300. On the third Friday in February 2002, the stock is trading above $45, and the option expires worthless. You would report a $300 short-term capital gain on your 2002 tax return.

While the tax implications of options strategies seem relatively straightforward, keeping all your transactions straight can get very complicated when you lay on multiple positions and unwind them at different times. Here are some basic rules to remember when calculating your gain or loss for tax purposes:

If you buy an option contract and it expires worthless, it is reported as a capital loss in the year it expires.

If you buy and sell an option contract (regardless of which order you do it in), you report the gain or loss in the year in which you close out the position.

If you sell an option and it expires worthless, it is taxed as a short-term gain in the year it expires, even if it covered a period of more than a year.

When options are exercised, the option premium is not considered income but rather changes either the basis or the net proceeds from the stock:

If you exercise a call, your basis in the stock is the cost of the stock plus the cost of the option.

If you exercise a put, your net sales proceeds equal the amount you received for the stock less the option premium paid.

If the call you wrote is exercised, your net sales proceeds equal the amount you received for the stock plus the option premium received.

If the put you wrote is exercised, your basis is the cost of the stock less the option premium received.

Writing off Investment Expenses

As a general rule, the IRS lets you deduct expenses incurred in the process of earning income. This is certainly the case for businesses. It is also true for investing, but special rules apply. We will be covering the specific rules for bonds and mutual funds in the chapters that follow. For stocks, you will be concerned with the following investment expenses.

Commissions

As noted earlier, trading commissions—the fees paid to your broker to execute orders to buy or sell shares of stock—are added to your basis or subtracted from your sales proceeds in determining your capital gain or loss.

Example

You buy 100 shares of XYZ at $50 and sell it 3 months later at $55. You pay a brokerage commission of $30 on each trade. When reporting this transaction, your basis will be $5,030 ($5,000 + $30), and your sales proceeds will be $5,470 ($5,000 − $30), for a net gain of $440 ($5,030 − $5,470 = $440).

Investment Interest

If you borrow money and use it to buy investment property, the interest you pay is deductible up to the amount of your investment income. You must itemize deductions in order to take advantage of this deduction. However, this deduction is not subject to the 3-percent reduction of itemized deductions if your AGI exceeds $132,950. Since there are many kinds of loans and many different ways you can use the proceeds, you will need to keep careful records showing that the money you borrowed was indeed used to acquire investment property. Otherwise, the interest will not be deductible.

MARGIN LOANS

The most common type of loan for buying stocks is a *margin loan*—this is the money your brokerage firm lends you with your securities pledged as collateral. As long as you use the money to buy securities and not living-room furniture, the interest you pay on a margin loan qualifies as investment interest. However, you actually must pay the interest during the tax year in order to deduct it. If the interest is merely added to the loan, you may not deduct it. If you do not have the cash to pay it, you can borrow it—but not from the same lender. You will need to borrow from another lender in order to write off investment interest you cannot afford to pay during the tax year.

PERSONAL LOANS

As you probably know, the interest on credit cards, automobile loans, and other personal loans is not deductible. What determines whether or not any loan interest is deductible as an investment expense is how you use the proceeds. If you take out a personal loan and use the proceeds to buy investment property, the interest would qualify as investment interest. What if you take out a loan and split the use of proceeds, using part of it to buy stocks and part to buy a new couch? Only the interest paid on the part allocated to the stocks would qualify as investment interest expense. To avoid accounting nightmares, put loan proceeds into segregated accounts based on their intended purpose. By keeping the stock money in a separate account, you can show that all the disbursements from that account were used to acquire investment property and safely write off the interest on that part of the loan.

Example

You borrow $20,000 intending to use $15,000 to invest in stocks and $5,000 for a new couch. Your annual interest cost on the 9-percent loan is $1,800. Since three-quarters of the loan proceeds were used to buy stocks, you can write off three-quarters of the interest expense, or $1,350 ($1,800 − 0.75 = $1,350).

MORTGAGE LOANS

Home mortgage interest is deductible anyway and is not deductible as investment interest, even if you take out a home equity loan and use the proceeds to buy investment property.

Dividends on Short Sales

As noted in the section on short selling, when you short a stock, you must pay the broker the dividends that the buyer is entitled to receive. If you itemize deductions, you may treat these dividend payments as investment interest expense, provided the short sale is held open at least 46 days. If the position is held open less than 46 days, the payment is not deductible as an expense but instead is added to your basis.

Example

You sell short 1000 shares of XYZ at $50 per share on July 1, 2001. On August 1, 2001, you cover your position at $45. While you were short the stock, the company paid a quarterly dividend of 25 cents a share, or $250 on your 1000 shares. Since the short position was open less than 46 days, the $250 is added to your basis. Your new basis becomes $50,250 ($50,000 + $250), giving you a capital gain of $5,250 ($50,250 − $45,000).

Miscellaneous Deductions

If you subscribe to newsletters or research services or incur other types of expenses in the pursuit of investment income, you may deduct only the amount that exceeds 2 percent of your AGI. For example, if your AGI is $60,000 and you spend $800 on newsletters, you would not get to deduct any of it (2 percent of $60,000 is $1,200). If you spent $1,500, you could deduct $300 ($1,500 − $1,200 = $300). Cruises are not deductible as an investment expense, even if you attend an investment seminar while on board.

Investment Income

The thing to remember about deducting investment interest is that you may not deduct more than you receive in investment income. If you pay $500 in investment interest and receive only $200 in investment income, you may deduct only $200 in interest expense. Any amount not deducted (the remaining $300 in this case) may be carried over to the next year.

Investment income usually is defined as interest, dividends, or short-term capital gains. It does not include *net capital gains*, which in this definition means the excess of long-term capital gains over short-term capital losses. You can make the election to include long-term capital gains in investment income for the purpose of deducting investment interest. However, you will be giving up their favorable tax treatment. This may be worth it if you have a lot of investment interest expense that you do not expect to be able to deduct in the next year or two. However, you should always think carefully before converting long-term capital gains into ordinary income and consider the impact on your overall taxes, not just this year, but in subsequent years as well.

Do You Qualify as a Trader?

If you qualify as a trader, you may be able to write off more of your investment expenses than the preceding guidelines suggest. A trader must meet two tests: the trading activity test and the substantial activity test. We will cover this subject in more depth in Chapter 13. For now, suffice it to say that you must have many, many short-term trades in a year to qualify as a trader.

Foreign Tax Credit

If you invest in overseas stocks, either through American depositary receipts (ADRs) or actual foreign shares, the country of origin will withhold taxes on your dividends. The amount withheld varies by country but is commonly 15 percent. Thus, for example, if you are entitled to a dividend of $100, you will actually receive $85. When you file your U.S. tax return, you must report the full $100 as income. You get the 15 percent back by filing for the foreign tax credit using form 1116. If you qualify for the *de minimis* foreign tax credit—which means your foreign dividends did not exceed $300 ($600 for married couples filing jointly), you can claim the foreign tax credit on line 43 of form 1040 without filing form 1116.

Tax Points to Remember when Investing in Stocks

- Hold stocks at least one year and a day to qualify for favorable long-term capital gains tax treatment: 20 percent for investors in the 27-percent tax bracket or higher or 10 percent for those in the 15-percent tax bracket or lower.

- Sell unprofitable stocks before the one-year anniversary date to capture short-term losses that can be used to offset short-term gains or up to $3,000 of ordinary income ($1,500 for married filing separately).

- Hold stocks more than five years to qualify for the five-year capital gains rate: 18 percent for investors in the 27-percent tax bracket or higher or 8 percent for those in the 15-percent tax bracket or lower.

- Defer capital gains taxes by holding stocks indefinitely.

- Do not let tax considerations overrule investment considerations: Market movements often exceed any amounts you stand to save in taxes.

CHAPTER 3

Investing in Bonds

U nless you are a buy-and-hold kind of investor, tax planning with stocks can be difficult because you never know for sure how your trading activity will net out until the year is over. Bonds are a different story, however. Most people invest in bonds for the income, which is largely predictable in advance. This predictable income stream not only makes your life easier because you know how much money you have coming in every year, but it also makes investment and tax planning easier. When considering a bond purchase, you can ask how much interest you will receive each year and refer to your tax bracket to determine the amount of after-tax income you will have.

Example

You are considering investing $50,000 in bonds that pay 7-percent interest, for a total of $3,500 per year in taxable income. If you are in the 27-percent tax bracket, you can calculate that $945 will be lost to taxes ($3,500 × 0.27). This information can help you decide if you want to invest in these bonds and, if you do, how much you will need to set aside for taxes.

Bond Basics

You may already know what a bond is, but to get all our readers on the same page and make sure everyone understands the terminology we will be using throughout this chapter, let us do a quick review.

A *bond* is evidence of a debt obligation, sort of like an IOU. When you buy a bond, you are actually lending money to the bond's *issuer*. The issuer may be a corporation, a municipality, or the U.S. government or one of its agencies. The bond is the physical certificate that serves as evidence of the loan and states all its terms. (If you hold your securities at your brokerage firm in *street name,* you will not receive the certificate, and in fact, many bonds today are electronic or so-called book-entry bonds.) The key terms of a bond are its *face amount* (also called *par value*), *interest rate*, and *maturity date*. These three pieces of information tell you how much you will be investing, the amount of interest you will receive each year, and when you will get your original investment back. For example, if you are looking at a bond that has a $1,000 face amount, pays 7-percent interest, and matures in 2021, you know that for each bond you buy you will be investing $1,000 and will receive $70 per year ($1,000 × 0.07). In 20 years you will get your $1,000 back—assuming that you do not sell it before then.

Yield and Price

If you do sell your bonds before maturity, you probably will get more or less than the amount you invested. As with stocks, bond prices are constantly moving up and down (although usually in a narrower range). Unlike stocks, however, whose prices are determined by many, many factors, including the outlook for the company, the industry, and the overall economy, the key thing affecting bond prices is interest rates. When an investor is deciding whether or not to pay par value ($1,000) for your 7-percent bond maturing in 20 years, he or she will look at what is available in the current marketplace. If interest rates have fallen since you bought your bond so that equivalent 20-year bonds are now yielding 6 percent, your 7-percent bond will be priced higher than $1,000 to make the income equal to 6 percent. This would make your bond worth $1,166 ($70 annual interest ÷ $1,166 purchase price = 6-percent yield). Conversely, if interest rates have risen to 8 percent since you bought your bond, the price will be discounted to make the $70 interest payments equal to 8 percent. This would put the price at $875 ($70 ÷ $875 = 8 percent). Bonds selling for less than par value are said to be selling at a *discount*, whereas bonds selling for more than par value are selling at a *premium*. Keep in mind, however, that if you hold your bonds to maturity, you need not worry about these price changes. Only if you decide to sell do you need to be concerned about getting more or less than your original investment back.

Bond yields may be expressed in different ways. First, there is the *coupon rate,* which is the contractual rate of interest stated on the bond. When you buy a new-issue bond and pay par for it (the same as the face amount), your yield will be the same as the coupon rate. The coupon rate is stated as a percentage of the face amount. A 7-percent coupon on a $1,000 bond means that interest payments will be $70 per year. Then there is the *actual yield,* which is what investors care most about. If interest rates go up, a bond having a 7-percent coupon will be discounted, as just discussed. A 7-percent coupon bond priced at $875 will have an *actual yield* of 8 percent. And finally, there is the *yield to maturity*, which represents the total rate of return on the bond if it is held to maturity. This takes into account both the interest payments and any difference in price between the amount you paid and the amount you receive at maturity. For example, if you pay $875 for a 20-year bond and receive $1,000 at maturity, a portion of the $125 difference (in this case, one-twentieth, or $6.25) is added to your annual interest payments to determine your yield to maturity. When you buy a bond at a discount, your yield to maturity will be more than your actual yield. If you pay a premium for the bond—say, $1,166 for $1,000 in face amount —the amount you paid over par is divided by the number of years remaining and subtracted from your annual interest payments to determine your yield to maturity. In this case, your yield to maturity will be lower than your actual yield. Bonds that have call provisions (discussed later) may be redeemed prior to maturity. These bonds also have a *yield to call*, which indicates your total return if the bond is called on the earliest possible date.

Some bonds have a coupon of zero and are called, appropriately enough, *zero-coupon bonds*. With these bonds your entire yield comes from the difference between the amount you invest and the amount you receive on sale or maturity. Zero-coupon bonds are great for long-term planning because you know exactly how much you will get back on a specific date in the future, making them suitable for college saving or retirement planning. However, taxable zero-coupon bonds do have undesirable tax consequences, which we will get to in a moment.

Floating-rate bonds do not have a fixed coupon rate, but rather the interest rate is pegged to a certain key interest rate and adjusted periodically. Because of these interest-rate adjustments, prices on floating-rate bonds seldom drift very far from par, making them good short-term investments. Compared with long-term bonds with fixed rates, however, the yields are substantially lower because of the reduced risk.

Maturity

A bond's *maturity* is the date the issuer plans to pay off the debt and *redeem* the bond. If you are still holding the bond at maturity, you will be paid the face amount, usually $1,000 for each bond. Bonds maturing in two to three years are considered *short-term* bonds; those maturing in 3 to 10 years are *intermediate-term* bonds, and those maturing in 10 or more years are *long-term* bonds. A bond's maturity affects its pricing. Under normal circumstances, long-term bonds carry higher yields than short-term bonds due to the higher risk associated with waiting to get your money back. On a 30-year bond, any number of things can happen between now and then to threaten the security of your investment, from the issuer's possible financial ruin to rampant double-digit inflation. This is why long-term bonds tend to yield more than short-term bonds and is why their prices tend to be more volatile.

The relationship among bond yields and maturities is reflected in the *yield curve*, which is published every day in the *Wall Street Journal.* The horizontal axis represents years to maturity. The vertical axis represents yield, from low to high. A normal yield curve shows short-term rates having the lowest yields, with the curve sloping gradually upward and flattening out for bonds further out on the maturity scale. Sometimes the yield curve becomes inverted. This can happen when investors are uncertain about the economy and want to keep their money in short-term instruments in order to maintain flexibility. Generally, though, the longer the maturity, the higher is the yield.

One thing you must watch out for are *call provisions*. Some issuers (corporations and municipalities, not the U.S. government) reserve the right to call the bonds early. They may exercise this call privilege if interest rates fall below the coupon rate, allowing them to obtain cheaper financing elsewhere—just as you refinance your mortgage when interest rates drop. A called bond is bad for you as an investor because it means that you have to reinvest your proceeds at a time when interest rates are low. In addition, the profit potential in your bond will be limited by the call provision. Normally, a steep drop in interest rates would result in a steep rise in bond prices, giving you a nice profit if you were to sell. However, if a bond is callable at par, investors know it is likely to be called in the face of dropping interest rates and will not pay as much as they would for a noncallable bond. Moreover, if you were unlucky enough to pay a premium for a bond that gets called, you likely will have a loss because most bonds are called at par or slightly above. Be wary of call provisions, and if you do buy a callable bond, be sure to evaluate its yield to call, not the yield to maturity. The flip side of call provisions are *put provisions*. These are beneficial to investors and allow you to sell the bonds at par back to the issuer after a stated number of years. Put provisions offer some protection against being locked into a low rate and take some of the risk out of investing in long-term bonds.

Quality

A fourth aspect that is not a bond term per se but that affects bond pricing significantly is the *quality* of the bond, or the likelihood that the issuer will make good on its promise to pay the stated interest rate and return the full principal amount to investors when the bond matures. Bond quality is a subjective judgment, but rarely do investors have to evaluate quality themselves. Rating services, such as Standard & Poor's (S&P) and Moody's, do extensive research on the financial strength of bond issuers. They assign ratings that distill reams of quantitative research down to a few simple letters, ranging from AAA (highest) on down through AA, A, BBB, BB, B, CCC, and so on. Bond investors rely heavily on these ratings, and a survey of the bond market at any given time would show the inverse relationship between bond yields and quality: The higher the quality, the lower the yield, and vice versa.

The federal government can be counted on absolutely to fulfill its promises to bondholders not just because this is a great country we live in but also because the government has taxing authority. Unlike a corporation, which could simply run out of money if business goes bad, the federal government will never run out of money because it can make people like you and me pay more in taxes. This is the theory, anyway, behind the AAA rating bestowed on U.S. Treasury securities—the highest rating a bond can get. A few other issuers have AAA ratings, but for most it goes downhill from there. The four highest ratings—BBB and above—are considered investment grade. Practically speaking, this means that you are pretty likely to get all the interest and principal you are entitled to (although AAA is the only rating offering ironclad assurance). When you get into the lower ratings, you are taking more of a chance, but you will be rewarded for your bravado: Low-rated bonds carry much higher yields. Whenever you hear the term *high-yield bonds*, you know that somebody is trying to make *junk bonds* sound good. This does not mean that they are necessarily bad investments, just risky. If you are going to venture into the junk bond universe, be sure to diversify so that if one bond goes bad, you will not lose all your money. Consider mutual funds for your high-yield bond investments.

While we are on the subject of quality, we should note that bond prices are affected not only by changes in the general level of interest rates but also by changes in ratings. In other words, the quality you think you are getting could change. Even if interest rates remain unchanged, a bond whose rating drops from A to BBB due to negative circumstances affecting the issuer most certainly will fall in price. Let this be a warning to anyone who buys a bond believing that its high rating is cast in stone. Except for U.S. Treasury securities, all bonds are subject to some degree of risk arising from unforeseen circumstances.

When we talk about comparing bonds throughout this chapter, we use the term *equivalent bonds*. Equivalent bonds are similar in quality and maturity. If you are evaluating taxable versus tax-free bonds, for example, it is fair to compare an AAA U.S. Treasury bond maturing in 20 years with an AAA municipal bond maturing around the same time. However, do not try to compare a B-rated corporate bond against an AAA municipal bond because too many other factors will influence their respective yields. (See Table 3.1.)

Taxes

Taxes play an important role in bond strategies because bonds typically (but not always) generate substantial current income. Whereas you can buy a portfolio of nondividend-paying stocks, forget about them, and not worry about taxes until you sell decades later, bonds usually create some type of taxable event, usually every year, unless you are careful to arrange otherwise. First we will cover the general rules concerning taxation of bond income. Then we will go into the many

TABLE 3.1   Bond Ratings

MOODY'S	S&P	DEFINITION
Aaa	AAA	High-grade investment bonds. The highest rating assigned, denoting extremely strong capacity to pay principal and interest. Often called "gilt edge" securities.
Aa	AA	High-grade investment bonds. High quality by all standards but rated lower primarily because the margins of protection are not quite as strong.
A	A	Medium-grade investment bonds. Many favorable investment attributes, but elements may be present that suggest susceptibility to adverse economic changes.
Baa	BBB	Medium-grade investment bonds. Adequate capacity to pay principal and interest but possibly lacking certain protective elements against adverse economic conditions.
Ba	BB	Speculative issues. Only moderate protection of principal and interest in varied economic times. (This is one of the ratings carried by junk bonds.)
B	B	Speculative issues. Generally lacking desirable characteristics of investment bonds. Assurance of principal and interest may be small; this is another junk bond rating.
Caa	CCC	Default. Poor-quality issues that may be in default or in danger of default.
Ca	CC	Default. Highly speculative issues, often in default or possessing other market shortcomings.
C		Default. These issues may be regarded as extremely poor in investment quality.
	C	Default. Rating given to income bonds on which no interest is paid.
	D	Default. Issues actually in default, with principal or interest in arrears.

Source: Moody's Bond Record and Standard & Poor's Bond Guide

exceptions and special situations that make bond investing a rather complex endeavor. It is this complexity, however, that allows investors to design bond strategies perfectly suited to their needs—to meet both current income requirements and tax minimization where appropriate.

Interest Income

The interest on bonds may be either taxable or tax free depending on the issuer. Special rules apply to bonds that do not pay current interest income but rather accumulate the interest and pay it all out at maturity. We will cover these in a later section entitled "Premium and Discount Bonds."

CORPORATE AND GOVERNMENT AGENCY BONDS

The interest on bonds issued by corporations or agencies of the U.S. government is fully taxable as ordinary income on both federal and state tax returns in the year it is received. For example, if you invest $10,000 in 7-percent corporate bonds, you will receive $700 per year in interest, typically in two semiannual payments of $350 each. At the end of the year, you will receive form 1099-INT stating the amount of interest you received for the year. You report this on line 8a of your form 1040. If you have more than $400 in interest income, you also have to fill out schedule B, listing the sources of all your interest income, and transfer the total amount to line 8a.

TREASURY SECURITIES

The interest on U.S. Treasury securities is taxable at the federal level but is not subject to state or local taxes. Treasury securities are divided into three categories—bills, notes, and bonds—as defined by their maturity date. *Treasury bills* (T-bills) mature in one year or less and do not carry a coupon rate, as do ordinary bonds. Instead, you buy a T-bill for less than its face value and receive the face value at maturity. The difference between the purchase price and the redemption amount represents your interest. For example, if you paid $9,650 for a one-year T-bill and received $10,000 at maturity, your interest would be $350. This is reported on your tax return in the year the T-bill comes due. Some people buy T-bills as a way to defer interest income into the next year. Treasury *notes,* maturing in 2 to 10 years, and Treasury *bonds,* maturing in 10 or more years, both pay a fixed rate of interest every six months that is federally taxable in the year it is received.

TAX-EXEMPT MUNICIPAL BONDS

The interest on tax-exempt municipal bonds is not taxable at the federal level, and if the bonds are issued in the state where you live, the interest is not taxable at the state level either. Thus, if you buy $50,000 worth of California municipal bonds while you are living in California, the interest will be free from both state and federal income tax. However, if you move to New York, the interest on those bonds will now be subject to state tax. Understanding the yield differential between equivalent taxable and tax-free bonds for your tax bracket is a key aspect of investing in bonds and will be covered in the section entitled "Municipal Bonds."

Capital Gains

Bonds are considered capital assets, so if you sell your bond prior to maturity and receive more or less than the amount invested, you will incur a capital gain or loss, just as we discussed in Chapter 2. The tax will be based on the difference between your cost basis and your sales proceeds. Your holding period starts on the day after you buy the bond and ends on the day you sell it. As with all capital assets, bonds held for more than one year are subject to long-term capital gains rates: 20 percent for investors in the 27.5-percent tax bracket or higher or 10 percent for investors in the 15-percent tax bracket or lower. Thus, if you buy a bond for $1,000 and sell it for $1,200 two years later, you will have a $200 long-term capital gain. As with stocks, any trading costs you incur are added to your basis and subtracted from your sales proceeds. Since bonds usually include the dealer's markup in their price, this may be done automatically for you.

The actual calculation for determining gains and losses on bonds is not quite as simple as it is for stocks because of special rules applying to accrued interest and to bonds purchased at a discount or premium, as we will see in the sections that follow.

Investing in Bonds

To buy a bond, you have to go through a broker, except for U.S. Treasury securities, which may be bought directly from the Federal Reserve Bank (brokers also trade in Treasuries and charge a small markup). If you are able to buy a new issue, your purchase price will be the same as the face amount, and your yield will be the same as the coupon rate. However, if you are looking for a particular type of bond (Treasury, government agency, corporate, or municipal) and want to specify a particular quality and maturity date, you will find a larger selection in the secondary market. The secondary market for bonds is vast, comprising virtually every bond that has ever been issued that has not reached maturity yet. However, it is not like the stock market, where a ready buyer or seller usually can be found for even small holdings. The bond market is largely institutional, composed of professional traders who every day buy and sell millions of dollars worth of bonds for pension funds, mutual funds, insurance companies, and banks. Individual investors are small potatoes in the taxable bond market, although they do make up the bulk of the municipal bond market.

Bonds are sold through dealers, who maintain an in-house inventory of bonds and charge a markup on each sale, just like your local retailer. The larger brokerage firms that deal in bonds have their own inventory and also act as agents who buy bonds from other dealers on behalf of customers when they do not have the desired bonds in inventory. Individual investors who buy bonds through brokers usually specify the type of bond they want (Treasury, agency, corporate, or municipal), the lowest rating they are willing to accept, and the approximate maturity date they want. The broker calls around and comes back to them with a list of bonds specifying the exact terms of the bonds he or she has found, including the issuer, coupon rate, and maturity, along with the price of the bond and the current yield. The price is usually quoted *net*, which means that it includes the dealer's markup. Bond prices are quoted in two or three digits and represent a percentage of par. For example, a quote of 98 means 98 percent of the $1,000 face amount, or $980 per bond. A quote of 106 means 106 percent of the $1,000 face amount, or $1,060 per bond. If you buy 50 bonds at 96, your total investment will be $48,000 (50 × $960 = $48,000). If the bond carries a coupon of 7 percent, your annual income will be $3,500 ($70 per bond × 50 bonds = $3,500). On your $48,000 investment, this gives you a current yield of 7.29 percent ($3,500 ÷ $48,000 = 0.0729).

Accrued Interest

Most bonds pay interest just twice a year. However, you are entitled to interest every day you own the bond (based on a 360-day year), so adjustments for accrued interest are made at the time of purchase and sale. For example, if you buy a bond on April 1 that pays interest on January 1 and July 1, you will receive the regular interest payment in July, but you will be entitled to only part of it because you will not have owned the bond for the full six-month period. Conversely, when you sell a bond, you will not be around to receive the next interest payment, but you would be entitled to the interest that has accrued to you since the last interest payment. Thus a part of each bond purchase and sale includes an adjustment for accrued interest. When you buy a bond, you must pay the portion of the next interest payment to which you are not entitled, and when you sell a bond, you will receive the portion of the next interest payment to which you are entitled. When reporting the transaction for tax purposes, you will need to separate out the portion attributable to accrued interest. What is left will be your cost basis or sales proceeds, depending on whether you bought or sold. As with stocks, these number are subtracted from each other to determine your capital gain or loss.

Example

Buy bonds, pay accrued interest. On April 1 you buy $10,000 worth of 7-percent bonds priced at par (par means the bonds are priced the same as their face value). The $700 in annual interest is payable semiannually: $350 on January 1 and $350 on July 1. Since you are not entitled to interest from January 1 through March 31, your purchase price will include $175 in accrued interest, making your total investment $10,175. On July 1, you will receive the regular $350 interest payment. At the end of the year, you will receive a form 1099-INT reporting $350 in interest income. On schedule B you will report the full $350 in interest and on the line underneath subtract the $175 in accrued interest, making your taxable interest for the year $175 ($350 − $175 = $175). When determining your basis for gain/loss purposes, you will subtract the $175 in accrued interest from the total amount paid, giving you a basis of $10,000 ($10,175 − $175 = $10,000).

When you sell a bond, the accrued interest is calculated in the opposite manner. In addition to your bond proceeds, you will receive the amount of interest that has accrued to you as of the date of sale.

Example

Sell bonds, receive accrued interest. Using the same example, let us say that your bond is worth $9,500 on December 1 and you decide to sell it so that you can establish a loss for tax purposes. Since you will not be around to receive the next interest payment on January 1, you will receive accrued interest of $292, giving you net proceeds of $9,792. Again, you must separate out the accrued-interest portion. You will report the $292 on schedule B and pay ordinary income tax on the accrued interest. When calculating your short-term loss, you will subtract the $292 from your total sales proceeds: $9,792 − $292 = $9,500. To calculate your loss, subtract this amount from your basis: $10,000 − $9,500 = $500. Since you owned the bond for less than one year and a day, your loss would be short term.

REDEMPTIONS

If your bond is called prior to the maturity date, you may receive interest for a period that you did not own the bond. This extra payment is considered a capital gain, not interest income.

Example

You hold a $10,000, 7-percent bond with interest payable January 1 and July 1. The company has the right to call the bond on any interest date. In May, the company announces that it will redeem the bonds on July 1, but you are allowed to turn it in early and receive the full interest payment. On June 1, you present the bond and receive $10,350—($10,000 principal, $292 interest to June 1, and $58 interest to July 1). The $58 is treated as a capital gain; the $292 is interest.

Premiums and Discounts on Bonds

Unless you buy a new issue, you probably will pay more or less than the face amount when you buy a bond. Yet, if you hold the bond to maturity, you will receive the face amount regardless of what you paid. The premium or discount representing the difference between the amount you paid and the face amount has special tax implications.

PREMIUMS

Let us say that taxable bonds with the quality and maturity you are looking for are currently yielding 7 percent. Either you could buy a new bond and pay $1,000 for each $1,000 in face amount, or you may choose to buy an older bond—one that has been on the market for a while. If interest rates are lower now than they were, say, a year ago, you may find a bond with an 8-percent coupon selling for a premium. The premium is the additional amount tacked onto the price of the bond to make the interest payments equivalent to the going rate in the marketplace. In this case, a bond with an 8-percent coupon paying $80 a year in interest would be priced at $1,142 to make the yield 7 percent ($80 ÷ $1142 = 7 percent). If you buy this bond, you will pay $1,142, but you will only get back $1,000 at maturity. Normally this would create a $142 capital loss realized at maturity. However, you may choose to amortize the premium over the life of the bond, deducting a portion of the $142 each year until it is all gone. When you redeem the bond at maturity, your basis will have been reduced to $1,000, and you will have neither a capital gain nor a loss. If you happen to sell the bond prior to maturity, you will subtract the new basis (which is going down little by little every year) from your sales proceeds to determine your capital gain or loss. The calculations are rather complicated and differ for bonds issued before September 28, 1985 versus those issued after September 27, 1985. See Internal Revenue Service (IRS) Publication 1212 or consult a tax professional if you choose to amortize bond premiums. You do not have to do it, but it can help offset your annual interest income and reduce your taxes.

Please note that this premium amortization applies only to taxable bonds. You may not claim a deduction for a premium paid on a tax-exempt bond.

DISCOUNTS

Bond discounts are the opposite of bond premiums. They are the amount by which a bond is priced under par. There are two kinds of bond discounts: market discounts and original issue discounts (OID).

Market Discounts

Bonds are subject to market discounts when interest rates go up and the price is reduced to make the fixed interest payment equal to the going yield in the marketplace. Let us again say that the current yield for the bonds you are looking for is 7 percent. However, this time let us say that interest rates have risen in recent years so that you can buy a bond with a 6-percent coupon priced at $857 for each $1,000 in face amount ($60 ÷ $857 = 7 percent). When you redeem the bond at maturity, the difference between the price you paid ($857) and the amount you receive is not considered a capital gain but rather is taxed as ordinary interest income. You can elect either to have this amount taxed in the year of disposition or report it annually.

If you report it annually, you must calculate the *accrued market discount* through one of two methods. The basic method, called the *ratable accrual method*, is figured by dividing the discount, $143 in this case ($1,000 − $857 = $143), by the number of days between the date you bought the bond and the date of maturity. This daily amount is then multiplied by the number of days you held the bond to determine your accrued discount. Thus, if there are, say, 800 days between the date you bought the bond and the date it matures, the daily accrual rate would be $0.1788 ($143 ÷ 800). If you disposed of the bond after 600 days and sold it for more than you paid, $107.25 would be attributable to market discount and taxable as interest income (600 × $0.1788).

The other method for figuring the accrued market discount is the *constant-yield method.* This method initially provides a smaller accrual of market discount than the ratable method, but it is more complicated to figure. Again, see IRS Publication 1212 or consult a tax professional.

Original Issue Discounts (OIDs)

Some longer-term bonds pay all the interest at maturity, similar to Treasury bills, as noted earlier. These are called *zero-coupon bonds* or *original issue discount* (OID) *bonds.* For example, you may invest $5,200 in a zero-coupon bond that matures in 10 years and pays $10,000 at maturity. The $4,800 difference is considered interest (not capital gain), and a portion of it must be reported each year as interest income. Note that you must pay taxes on the income even though you will not receive it until the bond matures (this is sometimes called *phantom income*). To avoid paying tax on phantom income, most people invest in zero-coupon bonds in tax-sheltered accounts, such as individual retirement accounts (IRAs) and retirement plans (more on these in Chapter 7).

If you do invest in OID bonds in a regular taxable account, your broker will calculate the amount of income you must report and issue you a 1099-OID. This amount may be reduced if you bought the security at a premium (that is, if interest rates have fallen since the bond was issued). See IRS Publication 1212 to find out how to recompute the OID in this case.

STRIPS, CATS, and TIGRS

Brokers holding large amounts of coupon bonds may separate or strip the coupons from the bonds and sell the coupons to investors. Examples include zero-coupon instruments sold by brokerage houses that are backed by U.S. Treasury bonds (such as CATS and TIGRS). The U.S. Treasury also offers its version of zero-coupon instruments, with the name STRIPS, that are available from brokers and banks. If you buy a stripped coupon, the spread between the cost of the coupon and its higher face amount is treated as an OID. This means that you annually report a part of the spread as interest income.

Discounts on Tax-Exempt Bonds

When a tax-exempt bond is issued with an OID, the difference between your cost and the redemption amount is not taxable. Thus, if you buy a zero-coupon municipal bond when it is first issued and hold it to maturity, there is no tax to pay.

However, if you sell the bond prior to maturity, and if you sell it for more than the accrued OID amount, you must pay tax on the excess at ordinary income tax rates.

Characteristics of Bonds

The four types of bonds—U.S. Treasury, agency, corporate, and municipal—each have special characteristics that distinguish them from one another in meeting various tax and investment objectives. Municipal bonds are especially appealing to high-income investors, whereas U.S. savings bonds, although technically not tradable securities, offer their own unique brand of tax benefits.

U.S. Treasury Securities

The market for Treasury securities is large, active, and liquid. As long as the U.S. government has borrowing needs, conservative investors will find a ready source of fixed-income securities that generate interest free from state taxes. Whatever will they do if the government pays all its bills and gets out of debt? Now there is a frightening thought.

Treasury bills mature in one year or less and pay interest at maturity. Treasury notes and bonds mature in 2 to 30 years and come in two varieties: fixed-principal and inflation-indexed. Both pay interest twice a year, but the principal value of inflation-indexed securities is adjusted to reflect inflation as measured by the consumer price index (CPI)—the Bureau of Labor Statistics' consumer price index for all urban consumers (CPI-U). With inflation-indexed notes and bonds, your semiannual interest payments and maturity payment are calculated based on the inflation-adjusted principal value of the security.

There are two kinds of inflation-indexed securities: I-bonds and Treasury inflation-protected securities (TIPS). I-bonds are a type of savings bond and are covered in the section entitled "Savings Bonds." TIPS are securities sold in 5-, 10-, and 30-year maturities. Like any other Treasury bond, they pay a fixed rate of interest semiannually that is taxable at the federal level and free from state and local taxes. The difference is in the face amount, which is adjusted every year for inflation. Let us say that you decided to buy $10,000 worth of TIPS maturing in January 2011. Your coupon rate might be 4 percent. This means that you would receive $400 in interest your first year, just like a regular bond. Where TIPS differ from a regular bond is that every year your principal would be adjusted based on the preceding year's change in the CPI. Thus, if the CPI rose by, say, 3.2 percent, your principal that first year would rise to $10,320. This would give you an overall yield of 7.2 percent—4 percent in interest payments and 3.2 percent in principal adjustment. If inflation continued to rise by 3.2 percent every year, your bond would be worth approximately $13,700 at maturity. It is important to note that the annual principal adjustments are federally taxable each year, even though you will not be receiving the money until maturity.

For this reason, TIPS are often purchased in retirement accounts or children's education accounts, where taxes are not an issue.

STRIPS, also known as zero-coupon securities, are Treasury securities that do not make periodic interest payments. Market participants create STRIPs by separating the interest and principal parts of a Treasury note or bond and selling the individual interest and principal payments to investors. For example, a 10-year Treasury note consists of 20 interest payments—one every 6 months for 10 years—and a principal payment payable at maturity. When this security is "stripped," each of the 20 interest payments and the principal payment become separate securities and can be held and transferred separately. STRIPS can only be bought and sold through a financial institution, broker, or dealer and held in the commercial book-entry system.

Agency Securities

Agency bonds are debt securities issued by various agencies and organizations of the U.S. government, such as the Government National Mortgage Association (GNMA) and Student Loan Marketing Association. Since agency issues are not direct obligations of the U.S. Treasury, they are not backed by the "full faith and credit of the United States government" and therefore technically are not as secure as Treasury securities. However, for all intents and purposes, they are as safe as Treasuries and offer slightly higher yields. Some agency securities, such as those issued by GNMA ("Ginnie Maes"), may return a portion of your principal with each interest payment. This principal portion is not taxable because it is considered a return of capital. Ginnie Maes consist of large pools of mortgages. As people refinance their mortgages or sell their homes and pay off the mortgages, these lump sums come back to investors. Even though a Ginnie Mae may have a maturity date 30 of years, you could receive all your principal back before that time. The biggest risk with Ginnie Maes is reinvestment risk because mortgage holders are more likely to refinance when interest rates are low, forcing you to find another investment in a low-interest-rate environment.

Corporate Bonds

As long as there are plenty of corporations with borrowing needs, there will be plenty of corporate bonds available for investors who are willing to take a little more risk in exchange for the opportunity to earn higher yields. Unlike Treasury securities, which are backed by the full faith and credit of the U.S. government, and agency bonds, which are backed by something close to that, corporate bonds are backed only by the promises (and the assets, if there are any) of the companies issuing them. Corporate bonds, also called *debentures*, are considered *senior* securities, which means that in the case of liquidation bondholders would receive their money before stockholders. However, this is little reassurance in the case of companies whose primary "assets" consist of the brainpower of fickle knowledge workers and a bank of used computers that may bring pennies on the dollar in a bankruptcy liquidation.

Nevertheless, corporate bonds are popular with investors looking for current income, a play on interest rates, or both. Strategies range from very conservative to very aggressive. A conservative strategy might be to buy only the highest-rated bonds and hold them to maturity. A slightly more aggressive strategy is to buy BBB-rated bonds and enjoy the higher yields associated with these lower-rated securities. An aggressive strategy might be to buy low-rated bonds with long maturities in the hope of selling them for a profit if interest rates decline.

The secondary market for corporate bonds is not as active and liquid as it is for Treasuries. This generally means that you will pay a higher markup when you buy and could have trouble selling your bonds in the future. Because the bond market is dominated by institutional investors and is not the place for small-fries, many people do their bond investing through mutual funds. Although mutual funds do not offer the flexibility and customization of managing your own portfolio of bonds, they do offer economies of scale, broad diversification (very important when investing in lower-rated bonds), and professional management. More will be said about mutual funds in Chapter 4.

Municipal Bonds

The interest on state and local obligations, commonly called *municipal bonds* (or *munis*), is not subject to federal income tax. It is also exempt from taxation in the state in which the obligations are issued. The terms *tax-free* and *tax-exempt* are used interchangeably and refer to bonds whose interest is federally tax-exempt (and may or may not be state tax-exempt). The proceeds from these bonds typically are used to build schools, bridges, hospitals, and other public works. Like any bond, municipal bonds have a face amount, an interest rate, and

Example

You are considering investing $1,000 in an AA-rated 7 percent taxable bond maturing in 20 years. This bond would entitle you to $70 in income before tax. At your 30-percent tax bracket, you would pay $21 in taxes ($70 × 0.30 = $21), which would reduce your after-tax return to $49 ($70 − $21 = $49). Divide $49 by $1,000, and you can see that earning $49 in after-tax interest on a $1,000 bond would make the tax-free equivalent yield 4.9 percent. Now you can check yields in the muni market to see if AA-rated tax-free bonds maturing in 20 years are yielding more or less than 4.9 percent. If more, you obviously are better off buying the muni.

a maturity date. The main difference is that the interest rate reflects their tax-exempt status, which means that yields are lower than for similar taxable bonds. Thus, if taxable bonds are yielding, say, 7 percent, an equivalent tax-free bond having the same quality and maturity may yield just 4.9 percent. For an investor in the 30-percent tax bracket, these two yields are the same after tax. You can compare taxable and tax-free yields by subtracting taxes at your bracket from the taxable bond and comparing the result to what you can get in an equivalent tax-free bond.

The higher your tax bracket, the greater is the differential between taxable and tax-free yields. Let us say that you are in the 35-percent tax bracket and comparing a taxable bond yielding 7 percent against a tax-free bond yielding 4.9 percent. In this case, you would pay $24.50 in taxes on the $70 interest generated by the taxable bond ($70 × 0.35 = $24.50). This would reduce your after-tax return to $45.50 ($70 − $24.50 = $45.50). On a $1,000 investment, this translates to a 4.55-percent yield. Clearly, you will end up with more money in your pocket by investing in the tax-free bond: A 4.9-percent tax-free yield is better than the 4.55-percent after-tax yield from the taxable bond.

In the marketplace, the yield differential between taxable and tax-free bonds is constantly changing depending on the outlook for interest rates, the outlook for tax rates, and even the general economy as it affects state and local municipalities (for example, California's recent power problems have pushed the state's bond prices lower, which in turn has made yields higher). As a general rule, investors in the 30-percent tax bracket or higher should think about tax-free bonds for their bond investments, whereas those in lower brackets are usually better off buying taxable bonds and paying the tax. However, you really should do the calculation at the time you make the investment because, as noted, the differential is constantly changing in the marketplace. The formula is easy enough to do.

STEP 1: Find the inverse of your tax bracket by subtracting your tax bracket from 1. Here, we will do it for you:

IF YOUR TAX BRACKET IS	THE INVERSE OF YOUR TAX BRACKET IS
27.0%	0.73
30.0%	0.70
35.0%	0.65
38.6%	0.614

STEP 2: Find the taxable equivalent of the current tax-free yield for your tax bracket by dividing the current yield on tax-free bonds by the inverse of your tax bracket.

> **STEP 2 Example 1**
>
> AA 20-year munis currently are yielding 4.9 percent. You are in the 35-percent tax bracket. Divide 0.049 (the current muni yield) by 0.65 (the inverse of your tax bracket). The result is 7.54 percent.

STEP 3: Survey the taxable bond market and compare yields.

> **STEP 3 Example 1**
>
> A survey of the bond market shows that AA 20-year taxable bonds are currently yielding 6.75 percent. In step 2 you found that you would have to earn 7.54 percent in a taxable bond in order for it to be equivalent to a 4.9-percent tax-free bond. Therefore, buy the muni.

	A TAX-EXEMPT YIELD OF					
IF TOP INCOME TAX RATE IS:	3%	4%	5%	6%	7%	8%
	IS THE EQUIVALENT OF THESE TAXABLE YIELDS:					
27.0%	4.16	5.56	6.94	8.33	9.72	11.11
30.0%	4.29	5.71	7.14	8.57	10.00	11.43
35.0%	4.62	6.15	7.69	9.23	10.77	12.31
38.6%	4.89	6.51	8.14	9.77	11.40	13.03

When doing the taxable versus tax-free comparisons, be sure to consider your tax rate in future years. Keep in mind that the Economic Growth and Tax Relief Reconciliation Act of 2001 calls for lower tax rates in the years ahead. Here's the schedule of expected rate reductions:

CALENDAR YEAR	28% RATE REDUCED TO	31% RATE REDUCED TO	36% RATE REDUCED TO	39.6% RATE REDUCED TO
2002–2003	27%	30%	35%	38.6%
2004–2005	26%	29%	34%	37.6%
2006 and later	25%	28%	33%	35%

These expected rate reductions would imply that if you are on the borderline now between taxable and tax-free, you may be better off going with the taxable bond because tax rates will be reduced in future years. Of course, another key element is your own personal situation. Will your income be going up in future years? Are you planning any major life changes, such as retirement, that might put you in a lower tax bracket? You should evaluate your bond holdings periodically to make sure that they are still appropriate for you in light of changing circumstances. If you buy tax-free bonds now because you are in a high tax bracket and then suddenly find yourself in a low bracket due to a job loss or other unexpected event, you may want to swap your munis for taxable bonds. How quickly you act will depend on how long you expect to remain in the low tax bracket. If it is just for a year or so, it may not be worth the cost of the transaction, but if it is likely to be permanent, you will want to switch to the higher after-tax yield available in taxable bonds.

Please note that only the *interest* is free from tax on municipal bonds. If you sell your bonds for a profit, the transaction may be taxed at regular capital gains rates. Please see the special rules for tax-exempt bonds purchased at a discount in the section entitled "Premium and Discount Bonds." Also, be aware that you have to report tax-free interest on your tax return (line 8b of form 1040) even though it will not be taxed.

TYPES OF MUNICIPAL BONDS

Municipal bonds are brought to market as either general obligation or revenue bonds. *General obligation bonds* are backed by the full faith, credit, and taxing power of the issuer. *Revenue bonds*, in contrast, are serviced by the income generated from the specific income-producing projects, such as toll roads, that the bonds support. Revenue bonds make up the bulk of the municipal bonds issued today, so it is important to understand that an issuer is obligated to pay the principal and interest *only* if the project generates a sufficient level of revenue. General obligation bonds, in contrast, do not hinge on a specific amount of revenue but rather are general debts of the state or municipality. Because it is always possible that revenue bonds will not generate the amount of revenue necessary for fully servicing the bond, revenue bonds are riskier than general obligation bonds and therefore carry higher yields. Investors rely heavily on ratings when investing in revenue bonds.

One way in which a revenue bond can get a high rating is to obtain a third-party guarantee that interest and principal will be paid over the life of the bond. The three principal insurers are the Municipal Bond Investors Assurance Corporation (MBIA), the American Municipal Bond Assurance Corporation (AMBAC), and the Financial Guaranty Insurance Company (FGIC). A revenue bond that carries insurance usually has an AAA rating and is traded more actively in the secondary market than revenue bonds not carrying such guarantees.

MUNICIPAL BONDS THAT MAY BE TAXABLE

Although the term *municipal bonds* usually refers to tax-exempt bonds, there are some munis that may be taxable. These include the following.

Private-Activity Bonds

A private-activity bond is any bond where more than 10 percent of the issue's proceeds are used by a private business whose property secures the issue or where at least 5 percent of the proceeds (or $4 million if less) is used for loans to parties other than governmental units. However, there are exceptions where bonds technically may be in the category of private-activity bonds but are tax-exempt. These include qualified student loan bonds, exempt-facility bonds, qualified small-issue bonds, qualified mortgage bonds and qualified veterans' mortgage bonds, qualified redevelopment bonds, and qualified 501(c)(3) bonds issued by charitable organizations and hospitals. While interest on these bonds is not subject to regular tax, the interest may be considered a tax preference item and subject to the alternative minimum tax (see Chapter 11). Always check with the issuer of a private-activity bond to find out if it is tax exempt.

Federally Guaranteed Obligations

Interest on state and local obligations issued after April 14, 1983 generally is taxable if the obligation is federally guaranteed. However, there are exceptions allowing tax exemptions for obligations guaranteed by the Federal Housing Administration, Department of Veterans Affairs, Bonneville Power Authority, Federal Home Loan Mortgage Corporation, Federal National Mortgage Association, Government National Mortgage Corporation, Resolution Funding Corporation, and Student Loan Marketing Association. Again, check with the issuer to verify the tax-exempt status of a federally guaranteed obligation.

Mortgage-Subsidy Bonds

Interest on bonds issued by a state or local government after April 24, 1979 may not be tax-exempt if funds raised by the bonds are used for home mortgages. There are exceptions for certain qualified mortgage bonds and veterans' bonds. Check on the tax-exempt status of mortgage bonds with the issuing authority.

TAX-EXEMPT INTEREST AND TAXATION OF SOCIAL SECURITY BENEFITS

Although tax-exempt interest is indeed not taxable, it is used in calculating *provisional income* to determine if Social Security benefits are taxable. For anyone *not* receiving Social Security, the number that goes on line 8b of form 1040 is essentially ignored by the IRS. However, if you do receive Social Security benefits and also earn tax-exempt interest, the number on line 8b must be counted when computing your provisional income for the purpose of determining tax on Social Security benefits. (The interest itself is not taxable, however.)

Your provisional income includes all your taxable income, all your tax-exempt interest, and one-half your Social Security benefits. If your provisional income is less than the *base amount*, none of your Social Security benefits are taxable. The base amount is $25,000 (single, head of household, or married filing separately and living apart from your spouse the entire year), $32,000 (married filing jointly), or 0 (married filing separately and living with spouse). If your provisional income is over the base amount, either 50 or 85 percent of your Social Security benefits are taxable depending on the amount of provisional income over the base amount. If you are single or filing as head of household and your provisional income is between $25,000 and $34,000, 50 percent of your benefits are taxable, and if your provisional income is more than $34,000, 85 percent of your benefits are taxable. For married couples filing jointly, if your provisional income is between $32,000 and $44,000, 50 percent of your benefits are taxable, and if your provisional income is more than $44,000, 85 percent of your benefits are taxable. If you are married filing separately and living with your spouse all or part of the year, 85 percent of your Social Security benefits are taxable regardless of your income. Please see IRS Publication 915, "Social Security and Equivalent Railroad Retirement Benefits," for detailed information on calculating the tax on Social Security benefits. For now, just understand that tax-exempt interest does figure into the calculation, even though the income itself is not taxable.

Savings Bonds

Savings bonds are more like savings accounts than the tradable securities we have been talking about in this chapter. However, they do have some features in common with Treasury securities, including the fact that interest is taxable at the federal level and tax exempt at state and local levels.

SERIES EE/E SAVINGS BONDS

Series EE/E bonds are sold on a discount basis, similar to Treasury bills. That is, you buy them for a percentage of face value and get back face value at maturity. The difference between the amount you invest and the amount you receive represents your interest. The beauty of this type of investment is that it allows you to defer the tax on the interest. With Treasury bills, you cannot defer the interest more than a year due to their limited maturities. However, with Series EE/E bonds you can defer the tax up to 30 years. As you hold these bonds, interest is added periodically to the amount you paid originally to establish their current redemption value. As this interest accrues, the value of your bond increases. When you cash a Series EE/E bond or savings note, you receive this redemption value, which represents the return of your original investment plus the interest that you earned while you held the bond.

Series EE/E savings bonds are sold at half their face value and are available in denominations ranging from $50 to $10,000. Those bought on or after May 1, 1997 earn interest based on five-year Treasury security yields. Rates are announced each May and November and equal 90 percent of the average yield on five-year Treasury securities for the preceding six months. The value of the bonds is adjusted every month, and interest is compounded semiannually. You can cash Series EE/E bonds any time after six months. However, a three-month interest penalty applies to bonds cashed in before five years. Because Series

EE/E bond interest is pegged to market rates every six months, there is no way to predict when a bond will reach its face value. In the unlikely event that rates are so low that a bond does not reach face value by the time it is 17 years old, the Treasury will make a one-time adjustment to increase the bond's value to face value at that time.

You have the choice of reporting interest earned on your savings bonds each year or deferring interest reporting until your bond is cashed, stops earning interest at final maturity, or is disposed of in some other way (such as an ownership change through a reissue transaction). Whenever you report savings bonds interest, it should be included with other interest income on your federal income tax return. If you choose to report interest annually, you may want to get a copy of Public Debt Form 3501. This table compares the value of your bonds from one year to the next and will help you determine how much interest you should report. When you cash your bonds, all the interest they have earned will be reported to the IRS. Therefore, you should keep good records so that you can show the IRS that you have been reporting all along.

If you start out deferring interest reporting, you can begin to report interest annually at any time. In the year you want to start annual reporting, you will need to report all interest earned to date (and not previously reported) for all your savings bonds and notes. Once you start annual reporting, you must continue to report interest earned annually for all savings bonds and notes you own and any you may acquire. In order to change from annual reporting back to deferred reporting, you must get approval from the IRS (refer to IRS Publication 550, "Investment Income and Expenses"). Most people choose to defer the tax on the interest. Indeed, this is one of the key benefits of Series EE/E savings bonds.

In addition to the tax deferral, there are also special tax benefits available for education savings. If you qualify, you can exclude all or part of the interest earned on Series EE/E bonds from income when the bonds are redeemed to pay for post-secondary education tuition and fees. More will be said about this in Chapter 8.

SERIES H AND HH SAVINGS BONDS

Series H and HH bonds are current-income securities. The redemption value of the bonds remains constant at exactly the amount you invested, and your interest is paid to you every six months. When you cash a Series H or HH bond, you receive your original investment back. Series H and HH bonds are issued in face amounts of $500, $1,000, $5,000, and $10,000. They pay interest at a fixed rate set on the day you buy the bond. The current rate of 4 percent has been in effect since March 1, 1993. Interest rates are reset on the tenth anniversary of the bond's issue date.

You cannot buy Series HH bonds for cash. You can get them only in exchange for Series EE/E bonds and savings notes or on reinvestment of the proceeds of matured Series H bonds. By exchanging Series EE/E bonds for Series HH or H bonds, you can continue to defer the taxes on the interest accrued on the Series EE/E bonds or savings notes until you cash the Series HH bonds, they reach final maturity, or the bonds are reissued in a reportable event.

I-bonds

I-bonds are a new type of bond designed for investors seeking to protect the purchasing power of their investment and earn a guaranteed real rate of return. I-bonds are an accrual-type security, meaning that interest is added to the bond monthly and paid when the bond is cashed. I-bonds are sold at face value—you pay $50 for a $50 bond—and they grow in value with inflation-indexed earnings for up to 30 years.

The earnings rate of an I-bond is a combination of two separate rates: *a fixed rate of return* and a *variable semiannual inflation rate*. The fixed rate remains the same throughout the life of the I-bond, whereas the semiannual inflation rate can vary every six months. The fixed rate of return is announced by the Treasury Department each May and November. The fixed rate of return announced in May of a given year is the same over the entire life of the I-bonds you purchase between May 1 and October 31 of that year. Likewise, the fixed rate of return announced in November of a given year applies to the entire life of I-bonds you purchase between November 1 and April 30 of the following year.

The semiannual inflation rate is also announced each May and November by the Treasury Department. The semiannual inflation rate is based on changes in the CPI-U, which is reported by the Bureau of Labor Statistics. The semiannual inflation rate announced in May is a measure of inflation over the preceding October through March; the inflation rate announced in November is a measure of inflation over the preceding April through September.

The semiannual inflation rate is combined with the fixed rate of an I-bond to determine the I-bond's earnings rate for the next six months. I-bonds increase in value each month, and interest is compounded semiannually. In the rare event that the CPI-U is negative during a period of deflation and the decline in the CPI-U is greater than the fixed rate, the redemption value of your I-bonds will remain the same until the earnings rate becomes greater than zero. As with all savings bonds, earnings are exempt from state and local income taxes. Federal income taxes can be deferred for up to 30 years or until redemption or other taxable disposition, whichever comes first.

I-bonds are sold at face value in denominations of $50, $75, $100, $200, $500, $1,000, $5,000, and $10,000. You are limited to purchasing $30,000 in I-bonds each year. You can order I-bonds at most local financial institutions. You just fill out a simple purchase order, pay for the bond, and your I-bond will be mailed to you within three weeks. You can cash an I-bond anytime six months after the issue date to get the original investment plus the earnings. However, I-bonds are meant to be longer-term investments. Thus, if you redeem an I-bond within the first five years, there is a three-month earnings penalty.

Tax-Saving Bond Strategies

Choosing the right type of bond for your tax situation is the most important consideration when investing in bonds, specifically the choice between taxable and tax-exempt bonds. Since bond portfolios tend not to be as actively managed as stock portfolios, there are fewer opportunities for fancy tax-saving maneuvers. However, there are a few key strategies that can help you save taxes.

Bond Swapping

Bond swapping is a very popular strategy during periods of rising interest rates because it allows you to take a tax loss on bonds that have declined in value and replace them with other bonds that are very similar but do not violate the wash sale rule. Please note that Series EE/E, HH, and I-bonds are not tradable securities and would not qualify for bond swapping. However, the other types of bonds discussed in this chapter all trade on the secondary market and therefore would be candidates for swapping.

You will recall from our discussion of the wash sale rule in Chapter 2 that if you sell a security for a loss and buy a *substantially identical* security within 31 days, you are not allowed to deduct the loss. However, the definition of *substantially identical* is much more liberal in the bond world. You can sell a bond at a loss and buy another bond with a similar interest rate and maturity date but with a different issuer, and you will have avoided the wash sale rule without substantially changing the nature of your investment. The exact name of the issuer is less important with bonds than it is with stocks. What matters most are the type of bond it is (Treasury, agency, corporate, or municipal), the interest rate, the maturity date, and the quality of the bond.

To avoid the wash sale rule, at least two of the following factors must be different: issuer, coupon rate, maturity, or call feature. Thus you could swap Ford

---

Example

In January 2002, you invest $10,000 in XYZ 7-percent bonds due in 2021. By October, general interest rates have risen, and your bonds are now worth $9,000. You sell the bonds to establish a $1,000 short-term capital loss and invest the proceeds in ABC 7-percent bonds due in 2020. Because the new bonds are priced similarly to the old bonds (they also went down after interest rates went up), you will not have to come up with much, if any, extra cash to make the new investment. You will receive the same interest payments as before and can count on getting your original principal back around the same time. In other words, you will not have changed the character of your investment substantially, but you get to take a loss for tax purposes.

bonds for Chrysler bonds. Or you could swap a 6-percent Treasury maturing in 2009 for a 6.5-percent Treasury maturing in 2010. Or in the municipal arena, you could swap a sewer bond maturing in 2015 for a water bond that matures in 2016. Any of these swaps would not change the character of your portfolio substantially but would allow you to take a loss without violating the wash sale rule. With bonds, it is very easy to find similar but not substantially identical securities, which means that there is no reason not to realize the loss if interest rates have gone up since you bought your bonds. Some people do bond swaps nearly every year, capturing even small losses for tax purposes. The only thing that might discourage you would be trading costs: If the tax benefit is so slight as to be worth less than the cost of the trade, then obviously it is not worth it to do the swap.

Other Tax-Saving Bond Strategies

Other than tax swapping, keep in mind the characteristics of the types of bonds discussed in this chapter, and focus on those that meet your investment objectives in the most tax-efficient manner.

- If you are in a high tax bracket and want to earn current income, invest in tax-exempt municipal bonds.
- If you live in a high-income-tax state, buy Treasury securities, whose interest is free from state income tax.
- If you like the predictability of zero-coupon Treasury bonds but do not want to pay tax on phantom income, buy them in a retirement or other nontaxable account.
- If you do not need current income and want a conservative, tax-deferred investment, consider buying U.S. savings bonds.

And always keep in mind the overarching rule noted in Chapter 2: Always balance investment considerations with tax considerations and follow the strategy that offers the highest after-tax return consistent with your risk tolerance and time horizon.

CHAPTER 4

Investing in Mutual Funds

If you are like the majority of investors, you do most of your investing through mutual funds rather than buying and selling individual stocks and bonds. For busy people who have neither the time nor the inclination to research individual securities, hiring a professional portfolio manager to comb through the data, analyze the numbers, and enter timely buy/sell orders makes a lot of sense. With mutual funds, you also get automatic diversification, enabling you to own a small interest in hundreds of issues rather than placing a few big bets that could devastate you financially if they did not pan out. And mutual funds are easy to buy and sell: You can invest small amounts on a regular basis and have distributions reinvested so that you do not have to go searching for another investment each time you receive a small dividend.

From a tax standpoint, however, mutual funds can be rather complicated. In addition, you often do not discover these complications until after you have already invested and later find out that you owe tax on a fund that has dropped in value or that you should have kept all those statements showing reinvested dividends over the years. If you skipped over the stock and bond chapters (Chapters 2 and 3) because you are exclusively a mutual fund investor, you may want to go back and brush up on the basic rules concerning the taxation of dividends, interest, and capital gains. Even though you do not own securities directly, the same tax rules that apply to holders of individual securities also apply to mutual funds, which are required to pass through to shareholders at least 95 percent of the investment income earned during the year. In other words, if you make money on a stock, whether it is through direct ownership of the company's shares or ownership of fund shares, you must pay capital gains tax. There are special rules that apply to mutual funds, which is what this chapter is about. However, it is also important to understand the basic taxation of stocks and bonds and how portfolios can be managed for maximum tax efficiency because the same guidelines for reducing taxes on stock and bond portfolios also apply to mutual funds. Just because someone else is managing the portfolio does not mean you cannot manage the tax impact by choosing tax-efficient funds and carefully timing your purchases and sales to minimize taxes.

It goes without saying that if you do all your mutual fund investing through retirement accounts or other tax-sheltered plans, you do not need to be concerned with taxes. Retirement-plan assets are taxed when the money is withdrawn. Annual investment income is neither reported nor taxed. We will be covering retirement plans in more detail in Chapter 7. This chapter is only for people who invest in mutual funds in taxable accounts.

Mutual Fund Basics

A mutual fund is a large portfolio of securities that have been selected by a professional portfolio manager or group of portfolio managers. The portfolio is divvied up into *shares* that are sold to the public. The price per share, also called *net asset value* (NAV), is the value of the portfolio on any given day divided by the number of shares outstanding.

Example

XYZ Mutual Fund owns 150 different stocks, including 9,000 shares of Microsoft and 8,000 shares of AOL, among many others. The value of the entire portfolio is $100 million. The portfolio has been divided into 10 million shares, which makes the NAV of each share equal to $10.

Buying a Mutual Fund

When you invest in a mutual fund, either through a broker or directly with a fund company, you usually specify the dollar amount you wish to invest. The fund com-

---

Example

On January 2, 2001, you decide to invest $10,000 in XYZ Mutual Fund. If this is a *no-load* fund (meaning no sales charge) and today's NAV is $10, you will get 1,000 shares. When your first statement comes, it will show your initial purchase: 1,000 shares at $10 per share. In the right-hand column, your share balance will be listed as 1,000 shares.

pany divides the dollar amount by that day's NAV (plus any *loads*, or sales charges, that may apply) to determine how many shares you will get.

As the stocks in the portfolio move up and down in price, the NAV fluctuates each day (mutual funds are priced daily after the stock markets close). Tomorrow it might be $10.01. The day after that it might be $9.98. You may not even be aware of these daily price fluctuations unless you follow your fund in the newspaper or on the Internet. As the portfolio earns investment income, including dividends and interest, the income is added to the pot, which increases the NAV.

Example

After three months, the appreciation of the securities has caused the NAV to rise by $0.20. In addition, the accumulation of dividends and interest has caused it to rise by $0.15, for a total NAV of $10.35. Your share balance remains constant at 1,000 shares, but the value of your investment is now $10,350 (1,000 × $10.35).

Receiving Distributions

Mutual funds are required to distribute income to shareholders periodically. This income must be reported on your tax return according to what kind of income it is. Please note that even if you are reinvesting your distributions, you need to report mutual fund income just as if you had received a check.

ORDINARY DIVIDENDS

Ordinary dividends consist of taxable interest and dividends and short-term capital gains. Unlike short-term gains you realize on individual stocks, short-term gains realized by the fund and included in ordinary dividends may not be used

Example

On March 31, XYZ Fund pays a dividend of $0.15 per share. This distribution causes the NAV to drop by $0.15, so the NAV is now $10.20 ($10.35 − $0.15). On your 1,000 shares, the dividend amounts to $150 (1,000 × $0.15). However, you have already told the fund that you do not want to receive your distributions in cash but would rather reinvest them back into the fund. Thus, on the day the dividend is paid, the fund takes your $150 and buys 14.71 shares at $10.20 per share ($150 ÷ $10.20 = 14.71). Now you own 1,014.71 shares at $10.20 per share, for a total value of $10,350. As you can see, the payment of the dividend did not change the value of your investment. You now own slightly more shares, each share worth slightly less than before.

to offset investment losses. For tax purposes, they are treated as ordinary income.

A typical growth-and-income fund might distribute dividend income four times a year. Whenever a distribution is made, that money is permanently removed from the portfolio, so the NAV drops by the amount of the distribution.

CAPITAL GAIN DISTRIBUTIONS

Periodically (or maybe fairly often), the portfolio manager sells profitable stocks and realizes capital gains. The realization of gains does not change the NAV because the stocks simply are exchanged for cash; their current value was already reflected in the NAV. However, this capital gains income must be distributed to shareholders because somebody has to pay taxes on it. Mutual funds generally do not pay taxes but rather pass the income through to shareholders who report the income on their own tax returns. Mutual funds typically distribute capital gains income once a year in the fall.

Example

Let us say that it is now November 30. In June and September you received another $0.15 per share dividend, which you reinvested into more shares, so on the morning of November 30, you have 1,043.92 shares, each worth $10.60, making your total investment worth $11,065.55 (1,043.92 × $10.60). This $10.60 NAV includes $0.60 in realized capital gains for the year (i.e., the portfolio manager has already sold the profitable stocks). In the afternoon, the fund pays all this accumulated capital gains income out to shareholders. On your 1,043.92 shares, this is a check for $626.35 (1,043.92 × $0.60). This $0.60 capital gains distribution knocks the NAV back down to $10. Because you have directed the fund to reinvest your distributions, it takes your $626.35 and buys 62.64 shares ($626.35 ÷ $10). Now you have 1,106.56 shares, each worth $10 per share. The total value of your investment has not changed from this morning; it is still $11,065.20 (1,106.52 shares × $10 per share). However, you now have a bigger a tax liability than you had before. When you file your income tax return for the year, you will need to report $626.35 in long-term capital gains. You also will need to report the total dividend income for the year. Assuming that the fund pays another $0.15 per share dividend on December 31 on your now 1,106.56 shares, you will have received a total of $622.59 in dividends for the year. This amount will have to be reported on your tax return as well. The total tax on the capital gains and dividend income, assuming that you are in the 27-percent tax bracket, will be $293.37. This breaks down as follows:

$626.35 in long-term capital gains taxed at 20 percent = $125.27.
$622.59 in dividend income taxed at 27 percent = $168.10.
Total tax due by April 15 = $293.37.

Capital gain distributions from funds are taxed as long-term capital gains, even if you have not owned the fund more than one year. As you know, long-term capital gains are taxed at favorable rates (20 percent for investors in the 27-percent tax bracket or higher or 10 percent for investors in the 15-percent tax bracket or lower). When reporting long-term capital gains from mutual funds, be sure to follow the instructions on the tax form for computing the tax on long-term gains. Otherwise, you will pay too much in tax.

Once a distribution is made, the deed is done no matter what happens to the fund after that. In our example, you will be starting the new year with 1,122.83 shares (the December dividend bought another 16.27 shares), each share worth $10, for a total value of $11,228.30. If the market tanks in January, the NAV could fall to, say, $8. Now your investment would be worth $8,982, or $1,018 less than your original $10,000. However, you would still have to report the $626.35 in capital gains income and the $622.59 in dividend income for the preceding year and pay the tax of $293.37 in April. As anyone who has been in this situation will attest, it is pretty hard to write out that tax check when your investment is down in value. However, once you understand the nature of fund accounting, you see how it can happen. There is no better lesson in the realities of mutual fund taxation than to have to write a check for income that has disappeared. It will make you go on the search for a more tax-efficient fund. We will talk more about this later.

OTHER TYPES OF MUTUAL FUND DISTRIBUTIONS

Ordinary dividends and capital gain distributions are by far the most common types of mutual fund distributions. However, there are other types of distributions you may need to know about.

Exempt Interest Dividends

Mutual funds that invest in tax-exempt securities pay income that is tax-exempt on the federal level and may or may not be tax-exempt at the state level. Exempt interest dividends must be reported on your tax return, even if they do not affect the amount of tax you pay. As we discussed in Chapter 3, tax-exempt interest is used to calculate tax on Social Security benefits. Also, exempt interest dividends may affect your deduction for investment interest expense (you may not write off the interest on loans used to invest in tax-exempt securities). In addition, some or all of your exempt interest dividend may be subject to state income tax. Also keep in mind that even tax-exempt funds sometimes distribute a small amount of taxable income, so pay attention to any form 1099-DIVs you receive at the end of the year.

Nontaxable Distributions: Return of Capital

Mutual funds sometimes make nontaxable distributions that are considered part of your investment in the fund—in other words, it is your own money coming back to you. These distributions are not taxable and are sometimes referred to as *return-of-capital distributions.* They are reported on form 1099-DIV in a box labeled "Nontaxable distributions." You do not have to report these nontaxable distributions, but you do need to lower your basis in your shares by the amount of the distribution. If the accumulation of these distributions drives your basis down to zero, you have to start paying taxes on them. They are taxed as capital gains, either long- or short-term depending on how long you held the shares to which the distribution relates.

Capital Gain Allocations

Sometimes a fund will sell profitable stocks and keep the proceeds in the fund rather than making a capital gain distribution to shareholders. When they do this, they pay tax on the gain (at the 35 percent rate) and allocate your portion of the gain on form 2439. When you get this form, you will report the capital gain on your income tax return for the year and do the long-term capital gains tax rate calculation as just noted. Because the fund paid more in tax than you will owe (35 versus 20 percent), you can claim a credit for the tax paid by the fund. Before you are finished, be sure to adjust the basis of your shares in the fund. This will save taxes when you sell. You can increase your basis by 65 percent of the amount of the allocation (the amount left after you get credit for the 35 percent tax paid by the fund).

Save Your Documents

Mutual fund shareholders get so much mail in December and January that it can be hard to know what to keep for current tax reporting and what you will need to save for later.

FORM 1099-DIV (OR SUBSTITUTE)

Form 1099-DIV is the biggie. This is the official document stating your taxable income for the year. Both you and the Internal Revenue Service (IRS) receive copies of this form from the mutual fund. If the amount you report does not jibe with the amount the IRS thinks you should be reporting, you may get a friendly letter asking you to explain. If the amount appears wrong or you have a question about it, do not hesitate to call the fund for clarification.

INFORMATION STATEMENTS

If there is anything special you need to know about your mutual fund income that the fund company does not need to tell the IRS about, you will receive it in a separate statement. For example, if some of your interest came from U.S. Treasury securities and therefore is not taxable at the state level, you will be informed of this in an information statement. Likewise, if you received exempt interest dividends that are tax-exempt at the federal level and may or may not be tax-exempt at the state level, you will receive information about this in a separate statement.

MUTUAL FUND STATEMENTS

Whenever there is activity in the fund, such as when you buy shares, receive a distribution, or redeem shares, you will receive a statement from the fund. These statements are not so important for reporting annual distributions because form 1099-DIV is your official statement for that purpose. However, if you sell shares during the year, you will need to report the transaction on your tax return and will need your statements to determine your basis (covered in the next section). Most funds issue a cumulative statement at year end listing all the year's activity, so when that one comes, you can throw out all the interim statements that came throughout the year. Keep these year-end mutual fund statements for as long as you own the fund.

Selling a Mutual Fund

Selling mutual fund shares is a taxable event, just as it is with any other capital asset such as stocks and bonds. If your sales proceeds exceed your basis, you will have a capital gain, long term if you held the shares more than one year or short term if you held them one year or less. As noted in Chapter 2, long-term gains are taxed at favorable rates, 20 percent for investors in the 27-percent tax bracket or higher or 10 percent for investors in the 15-percent tax bracket or lower. Short-term gains are taxed at your marginal tax rate. Likewise, if you have a loss on your sale of fund shares, that is, your basis exceeds your sales proceeds, you may use it to offset other gains or up to $3,000 of ordinary income. Gains

Example

Using our same example, you would have made five separate share purchases during your first year. Your initial purchase plus the reinvestment of four quarterly distributions would look like this:

DATE	AMOUNT OF DISTRIBUTION	TRANSACTION	SHARE BALANCE
1/2/01		1,000 shares @ $10.00	1,000.00
3/31/01	$150.00	14.71 shares @ $10.20	1,014.71
6/30/01	$152.21	14.64 shares @ $10.40	1,029.35
9/30/01	$154.40	14.57 shares @ $10.60	1,043.92
11/30/01	$626.35*	62.64 shares @ $10.00	1,106.56
12/31/01	$165.98	16.27 shares @ $10.20	1,122.83

*Capital gains distribution

and losses are reported on schedule D and matched against each other, as discussed in Chapter 2.

Where mutual fund taxation gets complicated is in the calculation of basis. Going back to the example we have been using, calculating your basis on your first 1,000-share purchase is easy: It is clear from your initial statement that you bought 1,000 shares at $10 per share. If you sell these particular shares for, say, $10.20 per share and receive proceeds of $10,200, your capital gain is $0.20 per share ($10.20 − $10.00), or $200 ($10,200 − $10,000). No problem there. However, what if you sell some of the shares you acquired through reinvested dividends? Each of those reinvested dividends represented a separate transaction and established a different cost basis for the shares acquired. For example, your first dividend of $150 was used to purchase 14.71 shares at $10.20 per share. If you sell any of those shares at, say, $10.20 per share, you have neither a gain nor a loss. The June, September, and December distributions were all reinvested at different share prices, giving each batch of shares a different basis.

CALCULATING COST BASIS

NOTE

Because our share price is not fluctuating very much and we are using a short time frame, the differences among the following examples are not very dramatic. You must consider all four methods for your situation and choose the one that gives you the most favorable tax result.

In order to calculate your gain or loss on mutual fund sales, you need to know which shares you are selling, the date they were purchased, and their basis. There are four ways to identify fund shares when selling:

- First-in, first-out (FIFO) method
- Specific identification method
- Single-category, or "regular," average basis method
- Double-category average basis method

First In, First Out (FIFO)

This method assumes that you are selling the earliest acquired shares first.

In a rising market, FIFO creates the biggest tax bill because the earliest-acquired shares usually are purchased at the lowest cost. However, the disadvantage of selling shares with a lower basis must be balanced against the favorable tax treatment afforded long-term capital gains. The best way to determine which shares to sell is to actually do the tax calculation and choose the most favorable method. The IRS considers FIFO to be the default method. In other words, if you do not select one of the other three methods *at the time of sale*, it will be presumed that you sold the oldest shares first.

Example

On January 15, 2002, you decide to sell 1,100 shares at $10.20 per share, receiving net proceeds of $11,220. Using the FIFO method, these are the shares you would sell:

1,000 shares purchased 1/2/01 @ $10.00 (total cost: $10,000)
14.71 shares purchased 3/31/01 @ $10.20 (total cost: $150)
14.64 shares purchased 6/30/01 @ $10.40 (total cost: $152)
14.57 shares purchased 9/30/01 @ $10.60 (total cost: $154)
56.08 shares purchased 11/30/01 @ $10.00 (total cost: $561)

Note that your first batch of shares, the 1,000 shares purchased on 1/2/01, has been held for longer than one year. Thus, for these shares, you would report a $200 long-term capital gain.

```
  $10,200  (sales proceeds, 1,000 shares × $10.20 per share)
−$10,000  (cost basis, 1,000 shares × $10 per share)
─────────
    $200  (long-term capital gain)
```

The remaining 100 shares were held for less than one year. Thus your short-term gain would be calculated as follows:

```
  $1,020  (sales proceeds, 100 shares × $10.20 per share)
−$1,017  (total investment, $150 + $152 + $154 + $561 = $1,017)
────────
     $3  (short-term capital gain)
```

After the sale, you would have 22.83 shares remaining—the balance of the shares acquired by the November distribution (6.56) and all the shares acquired with the December reinvested dividend (16.27).

Specific Identification Method

Under this method, you specify exactly which shares you are selling.

There is no question that the specific identification method offers the greatest flexibility because it allows you to pick and choose which shares you want to sell for the greatest tax benefit. However, it does require a little more effort. To use the specific identification method, you must tell your broker or the fund company which shares you are selling by specifying the date and purchase price of those specific shares. *You must do this at the time you sell the shares.* You also must receive written confirmation of your instructions from the broker or fund company. If you do not receive written confirmation, at least keep a record of your instructions so that it will be clear which shares you intended to sell.

> ### Example
>
> Using our same example, you would choose to sell your longest-held shares first because they qualify for long-term capital gains treatment. Next, you would choose those shares with the highest cost basis.
>
> *Sell 1,000 shares purchased on January 2, 2001 at $10.00 per share:*
>
> $10,200   (sales proceeds, 1,000 shares × $10.20 per share)
> −$10,000   (cost basis, 1,000 shares × $10 per share)
> $200   (long-term capital gain)
>
> *Sell 14.57 shares purchased on September 30, 2001 at $10.60 per share:*
>
> $154.40   (cost basis, 14.57 shares × $10.60 per share)
> −$148.61   (sales proceeds, 14.57 shares × $10.20 per share)
> $5.79   (short-term capital loss)
>
> *Sell 14.64 shares purchased on June 30, 2001 at $10.40 per share:*
>
> $152.26   (cost basis, 14.64 shares × $10.20 per share)
> −$149.33   (sales proceeds, 14.64 shares × $10.20 per share)
> $ 2.03   (short-term capital loss)
>
> *Sell 14.71 shares purchased on March 31, 2001 at $10.20 per share:*
>
> $150.04   (sales proceeds, 14.71 shares × $10.20 per share)
> −$150.04   (cost basis, 14.71 shares × $10.20 per share)
>   0   (no gain or loss)
>
> *Sell 16.27 shares purchased on December 31 at $10.20 per share:*
>
> $165.95   (sales proceeds, 16.27 shares × $10.20 per share)
> −$165.95   (cost basis, 16.27 shares × $10.20 per share)
>   0   (no gain or loss)
>
> *Sell 39.81 shares purchased on November 30 at $10 per share:*
>
> $406.06   (sales proceeds, 39.81 shares × $10.20 per share)
> −$398.10   (cost basis, 39.81 shares × $10 per share)
> $7.96   (short-term capital gain)
>
> The net result is a $200 long-term capital gain. The short-term gains and losses offset each other.

Here is an example of where the specific identification method can help you taxwise (and help save you from a common mutual fund blunder).

Example

Using our same example, let us say that you invested an additional $15,000 in XYZ Fund just before the capital gains distribution in November when the NAV was $10.75. This purchase would give you 1,395 shares ($15,000 ÷ $10.75). If you sell 1,100 shares in January at $10.20, it would be in your best interests to sell the shares purchased in November at $10.75 rather than the ones purchased in January 2001 at $10. Identifying these recently purchased shares would give you a loss of $605. However, there is a special rule that says you may not claim a short-term loss on shares held for less than six months if you have received a capital gain dividend on those shares. In this case, the loss was less than the dividend, so all of it must be treated as a long-term loss; if the loss had been more than the dividend, the amount exceeding the dividend could be treated as a short-term loss.

> $11,825   (cost basis, 1,100 shares × $10.75 per share)
> −$11,220   (sales proceeds, 1,100 shares × $10.20 per share)
> _____
> $605   (long-term capital loss)

This example shows the hazards of investing in a fund just before the annual capital gains distribution. A $15,000 investment in November would generate an additional $837 in capital gains income for 2001 (1395 shares × $0.60 per share). The January 2002 sale would generate a long-term capital loss, but you could not use it to offset any of the 2001 gains because it is in a different tax year. Never buy a mutual fund in the fall without calling the fund to find out if it has made its annual capital gains distribution. After the distribution has been made and the share price has dropped, you are free to buy.

Single-Category Average Basis Method

With this method, you simply figure your average basis for all shares owned. For holding-period purposes, it is assumed you are selling the oldest shares first.

Although the difference is slight, these examples show that the single-category average basis method would result in slightly higher tax than the FIFO method: a $180 long-term capital gain and an $18 short-term capital gain versus a $200 long-term capital gain and a $3 short-term capital gain.

Practically speaking, the single-category average basis method is the easiest to use because the mutual funds report these numbers on your mutual fund statements, saving you the burden of calculating the average basis yourself. However, this method may not be the most favorable taxwise, especially if your fund has fluctuated a lot in price and you have many dollars invested. Then again,

Example

Let us go back to our previous example that did not include the additional $15,000 investment in November. If you add up your original $10,000 investment plus all your reinvested distributions, you see that you have invested a total of $11,240 ($10,000 + $150 + $152 + $154 + $626 + $166 = $11,248). If you divide this by your ending share balance of 1,122.83, you come up with an average cost of $10.02 per share. ($11,248 ÷ 1,122.83 shares = $10.02). Now if you sell 1,100 shares for $10.20 in January, your gain will be as follows:

Shares held more than a year:

$10,200 (sales proceeds on shares held long term, 1,000 shares × $10.20 per share)

−$10,020 (average basis, 1,000 shares × $10.02 per share)

$180 (long-term capital gain)

Shares held a year or less:

$1,020 (sales proceeds on shares held short term, 100 shares × $10.20 per share)

−$1,002 (average basis, 100 shares × $10.01 per share)

$18 (short-term capital gain)

you may want to add the value of your time or your accountant's time to the equation when deciding which method to use. If it looks like it will cost you more to calculate than you stand to save in taxes, take the easy route and use the single-category average basis method. On schedule D, simply write "single-category average basis method." However, be aware that if you use this method for a particular fund, you must continue to use it for all future sales of that fund (other funds are not affected).

Double-Category Average Basis Method

With this method you separate shares into two pools—one consisting of all long-term shares and the other consisting of all short-term shares. Each time you sell, you calculate the average per-share basis for each pool. You can then sell strictly out of one pool or the other or mix and match as you see fit.

If you were selling for a loss (say, the NAV really did drop to $8 in January 2002), you would want to sell your short-term shares first to establish the short-term capital loss. This ability to choose between short-term shares and long-term shares depending on your tax situation is the main advantage of the double-

> ## Example
>
> Using the same example as earlier, if you group your shares into pools, you have 1,000 long-term shares (your original purchase in January 2001) and 122.83 short-term shares (all acquired through dividend reinvestments in March, June, September, November, and December). The average cost basis for your long-term shares is $10 ($10,000 ÷ 1,000). The average basis for your short-term shares is $10.18 ($1,250 in total distributions divided by 122.83 shares). If you sell 1,100 shares in January 2002, you can choose which pool of shares you are selling from. If you sell for a gain ($10.20 in our example), it makes sense to sell from the long-term pool first, so you would specify 1,000 shares from the long-term pool and 100 shares from the short-term pool.
>
> *Long-term pool:*
> $10,200 (sales proceeds, 1,000 shares × $10.20 per share)
> −$10,000 (cost basis, 1,000 shares × $10.00 per share)
> $200 (long-term capital gain)
>
> *Short-term pool:*
> $1,020 (sales proceeds, 100 shares × $10.20 per share)
> −$1,018 (cost basis, 100 shares × $10.18 per share)
> $ 2 (short-term capital gain)

category average basis method. However, the specific identification method accomplishes the same thing and offers greater flexibility without much more trouble, which is why the double-category average method is not used very much.

The Easy Method

Want to sell all your fund shares and not bother with any of these methods? First, cancel your automatic dividend reinvestment election so that when you sell your shares a year from now, all of them will be long term (it is those pesky dividend reinvestments that make all this so complicated; they do help you build wealth over time, however, so keep them going if you do not plan to sell your shares for a long time). When you sell your shares a year later, gather up all your fund statements and add up the dollar amount of all your investments, including all reinvested distributions, and subtract the total dollar amount from your sales proceeds. With this method you are not dealing with holding periods or share prices, just dollar amounts.

Example

In January 2002 you cancel your dividend reinvestment instruction and receive all subsequent distributions in cash, which you immediately squander on fancy dinners out to celebrate your investing prowess. In January 2003 you sell all your shares. You have the same 1,122.83 shares that you had a year ago, and all of them are now long term. Let us say that the share price has risen to $11.00 Your sales proceeds will be $12,351.13 (1,122.83 × $11). To calculate your long-term gain, you would add up your original $10,000 investment plus all dividends received and reinvested in 2001 ($1,248.94) and subtract the total from your proceeds. What could be easier?

  $12,351.13 (sales proceeds, 1,122.83 shares × $11 per share)
−$11,248.94 (cost basis, $10,000 + $1,248.94)
   $1,102.19 (long-term capital gain)

This method is especially good for people who have owned their funds for a long time and may not have all their mutual fund statements but do have all their tax returns. You do not need to know the price at which you reinvested your dividends; all you need to know is the dollar amount of dividends you have received over the years. Your tax returns should have this information.

Exchanging Shares

Many fund groups offer the opportunity to exchange shares simply by picking up the phone. Say that you are worried about the stock market and want to shift some money from XYZ Stock Fund into XYZ Bond Fund. No problem. All you have to do is specify the amount of dollars or shares you want to shift, and the fund will automatically liquidate the proper number of shares from the stock fund and buy the appropriate number of shares in the bond fund.

The ease with which you are able to exchange mutual fund shares belies the effort you will expend later because the exchange of mutual fund shares is a taxable event. You will need to report the sale of the stock fund in the year it occurs and calculate the short- or long-term gain or loss using one of the four methods for calculating basis just described. When you purchase the bond fund, you will be establishing a new cost basis in a new investment and will need to keep your paperwork so that when you are ready to sell, you will have the records you will need for determining your basis.

> **Example**
>
> You want to move $5,000 from XYZ Stock Fund (NAV $10.20) to XYZ Bond Fund (NAV $12.00). After you give the fund company your instructions, the fund will liquidate 490.20 shares of the stock fund ($5,000 ÷ $10.20) and buy 416.67 shares of the bond fund ($5,000 ÷ $12). If you want to use the specific identification method for determining basis, you will need to indicate at the time you place the order which shares of the stock fund (date, purchase price) you are selling. You will then report the transaction on your tax return.

Writing Checks

Some mutual funds make it easy to take money out of your account simply by writing a check. When your check clears the mutual fund, it will redeem or sell enough shares to cover the check, thus creating a taxable event, as with any other sale.

Systematic Withdrawals

A popular strategy among retirees who are living off their investment income is to request monthly automatic withdrawals in an amount that fits their budget. For example, you may invest $500,000 in a bond fund that is currently yielding 6 percent, or approximately $30,000 a year. You do not want to withdraw all the income the fund is generating because you want to keep some of it growing and compounding for the future. Thus you request a systematic withdrawal of $1,500 per month. The fund will continue to reinvest your distributions (approximately $2,500 per month if the fund continues to earn 6 percent), purchasing new shares with each distribution. Then each month it will redeem enough shares to pay you $1,500. This results in a lot of purchases and sales, but if you keep your statements, you should have no trouble calculating the tax.

Tax-Free Mutual Funds

Keep in mind that although distributions from tax-free mutual funds are indeed tax-free, when you sell your shares, you may incur a capital gain or loss.

Tax-Saving Mutual Fund Strategies

One of the disadvantages of investing in mutual funds as opposed to buying and selling individual securities is that you do not have as much control over taxes.

As we discussed in Chapter 2, there are several ways to minimize taxes when managing a portfolio of securities:

- Defer capital gains taxes on profitable securities by not selling.
- Hold profitable securities more than one year and a day to qualify for favorable long-term capital gains treatment.
- Sell losing securities before the one-year anniversary date to realize short-term losses.
- Manage the overall portfolio for tax efficiency by taking gains and losses as appropriate (that is, if you have short-term losses, feel free to take short-term gains; if you want to realize gains on profitable stocks, look for offsetting losses).
- Reduce exposure to dividend-paying stocks to minimize ordinary income.

The problem with mutual funds is that they do not always follow these tax-saving strategies when managing the fund portfolios. Some funds are very conscientious about taxes and may even be called *tax-managed funds*. Other funds pay no attention to taxes and justify it by saying that most of their shareholders are investing in tax-deferred accounts. They say that these investors want the highest returns possible consistent with the fund's other objectives and that taxes should not enter into the picture because they do not matter anyway. Some industry professionals have called for two classifications of funds: one designed strictly for retirement plans where taxes are not an issue and the other designed for taxable accounts. So far this has not happened, but the industry has taken a big step in the right direction with the enforcement of a new Securities and Exchange Commission (SEC) directive that requires mutual funds to post after-tax returns along with their regular performance numbers.

While these after-tax returns can be helpful for investors comparing similar funds, they also may be misleading. First, the funds are required to use the highest tax bracket or "worst-case scenario," as the SEC put it. Thus the after-tax returns you are looking at will assume a tax rate of 38.6 percent on ordinary income. Unless your taxable income is over $297,350, this is not you. Also, the after-tax returns do not take state income taxes into account, and you may live in a high-income-tax state. The bottom line is that the tax impact implied in the numbers will be different for you. Still, the after-tax returns can be helpful if you use them to compare similar funds.

The second and more serious problem associated with after-tax performance figures is that a mutual fund's so-called tax efficiency can create a real paradox. While it is true that a fund manager who manages for tax efficiency is likely to continue the practice in the future, some tax-efficient funds are sitting on a ticking tax bomb in the form of unrealized capital gains. A fund that maintains low turnover—that is, holds stocks instead of taking profits and distributing the gains—is indeed meeting a key tax-efficiency guideline. However, at some point those gains are going to have to be realized, and whoever owns the fund at the time the stocks are sold will pay the price. New shareholders to old funds are especially susceptible to these *embedded gains*. While it is possible for a fund to go years without having to sell highly appreciated stocks, sometimes it cannot be avoided, such as when a bear market sets in, shareholders panic, and massive redemptions force the fund to liquidate securities it had no intention of selling. In this situation, you could get hit with a large capital gain distribution at the same time the fund is plummeting in value, putting you in that unfortunate position of having to write a check to the government while you are staring at a mutual fund statement that tells you that you have lost money. Thus the paradox with mutual fund tax reporting is that the more tax-efficient a fund is, the more accumulated gains it may be holding and the *more* dangerous it may be taxwise for investors in the future. Conversely, a fund that is not very tax-efficient, one that is constantly ridding itself of accumulated capital gains, could be more favorable for investors in the future because it is less likely that shareholders will be hit with a large, unexpected capital gain distribution.

Now that we have issued the caveat about after-tax performance figures—along with the biggest caveat, of course, which is that past performance is no guarantee of future results—let us talk about how you can pursue a tax-savvy mutual fund investing strategy.

Investing in Tax-Efficient Funds

Your first order of business when choosing tax-efficient mutual funds is to identify those funds which are at least somewhat conscious of the tax impact of their portfolio operations. Funds held largely in pension funds and retirement accounts do not (and should not have to) pay attention to taxes. They manage for the highest returns possible consistent with the fund's other objectives, and this is what you want when you are investing in a tax-sheltered account. However, it is not what you want for your taxable account. Although investment considerations should always take precedence over tax considerations, it is easy enough to follow a tax-savvy strategy without sacrificing investment returns. Begin your search by honing in on those funds which pay at least some attention to taxes.

Know Your Objectives

When we talk about tax efficiency, we are usually referring to growth funds. The assumption is that you are still in the wealth-building stage of your life and do not want to receive current income (which you are reinvesting anyway) because you will just have to pay taxes on it. However, if you are retired or otherwise living off your investments, you may indeed want current income from your funds.

INVESTING FOR INCOME

If you are investing for current income, there are two ways to go about it using mutual funds. First, you can invest in a money market fund or a bond fund that generates current income that you have sent to you every month or quarter. Second, you may invest in funds whose primary objective is not strictly current income but rather a combination of growth and income, or what is called *total return*. You can then draw income from these funds in whatever amount you wish.

Money Market Funds

People tend to think of money market funds as savings accounts because there is no risk to principal and the yields are in the same neighborhood. In reality, money market funds are mutual funds that invest in short-term securities such as Treasury bills and commercial paper. Tax-exempt money market funds invest in short-term municipal obligations. In both cases, the funds are managed in such a manner as to keep the share price (NAV) at $1.00. When you put a dollar in and take a dollar out, you are actually buying shares at $1 and selling them at $1. This results in no capital gain or loss. The dividends you receive may be fully taxable, federally taxable but state tax-free, federally tax-free but taxable by the state, or completely tax-exempt. Your 1099-DIV will tell you.

Bond Funds

Bond funds invest in a portfolio of bonds. Usually these funds focus on a particular type of bond, such as Treasury bonds, high-yield corporate bonds, or tax-exempt municipal bonds. Bond funds must be considered not only for the amount of income they generate, but also for the tax impact of that income as well as the fund's risk factors. For example, funds that invest exclusively in Treasury securities generate interest income that is taxable at the federal level but not at state and local levels. Treasuries are considered the safest of all securities. Corporate bond funds generate interest income that is fully taxable at both state and federal levels. These funds offer higher yields but also involve more risk. Municipal bond (muni) funds generate interest income that is federally tax-free, and if all the securities in the portfolio are issued in the state where you live, the interest is free from state tax as well. Some municipal bond funds focus exclusively on insured issues and therefore are safer than those which invest in lower-rated munis. In other words, the tax and risk features of bonds that we talked about in Chapter 3 apply to bond mutual funds as well. Thus, when investing in bond funds, you will need to consider your income needs, tax bracket, and risk tolerance.

If you are in a high tax bracket—generally 30 percent or higher—you will want to consider municipal bond funds. And if you live in a state that has a high income tax, you will want to focus on muni funds that invest in bonds issued in your state. You can use the same formula described in Chapter 3 to compare taxable and tax-free yields for your bracket. As with individual bonds, you will want to compare funds that are similar in quality and maturity. Maturity, of course, refers to the average maturity of the bonds in the portfolio, since mutual funds themselves have no maturity. As the bonds in the portfolio mature or are sold, new bonds are purchased. For this reason, the income is not fixed, as it is with most individual bonds. In a declining interest-rate environment, the portfolio manager is forced to buy lower-yielding bonds; eventually, this can cause the income to fall. However, it also works the other way: in a rising interest-rate environment; new bonds coming into the portfolio will generate higher income, which eventually will show up in higher dividend checks. (*Note:* Mutual fund distributions are often called *dividends,* even though they may consist of interest income.)

Bond funds can generate capital gains income as well as interest income. When interest rates fall, the bonds in the portfolio rise in price. If these bonds are sold, a capital gain occurs and is passed onto shareholders. Tax-exempt funds usually try not to generate capital gains income because they know shareholders are investing in the fund precisely because they *do not* want taxable income, but it *can* happen

Total-Return Funds

Some investors seeking income invest in growth funds or growth and income funds and take monthly withdrawals to meet their income requirements. As long as a fund is growing by more than the amount you are taking out, your investment will increase in value. Investors taking this approach are more concerned with total return than with pure yield. They do not care where the return comes from—it could be interest from bonds, dividends from stocks, or capital gains from the sale of profitable bonds or stocks. Of course, capital gains income is not as reliable as interest or dividend income, so this strategy involves more risk than sticking with bond funds and living off the interest income. However, retirees who are concerned about inflation eroding the purchasing power of their money may want to opt for this approach.

The tax impact could be less than with taxable bond funds because a greater portion of the total return will consist of capital gains. Any capital gains that remain in the fund (that is, where profitable securities are not sold) are not taxable, of course. And when capital gains are distributed to shareholders, they are long term and therefore taxable at a more favorable rate. When looking for a fund, you can use the same criteria growth investors look for when seeking a tax-efficient fund (which we will cover in a moment). As noted earlier, the actual mechanics of taking systematic withdrawals from a total-return fund involve reinvesting all distributions and then selling enough shares each month to give you the income you need. The tax impact of these transactions will vary depending on how the share price fluctuates, but by using the specific identification method for determining basis, you can pick and choose which shares you want to sell and thereby have a significant influence on the overall tax impact. If you work it right, during certain periods you might be able to have *no* taxable income even as you draw a check every month.

INVESTING FOR GROWTH

If you are investing for growth—that is, not taking current income but rather wanting your portfolio to increase in value in the years ahead—you will want to minimize taxable income as much as possible. After all, if you do not need the income, there is no point in paying taxes on it. We must reiterate that taxes are only one consideration when choosing a mutual fund. You also want to consider a fund's appreciation potential in light of your risk tolerance and time horizon and how the fund fits with the rest of your portfolio. This said, you will still want to evaluate the tax efficiency of a fund, especially when comparing funds within the same category (such as large-cap stock funds, international funds, and so on).

Tax efficiency is measured by dividing a fund's pretax return by its after-tax return. The after-tax return is what an investor in the highest federal tax bracket would be left with after paying taxes on the year's distributions.

> **Example**
>
> XYZ Fund has established a pretax return of 11 percent. Its after-tax return is 10.5 percent. To determine the fund's tax efficiency ratio, you would divide the fund's after-tax return by the pretax return: $0.105 \div 0.11 = 0.95$. The fund's tax efficiency ratio therefore is 95 percent. A tax efficiency ratio of 90 percent or better is considered good.

A fund that pays out a lot in dividends and capital gains would have a lower tax efficiency ratio than one that is managed in such a way as to minimize taxable distributions to shareholders. Of course, one reason a fund could have a low tax efficiency ratio is if it is losing money: If there are no profitable stocks, there will not be many capital gains distributions. This kind of "tax efficiency" will be obvious from the fund's performance record, so presumably you will be passing over these funds. What you are really looking for when you evaluate tax efficiency is how similar funds performed on a before-tax and after-tax basis. If two funds have the same before-tax performance and one has significantly higher after-tax performance—that is, it gave up less of its profits to taxes—you may be inclined to pick that fund over the other (understanding the previously stated caveat about embedded gains, which we will revisit again in a moment).

Looking at a fund's tax-efficiency ratio, or comparing the after-tax returns of similar funds, is really only a starting point for understanding what your tax impact will be going forward. Remember, these performance figures are based on the past. They may bear little resemblance to what you will experience if you invest in a fund now. The main advantage is that they may tell you which funds pay attention to taxes so that you can separate them from those which do not. Otherwise, you will want to look more deeply into the portfolio so that you can get an idea of the kind and amount of taxable income you are likely to receive going forward.

Obtaining current portfolio information is not always easy. Most funds publish the full list of securities holdings only once or twice a year, so by the time you get the annual or semiannual report, the portfolio may have changed. Also, some funds engage in a little (or a lot of) portfolio window dressing just before the period ends, so what you see may not reflect what the fund owned during most of the period. Some funds are very good about describing their investment approach and philosophy, and as long as they remain true to their principles, you can rely on this information to guide you in your search for tax-efficient funds. Read the prospectus and marketing literature and focus on funds that seem truly interested in helping prospective investors better understand their funds. (Some funds communicate only enough to meet minimum SEC disclosure requirements and are not very helpful at all.)

Also rely on independent research services such as Morningstar. Morningstar (www.morningstar.com) provides a wealth of data on mutual funds, including information on tax efficiency. When using Morningstar, do resist the temptation to rely too much on its star rating system or even some of its at-a-glance ratios. As we have discussed, there is more behind a fund's tax-efficiency ratio than meets the eye. Sometimes a more qualitative approach is called for. Here are some things to look for:

Kinds of securities the fund owns. Mutual funds that invest in bonds and dividend-paying stocks generate more ordinary income than those which invest in non-dividend-paying stocks. Yield information is readily available on Morningstar's site, or you can call the fund. If you are interested in keeping taxable income to a minimum, look for funds with very low yields. As we discussed in Chapter 2, companies that do not pay dividends tend to be more growth-oriented and may even be speculative, so you will need to balance the fund's risk factors against your desire to save taxes.

Portfolio turnover. It is believed generally that a fund that uses a buy-and-hold strategy will be more efficient from a tax standpoint than one that is constantly buying and selling stocks. After all, it works for your own portfolio: You do not pay capital gains tax on appreciated gains until you sell. For this reason, tax-savvy investors look for funds having low portfolio turnover, say, 50 percent or less, which means less than half the stocks in the portfolio have been replaced in a given year. Portfolio turnover can be misleading, however. For one thing, it may mean that a portfolio manager is not harvesting losses to the extent that he or she could in order to offset realized gains. Second, lack of turnover can lead to the dreaded buildup of unrealized capital gains.

Capital gains exposure. As we have been discussing, embedded capital gains —that is, stocks that have greatly appreciated in value since the fund originally purchased them—are like a ticking tax bomb for new investors. When they are finally sold, they will generate a capital gains distribution for whoever owns the fund at the time. This means that you could inherit someone else's tax bill without the benefit of all that appreciation. There is no telling when the fund will realize the gains or even if it will happen while you own the fund. Certainly, most funds with large capital gains are sensitive to the problem. However, if the fund is small and a lot of people want to redeem their shares at once, the fund may have no choice but to sell some of those highly appreciated stocks to raise cash for redemptions. Morningstar's fund snapshots give each fund's capital gains exposure. The number is stated as a percentage and indicates how much of a fund's assets would be subject to taxation if the fund were to liquidate today. The information is taken from the fund's last annual report. The paradox with capital gains exposure is that the higher the number, the more successful the fund has been both in choosing profitable stocks and in reducing capital gains taxes for investors. Funds with negative capital gains exposure have losses on the books. This can be positive taxwise because the losses can be used to offset future gains. However, it does not speak very well for the stock-picking ability of the managers. One way to avoid embedded capital gains is to buy newer funds, perhaps a clone of a previously successful fund. In this way, you are starting fresh but with a portfolio manager who has already proven himself or herself. Be careful with funds that have just changed managers: A new manager who is not sensitive to taxes may "clean house" on taking over, sell appreciated stocks, and replace them with his or her favorites.

Tax-managed funds. Some funds make the search easy by calling themselves *tax-managed funds.* These funds make tax efficiency a priority by following the guidelines noted at the beginning of this section: holding securities to defer gains, matching gains and losses, minimizing ordinary income, and the others. This is not to say that funds not calling themselves tax-managed do not do those things. However, if you want to be sure you are buying a tax-efficient fund, you can pretty well rely on one that has the words *tax-managed* or *tax-advantaged* in its name.

Index funds. Index funds maintain a portfolio of securities that attempts to mimic one of the major indexes, such as the Standard & Poor's 500, an index of the 500 largest companies in America. Because these funds are not trying to outperform the market (the index is presumed to be "the market"), they do very little buying and selling. In fact, the only time they make changes to the portfolio is when changes are made to the index—then they are forced to sell the securities that are no longer in the index and buy the newly named ones. The very low turnover of most index funds means that there is minimal capital gains impact.

Exchange-traded funds (ETFs). Exchange-traded funds are similar to index funds but come in more varieties, including foreign indexes and specific market sectors. ETFs trade on the major stock exchanges similar to stocks, which means that they are priced throughout the day (as opposed to once a day for regular mutual funds), and you pay a commission each time you buy and sell. The tax benefits in ETFs come from the fact that the portfolio does not turn over very often—securities are sold only when changes are made to the index on which it is based. ETF managers give the specialists stock, not cash, to meet redemptions, so the fund need not incur a tax liability if lots of investors want to get out at once.

Buying and Selling Mutual Funds

Choosing a tax-efficient fund is probably the most significant thing you can do to minimize taxes on mutual fund investments, especially if you are a passive investor who does not want to spend a lot of time on your investments. However, there are some things you can actively do to manage a mutual fund portfolio to minimize the taxes.

Sell Losing Funds

Although regular mutual funds (not ETFs) were not designed for trading, if you have a loss on a fund, either due to a poor choice or a lousy market, you might as well make the best of it by selling your shares so that you can deduct the loss. Again, you will have to check redemption fees; however, some fund families will let you switch to another fund within the same family without paying any fees. ETFs, of course, are as easy to trade as stocks, and many investors do not hesitate to bail out of losing positions so that they can deduct the loss.

Match Gains with Losses

You may not want to sell all your shares in a losing fund but rather just enough to offset some of your other gains. Indeed, if you have owned a fund for a long time, you may have an overall profit in the fund, with just a handful of losses on your most recently purchased shares. By selling part of your holdings and using the specific identification method to sell those high-basis shares, you can realize as much of a loss as you need to cancel out other gains or reduce some of your ordinary income.

Watch Out for the Wash Sale Rule

You will recall from Chapter 2 that if you repurchase substantially identical securities within 30 days before or after you sell for a loss, you are not allowed to deduct the loss. This rule applies to mutual funds too. If you want to take a loss and stay in the market, you can always buy a different fund with similar objectives, so it is pretty easy to get around the wash sale rule with mutual funds. However, watch out for reinvested dividends. As we have seen, reinvested dividends constitute a new purchase, so if you sell some of your XYZ Fund for a loss and continue to hold some shares, be sure to cancel the automatic dividend reinvestment during that 61-day period, or part of your loss may be disallowed.

Do Not Buy the Dividend

Earlier in this chapter we gave an example of investing $15,000 in a fund just before the capital gains distribution on November 30. The distribution of $0.60 per share represented all the fund's realized capital gains for the year. Right after the distribution was made, the share price dropped by the same amount. When you invest in a fund just before the annual capital gains distribution, you have to pay taxes on gains that were realized before you got there. It is like getting some of your own money back and having to pay taxes on it. On the record date for determining which shareholders receive the fund's dividends and capital gain distributions, the value of the fund's shares drops by the amount of the distributions. If you buy just before this, the higher cost for your shares will be offset by the distributions you receive, but you will have to pay tax on the distributions. On the other hand, because you paid the higher predistribution price, your higher basis will reduce any capital gain on a later sale or increase any capital loss. Still, it is better to put off paying tax as long as possible, so if you are considering investing in a fund in September through December, call the fund to find out when it intends to make its capital gains distribution for the year, and then wait until after that to buy your shares. If you make a blunder and buy into a fund before the capital gains distribution, consider selling your shares at a loss before the end of the year. However, remember that all or most of it would be a long-term capital loss if you have owned the shares for less than six months. (This restriction does not apply to dispositions under periodic redemption plans.) Also, you should be sure to see if there are redemption fees or other negative consequences of selling so soon. Although quarterly dividends are not as significant, the same principal applies. There is no point in buying a fund just before it goes ex-dividend when you can wait a week or two and avoid the taxable income.

Sell Before the Dividend

If you find that you have walked into a ticking tax bomb, you may want to bail before the bomb goes off. Call the fund and ask about "realized but undistributed gains." Unlike unrealized gains, which may not be realized for a long, long time, realized gains are just sitting there waiting to be paid out. If the amount is significant and consists of a lot of short-term gains, consider selling your shares before the fund goes ex-dividend. Of course, you may incur a capital gain on the sale of your shares, so you will have to take that into account. However, if you have a relative small gain, selling the shares to avoid a much larger distribution may make sense.

Give Away Low-Basis Shares

If you are considering making a gift to a grandchild or to charity, do not give cash. Give your low-basis mutual fund shares, and let somebody else worry about the taxes.

Hire a Professional Money Manager

When you invest in a mutual fund, your money is pooled with everyone else's, and the fund manager has no choice but to try to make everyone happy regardless of their tax situation. When you hire your own professional money manager, your portfolio is kept in a separate account, and the manager is there to serve you and you alone. If you are investing after-tax money and are in a high tax bracket, the manager will manage your portfolio for tax efficiency by harvesting losses and following other strategies noted in this chapter. One question you might ask when interviewing managers is what tax-saving strategies they employ. Money managers impose rather high investment minimums, so if you have less than $100,000, you are probably better off sticking with mutual funds.

CHAPTER 5

Investing in Real Estate

Real estate differs from securities, such as stocks and bonds, in one important way: It is tangible. You can see it, touch it, walk around in it (or on top of it, if raw land), and make improvements to it. Whether you use it for your own enjoyment or keep it strictly for investment, real estate offers powerful tax benefits. And its use of leverage—where you put up a small initial investment yet benefit from the appreciation on the entire value of the property—makes it very attractive from an investment standpoint.

Real estate is not as easy to buy and sell as stocks and bonds. It takes time to find the right property and put a deal together, including financing, inspections, appraisals, and other such details. In addition, if you are buying it for an investment, you must consider the monthly expenses, such as mortgage payments, property taxes, and property maintenance, in addition to the income. Rental properties often have negative cash flow in the beginning. The tax benefits will help, but it is crucial to understand the many factors that will influence your investment returns, including the value of the tax benefits to you personally.

One issue that is bound to cause confusion in the years ahead is the phaseout of deductions for high-income taxpayers. Currently, if your adjusted gross income (AGI) is over $132,950, you must reduce your itemized deductions by 3 percent of the amount by which your income exceeds the stated amount. For example, if your AGI is $200,000 and you have $30,000 in deductions for mortgage interest, property taxes, state income taxes, and charitable contributions, your deductions will be reduced by $2,011, allowing you to deduct only $27,989 ($200,000 − $132,950 = $67,050 × 0.03 = $2,011 and $30,000 − $2,011 = $27,989). The

Economic Growth and Tax Relief Reconciliation Act of 2001 calls for the gradual reduction of these phaseouts: They are scheduled to be reduced by one-third in 2006 and 2007, by two-thirds in 2008 and 2009, and eliminated entirely in 2010. Since so many of the benefits of real estate investing are derived from the tax benefits, high-income investors will have to pay close attention to the phaseout rules. Another thorn in real estate investors' sides is the alternative minimum tax (AMT), which disallows some common deductions. We will be covering the AMT in Chapter 11.

In this chapter we will cover the tax implications of four common ways to invest in real estate:

- Principal residence
- Vacation homes
- Rental property
- Real estate investment trusts (REITs)

Principal Residence

Most people do not think of their homes as an investment, but the reality is that a home often ends up being a family's best investment. The real estate boom that has been going on in many parts of the country in the last few years has made many people rich beyond their wildest dreams. In some areas, a home purchased for $150,000 in the 1970s now sells for $600,000 or $700,000 or more. Empty nesters can take that equity, move to a less expensive retirement community, and have a very comfortable lifestyle. The lucrative real estate market has bailed out many retirees who perhaps were not able to save very much while they were meeting the high expenses of raising a family. In many cases, a couple's home equity exceeds the value of their retirement accounts. And the best part is that they had a place to live while all that appreciation was taking place.

From a tax standpoint, home ownership cannot be beat. The mortgage interest deduction is sacrosanct in Washington, and pundits say that it will never be repealed. This deduction saves homeowners thousands of dollars a year in taxes. And what other investment lets you exclude a huge chunk of gains from taxes? Since 1997, single taxpayers have been able to exclude $250,000 and married couples $500,000 when selling their homes for a profit. Before this ruling, the only way a homeowner could defer capital gains taxes on the sale of a home was to buy another home of equal or greater value (with the exception of people over age 55, who could exclude $125,000 in gains if they downsized into a smaller home).

Home Mortgage Interest Deduction

Home mortgage interest is one expense people do not seem to mind paying because Uncle Sam shares the cost in the form of a tax deduction. If you borrow, say, $200,000 at 7.25 percent for 30 years, your monthly payments will be $1,364. Your first payment comprises $1,208 in interest, whereas just $156 goes toward principal. If you are in the 27-percent tax bracket, your $14,496 in annual interest ($1,208 × 12) knocks $3,914 off your tax bill. Some people like to convert the tax savings to a monthly amount so that they can compare their after-tax mortgage payment with what they would pay in rent. In this case, the tax deduction knocks off $326 a month, making a $1,364 mortgage payment equivalent to $1,038 in rent ($1,364 − $326). This comparison of monthly payments does not take into account the extra costs of home ownership, such as taxes, insurance, and maintenance, nor does it factor in future home appreciation or rent increases. However, understanding the actual amount of tax savings certainly can help you make a decision about whether or not to buy a home and help you determine how much house you can afford. The calculators at www.timevalue.com can tell you what part of your mortgage payments will be allocated to interest versus principal so that you can estimate your tax savings.

If your mortgage is amortized in the usual way, your interest payment goes down a little each month, whereas the amount that goes toward principal increases gradually. After 10 years, for example, you are paying $1,033 in interest and $331 in principal. After 20 years, it is about even: $682 goes toward interest and $682 goes toward principal. Your last payment in the thirtieth year, just before you burn the mortgage papers, is $8 in interest and $1,360 in principal. At this point you say goodbye to your tax deduction and enjoy living in the home payment-free. Most people never get to this point, either trading homes after a number of years or refinancing after building up some equity. The home refinancing business has been booming lately as people trade in their high-interest mortgages for low-interest ones and pull cash out of their homes to pay off credit card debt (whose interest is not tax deductible) or send their kids to college.

WHAT IS HOME MORTGAGE INTEREST?

According to the Internal Revenue Service (IRS), home mortgage interest is any interest you pay on a loan secured by your home (main home or a second home, but not a third, fourth, or fifth home). The loan may be a mortgage to buy your home, a second mortgage, a line of credit, or a home equity loan. You can deduct home mortgage interest only if you meet all the following conditions:

- You must file form 1040 and itemize deductions on schedule A. (If your itemized deductions in 2001 are less than $4,550 if single or $7,600 if married filing jointly, you will take the standard deduction and therefore will derive no additional tax benefit from home ownership.)
- You must be legally liable for the loan. You cannot deduct payments you make for someone else if you are not legally liable to make them. Both you and the lender must intend that the loan be repaid. In addition, there must be a true debtor-creditor relationship between you and the lender.

- The mortgage must be a *secured debt* on a *qualified home*. (These terms are explained below).

You can deduct all your home mortgage interest if all your mortgages fit into one or more of the following three categories:

- Mortgages taken out on or before October 13, 1987 (called *grandfathered debt*).
- Mortgages taken out after October 13, 1987 to buy, build, or improve your home (called *home acquisition debt*), but only if these mortgages plus any grandfathered debt total $1 million or less ($500,000 or less if married filing separately).
- Mortgages taken out after October 13, 1987 other than to buy, build, or improve your home (called *home equity debt*) but only if throughout the tax year these mortgages totaled $100,000 or less ($50,000 or less if married filing separately) and if the total of all loans (including the two loans described above) did not exceed the fair market value of your home.

Most people will not have to worry about their mortgage debt exceeding $1 million. However, many people may not be aware of the third point. Although the mortgage interest deduction makes it convenient for people to swap non-deductible credit card debt for deductible home equity debt by refinancing their homes, keep in mind that you are limited to $100,000 ($50,000 if married filing separately). If you borrow more than that, the interest is not deductible. Also be aware that if you have an adjustable-rate mortgage that allows for negative amortization (that is, monthly payments are not enough to cover principal and interest), it is possible for the total of all loans to exceed the market value of your home.

Secured Debt

You can deduct your home mortgage interest only if your mortgage is a secured debt. A *secured debt* is one in which you sign an instrument (such as a mortgage, deed of trust, or land contract) that

- Makes your ownership in a qualified home security for payment of the debt
- Provides, in case of default, that your home could satisfy the debt
- Is recorded by the appropriate governmental agency

In other words, your mortgage is a secured debt if the home serves as collateral to protect the interests of the lender and the home can serve as payment to satisfy the debt. (Scary thought, isn't it?).

Qualified Home

In order to take the home mortgage interest deduction, your debt must be secured by a qualified home. A *qualified home* is your main home or your second home. A home includes a house, condominium, cooperative, mobile home, house trailer, boat, or similar property that has sleeping, cooking, and toilet facilities. You can have only one main home at any one time. Generally, this is the home where you spend most of your time. The rules for second homes are discussed in the section entitled "Vacation Homes."

Special Situations

The following special situations may raise questions as to deductibility. For more information, see IRS Publication 936, "Home Mortgage Interest Deduction."

Late payment charge on mortgage payments. You can deduct a late payment if it was not for a specific service in connection with your mortgage loan.

Prepayment penalty. If you pay off your mortgage early, any prepayment penalties you pay are deductible.

Sale of home. If you sell your home, you can deduct home mortgage interest paid up to, but not including, the date of the sale. For example, if you sell your home on May 7, your settlement sheet may include interest charged for the six-day period since your last payment. This charge is deductible.

Prepaid interest. You can deduct in each year only the interest that qualifies as home mortgage interest for that year. However, there is an exception that applies to points, discussed later.

Mortgage proceeds invested in tax-exempt securities. You cannot deduct home mortgage interest if the loan proceeds were used to buy tax-exempt securities.

POINTS

Points are certain charges you may pay in order to obtain a home mortgage. They may be called *loan origination fees* or *discount points.* A point is equal to 1 percent of the loan amount. Thus, if a lender charges, say, 1.5 points on a $200,000 loan, you would pay a sum of $3,000 ($200,000 × 0.015). Generally, points are deductible in the year they are paid in the case of a home purchase but not on a refinance *unless* it is a home-improvement loan as discussed below. According to the IRS, you can fully deduct points in the year paid if you meet all the following tests:

1. Your loan is secured by your main home.
2. Paying points is an established business practice in the area where the loan was made.
3. The points paid were not more than the points generally charged in that area.
4. You use the cash method of accounting. This means that you report income in the year you receive it and deduct expenses in the year you pay them. Most individuals use this method.

5. The points were not paid in place of amounts that ordinarily are stated separately on the settlement statement, such as appraisal fees, inspection fees, title fees, attorney fees, and property taxes.

6. The funds you provided at or before closing, plus any points the seller paid, were at least as much as the points charged. The funds you provided do not have to have been applied to the points. They can include a down payment, an escrow deposit, earnest money, and other funds you paid at or before closing for any purpose. You cannot have borrowed these funds from your lender or mortgage broker.

7. You use your loan to buy or build your main home.

8. The points were computed as a percentage of the principal amount of the mortgage.

9. The amount is clearly shown on the settlement statement as points charged for the mortgage.

If you meet all of these tests, you can fully deduct the points in the year they are paid.

Points you pay to refinance a mortgage generally are not deductible in full in the year you pay them; they must be deducted over the life of the loan. However, if you use part of the refinanced mortgage proceeds to improve your main home and you meet the first six tests listed above, you can fully deduct the part of the points related to the improvement. You must pay the points with your own funds; they cannot be added to the loan.

Any amounts charged by the lender for services, such as appraisal fees, notary fees, and mortgage insurance premiums, are not deductible either in the year paid or over the life of the mortgage.

REPORTING MORTGAGE INTEREST

Your lender will send you a form 1098, "Mortgage Interest Statement," stating the amount of mortgage interest you paid during the tax year. If you purchased a main home during the year, it also will show the deductible points paid during the year. To deduct this on your tax return, enter the amount of deductible interest on line 10 of schedule A. If you paid any interest that was not reported on form 1098, enter this amount on line 11.

Real Estate Taxes

Most state and local governments charge an annual tax on the value of real property. This is called a *real estate tax* or *property tax* and is fully deductible. Enter the amount on line 6 of schedule A.

Business Use of Home

If you work from home, you may deduct part of your housing costs as a business expense. If you meet the qualifications (see IRS Publication 587, "Business Use of Your Home"), you may allocate part of your mortgage interest, property taxes, and any casualty losses to business expenses. In addition, you may deduct expenses for depreciation, insurance, utilities, and repairs relating to business use of your home. Please note that if you claim a deduction for depreciation, you must adjust (reduce) your cost basis by that amount. When you sell the property, you would not be allowed to exclude the depreciated portion from capital gains taxes, as discussed in the next section.

Capital Gains Exclusion

When you sell your home, you may exclude up to $250,000 ($500,000 on a joint return) in gains from capital gains taxes. Naturally, there are all sorts of rules that go along with this rather generous tax break.

OWNERSHIP AND USE TESTS

To claim the exclusion, you must meet the ownership and use tests. This means that during the five-year period ending on the date of the sale, you must have

- *Owned* the home for at least two years (the *ownership test*)
- *Lived in* the home as your main home for at least two years (the *use test*)

Following are some of the conditions to keep in mind:

- If you had to sell the home due to a change in health, a change in place of employment, or other unforeseen circumstances and therefore could not meet the ownership and use tests for the full two years, you may be able to claim a partial exclusion.
- The required two years of ownership and use do not have to be continuous. You meet the tests if you can show that you owned and lived in the property as your main home for either 24 full months or 730 days (365 × 2) during the five-year period ending on the date of sale.
- Short temporary absences for vacations or other seasonal absences, even if you rent out the property during the absences, are counted as periods of use.
- You can meet the ownership and use tests at different times.
- If you postponed the gain on a previous home to buy this one, you may be able to count the time you owned and lived in the previous home in meeting the ownership and use tests.
- If you and your spouse file a joint return for the year of sale, you can exclude gain if *either* spouse meets the ownership and use tests.

Example

One spouse sells a home. Emily sells her home in June 2001. She marries Jamie later in the year. She meets the ownership and use tests, but Jamie does not. Emily can exclude up to $250,000 of gain on a separate or joint return for 2001.

Each spouse sells a home. The facts are the same as in Example 1 except that Jamie also sells a home. He meets the ownership and use tests on his home. Emily and Jamie can each exclude up to $250,000 of gain.

- If your home was transferred to you by your spouse (or former spouse if the transfer was incident to divorce), you are considered to have owned it during any period of time when your spouse owned it.
- If you continue to own all or part of the home after a divorce and your spouse continues to live in it as part of the divorce agreement, you are considered to have used the property as your main home.

Example

You and your spouse get divorced in October 2001. You move out of the home but continue to own it jointly with your former spouse. Your divorce agreement states that your former spouse may live in the house for another 10 years. When the house is sold in 2011, you would qualify for $250,000 in capital gains exclusion.

- You may not take the capital gains exclusion more than once every two years.
- You may not claim a tax deduction if you sell your home for a loss.

Calculating Your Basis

Although the $250,000/$500,000 capital gain exclusion has greatly simplified record keeping, you still should keep any records that will affect the basis of your home. After all, real estate values could soar in the years ahead, making the $250,000 exclusion insufficient to cover all your gains. Maybe your house is already worth more than $250,000 (or $500,000) more than you paid for it. Maybe you have been rolling over gains from previous homes you have sold, which means you have a very low basis in your present property.

Determining your gain on the sale of your house involves subtracting your basis from your net proceeds, as with any other capital asset. Your basis starts with the amount you paid for the home. This usually includes your down payment and any debt you assumed. If you contracted to have your home built on land you already owned, your basis is your basis in the land plus the amount you paid to have the home built, including the cost of labor and materials, utility connection charges, and legal fees. (If you did part of the work yourself, you cannot include the value of your labor in your basis no matter how much you value your time.)

Increases to Basis

Beginning at the time of sale and all throughout the period that you own the property, you will have opportunities to increase your basis. Increasing your basis eventually reduces the amount of gain, so do not discard any documents that can help you do this. The following items may serve to increase your basis:

Settlement or closing costs. The only closing costs you may deduct on schedule A are your mortgage interest and certain real estate taxes, as discussed earlier. However, if you paid additional costs such as legal fees, recording fees, surveys, transfer taxes, or title insurance, you may add the cost of these items to your basis. (Charges connected with getting or refinancing a mortgage loan such as loan assumption fees, cost of a credit report, or appraisal fee required by the lender are not deductible and may not be added to basis.) If you paid any part of the seller's share of property taxes at closing, you can add that amount to your basis (you cannot deduct them as taxes paid).

Home improvements. An *improvement* adds materially to the value of your home, prolongs its useful life considerably, or adapts it to new uses. A *repair* keeps your home in ordinary, efficient operating condition and does not add to the value of the home or prolong its life. Improvements include putting a recreation room in your unfinished basement, adding another bathroom or bedroom, putting up a fence, putting in new plumbing or wiring, installing a new roof, and paving your driveway. Repairs include repainting your home inside or outside, fixing your gutters or floors, fixing leaks or plastering, and replacing broken windows. You cannot deduct either the cost of improvements or repairs. You may add the cost of improvements to your basis. You may *not* add the cost of repairs.

Decreases to Basis

If you have owned several homes over the years and, following the rules of the day, deferred the gains by moving into a more expensive house, you must decrease your basis by the amount of deferred gains.

Example

You sold your home in February 1996 for $150,000 and had a $50,000 gain. Within two years, you bought a home for $250,000. Because you followed the rules by buying a more expensive home within the required time period, the $50,000 gain was not taxed in 1996. You must subtract the $50,000 gain from the basis in your new home, giving you a new basis of $200,000 ($250,000 − $50,000).

KEEPING RECORDS

Keep all records associated with the purchase of your home, including the purchase contract and settlement papers. Also keep all receipts and associated paperwork (contracts, etc.) relating to home improvements. *Keep these documents for as long as you own your home.* You will need them to calculate your basis so that you can figure your gain when you sell. If you have been rolling over gains from previous homes, you will need to dig up your tax return for the year of your last sale, which should list the adjusted cost basis of your current home, taking into account any gains rolled over from previous residences.

REPORTING THE GAIN

You do not have to report the sale of your home unless you have a taxable gain —that is, you do not qualify for the capital gain exclusion or your gain exceeds the excluded amount. If you do have a taxable gain, report it on schedule D. To calculate the gain, you will need to know the selling price, the amount realized, and the adjusted basis.

Selling price. The selling price is the total amount you receive for your home. It includes money, all notes, mortgages, or other debts assumed by the buyer as part of the sale and the fair market value of any other property or any services you receive. It does not include the value of any personal property sold with the home, such as furniture, draperies, and lawn equipment.

Amount realized. The amount realized is the selling price minus selling expenses. Selling expenses include commissions, advertising fees, legal fees, and loan charges paid by the seller, such as loan placement fees or points.

Adjusted basis. As just discussed, your basis may be increased by the cost of improvements or decreased by deferred gains.

If the amount realized is more than the adjusted basis, the difference is a gain. If any or all of the gain cannot be excluded, either due to failure of the ownership and use tests or because it exceeds the $250,000/$500,000 exclusion, it is taxable as a capital gain and reported on schedule D. As with any other capital asset, if you have owned the home more than a year, any taxable gain is taxed at long-term capital gains rates: 20 percent if you are in the 27-percent tax bracket or higher or 10 percent if you are in the 15-percent tax bracket or lower. If you have owned the home a year or less, the gain is taxed at your marginal tax rate. Unfortunately, you may not deduct a loss on the sale of a principal residence.

Vacation Homes

If you own a vacation home, the tax rules you will need to follow depend on whether you mainly keep it for your own use, mainly rent it out, or do a fair amount of both. We will look at each of these three categories.

If You Keep It Mainly for Your Own Use

If you maintain a second home and do not rent it out more than 14 days a year, you may deduct the mortgage interest and property taxes as described earlier for principal residences (as long as the total amount of your mortgage loans does not exceed $1 million). What is more, any rental income you receive from renting out the home for 14 days or less does not have to be reported. This can be quite a bonus if the home is in a desirable location near a seasonal event such as the Pebble Beach Golf Tournament, when visitors are willing to pay very high prices for a two-week rental. You could conceivably earn two months' worth of mortgage payments in two weeks and not have to pay taxes on the income. Such a deal!

When you sell a vacation home, you generally would have to pay capital gains taxes on the gain because you would not meet the use test to qualify for the $250,000 or $500,000 exclusion. The IRS says that you can have only one main home, and it is the home where you spend most of your time. However, there may be nothing stopping you from moving into your vacation home for two years before selling it so that you can qualify for the exclusion. Some people play musical homes this way, living in one home for two years, then moving into another home for two years, and even another and another. The rules of the game are simple: You may take the capital gains tax exclusion once every two years, and you must own and live in the home two years out of the five years before sale. As long as you follow these rules, you can juggle multiple homes, keep the moving companies in business, and never pay any capital gains tax.

If You Mainly Rent It Out

If you keep your vacation home primarily as an investment, different rules apply. These rules apply to anyone who owns a second home that is rented out most of the time. Here are the rules: A vacation home is considered rental property if you it rent out for more than 14 days a year *and* if your personal use does not exceed 14 days or 10 percent of the rental days, whichever is greater. For example, if you rent out the house for 20 weeks, or 210 days, and if you stay in the house no more than 21 days (210×0.10), the house would be considered rental property. However, if you stay in the house 22 days or more, it falls into the third category discussed below.

As an owner of rental property, you must pay taxes on the rental income, but you also can write off certain expenses such as depreciation and maintenance costs. In fact, if your expenses exceed the rental income, you may be able to claim a loss on your tax return, which would reduce your other taxable income. If your modified adjusted gross income (MAGI) is less than $100,000, you can write off up to $25,000 in losses as long as you actively rent and maintain the property. (This is an exception to the rules concerning so-called passive-activity losses, which do not allow you to write off more than you earn in passive-activity income. Being actively involved means finding tenants and arranging for repairs; if you hire a property management company to do these things, you may not meet the requirement for the $25,000 deduction.) This tax benefit is phased out for incomes between $100,000 and $150,000: For every dollar of income over $100,000, the loss is reduced by 50 cents; at $150,000 it is eliminated entirely. For the purpose of the allowance phaseout, MAGI is the adjusted gross income shown on line 33 of your tax return but with certain items disregarded. These include deductible individual retirement account (IRA) contributions, the deduction for one-half of self-employment tax, deductible student loan interest, and taxable Social Security benefits. Any losses you are not able to write off may be carried over to a later year when you have enough passive-activity income to offset them.

TAX-DEDUCTIBLE EXPENSES

As a landlord, you can deduct the following expenses associated with maintaining rental property:

Mortgage interest and real estate taxes. You can deduct mortgage interest and real estate taxes, just as you can for a home you live in. However, you report them on schedule E, not schedule A. Other mortgage fees such as commissions and recording fees may not be deducted but are capital expenses that must be amortized over the life of the mortgage. Points are not deductible in the year you buy the property, as they are with your main home. Instead, you amortize them over the term of the loan. You may not deduct the portion of your mortgage payments going toward principal. You deal with this part of your cost through depreciation, as described below.

Repairs and improvements. As noted earlier, repairs keep the home in good working order, whereas improvements add to the value of the property. On your main home, you may not deduct either of these, but you can add the cost of improvements to your basis, which eventually may reduce the taxes you will pay when you sell. On your rental home, you can deduct the cost of repairs but not improvements. Improvements must be capitalized over the period of time you own the property.

Travel expenses. You can deduct the cost of travel for the purpose of collecting rental income or maintaining the property. Be sure to keep good records.

Depreciation. When you own property for the purpose of producing income, you are allowed to recover some or all of what you paid for the property through tax deductions. You do this by depreciating the property, that is, by deducting some of your cost on your tax return each year. Residential rental property is depreciated over 27.5 years (regardless of how long you actually own the property). The depreciation is based on your adjusted basis at the time you started renting it out (the building only, not the land). For example, if your adjusted basis is $100,000, you can write off $3,636 per year ($100,000 ÷ 27.5) in depreciation in addition to your other expenses.

When you sell rental property that you have owned more than 1 year, the difference between your sales proceeds and your basis is taxed as a long-term capital gain, *except* for the part attributable to depreciation. The amount of gain equal to the depreciation is taxed at a maximum rate of 25 percent rather than 20 percent. However, you can defer this tax if you do a like-kind exchange for property of similar value. More will be said about this in a moment.

By the way, if you use the property yourself for part of the year—the 14 days or 10 percent of rental days you are allowed, as noted at the beginning of this section—you may not write off the portion of mortgage interest attributable to the period you use the property. Remember, in this situation the property is not considered a principal residence, so the interest is deductible only as it relates to the production of rental income. Property taxes are fully deductible, however. To get the full deduction for mortgage interest, consider taking a longer vacation. By using the home more than the 14 days or 10 percent of rental days, you would fall into the next category.

If You Rent It Out and Use It More than 14 Days a Year

If you rent your vacation home more than 14 days a year and also use it more than 14 days or 10 percent of the number of rental days, the IRS considers it a personal residence (rather than rental property). This means that you can write off mortgage interest and property taxes for the portion attributable to your personal use. For example, if you use the property 75 percent of the time, you can write off 75 percent of the interest and property taxes. You must report and pay taxes on the rental income, but you may write off rental expenses (the balance of mortgage interest and property taxes plus maintenance costs that you otherwise would not be able to deduct for a personal residence) up to the amount of income. While this arrangement will not give you extra write-offs against other income, it will let you enjoy the house and earn a little extra money in rent, much of which will not be taxable if you can offset it with expenses.

Rental Property

Investing in income property is a lot like running a business. Unlike some of the more passive investments, where you pick a stock, say, and leave it up to someone else to run the company, real estate requires real hands-on involvement. The good part about this is that you can have more of an influence on how much money you make. The bad part is that these activities can take up a lot of your time, and if you are not careful about how you structure the deal and manage the property, you could end up with a losing investment. Although real estate ownership can take many forms, including skyscraper office buildings and multiunit apartment buildings, in this section we are limiting our discussion to simple income properties such as a home, a duplex, or a small apartment building that you rent to tenants.

When investing in rental property, your return on investment comes from the current rental income plus the eventual appreciation of the property when you sell. In both cases, the income is partially offset by tax-deductible expenses such as mortgage interest, maintenance costs, and depreciation. The value of the tax deductions will depend on your tax bracket and overall tax situation and is an important part of the formula. For example, if you are subject to the passive-activity loss (PAL) rules, which can happen if you do not actively participate in the real estate rental activities or your MAGI is over $150,000, you may not write off expenses in excess of income. However, if you are exempt from the PAL rules because your MAGI is less than $100,000 and you are actively involved with the property, you can write off up to $25,000 against other income. In the 27-percent tax bracket this is equivalent to $6,750 in saved taxes. If you are subject to the PAL rules, the deductions are not lost entirely but rather postponed until there is enough passive income to offset them (as rental income increases in future years) or you sell the property for a taxable gain. In any case, you will want to sharpen your pencil before investing in income property and take into account all the income, all the expenses, and all the tax breaks—along with your predictions for the rate at which rents and property values will appreciate in the years ahead.

Buying income property is not the same as buying a house to live in. Emotion is not part of the deal except for how an enchanting property might pull the heartstrings of a prospective renter and squeeze a few more dollars a month in rent out of him or her. Generally, the purchase of income property should be viewed as a financial proposition only. The following questions are pertinent to determining your return on investment:

- *How much does the property cost?* Every $1,000 you can shave off the purchase price adds to your return on investment. Be especially watchful for bargains, such as homes being sold by anxious sellers, fixer-uppers that will not cost too much to fix, and even foreclosures.

- *How much do you have to put down?* The less you put down, the greater is your leverage. If you put 10 percent down on a property that appreciates 10 percent, you have just doubled your money. However, a lower down payment will increase your monthly expenses.

- *What are the monthly expenses, including principal, interest, taxes, insurance, and maintenance costs?* If the monthly rental payments will not cover all these costs (often they do not in the beginning), you will be out of pocket some cash every month. You may get some of this back in the form of tax benefits, and the negative cash flow may turn positive in a few years as rents go up, but until then, you will have to cough up extra cash to keep your investment going.

- *How much can you depreciate every year?* The depreciation deduction is what makes negative cash flow worthwhile. Calculate the amount of depreciation you can take each year by dividing your basis by 27.5.

- *How much rent can you charge? What is the going rent in your area for this type of property?* Setting an accurate rental rate that is neither too high nor too low is crucial to both keeping the property rented and meeting your monthly expenses.

- *How much can you raise the rents every year? What is the outlook for inflation? What is the economic outlook for your region? What is the supply/demand balance for rental units? What is the average vacancy rate?* Try to get an idea of how much you can raise rents each year. Do keep in mind, however, that if you get a good tenant, you may not want to raise the rent as much as the market will bear.

- *How much do you expect the property to increase in value?* Again consider the outlook for inflation and economic growth in your area. Most of your return on investment will come from price appreciation, so this is an important part of the equation. You may not have a crystal ball, but if you can see that the outlook for real estate is grim in your area, you can invest in something else.

- *How will you deal with the risks, such as lengthy vacancy periods or destructive tenants?* Unexpected costs can turn a good investment into a bad one. Be aware going in that there is a possibility that the property could sit empty for awhile or you could face high repair costs. Of course, you will do everything you can to prevent these things from happening, but you should have extra funds set aside so that you will not lose your investment in the face of unforeseen circumstances.

Like-Kind Exchanges

If you become really successful in the real estate business, you may wind up with such a valuable property on your hands that you will not want to sell it for fear of triggering a gigantic capital gains tax. Uncle Sam understands your dilemma and is willing to wait. You can do a so-called like-kind exchange, also known as a *Section 1031 exchange*, where you swap one piece of real estate for another (and another and another, if you wish) and put off paying capital gains taxes until you finally sell the last property for cash. One reason like-kind exchanges are so popular with real estate investors is that writing off all that depreciation often reduces their basis to practically zero. Unfortunately, the low basis has to be carried over to the new property as well, so the tax pain is not eliminated, just postponed. To qualify as a like-kind exchange, you must satisfy these conditions:

- The property traded must be solely for property of a *like kind.* The words *like kind* are interpreted liberally. They refer to the nature or character of the property, not its grade, quality, or use. Examples of like-kind exchanges are farm or ranch for city property, unimproved land for improved real estate, or a rental house for a store building.

- The property exchanged must have been held for investment and traded for another property to be held for investment. In other words, rental property must be exchanged for rental property, not residential property.

- The trade generally must occur within a 180-day period, and property identification must occur with 45 days of the first transfer.

Selling for Cash

If you sell a rental property for cash, you determine your gain the usual way, by subtracting your basis from the amount realized from the sale. Obviously, you may not take the $250,000 or $500,000 capital gain exclusion for principal residences because it is not your principal residence. In addition, you must reduce your basis by the total amount of depreciation taken each year and pay tax on that amount at a rate of up to 25 percent. Is there any good news here? Yes and no. If you sell at a loss, you can deduct it on your tax return (you cannot do that with a personal residence). And anyway, large tax bills usually mean large profits, which cannot be all bad.

Real Estate Investment Trusts

If you like the idea of investing in real estate but do not want to get your hands dirty, work your calculator overtime, or come up with a boatload of cash, a real estate investment trust may be just for you. A real estate investment trust (REIT) is a type of closed-end mutual fund that invests in various kinds of real estate properties and/or mortgages. Professional managers choose the properties and manage them, passing 90 percent of the earnings through to shareholders. Shares are traded on the major stock exchanges as well as the over-the-counter market. These are the three main types of REITs:

- *Equity REITs* invest in properties such as apartments, office buildings, shopping centers, and hotels. They are by far the most common type.
- *Mortgage REITs* make both construction and mortgage loans to real estate investors.
- *Hybrid REITs* invest both in properties and in construction and real estate mortgage loans.

Equity REITs tend to be the most popular because they share directly in real estate growth. If rents go up, so will the dividend distribution. If property values increase, share prices will rise. REITs can be very different from one another depending on the types of properties in the portfolio. Some concentrate on specific types of properties such as shopping centers, whereas others maintain a diversified portfolio of residential and commercial properties. Choosing an equity REIT is like choosing a growth mutual fund: You will want to consider the types of investments it makes, the expertise of the managers, and the track record. Keep in mind that track records often reflect market conditions more than manager skills. Real estate tends to be cyclical, with fluctuating prices based on interest rates, inflation, the general economy, and the regional economy in which the properties are located. As with any mutual fund, the more concentrated the portfolio is in a particular geographic location or industry, the more risk is involved (and the higher the potential returns); diversification reduces risk but dilutes returns. Since REITs trade like stocks, their share prices are also influenced by stock market trends.

REITs carry generous yields because they invest in income-generating properties and pass much of the cash flow (called *funds from operations,* or FFO) through to shareholders. When evaluating REITs, you will want to consider the stability of the income (regional recessions and tenant bankruptcies can put the income in jeopardy), as well as the percentage of FFO it pays out to shareholders. The lower the percentage, the more cushion there is.

Mortgage REITs function similar to bond funds because the portfolio consists of debt instruments. Yields are usually higher than with equity REITs, and the risk lies in the possibility that borrowers will default, causing income to drop and share prices to plummet.

Because equity REITs take depreciation deductions, a portion of the income may not be taxable. The nontaxable portion of the dividend reduces your basis so that you have a larger capital gain (or smaller loss) when you sell. In addition, when REITs sell property on which depreciation deductions have been taken, part of the gain is taxable at the 25-percent maximum rate. This 25-percent income is passed through to shareholders and identified as such.

REIT Mutual Funds

REIT mutual funds invest in a portfolio of REITs. This "fund of funds" approach provides additional diversification and another layer of management skills because REITs are not all that easy for the average investor to analyze. Tax rules are the same as for all mutual funds.

Real Estate Mortgage Investment Companies

A real estate mortgage investment company (REMIC) holds a fixed pool of mortgages. Investors are treated as holding debt obligations. Interest income is reported on form 1099-INT and original issue discount (OID) on form 1099-OID.

Tips for Saving Taxes on Real Estate

Whether your only real estate investment is the home you live in or you consider yourself a minimogul, always pay close attention to taxes. Our tax laws naturally favor real estate, but often you have to structure your transactions carefully to take advantage of them. Here are a few tips for saving taxes:

- *Installment sale*. If your house is worth more than $250,000 ($500,000 for couples) over your basis, consider doing an installment sale to spread out your gain and defer your taxes over several years. Installment sales used to be quite popular when homeowners were not able to exclude such a large amount of capital gains from taxes. Lately they have fallen out of favor. However, if the real estate market has been booming in your area or you do not qualify for the exclusion, you may want to consult a professional about arranging an installment sale. Get good tax advice before you do this.

- *Keep an eye on your gain.* If real estate is booming in your area, consider selling your home when the appreciation approaches $250,000 (or $500,000 for couples) so that you can take the full capital gain exclusion and start over somewhere else. Alternatively, put in a tennis court or a fancy pool or build a new wing to increase your basis in the property.

- *Recharacterize property to suit your interests*. As we have seen in this chapter, personal residences carry certain benefits, such as the ability to write off mortgage interest and exclude up to $250,000 ($500,000 for couples) in capital gains from taxes. Rental property carries other benefits, such as the ability to write off expenses for maintenance and depreciation and to defer capital gains by exchanging it for a like-kind property. It is perfectly legal to recharacterize a property by moving out of a personal residence and renting it out or moving into a house that you have been renting to tenants previously. Get professional advice before engaging in any of these tricky maneuvers.

- *Be careful when taking a tax deduction for business use of your home*. This is especially applicable if you plan to sell your home in the near future. The portion of the home used for business purposes is not eligible for the $250,000/$500,000 capital gain exclusion. Also, the total amount of depreciation taken over the years may be subject to a maximum tax rate of 25 percent.

- *Become a pack rat.* Do not listen to those overzealous organizers who say you can throw out tax records as soon as you are safely out of the audit zone, normally three years after your return is due. As we have seen in this chapter, your cost basis in real estate is always changing, every time you do a major improvement to your main home or write off depreciation on rental property. You must keep the documents proving adjustments to basis for as long as you own the property.

CHAPTER 6

Investing in Tax Shelters

If the tax code has morphed into this tangled web of complicated rules and regulations that seem far more complicated than they need to be, part of the blame goes to tax-shelter promoters who over the years have pounced on every possible loophole only to have new regulations written to close it. The Internal Revenue Service (IRS) has done a good job of closing loopholes. Many of the tax shelters that for a while in the 1980s saved rich investors huge sums of money in schemes of dubious investment merit have been shut down. Some investors lost all their money. Some had to pay huge amounts of back taxes, along with penalties and interest (Willie Nelson was perhaps the most famous of these unwitting tax-shelter investors). Some promoters went to jail. The IRS's position, and rightly so, is that an investment should be made for its money-making potential, not its tax-saving benefits. This is why this chapter on tax shelters will be very short.

One of the biggest problems with tax shelters from the investor's standpoint is that the laws change. Most of the people who got burned in tax shelters in the 1980s were honest, hard-working people who went into these deals believing that they were complying with the law. And they were. Then the laws changed, and the investments that were supposed to provide good returns in the form of tax benefits provided no returns at all and in fact gobbled up the money they did invest. Let this be a lesson to anyone who pursues any course of action —including the ones recommended in this book—based on current tax laws. The laws can change with the stroke of a pen, as they just did with the Economic Growth and Tax Relief Reconciliation Act of 2001.

Then there is the problem of crooked promoters. Most tax shelters have taken the form of limited partnerships, where the general partner runs the show and the limited partners (the investors) collect their income (if there is any) and wait for their K-1 at the end of the year telling them how much they will save in taxes. The problem is that many general partners are not held accountable by the limited partners, so they charge high fees and make bad investments, and there is nothing the limited partners can do. It is pretty hard to get your money out of a limited partnership. Some brokers maintain a secondary market for some partnership units, but investors generally are not willing to pay very much, especially for a deal that has gone bad. If you have already invested in a partnership that has turned out to be a disappointment, consider taking action. Gather up your offering documents, and check to see if the general partner has complied with all the promises and fully disclosed the risk factors. If not, and if you think there may be fraud involved, contact your state securities commission and consider talking to an attorney about filing a lawsuit against the general partner.

When evaluating any investment that promises tax benefits, it is important to keep in mind the big picture. The IRS allows you to take legitimate tax deductions for expenses incurred in the pursuit of income. If you are actively involved in a business, your deductions may even exceed the amount of income generated by the venture. However, if you are not actively involved in the business, your tax deductions are limited to the amount of income earned from the business. This relates to the passive-activity loss (PAL) rules we discussed in Chapter 5. These rules are explained fully in IRS Publication 925, "Passive Activity and At-Risk Rules." Thus, if you are tempted to invest in a business in which you will not *participate materially* in the expectation of getting large tax deductions that will offset your salary or other income, you can pretty much forget about it.

If you read this book cover to cover, you will have a pretty good grasp of the basic tax breaks that go with the more common investments. For example, municipal bond interest is tax-exempt. Assets held more than one year are subject to favorable capital gains tax rates. Investment income earned in a retirement account is not taxable until it is withdrawn (see Chapter 7). If you encounter an investment opportunity that promises tax benefits based on established rules such as these, you can go into it with confidence—understanding that the rules could always change, of course, but also understanding that it probably does not involve any funny stuff that would be disallowed by the IRS.

Granted, it can be hard to evaluate tax-advantaged investments if you are not well versed on taxes. Imagine a novice investor being told by a broker that the interest on these special sewer bonds is entirely tax-free! Would he or she have reason to be skeptical? Of course. However, if the broker goes on to explain the tax-exempt status of municipal bonds and provides printed literature explaining the rules, the investor will accept the fact that his or her municipal bond interest will indeed be tax-free. So what happens when someone tells this investor about another tax-advantaged opportunity? Perhaps it is a special kind of offshore trust that the promoter says will allow the investor to avoid taxes on all his or her investments, including stocks and Treasury bonds, and that he or she can take as much income as he or she wants without paying taxes. Since the investor is not a tax expert and was once surprised to learn that municipal bonds paid tax-free interest, would it not be reasonable for him or her to assume that this latest idea offers tax savings that are also legitimate? The trust I just described is what the IRS calls an *abusive trust.* It is the latest scam being perpetrated on unsuspecting investors and is currently the target of a major IRS crackdown. By the time you read this, the offshore trust promoters may have all gone away. However, you can be sure that there will be other tax-avoidance schemes coming down the pike.

In its warnings on abusive tax shelters, the IRS says

> *Abusive tax shelters are marketing schemes that involve artificial transactions with little or no economic reality. They often make use of unrealistic allocations, inflated appraisals, losses in connection with nonrecourse loans, mismatching of income and deductions, financing techniques that do not conform to standard commercial business practices, or the mischaracterization of the substance of the transaction.*
>
> *Abusive tax shelters commonly involve package deals that are designed from the start to generate losses, deductions, or credits that will be far more than present or future investment. Or, they may promise investors from the start that future inflated appraisals will enable them, for example, to reap charitable contribution deductions based on those appraisals. They are commonly marketed in terms of the ratio of tax deductions allegedly available to each dollar invested. This ratio (or "write-off") is frequently said to be several times greater than one-to-one.*

The IRS recommends that you ask the following questions, which might provide a clue to the abusive nature of the plan:

- Do the tax benefits far outweigh the economic benefits?
- Is this a transaction you would consider seriously, apart from the tax benefits, if you hoped to make a profit?
- Do shelter assets really exist, and if so, are they insured for less than their purchase price?
- Is there a nontax justification for the way profits and losses are allocated to partners?
- Do the facts and supporting documents make economic sense? In this connection, are there sales and resales of the tax-shelter property at ever-increasing prices?
- Does the investment plan involve a gimmick, device, or sham to hide the economic reality of the transaction?

- Does the promoter offer to backdate documents after the close of the year? Are you instructed to backdate checks covering your investment?

- Is your debt a real debt, or are you assured by the promoter that you will never have to pay it?

- Does this transaction involve laundering U.S.-source income through foreign corporations incorporated in a tax haven and owned by U.S. shareholders?

There is really no need to invest in complex and possibly abusive tax shelters when there are plenty of other legitimate ways to work the tax laws to your advantage. If you were hoping to find some juicy tax-avoidance schemes in this chapter, we are sorry. However, you will find some other good ones throughout this book, such as matching gains and losses (Chapter 2), doing bond swaps (Chapter 3), investing in tax-efficient mutual funds (Chapter 4), contributing to retirement plans (Chapter 7), and shifting income to family members (Chapter 8), among others.

The Tax Benefits of Life Insurance

Before we leave the subject of tax shelters, it is worth mentioning a type of tax-avoidance scheme that has not been knocked down by Congress. It is the tax benefits of life insurance. It is with mixed feelings that we write about this because the life insurance industry is notorious for charging high fees and not being very up front about where an investor's money really is going. However, the tax benefits of life insurance cannot be denied. Thus it will be up to you to decide if the tax benefits are worth the fees. We will try to present both sides of the issue in as objective a manner as possible, which should not be hard because we are also torn. Most of the stories you read in the financial press about whole-life policies and tax-deferred annuities focus on the fees and imply that the fees alone make them bad deals. However, annuity sales through brokers are booming because advisors and their clients recognize that the tax savings are worth far more than the few percentage points a year they might pay in fees. It is true that brokers get paid very well for selling annuities: The sales charge can be 4 percent or more (but often the client does not pay it unless he or she withdraws his or her money during the first few years). The bottom line is that investors seem to be very happy with their tax-deferred annuities. Let us see what everybody is talking about.

Cash-Value Life Insurance

The two types of insurance contracts we will be discussing here are *cash-value life insurance* and *tax-deferred annuities.* These are the forms of life insurance that are sold as investments, as opposed to *term insurance,* which is purchased for pure protection. Anything said here about life insurance as an investment does not apply to its value as an essential way to replace the income of the family breadwinner in case of unexpected death. One of the problems plaguing the traditional life insurance industry is that the same policy is often sold for both its investment and insurance merits and often comes up short in both areas. However, if you evaluate these products based on their investment merits alone, and by this we mean their *after-tax* (and after fees) investment returns, and consider the risk-reward tradeoff as you would with any other investment, you may be able to rise above the controversy and see them in a clear light.

In a nutshell, life insurance has two key tax benefits: The investment earnings build up tax-deferred, and the insurance proceeds are tax-free to the beneficiary. As with other tax shelters that have been tried and disallowed, the life insurance industry has played around with these key tax benefits and attempted to design products that take advantage of them. For example, for a while *single-premium* life insurance policies were sold as a way for investors to deposit a lump sum of $50,000 or $100,000 or more, earn current returns similar to money market rates, not pay any current tax on the earnings, and if they die while the policy is still in force, have their beneficiaries receive all the insurance and cash buildup tax-free. These policies were cut back when it was discovered that people were using them as tax-free money market funds without sacrificing yield. Now the law sets limits on the amount of premiums that may be earmarked for the cash reserve. If these limits are violated, tax-free treatment for the proceeds may be lost.

Tax-Deferred Annuities

Tax-deferred annuities, on the other hand, are alive and well and in fact have been expanded in scope to offer many more investment options than the original "plain vanilla" fixed-rate formula they had in the beginning. Today, *variable annuities* are sold as "mutual funds with annuity wrappers." The word *variable* means that the returns are not fixed and in fact will vary based on how the underlying investments perform. (Fixed-rate annuities are still popular with conservative investors.) The term *mutual fund* is exactly what it implies: The portfolio is managed in the same manner as a mutual fund; in fact, investment companies offering them often create a clone of a successful fund, keeping the same manager and investment objectives and simply wrapping an annuity around it. In the annuity world, these "mutual funds" are called *subaccounts*. The term *annuity wrapper* implies the existence of a life insurance contract, which is what makes the whole thing legal as far as allowing the tax-deferred buildup of investment earnings.

Annuities are very simple to understand. You invest a lump sum of money (or make periodic payments) and sign a contract naming a beneficiary. This is the life insurance part that must be present in order to get the tax-deferred buildup of investment earnings. Critics of annuities say that this life insurance is too expensive, that you do not need it, and that you should not have to pay for it.

Proponents of annuities acknowledge that the insurance costs money, but it is the only way you can get the tax-deferred buildup, so you have no choice but to pay for it. Otherwise, you are investing in a regular mutual fund and paying income taxes on your investment earnings every year at rates as high as 38.6 percent (plus state taxes). What if the cost of the insurance skims 1 or 2 percent off your return if you are saving all that money in taxes? To be sure, all the squawking in the press has caused fees to come down in the last few years, so the critics have less to complain about now.

Annuities are designed to be long-term investments. In fact, they usually serve as a supplement to a person's retirement plans after the annual maximum has been contributed to 401(k)'s or other types of retirement plans. Annuities impose surrender charges in the early years that discourage investors from taking their money out within the first few years. Frankly, these surrender charges enable the insurance company sponsoring the annuity to recapture the sales charge paid to the broker or advisor. However, if you leave your money in long enough, you can get past the surrender charges, which usually start out at 7 percent or so and decline by 1 percent per year until they hit zero in the seventh year. Usually you can take out some percentage, such as 10 percent, without paying the surrender charge. Some annuities do not impose any sales charges. These are called *no-load annuities.*

Annuities charge annual fees, just as mutual funds do, although they are somewhat higher because of the mortality and expense (M&E) charge, which includes the cost of the life insurance. On average, M&E charges may run about 1.15 percent of assets, whereas annual fund-level charges vary according to the type of fund: As with mutual funds, specialized stock funds (such as small stock funds) charge more than bond funds, which charge more than money market funds. On average, total annual fees might run 1.65 percent for an annuity that invests in bonds to 2.75 percent for one that invests in stocks.

Withdrawals taken prior to age 59½ are subject to a 10-percent penalty, as with an individual retirement account (IRA). The rules for getting around the penalty are also the same as for an IRA: You have to die, become disabled, or set up a program of substantially equal payments designed to stretch over five years or until you turn 59½, whichever comes later. You do not have to start taking withdrawals at age 70½ as with an IRA. However, most annuity contracts require the *annuitant* (this is you, the investor) to begin taking withdrawals at a specified age, usually age 85.

While the investment earnings are building and compounding, there is no income to report or pay tax on. Furthermore, you can move your investment from one subaccount to another, and as long as it stays inside the annuity, it is not considered a sale or exchange as it would be for a mutual fund. There is even a special law that allows you to transfer from one annuity contract to another without triggering a taxable event. In this respect, annuities are very similar to retirement accounts: The IRS does not want to know and does not care how much money you are making as long as it all stays in the account. Once you start taking withdrawals, you have some explaining (and tax paying) to do.

Basically, there are two kinds of income that come out of an annuity contract. One is the money you put in. When this money comes back out, it is return of capital and not taxable. The other is the investment earnings, which are taxable as ordinary income (even if they came from portfolio operations that normally would be taxed as capital gains, such as stock sales). The proportion of each withdrawal—how much is return of capital and how much is investment earnings—depends on how you set up the withdrawals.

Nonperiodic distributions, where you request an occasional check from the insurance company, are considered last in, first out (LIFO). These partial withdrawals are viewed for tax purposes as coming first from any untaxed investment earnings in the contract and are taxed as ordinary income until they are exhausted. Once the inside buildup is exhausted, further withdrawals are viewed as a return of capital and are tax-free. If you set up a program of equal payments, part of each distribution is considered return of capital and part is taxable investment earnings.

So there you have it. The best part about annuities is their tax-deferred growth. The worst part is their fees. Some would say that the fact that all the income is eventually taxable at ordinary income tax rates (as opposed to capital gains rates) is a big negative, but for our money, we would rather pay ordinary income tax later than capital gains tax now. (And those who say you can defer the tax *and* pay it at capital gains rates by sitting on a portfolio of stocks are not considering the fact that stock portfolios really should be *managed*— very few of us can pick companies that will be going just as strong in 30 years as they are now.)

One of the biggest questions to ask before investing in an annuity is how long you are prepared to leave the money invested. Consider the initial surrender charges and the 10-percent penalty for withdrawals before age 59½. Can you get over these humps? If so, and if you have fully funded all the retirement plans you are entitled to (see Chapter 7), take a hard look at annuities and consider investing.

Retirement Accounts

Of all the tax breaks mentioned in this book, you will find the best ones in this chapter. By doing all your investing in a retirement account, you can earn all the ordinary income you want and never see a form 1099-DIV. You can trade stocks a hundred times a day and never have to look at a schedule D. You need not worry about gains or losses, long or short term, or ordinary income or capital gains. None of this matters because all investment activity inside a retirement account is kept secret from the Internal Revenue Service (IRS). Your brokerage firm, mutual fund, employer, or whomever you have your account with will not be reporting how much income you have earned for the year, and you do not have to say anything on your tax return either. This is your chance to go for the big bucks (within your risk tolerance, of course) and not give a whit about taxes. Of course, Uncle Sam will not be helping you out with losses either, so some prudence is advised. However, when investing retirement assets, you can break free from the shackles of the tax laws and seek high returns without worrying about what it will cost you next April 15.

The only time the IRS is interested in knowing about your retirement account activity is when you take money out. And then their ears perk up big time. The IRS wants to know how much you took out and what kind of account it was taken from, and there is no keeping that a secret because your brokerage firm, mutual fund, or employer is obliged to tell. Then the IRS will want to know what you did with the money. If you put it into another type of retirement account within 60 days, the IRS will go back to sleep and not bother you again. If not, the IRS will be looking for it somewhere amidst the taxable income on your form 1040. In addition, if you are under age $59\frac{1}{2}$ and did not make special arrangements to get around the premature distribution penalty (covered later), you will have to pay a 10-percent penalty tax as well. The IRS giveth, and it taketh away. In this case, however, the giveth part is so substantial and the taketh part so easy to manage that all you can say about retirement accounts is that they are wonderful.

So wonderful, in fact, that there are limits to what you can do with them. As much as you may want to put all your investable funds into retirement accounts, the government says that there is a limit. Otherwise, it would miss out on all that tax money it collects from successful investors every year. Each type of retirement account has its own rules about how much you can contribute. When we talk about "maxing out" your retirement plans, we mean that you should contribute the maximum amount you are allowed to all the retirement accounts for which you are eligible before adding money to after-tax accounts. The tax breaks are so good that it sometimes makes sense to put money into retirement accounts even if you know you cannot leave it there until age 59½. You will have to run the numbers yourself to see if the tax savings would offset the penalties (usually they do if you leave the money in at least five years). However, it still should be remembered that the purpose of retirement accounts is to get you to save for retirement and to encourage you to use the money for that purpose.

How You Save Taxes with Retirement Accounts

There are two main ways to save taxes with retirement accounts. You get (1) a tax deduction against current income and (2) tax-deferred buildup of investment earnings. Some accounts offer both; others, just one. A relatively new type of account, the Roth IRA, offers tax benefits at the other end: You do not get a tax deduction up front, but you can take out your money tax-free. We will be talking more about each type of retirement account later. First, however, let us understand how you save taxes by contributing to retirement plans.

Current Tax Deduction

If you contribute to a plan that offers a current tax deduction, you may subtract the amount of the contribution from your taxable income. To see how much this saves you in income tax, simply multiply the amount times your tax bracket. For example, if you contribute $5,000 to a 401(k) plan and you are in the 27-percent tax bracket, you will save $1,350 in taxes. There are two ways you can look at this. First, the $5,000 contribution really only cost you $3,650; you have $5,000 in your account but only had to lay out $3,650. Second, you have an extra $1,350 in your pocket; you can either invest it in a regular taxable account and build your savings even faster or buy that big-screen TV you have been wanting.

To determine the lifetime value of this tax deduction, multiply each year's contribution times the number of years you will be contributing. Let us say that you contribute $5,000 a year for 30 years. If your tax bracket stays the same (we know it will not, but let's keep this simple), the total of your tax deductions will be $40,500 ($1,350 × 30). And we have not even counted the burgeoning amount of money in your retirement account. We will get to that in a minute. Come to think of it, your salary probably will not stay the same for 30 years (let's hope not), so let us assume that you increase your contributions by 6 percent a year. In the second year you will contribute $5,300, the third year $5,618, the fourth year $5,955, and so on. By the thirtieth year, you will have contributed a total of $395,290 and saved $106,728 in taxes. With the tax savings alone you could buy big-screen TVs for all your friends or triple it by investing it each year at a compound annual return of 8.5 percent. What you do with the tax savings from your retirement plan contributions is your business. Just do not ignore them because they represent a significant return on your investment.

Tax-Deferred Compounding

The other major benefit of retirement accounts is the tax-deferred buildup of investment earnings. Here we will be looking at some pretty big numbers that may appear unreal to you. Of course, it must be remembered that we are talking tax-*deferred*, not tax-free (except for the Roth IRA), so eventually you will have to pay the piper on the money you are earning. Still, at the other end there are ways to arrange your withdrawals to minimize the tax impact; we will be talking about these later in this chapter. For now, let us understand how much investment income you will *not* be reporting on your tax return as long as you leave your savings in the retirement account.

If you invest $5,000 a year for 30 years and do *not* increase the savings by 6 percent a year as in our first example, and if you earn an average annual return of 8 percent a year, you will earn a total of $416,416 in investment earnings (thanks to Quicken's calculator for this and other calculations used in these examples). You actually will have $566,416 in the account, but we took out your $150,000 in contributions ($5,000 × 30 years) to see how much investment earnings you have *not* had to pay taxes on. In the 27-percent tax bracket, investing your savings in a retirement account instead of a regular taxable account saved you a total of $112,432 in taxes ($416,416 × 0.27). If you inflate your contributions by 6 percent a year, the investment earnings amount to $684,501, saving you $184,815 in taxes. Big-screen TVs for all!

If you invest the tax savings instead of blowing it on electronic gadgets, you will have plenty of funds available to pay the taxes when the money comes out of the retirement account. Remember, these big numbers we are throwing at you represent taxes saved by not reporting the investment income every year. Eventually, you will have to pay taxes on that income. However, by deferring the tax, you have use of the money that ordinarily would go to Uncle Sam every year. The smart thing to do is invest it. Just imagine your rich uncle lending you $184,815 to invest; he tells you that you have to pay it back later, but you can keep the investment earnings for yourself. Who would turn down an offer such as this? (And who would blow the money knowing that eventually it had to be paid back?)

The purpose of these examples is to show you how the numbers work. Your situation will be different, of course, and you are encouraged to do your own calculations to understand the tax savings based on the annual amount of your contribution and number of years you will be contributing. Obviously, the more you contribute, the more taxes you will save both through the tax deduction and the tax deferral on the investment earnings.

Or you could let the calculator rest, take our word for it that retirement accounts are a great way to save taxes, and max out your retirement plans to the fullest extent possible.

Maxing out Your Retirement Plan Contributions

Retirement plans are associated with earned income—that is, earnings derived from your own labor as opposed to investment earnings such as dividends and capital gains that you do not have to work for (managing an investment portfolio apparently is not considered work). Thus you are allowed to contribute to retirement plans in the first place only if you have earned income (with the exception of spousal IRAs, which we will get to in a moment). Contribution limits are based on a percentage of your salary with a maximum dollar limit. For example, the annual contribution limit for IRAs is 100 percent of compensation to a maximum of $2,000 in 2001. For profit-sharing Keogh plans, the limit in 2001 is 15 percent of salary to a maximum of $35,000. In this case you would figure your maximum contribution by multiplying your income by 0.15, comparing it with the dollar maximum, and contributing the lesser amount. For example, if your income is $90,000, you would multiply it by 0.15 to get $13,500 and contribute that amount. Remember, you can always contribute less than the maximum (you do not have to contribute anything at all!). However, to maximize your tax benefits, you will want to contribute the maximum to as many plans as you are eligible for.

Employer-Sponsored Retirement Plans

The most popular way for people to contribute to retirement plans is through their employers. In the most common type of plan, the 401(k) plan (403[b] for nonprofit organizations and 457[b] for government agencies), your employer establishes the plan (complying with a mountain of governmental regulations and administrative details just so that you can have a happy retirement) and takes care of pulling the money out of your paycheck and putting it into a special account earmarked just for you. Employers have some flexibility in the way they set up the plans. Some are more generous than others, offering to match part of your contribution. (We did not even consider the employer match in our discussion of tax benefits, but needless to say, this benefit can be sizable.) Your employer will tell you how much you can contribute and what your investment options are. Then you will check a few boxes on your enrollment form and forget about it. You will not even think about the money that will be missing from your paycheck because you know that you are doing the right thing. Moreover, if you come up a little short that first month—well, you will figure out a way to manage.

The contribution limit for 401(k), 403(b), 457(b), and simplified employee pension (SEP) plans was raised with the Economic Growth and Tax Relief Reconciliation Act of 2001. Here are the contribution limits through 2006:

YEAR	LIMIT
2002	$11,000
2003	$12,000
2004	$13,000
2005	$14,000
2006	$15,000

After 2006, future increases will be indexed for inflation.

Also, beginning in 2002 there is a catch-up provision that allows people over 50 to make additional contributions:

YEAR	LIMIT
2002	$1,000
2003	$2,000
2004	$3,000
2005	$4,000
2006	$5,000

After 2006, the catch-up limit will be indexed to inflation in $500 increments. However, your employer may not have immediately updated your plan to include these higher limits. Indeed, unless you earn one of the top salaries at your company, you may not even have reached the old limit, which was $10,500 in 2001.

What happens if you leave the company? This is one of the best features of the 401(k) plan: You can take it with you. Actually, you have three options: (1) If you like where it is invested and feel comfortable leaving it where it is, you can leave it with your former employer (if it is more than $5,000, the company has to let you do this). (2) You can have it transferred to your new employer's plan (this may be difficult if your new employer does not have a 401[k] plan [then why are you working for them?] or you have to wait a year before becoming eligible for it). (3) You can have it transferred to an IRA rollover account established at a mutual fund or brokerage firm. This third option is the most likely for people who are serious about saving taxes and building a retirement nest egg. In fact, the law now requires employers who have a "cash out" provision—meaning that balances under $5,000 must be taken by the departing employee and not left in the plan—to transfer those balances automatically to an IRA account (unless the account balance is $1,000 or less).

As you progress in your career and move from employer to employer, it is critical that you preserve the tax-exempt status of your retirement funds. Whether you do this by transferring your balance to your IRA rollover account each time you change jobs or maintain small account balances with employers all over town, keeping the funds underneath the tax-sheltered umbrella will save you from paying unnecessary taxes and penalties. Unfortunately, too many people do not realize what they are giving up when they leave a job and take that "little" $10,000 balance and use it to remodel the kitchen. First, if you are under age 55, you will owe a premature distribution penalty of 10 percent. This knocks $1,000 off the $10,000 and leaves you with $9,000. (*Note:* If you are not leaving the company, the premature distribution penalty applies if you are under age 59½.) Next, you will pay ordinary income tax on the full $10,000. If you are in the 27-percent tax bracket, this will cost you $2,700 (plus state income tax, if any). Now you are down to $6,300 ($10,000 − $1,000 − $2,700). Still want to remodel the kitchen? However, the worst part about taking the money out of the plan is that it is now forever outside the tax-sheltered umbrella, and there is no getting it back in. All future tax-deferred appreciation is lost. What will this cost you? Oh, about $11,000 after 10 years or $35,000 after 20 years or $90,000 after 30 years, assuming compounded investment returns of 8 percent—plus the $10,000, of course— which was lost to taxes, penalties, and that new kitchen, which, when you add everything up, turned out to be awfully expensive. Once again, we encourage you to run the numbers for your own situation. Or you could take our word for it and accept the fact that cashing in your retirement plan when you change jobs is a bad idea.

Depending on the generosity of your employer, you also may qualify for other retirement benefits. Some employers still offer traditional pension plans where they take full responsibility for funding the plan and investing the portfolio such that the benefits will be there when you retire. There is not much you can do to maximize your benefits except to be aware of age and service requirements and stick around long enough to qualify for your full pension. If you are getting close to retirement and the benefit is based on your final years' salary, you may want to claw your way into a higher-paying position. In any case, if you leave the company and are eligible for pension benefits, you will need to consider your options carefully, including the after-tax consequences of each, and keep deferring taxes as long as possible. If you are offered a lump sum at retirement (as opposed to a monthly pension), you can have it transferred to an IRA rollover account to escape immediate taxation.

Retirement Plans for Small Businesses and Self-Employed Individuals

If you run your own show as either a small business owner or self-employed individual, there are several types of retirement plans available to you. The actual mechanics of starting one of these plans begin with a trip or a call to a financial institution such as a brokerage firm or mutual fund. Firms offering retirement plans have taken care of getting the Internal Revenue Service (IRS) approvals, so all you have to do is choose the type of plan you want and fill out the paperwork. Some business owners go to the trouble and expense of hiring an attorney or pension administrator to design a custom plan, but we will assume that you are not big enough or picky enough to do that. Do keep it mind as an option, however, if your situation is complicated.

An important thing to keep in mind concerning retirement plans is that if you have employees, you have to share the wealth. No fair starting a plan that allows you to contribute a big portion of your salary without contributing the same percentage for your employees too. The following descriptions hit the highlights of each type of plan. You can get more information from the brokerage firm or mutual fund that will be administering the plan. Be especially careful if you have employees because the rules can be tricky and the plan can end up costing you a lot if you are not careful. Strict antidiscrimination rules prevent business owners from using retirement plans exclusively for their own benefit, so if you have employees, you must strike a balance between your own objectives (saving taxes) and what the business can afford to contribute for employees. Get help with this.

SIMPLIFIED EMPLOYEE PENSION (SEP-IRA)

Simplified is the operative word here because a SEP-IRA is the easiest type of plan to open and maintain. If you are self-employed, you can contribute up to 13.04 percent of your salary to a maximum of $25,500 in 2001. If you are an employee of the business (this includes being the owner), you can contribute up to 15 percent to a maximum of $25,500. If you are reading this after December 31, 2001 and before April 15, 2002, you are in luck because the SEP-IRA is the only type of plan that you can open and fund as late as April 15 and still get a deduction for the 2001 tax year. Unlike some other plans, you do not have to make a contribution every year, so if your business is variable, you need not worry about locking yourself into a contribution schedule that may be hard to stick to. You must contribute for all employees who have worked for you for three of the past five years and who earned at least $450. The contribution percentage must be the same for them as it is for yourself. The money actually goes into each employee's SEP-IRA account, which immediately becomes the property of the employee. Each employee is responsible for managing his or her account.

SAVINGS INCENTIVE MATCH PLAN FOR EMPLOYEES (SIMPLE IRA)

A SIMPLE IRA is a good way to let employees contribute to their own accounts (similar to a 401[k] but for small businesses), but the main drawback is that it does not let you, the owner, contribute very much for yourself. Employees (including you) may contribute up to $6,500 plus a match of up to 3 percent from the employer (you). Chances are that you will be looking to put away more for yourself than would be allowed under this plan. Under the new tax law, the limits will be going up in future years:

YEAR	LIMIT
2002	$ 7,000
2003	$ 8,000
2004	$ 9,000
2005	$10,000

After 2005, the $10,000 limit will be indexed for inflation.

PROFIT-SHARING/MONEY-PURCHASE PLANS

Profit-sharing/money-purchase plans (often called *Keogh plans*) offer a lot of flexibility and generous contribution limits. You can have a profit-sharing plan only, which lets you vary your contribution if business fluctuates from year to year, or pair it with a money-purchase plan to have a higher contribution limit. Just be aware than while contributions to a profit-sharing plan are optional in any given year, once you set up a money-purchase plan, you are committed to contributing the stated percentage every year. The term *profit-sharing* is really a misnomer because the contribution is based not on the profits of the business but rather on a percentage of salary. With a profit-sharing plan, you may contribute from 0 to 15 percent of salary to a maximum of $25,500 in 2001. If you pair it with a money-purchase plan, you may contribute a total of 25 percent of salary to a maximum of $35,000 in 2001. In 2002, the contribution limit rises to 100 percent of salary or $40,000. Whatever percentage of salary you contribute for yourself must be contributed for each eligible employee as well.

DEFINED-BENEFIT PLAN

A defined-benefit plan uses a different method of computing the contribution amount. Rather than a percentage of your salary, it specifies the ultimate benefit you want to have at retirement and works backward to figure out how much you need to contribute to get to that amount. It is a more complicated process that requires the services of a professional actuary. However, if you are over age 40 and earn a high salary, it can allow you to make the highest contribution. The benefit can be set as high as 100 percent of your average compensation for your highest three consecutive earning years or $140,000, whichever is lower (this amount rises to $160,000 in 2002 and will be indexed to inflation in $5,000 increments after that). If you are late getting started planning for retirement and want to sock the most away, or if you are simply looking for a mega-tax deduction, a defined-benefit plan may be for you. Keep in mind that contributions will be higher for older employees, so if you have any geezers there besides you, you will need to contribute a hefty amount for them as well. Also, defined-benefit plans are more expensive to administer due to all the actuarial work involved.

401(K) PLAN

If you have several employees who have read this book and are bugging you to start a 401(k) plan, well, maybe you should. The beauty of 401(k) plans is that the employees make the bulk of the contributions. You can offer to match a percentage of their contributions, but you do not have to. The downside is that 401(k) plans are somewhat costly to administer. Also, you personally probably will not be able to contribute (and tax deduct) as much as with one of the other plans. As noted earlier, the 401(k) contribution limit for employees is $10,500 in 2001 and $11,000 in 2002. The combined employer/employee contribution cannot exceed $30,000 or 25 percent of salary in 2001.

What to Do with Your Retirement Account at Retirement

When you retire, you will be offered several options with regard to your retirement distribution, depending on the type of plan and your employer's policies. If it is your own small business plan, you get to set the policies. The two main options are an annuity or a lump-sum distribution (you may be offered one or both of these options). If you take the annuity, you will receive monthly payments for the rest of your life. You also may arrange to have payments continue for as long as your spouse is alive. When both of you go, the money is gone. Each monthly payment will be fully taxable if your entire retirement account consists of money that has never been taxed before. If you were allowed to make after-tax contributions to the fund, a portion of your payments will be tax-free.

If you are offered a lump-sum distribution, you will have to deal with the taxes on it. Most people do not deal with them at all. Instead of taking receipt of the distribution, they have it transferred directly into an IRA rollover account, which continues to defer the tax. An IRA rollover gives you control over how and when you pay taxes on the distribution (until you get to age 70½, covered later) and how to invest the money because it is presumed that it will have to last you a long time. If you and your spouse both die, whatever is left will go to your heirs rather than disappearing, as it would with the annuity.

If You Were Born Before 1936

There is just one circumstance that might cause you to rethink the IRA rollover idea: if you were born before 1936 and qualify for 10-year forward averaging. Ten-year forward averaging is a special method of taxing retirement distributions that works as if you received the money over a 10-year period (although you pay the taxes all in one year). This method of taxation is being phased out and is only available to people born before 1936. The advantage is that it might result in a lower overall tax. The disadvantage is that after you pay the taxes on your lump-sum distribution, it is now after-tax money, and all investment earnings will be taxable. One other reason you might want to pay taxes on your lump-sum distribution as opposed to rolling it into an IRA is if part of your distribution is subject to capital gains tax rather than ordinary income. This is another tax aspect that is being phased out: Only the part before 1974 is eligible for capital gains treatment and only part of that. If you roll over your entire distribution to an IRA, you will lose that capital gains treatment. If any of these circumstances apply to you—you were born before 1936 and part of the pre-1974 portion of your distribution qualifies for capital gains tax treatment—you probably should not do an automatic rollover but rather should sit down with an accountant to see which option will result in less tax. The rollover may still be a better deal, but you should explore all your options well before receiving the distribution.

You Are Age 55 or Older and Leaving Your Company

If you are at least age 55 and leaving your company, you can take withdrawals from your employer-sponsored retirement plan without penalty. This exception to the 59½ rule acknowledges the fact that some people are ready to retire at age 55 (or at least their companies think they are). It is presumed that distributions at this age would be used for retirement and not a snazzy hotrod, so the premature distribution penalty does not apply. In any case, if you are retiring at age 55 and had been planning to roll your retirement distribution into an IRA, keep in mind that once the funds go into the IRA, you will be subject to the 59½ rule. If you will need to draw funds from your retirement accounts between the ages of 55 and 59½, consider leaving the account where it is until you get past the IRA penalty period (also see the rules on setting up substantially equal payments below).

You Are a Divorced Spouse and Are Receiving Distributions under a Qualified Domestic Relations Order

If you are named as an *alternate payee* in your former spouse's retirement plan under a qualified domestic relations order (QDRO), you can take distributions from the plan without penalty even though you may be under age 59. This classification as alternate payee is important. If you are classified as an active participant, you will be subject to the premature distribution penalty if you are under age 59. If you receive a portion of your former spouse's retirement assets and wish to continue deferring taxes, you may roll over all or part of the distribution to an IRA. However, you will then become subject to the 10-percent penalty if you take distributions before age 59. Rolling over retirement assets to an IRA is almost always a good idea, especially for divorced people who will need the money later on in retirement. However, if you have bills to pay, it is nice to know that you can escape the 10-percent penalty (but not taxes) on the amount you need immediately.

Individual Retirement Account

Individual retirement accounts (IRAs) are retirement accounts you open and maintain on your own through a financial institution rather than through an employer. As with all retirement accounts, you must have earned income to contribute to one. However, it does not take much: You can contribute up to 100 percent of your salary to a maximum of $2,000 in 2001. And guess what! The IRA contribution limit finally has been raised! After 20 years of being stuck at the same $2,000 (which is worth less than half what it was then as a result of inflation), Congress finally decided to raise the IRA contribution limits. Here they are:

YEAR	LIMIT
2002	$3,000
2003	$3,000
2004	$3,000
2005	$4,000
2006	$4,000
2007	$4,000
2008	$5,000

After 2008, the contribution limit will be indexed for inflation in $500 increments.

Granted, it is going up slowly, but at least it is a step in the right direction. In addition, beginning in 2002, people age 50 and over will be able to make additional catch-up contributions according to these limits:

YEAR	LIMIT
2002	$500
2003	$500
2004	$500
2005	$500
2006	$1,000

After 2006, the limit is $1,000.

There are three kinds of contributory IRAs: the traditional IRA, the nondeductible IRA, and the Roth IRA. You may contribute a maximum of $2,000 ($3,000 in 2002) to an IRA as long as you have at least that much in income. If you contribute to more than one kind of IRA, your total contribution cannot exceed $2,000 ($3,000 in 2002). You have until April 15 following the close of the tax year to contribute to an IRA (an extension to file your taxes does not buy you more time to make the IRA contribution, as it does with Keogh plans). You must be under age 70 to contribute to a traditional or nondeductible IRA; you can contribute to a Roth IRA at any age, as long as you have earned income.

Traditional IRA

Traditional IRAs (also called *deductible IRAs*) give you both of the powerful tax benefits we talked about at the beginning of this chapter: an up-front tax deduction and tax-deferred buildup of investment earnings. The only problem with traditional IRAs is that a lot of people are not eligible to contribute to them. If you are considered an active participant in another retirement plan *and* if your income is over a certain amount, you are not eligible to contribute to a deductible IRA.

HOW TO KNOW IF YOU ARE AN ACTIVE PARTICIPANT IN A RETIREMENT PLAN

Clearly, if you are making contributions to a 401(k) plan or other qualified plan, you are considered an active participant. If your employer is making contributions to a plan on your behalf, you are also considered an active participant, even if you are not vested yet. To be sure, look at your form W-2. If the "Pension Plan" box is checked, you are an active participant.

HOW TO DETERMINE YOUR INCOME FOR IRA ELIGIBILITY PURPOSES

Your income for the purpose of determining traditional IRA eligibility is your adjusted gross income (AGI), found at the bottom of page 1 (line 33) of your form 1040 but with certain items added back in to determine your modified adjusted gross income (MAGI). The items that must be added back in are the amount of the deductible IRA contribution itself, as well as other items that do not apply to many people such as Series EE savings bond interest used for higher education expenses. Also, Social Security recipients must use a different formula for determining MAGI. Please see IRS Publication 590, "Individual Retirement Arrangements," for details on determining your MAGI. For the sake of simplicity, we will refer to it here as AGI.

With your W-2 and 1040 in hand telling you if you are an active participant in a retirement plan and the amount of your AGI, you are ready to see if you are eligible to contribute to a traditional IRA.

If you are single or filing as head of household . . .

And you *do not* participate in a retirement plan—you *can* contribute to a traditional IRA and deduct the full contribution on your tax return no matter how high your AGI is.

And you *do* participate in a retirement plan *and* your AGI is *less than* $33,000 —you *can* contribute to a traditional IRA and deduct the full contribution.

And you *do* participate in a retirement plan and your AGI is *more than* $43,000 in 2001 ($44,000 in 2002), you *may not* contribute to a deductible IRA. However, you may contribute to a nondeductible IRA or a Roth IRA (discussed later).

And you *do* participate in a retirement plan and your AGI is *between* $33,000 and $43,000 ($34,000 and $44,000 in 2002), you can contribute the full $2,000, but you may only deduct *part* of your contribution.

If you are married filing jointly . . .

And *neither* you *nor* your spouse is a participant in a retirement plan—you *can* each contribute to a traditional IRA and deduct the full contribution no matter how high your AGI is. If one spouse does not have earned income, the other spouse may contribute the full $4,000 (putting $2,000 in each spouse's separate IRA) as long as he or she has that much earned income.

And *both* you *and* your spouse are participants in a retirement plan *and* your AGI as shown on your joint return is *less than* $53,000—you *can* each contribute to a traditional IRA and deduct the full contribution.

And *both* you *and* your spouse are participants in a retirement plan *and* your AGI as shown on your joint return is *more than* $63,000 in 2001 ($64,000 in 2002)—you *may not* contribute to a deductible IRA. However, you may contribute to a nondeductible IRA or a Roth IRA (discussed later).

And *both* you *and* your spouse are participants in a retirement plan *and* your AGI as shown on your joint return is *between* $53,000 and $63,000 ($54,000 and $64,000 in 2002)—you *can* each contribute the full $2,000 to a traditional IRA and deduct *part* of the contribution.

And *one* of you is a participant in a retirement plan and the other is not *and* your AGI is *less than* $150,000, the spouse not covered *can* contribute and deduct the full $2,000. Again, if the nonparticipant spouse does not have earned income, the working spouse can contribute $2,000 on his or her behalf. If AGI is *more than* $160,000, neither spouse may contribute to a deductible IRA. If AGI is *between* $150,000 and $150,000, the nonparticipant spouse may contribute the full $2,000 and deduct *part* of it.

If you are married filing separately . . .

And you *do not* participate in a retirement plan—you *can* contribute to a traditional IRA and deduct the full contribution no matter how high your AGI is.

And you *do* participate in a retirement plan *and* your AGI is more than $10,000—you *may not* contribute to a deductible IRA.

Nondeductible IRA

If you are not eligible to contribute to a deductible IRA, you can contribute to a nondeductible IRA. Frankly, with the introduction of the Roth IRA, nondeductible IRAs, which were never very popular to begin with, have fallen out of favor. If you cannot deduct the contribution, why would you want to contribute to an IRA whose investment earnings eventually will be taxable when you could take them out tax-free with a Roth IRA? Moreover, there is the nightmarish paperwork involved with nondeductible IRAs: You have to keep track of all your contributions over the years so that when you go to take withdrawals in 30 or 40 years, you will be able to ascertain the ratio between your after-tax contributions (which will not be taxable on withdrawal) and the investment earnings (which will be fully taxable). The only reason you might contribute to a nondeductible IRA is if your income is too high for a Roth. After all, a tax-deferred account is better than a taxable one if this is your only alternative.

Roth IRA

The Roth IRA is one of those gems that Congress comes up with every now and then. When it was first established for tax year 1998, lots of people wondered how it ever got through. Even now, some advisors are skeptical that it will not last in its present form and fear that Congress will take away the tax benefits in the future. The main advantage of a Roth IRA is that withdrawals are tax-free. This may not sound like a very big advantage when you are young and have only a few thousand dollars in your IRA, but as you get older and build up not only your IRA savings but also your other retirement plan assets that eventually may be transferred to an IRA rollover and converted to a Roth IRA, you could be talking big bucks. You could someday have a million dollars in your Roth IRA. If all of this were taxed at, say, the 25-percent tax rate when it came out, the Treasury would be $250,000 richer and you would be that much poorer.

Not everyone can contribute to a Roth IRA. Your AGI must be less than $110,000 if single or $160,000 if married filing jointly ($10,000 if married filing separately). If your income is less than $95,000 (single) or $150,000 (joint), you can make the full $2,000 contribution ($3,000 in 2002). If your income is between $95,000 and $110,000 (single) or $150,000 and $160,000 (joint), you can make a partial contribution.

As noted, you can convert a traditional IRA, either a contributory IRA or an IRA rollover that once held assets that came out of an employer-sponsored retirement plan, to a Roth IRA. To do this, you would pay taxes on the amount converted and then for the rest of time enjoy tax-free buildup of investment earnings. To do a conversion to a Roth IRA, your AGI must be less than $100,000, not counting the amount converted. You may not do a Roth conversion if you are married and file a separate return. If your AGI tends to be more than $100,000 and you have control over your income, you might want to think about arranging for a low-income year for the purpose of converting your IRA to a Roth IRA. In the long run it could pay off.

Rollover IRAs

Most retirees eventually end up with some kind of IRA. Usually it is a rather large IRA rollover account to which employer-sponsored retirement assets have been transferred. Whether you job hop frequently and dump accumulated retirement plan assets into your IRA rollover each time you change jobs or stay with the same employer and receive a large lump-sum distribution when you eventually retire, the prudent thing to do is to keep that money sheltered from taxes by having it transferred directly to an IRA rollover account. You actually have 60 days to take it out and get it back into the IRA rollover account, but if you take receipt of the money, 20 percent will be withheld for taxes. This means that in order to roll over the entire amount, you will need to come up with the missing 20 percent from somewhere else until you file your tax return and get a refund. To save cash juggling and reduce the risk that you might miscount the days ("Sixty-one days? Too bad. Tax due."), open your IRA rollover account with a financial institution and tell your retirement plan administrator to send the check there. You may have the same rollover account for all your retirement distributions. You can even put annual contributions into your one big IRA account (but not Roth contributions; a Roth is a different kind of IRA). Previously, you could not roll IRA assets back into an employer's plan, but that rule was changed recently.

Warning on Company Stock

One word of caution on transferring retirement assets to an IRA rollover account: If you are receiving a lump-sum distribution from your company's retirement plan (that is, the entire balance within a single tax year) that includes company stock that you do not intend to sell immediately, you may want to keep the stock outside the IRA (you can roll over everything else). Here is why: If you take receipt of the stock (that is, do not roll it over), you are taxed only on the cost basis of the stock when it went into the plan. The *net unrealized appreciation*, or the difference between the plan's cost and the market value on the day you receive it, is taxed at capital gains rates and not until you sell. If you roll it into the IRA, the entire gain will be taxable as ordinary income when the money eventually comes out of the account. There is no one right answer here. You must consider the stock's cost basis and weigh the current tax hit and lower long-term capital gains rate against the continued tax deferral from rolling it over. Certainly, if you do not plan to hold the stock, it makes sense to roll it to the IRA, sell it inside the IRA, reinvest the proceeds, and keep deferring taxes as long as possible. However, if you plan to hold the stock forever, perhaps even die with it, keep it outside the IRA because you will pay tax at lower long-term capital gains rates. Or your heirs will receive a step-up in basis and escape the capital gains tax entirely. Once again, we caution you against letting tax considerations rule over investment considerations. If your portfolio is overweighted in company stock, you may want to roll it over, sell, and diversify into other investments.

Retirement Savings Credit for Low-Income Savers

As part of the Economic Growth and Tax Relief Reconciliation Act of 2001, a special retirement savings credit was enacted for a limited time for low-income wage earners. From 2002 through 2006, you can take a tax credit (a deduction directly off your tax bill) if you contribute to an IRA or employer-sponsored retirement plan. If your AGI is less than $15,000 (single) or $30,000 (joint), you can take a credit of 50 percent of the amount of the contribution to a maximum of $2,000. If your AGI is between $15,000 and $16,260 (single) or $30,000 and $32,000 (joint), the credit is 20 percent. If your AGI is between $16,251 and $25,000 (single) or $32,500 and $50,000 (joint), the credit is 10 percent. In all cases, the maximum credit is $2,000.

How and when You Can Take Money out of Retirement Accounts

As you would expect with a tax break as generous as retirement accounts, there are a few rules you have to follow. The main one is that you have to use these accounts for which they were intended: to save for retirement. For this reason, taking withdrawals before you turn age 59½ is generally a no-no—that is, you will be slapped with a 10-percent penalty on such withdrawals in addition to ordinary income tax. However, there are ways to get around this penalty. We bring you these loopholes with mixed emotions because it really is a good idea to leave your retirement money invested until you retire. However, we know that life happens, and when it does, it may be better to take from your retirement account than to borrow at exorbitant rates.

These rules apply primarily to IRAs, including deductible IRAs, nondeductible IRAs, and IRA rollovers. They do not apply to Roth IRAs, which will be covered later. There are three key periods in a person's life to which these rules relate: (1) the period before you turn age 59½, (2) the period between the ages of 59½ and 70½, and (3) after you turn age 70½. Find the one that applies to you.

If You Are under Age 59½

Generally, if you take withdrawals from a retirement plan or IRA prior to age 59½, you must pay a 10-percent penalty on the amount withdrawn. You also must add the amount of the distribution to your taxable income for the year and pay tax at ordinary income tax rates. Now we will go into all the exceptions. Please note that these exceptions let you escape the penalty but not the tax. All distributions from a deductible or rollover IRA are taxable as ordinary income in the year they are taken. Distributions from a nondeductible IRA are partially taxable based on the ratio of contributions to investment earnings at the time you take the withdrawals.

YOU HAVE UNREIMBURSED MEDICAL EXPENSES THAT EXCEED 7.5 PERCENT OF YOUR AGI

You can avoid the 10-percent premature distribution penalty if you have medical expenses that exceed 7.5 percent of your AGI. Although you do not have to itemize deductions, the expenses must be of the kind that ordinarily would be deductible.

YOU LOST YOUR JOB AND HAD TO PAY FOR MEDICAL INSURANCE

You can avoid the 10-percent premature distribution penalty to pay for medical insurance as long as *all* the following conditions are met:

- You lost your job.
- You received unemployment compensation for 12 consecutive weeks.
- You receive the distributions the same year as the unemployment compensation or the following year.
- You receive the distributions no later than 60 days after you have been reemployed.
- You became disabled.
- You can avoid the 10-percent distribution penalty if you can furnish proof that you cannot do any substantial gainful activity because of your physical or mental condition. A physician must determine that your condition can be expected to result in death or to be of long and indefinite duration.
- You died.

Actually, it is your beneficiary who could take IRA distributions without penalty if you were to die. Your beneficiary also could roll over the assets to his or her own IRA, but once the rollover occurs, distributions prior to age 59½ will be subject to the usual 10-percent penalty. Again, rolling over an inherited IRA is usually the prudent thing to do to avoid a big tax hit and preserve the assets for retirement. However, penalty-free distributions are available if you need them. (More will be said about this later.)

YOU SET UP A PROGRAM OF SUBSTANTIALLY EQUAL PAYMENTS

You may avoid premature distribution penalties by establishing a program of substantially equal payments under Section 72(t) of the Internal Revenue Code. The payments must be based on your life expectancy (or the joint life expectancy of you and your beneficiary) and continue for at least 5 years or until you turn 59½, whichever period is *longer*. Thus, if you start the program when you are 57 years old, for example, you must continue until you are age 62. You must calculate the annual amount according to strict rules and adhere to the schedule to the letter. If you do not, you could find yourself liable for the 10-percent penalty on all amounts withdrawn before age 59½. After you have taken the required amount for the specified period, you are free to take any amount without penalty. There are three methods for calculating the payments; one of them is covered in IRS Publication 590, "Individual Retirement Arrangements." The other two are so complicated that even the IRS does not attempt to explain them. Get professional help with this.

YOU PAID HIGHER EDUCATION EXPENSES

If you paid expenses for higher education during the year, part (or all) of any of the distribution may not be subject to the 10-percent penalty. The education must be for you, your spouse, or the children or grandchildren of you or your spouse. Qualified expenses include tuition, fees, books, supplies, and equipment required for the enrollment or attendance of a student at an eligible educational institution. Room and board may be included if the student attends at least half time. An eligible educational institution is any college, university, vocational school, or other post-secondary educational institution eligible to participate in the student aid programs administered by the Department of Education. This includes virtually all accredited institutions.

YOU BOUGHT A FIRST HOME

You can take up to $10,000 out of an IRA without penalty to pay *qualified acquisition costs* for the main home of a *first-time home buyer* who is yourself, your spouse, your child, grandchild, or parent. If you and your spouse both have IRAs, you can each take up to $10,000 without penalty. Qualified acquisition costs include the costs of buying or building a home plus reasonable settlement or closing costs. A first-time home buyer is anyone who did not own a main home during the 2-year period ending on the date of acquisition of the home. If you are married, your spouse also must meet this requirement. The costs must be paid within 120 days after taking the distribution. You may use this penalty exemption once in a lifetime.

If You Are between the Ages of 59½ and 70½

You may take any amount out of any retirement account without penalty. Your only restrictions are the ones you impose on yourself to keep from draining the account too fast or paying too much in tax. Otherwise, the money is yours to do as you wish. The distributions must be added to your taxable income for the year and are subject to ordinary income tax. Enter the amounts on line 15a (IRA distributions) or line 16a (pensions and annuities) of form 1040.

If You Are over Age 70½

Once you turn 70½, you must begin taking required minimum distributions from your IRA. This is serious business. The penalty for not taking the required amount is 50 percent of the underwithdrawal, and there are no loopholes. The distribution can be taken any time during the tax year and must be completed by December 31. You have a grace period to April 1 of the following year on your first distribution, but taking advantage of it would subject you to two taxable distributions in one year because the next one must be completed by December 31. Thus, if you are anywhere near 70½, it is a good idea to plan ahead and take your first distribution before the end of the year in which you turn 70½.

The formula for calculating the required minimum distribution was simplified greatly in January 2001 and applies to IRA holders who were already taking distributions as well as new people just starting out. We will spare you the old rules and how complicated they were and difficult to apply and focus on the new streamlined rules that make calculating your required minimum distribution as easy as pie. All you have to do is look at your year-end account statement and divide the total value by your life expectancy as shown in the IRS table (Table 7.1). Write down that number, and make yourself a note to take at least that much out of your IRA before the end of the year. When you file your tax return, enter the amount of the distribution on line 15a of form 1040. That's it.

TABLE 7.1 IRS Life Expectancy Table

AGE	DISTRIBUTION PERIOD
70	26.2
71	25.3
72	24.4
73	23.5
74	22.7
75	21.8
76	20.9
77	20.1
78	19.2
79	18.4
80	17.6
81	16.8
82	16.0
83	15.3

(continues)

TABLE 7.1 IRS Life Expectancy Table *(Continued)*

AGE	DISTRIBUTION PERIOD
84	14.5
85	13.8
86	13.1
87	12.4
88	11.8
89	11.1
90	10.5
91	9.9
92	9.4
93	8.8
94	8.3
95	7.8
96	7.3
97	6.9
98	6.5
99	6.1
100	5.7
101	5.3
102	5.0
103	4.7
105	4.1
106	3.8
107	3.6
108	3.3
109	3.1
110	2.8
111	2.6
112	2.4
113	2.2
114	2.0
115 and older	1.8

Let us say that you will celebrate your seventieth birthday on October 2, 2001. This means that you will turn 70½ on April 2, 2002. When your 2001 year-end statement arrives sometime in January 2002, note the total value of your IRA as of December 31, 2001. If you have more than one IRA, add them all up. Now refer to the life expectancy table for age 70 and divide the total value of your IRA by 26.2 from the table. This is the amount you must take out before December 31, 2002 (or April 1, 2003 if you want to take advantage of the grace period). It does not matter if your IRA fluctuates in value during the year. For required minimum distribution purposes, the value of the IRA is set on December 31 of the year before the distribution must take place. Next year the distribution amount might be quite different depending on how your investments perform. And next year, of course, you will refer to age 71 on the life expectancy table and divide by 25.3. And so on. Once you have determined the amount of the required distribution, you can take it out anytime during the year: If you need the money to live on, you can set up a monthly withdrawal plan with the mutual fund or brokerage firm where you have your IRA. If you want to keep the money invested as long as possible, you can wait until the end of the year and take a single lump sum.

The life expectancy table as just revised by the IRS is based on the joint life expectancy of you and a beneficiary who is 10 years younger than you (regardless of how old your beneficiary actually is and even if you have not named a beneficiary). The one exception is if your beneficiary is your spouse and she or he is more than 10 years younger than you. In this case, you can use a more liberal table that would require an even smaller distribution (see Appendix E of IRS Publication 590). The goal in revising the table was to enable a couple to make IRA assets last as long as both people live. The old rules required a much faster drawdown and left some people in jeopardy of exhausting their IRA assets too soon. Keep in mind that what we are talking about here are required *minimums*. You can always take out (and pay taxes on) more than the minimum if you want to.

Taking Distributions from a Roth IRA

Everything we have said so far about distributions pertains to traditional IRAs, including deductible IRAs, nondeductible IRAs, and rollover IRAs. Roth IRAs have their own set of rules.

Contributions Are Tax-Free

You can take your own contributions out of a Roth IRA anytime you want without paying penalties or taxes. It does not matter how old you are or how long the money has been in the account. By *contributions*, we mean your annual $2,000 contributions as well as any amounts converted from a traditional IRA on which you have already paid taxes. When you take distributions from a Roth IRA, the first money that comes out is presumed to be your own contributions (annual contributions followed by converted contributions) and is therefore not taxable. For example, if you have contributed a total of $10,000 to a Roth IRA and the account is now worth $12,500, you can take a distribution of $10,000, and it will not be taxable or subject to the premature distribution penalty because it will be presumed to have come from your own contributions. If you take out $11,000, the $1,000 that exceeds your contributions is presumed to come from earnings and is subject to special rules.

Earnings Are Subject to Special Rules

Following are the Roth IRA rules pertaining to distributions from *earnings*.

ROTH IRAS HELD LESS THAN FIVE YEARS

If you have not held the account at least 5 years (which includes everybody right now, since 1998 was the first year you could contribute to a Roth), the portion attributable to earnings will be taxable regardless of your age. If you are under 59 1/2, the amount also will be subject to the 10-percent premature distribution penalty *unless* you qualify for one of the seven exceptions noted earlier for traditional IRAs: (1) death, (2) disability, (3) first-time home buyer ($10,000 limit), (4) substantially equal payments, (5) medical expenses over 7.5 percent of AGI, (6) health insurance premiums if unemployed, and (7) higher education expenses. Even if the 10-percent penalty is waived, you still must pay taxes on the distribution. Remember, we are talking about the earnings only. You can always withdraw your contributions tax-free.

The five-year holding period begins on January 1 of the tax year for which you made the first contribution. For example, if you made a Roth IRA contribution for tax year 1998, your five-year holding period begins January 1, 1998, even if you did not make the actual contribution until April 15, 1999. Also, the five-year holding period applies to the period of time you have owned the account, not how long the money has been in there. For example, if you started your Roth IRA on January 1, 1998 with a $2,000 contribution and five years later the account is worth $15,000, the entire balance would meet the five-year requirement.

ROTH IRAS HELD FIVE YEARS OR LONGER

If you are *over 59 1/2* and have held the account at least five years (meaning you are reading this after 2003 or are planning ahead), all distributions from a Roth IRA are tax-free and penalty-free. What is more, there are no minimum distribution requirements at age 70 1/2. Some people think that this is one of the best features of the Roth. By not having to take out a certain amount every year, you need not worry about exhausting your retirement fund too soon (or forgetting to take the required amount and having to pay that onerous 50-percent penalty).

If you are *under 59½* and have held the account at least five years, you will be subject to both tax and the 10-percent penalty on distributions from earnings *unless* you qualify for one of the exceptions. This gets complicated, so pay attention. In the case of the first three exceptions noted earlier—death, disability, and first-time homebuyer—the earnings are free from *both* tax and penalty. In the case of the other four exceptions—periodic payments, medical expenses, health insurance premiums, and higher education expenses—you can escape the penalty but not the tax. In the case of these last four exceptions, a Roth IRA is like a traditional IRA with respect to the earnings (remember, your own contributions to a Roth have already been taxed and are always tax-free and penalty-free). See Table 7.2.

TABLE 7.2 Roth IRA Contributions

REASON FOR DISTRIBUTION	ROTH IRA CONTRIBUTIONS RECEIVED BEFORE 5 YEARS		ROTH IRA CONTRIBUTIONS RECEIVED AFTER 5 YEARS	
	EARNINGS TAXABLE	SUBJECT TO 10% PENALTY	EARNINGS TAXABLE	SUBJECT TO 10% PENALTY
On or after age 59½	Yes	No	No	No
Before age 59½ (no exceptions)	Yes	Yes	Yes	Yes
Before age 59½ (exceptions)				
Death	Yes	No	No	No
Disability	Yes	No	No	No
First-time homebuyer ($10K limit)	Yes	No	No	No
Substantially equal periodic payments	Yes	No	Yes	No
Medical expenses over 7.5% of AGI	Yes	No	Yes	No
Insurance premiums by unemployed	Yes	No	Yes	No
Higher education expenses	Yes	No	Yes	No

Source: Gary S. Lesser, "The New Roth IRA Rules: A Small Price for the Benefits," *Journal of Taxation of Employee Benefits,* Vol. 6, No. 4, November–December, 1998.

What Happens to Your IRA When You Die?

When you die, the beneficiary (or beneficiaries) named on the account will inherit your IRA. If your will conflicts with your beneficiary designation, the beneficiary designation will prevail. It is a good idea to review beneficiary designations once a year or so and especially whenever there is a major event in the family such as a marriage, divorce, birth, or death.

Whoever ends up with your traditional IRA will at some point have to pay taxes on it: income taxes when the money is withdrawn (except for any part allocable to nondeductible contributions) and estate taxes if your estate is over the exemption equivalent ($675,000 in 2001, $1 million in 2002, and rising to $3.5 million in 2009). If there is a downside to having assets inside an IRA, this is it: The entire balance is subject to ordinary income tax. (Different rules apply to Roth IRAs; see below). Conversely, if you held highly appreciated stock outside an IRA, your heirs would receive a step-up in basis at your death, and all that appreciation would escape income tax. However, when you are making decisions about IRA rollovers, often the stock has not appreciated yet, so it is difficult to pass up the tax deferral in favor of a step-up in basis whose value is not apparent.

What Happens When You Inherit an IRA?

Here we will shift our point of view from the decedent, who will not be around anymore, to the beneficiary, who will have to deal with the newly inherited IRA and make some decisions about it.

If You Are the Surviving Spouse

Different rules apply to spouses as opposed to kids, friends, cousins, and the occasional pet (just kidding) who also may be named as beneficiaries on IRAs. These rules apply to spouses who are the sole beneficiaries of an IRA.

IF YOU INHERIT A TRADITIONAL IRA

By *traditional,* we mean any IRA other than a Roth IRA. This includes deductible IRAs, nondeductible IRAs, and IRA rollovers.

Treat the IRA as Your Own

When you inherit a traditional IRA, you may treat the IRA as your own by rolling it over into an IRA account in your name. Rolling over an inherited IRA continues to defer the tax. As your own IRA, it then becomes subject to all the rules we have been discussing in this chapter, such as the 10-percent premature distribution penalty if you are under 59½ and required minimum distributions starting when you turn 70½. If you treat the IRA as your own, you may name your own beneficiary. (If you leave it in your spouse's name, as discussed next, you may not name a new beneficiary; when you die, the assets would go to the contingent beneficiary named by your spouse.) If your spouse has already started taking minimum required distributions, the last distribution he or she would be required to take in the year of his or her death must be taken before you roll over the remaining amount. Rolling over an inherited IRA is the most common choice among surviving spouses because it offers the most flexibility.

Receive Distributions as Beneficiary

However, there may be a reason why you would not want to do an IRA rollover and instead keep the account in your deceased spouse's name and receive distributions as beneficiary. The main reason you might want to do this is if you are under 59½ and need money from the IRA. Distributions to a beneficiary are not subject to the 10-percent premature distribution penalty. If you choose this option, you must take minimum distributions according to your single life expectancy, as shown in Table 7.3. The calculation is the same as for determining required minimum distributions at age 70½: Add up the balance of the account on December 31 and divide by the divisor corresponding to your age in the table. You can always take out more than the minimum if you want. All distributions, except for any portion allocable to nondeductible contributions made by the IRA holder, will be taxable at ordinary income tax rates.

TABLE 7.3 Single Life Expectancy Table

AGE	DIVISOR	AGE	DIVISOR
35	47.3	73	3.9
36	46.4	74	13.2
37	45.4	75	12.5
38	44.4	76	11.9
39	43.5	77	11.2
40	42.5	78	10.6
41	41.5	79	10.0
42	40.6	80	9.5
43	39.6	81	8.9
44	38.7	82	8.4
45	37.7	83	7.9
46	36.8	84	7.4
47	35.9	85	6.9
48	34.9	86	6.5
49	34.0	87	6.1

(continues)

TABLE 7.3 Single Life Expectancy Table *(Continued)*

AGE	DIVISOR	AGE	DIVISOR
50	33.1	88	5.7
51	32.2	89	5.3
52	31.3	90	5.0
53	30.4	91	4.7
54	29.5	92	4.4
55	28.6	93	4.1
56	27.7	94	3.9
57	26.8	95	3.7
58	25.9	96	3.4
59	25.0	97	3.2
60	24.2	98	3.0
61	23.3	99	2.8
62	22.5	100	2.7
63	21.6	101	2.5
64	20.8	102	2.3
65	10.0	103	2.1
66	19.2	104	1.9
67	18.4	105	1.8
68	17.6	106	1.6
69	16.8	107	1.4
70	16.0	108	1.3
71	15.3	109	1.1
72	14.6	110	1.0

Disclaim the IRA

Under new rules, you may now disclaim an IRA left to you by your spouse. Why would you want to do this? If you do not need the money and do not want the assets added to your estate. To disclaim an IRA, you would name a different beneficiary (say, a child or grandchild), who would then have to take distributions under the rules for nonspouses (see below).

IF YOU INHERIT A ROTH IRA

If you inherit a Roth IRA from your spouse, the natural thing to do is to treat it as your own by rolling it into your own Roth IRA. Although you may choose to remain as beneficiary on your spouse's account and take distributions over your life expectancy (the same as for a traditional IRA), there is no reason to subject yourself to these schedules when a Roth IRA in your own name has no minimum distribution requirements. Putting your spouse's Roth IRA in your own name allows you to take withdrawals whenever you want or preserve the assets for your heirs.

If You Are a Beneficiary Other than a Spouse (or You Are the Spouse and There Are Other Beneficiaries Besides You)

The main rule here is that you may not roll over the IRA into your own IRA. Instead, you must follow distribution rules for nonspouse beneficiaries.

IF YOU INHERIT A TRADITIONAL IRA

If you are the sole beneficiary of a traditional IRA, you must take distributions from it according to your single life expectancy, as shown in Table 7.3. If you are one of two or more beneficiaries, the distribution rules will depend on whether the IRA account was segregated into separate accounts for each beneficiary. If the account *was* segregated, then each beneficiary must take distributions according to his or her own life expectancy. If the IRA was *not* segregated, the assets are distributed based on the life expectancy of the oldest beneficiary. Segregating the accounts is a good tax planning strategy because it allows younger heirs (children and grandchildren) to stretch out their withdrawals and defer the tax for a longer period of time.

IF YOU INHERIT A ROTH IRA

The rules for taking distributions from an inherited Roth IRA are the same as for a traditional IRA: You must take distributions over your life expectancy or, if there is more than one beneficiary and the accounts were not segregated, over the life expectancy of the oldest beneficiary. However, the five-year rule concerning taxation on earnings comes into play here. If it has not been five years since the Roth IRA holder made the first contribution, any distributions from earnings made during this time are subject to tax. Remember, however, that the first distributions taken from a Roth IRA are presumed to be from contributions, so if you take distributions according to your life expectancy as required, they likely will not be taxed.

Saving for Retirement: Which Plan Is Best?

Our advice to max out your retirement accounts may not seem so easy now that you know about all the various plans and the different rules associated with each. Which plan do you start with? How many plans should you contribute to? There is no one right strategy suitable for everyone, but here are some guidelines that can help you decide.

Employer-Sponsored Plans Take Precedence over IRAs

Qualified plans such as 401(k) plans for employees of corporations and Keogh plans for self-employed individuals offer more advantages than IRAs mainly because of their higher contribution limits. If your employer matches part of your contribution, this is all the incentive you need to contribute as much as you can to your 401(k) because it is only by contributing that you get this free money. So max out contributions to employer-sponsored plans (even if you are the employer and sole employee) before contributing to IRAs or after-tax savings plans.

Deductible IRAs Take Precedence over Roth IRAs (Usually)

An immediate tax deduction is usually worth more than the promise of tax-free income in the future. Thus, if you and/or your spouse is eligible to contribute to a deductible IRA, either because you are not covered by a retirement plan at work or your income is low enough to qualify, that should be your first choice. In fact, if you qualify for a deductible IRA, it is crucial that you take advantage of it because it means that you do not have much else working for you in building your retirement savings. In addition to the annual IRA contribution, also try to save an extra amount in an after-tax account—put away the annual tax savings or even more if you can swing it—so that you can live as comfortably in retirement as your 401(k) counterparts. Some advisors believe that Roth IRAs are better even than deductible IRAs, especially for young, low-income people to whom the tax deduction would not be very valuable or anyone who expects to be in a high tax bracket during retirement.

Roth IRAs Beat Nondeductible IRAs

If you are not eligible for a deductible IRA, it is better to contribute to a Roth IRA than a nondeductible IRA—as long as you meet the income requirements: AGI less than $110,000 if single or $160,000 if married filing jointly. The advantages of tax-free income and no minimum distribution requirements at age 70½ make the Roth a very popular savings vehicle.

Nondeductible IRAs Are Probably Better than Nothing

We say *probably* because although the tax-deferred buildup is nice, the record keeping can be a nightmare. When you start taking money out of a nondeductible IRA, part of each withdrawal will be tax-free and part will be taxable. The part attributable to your after-tax contributions will be tax-free, whereas the investment earnings that have been growing tax deferred will be taxable. (The order of withdrawals is not the same as for Roth IRAs, where the first money that comes out is presumed to be your own contributions.) This means that you have to keep careful records of all your nondeductible contributions over the years so that you will not be taxed on that money again when it comes out. When reporting the income, you have to calculate the ratio between after-tax and pre-tax money for the entire account and use the same ratio to determine the taxable portion of each withdrawal. To keep life simple, some people just invest in a tax-deferred annuity instead. By investing after-tax money in a tax-deferred investment, you get nearly the same benefits without having to adhere to annual contribution limits or worry about keeping careful records for the rest of your life.

You Likely Will Have an IRA Rollover in Your Future

Even if you choose not to contribute to an IRA right now but rather do all your saving through an employer-sponsored plan, you likely will end up with an IRA rollover triggered by a job change or retirement itself. Transferring retirement assets to an IRA rollover account keeps them growing tax deferred and allows you to control the way they are invested. One decision that you will need to make at some point is whether to convert your rollover IRA to a Roth IRA. You can make this decision at any time, but keep in mind that the larger the account grows, the more tax you will have to pay if and when you finally convert (however, you do not have to convert the entire amount at once). Also keep in mind that your AGI must be under $100,000 (single or married filing jointly) to do the conversion. In any case, you will be responsible for managing your IRA rollover account and arranging your withdrawals to achieve that delicate balance between meeting your ongoing living expenses and not paying too much in taxes.

Arranging Withdrawals in Retirement

When you finally reach that desired place where your nest egg is as large as it needs to be to sustain you during retirement, you will face a whole new set of challenges. Which accounts do you draw from first, the tax-deferred retirement accounts or your after-tax savings accounts? How much can you safely withdraw without being in danger of running out of money during your lifetime? How should you invest your after-tax savings to minimize taxes, keep the assets growing, and not subject your principal to too much risk? If you thought life would become simpler in retirement, you may be in for a surprise. Good thing you have all this time on your hands to figure it all out.

Depending on the complexity of your financial situation—how many accounts you have, where your assets are located, and your spending needs in retirement —arranging withdrawals in retirement can be quite tricky, even requiring the services of a professional. The first place to start is to estimate your annual spending needs. This in itself is not so easy if you plan a life of travel and expensive hobbies during the early years of retirement yet also want to prepare for possible declining health later on. Then there is inflation to think about. The amount you budget now may not be enough to sustain you in 5 or 10 years. You also must estimate your income from all sources, including Social Security, possible part-time work, and even inheritances or other windfalls that may come to you at unexpected times.

The next step is deciding how much you can withdraw safely. Many financial planners recommend withdrawals of 4 or 5 percent per year. This assumes that the assets are invested in a diversified portfolio of securities earning average annual returns of 8 or 9 percent. You do not want to withdraw as much as the portfolio earns in a year because next year's returns might be different. It is important to allow for variable investment returns from year to year and take out an amount that will not leave you in danger of dipping into principal several years in a row.

Finally, you will face the choice of which accounts to draw from: taxable or tax-deferred accounts. At first glance it may seem that drawing from the taxable accounts would be the best choice in order to keep the tax-deferred accounts growing as long as possible. However, you also must take into account the minimum distribution requirements at age 70½ on traditional IRAs. If there is a chance your IRA will become so large that the minimum distributions would throw you into a higher tax bracket, it may be better to begin drawing down these accounts before you need to. Also consider where your taxable accounts are invested and how portfolio activity may affect the availability of free funds. For example, if you are selling losing stocks for tax purposes, you might withdraw the proceeds from the stock sale instead of reinvesting them and taking the distribution from somewhere else. As you can see, the issues become very complicated, and it is impossible to make sweeping generalizations that apply to everyone. The best advice we can offer is to carefully consider all the budgetary, investment, and tax implications of cracking your nest egg.

CHAPTER 8

College and Family Planning

Besides retirement, what else are you investing for? If you have kids, it is probably college. And paying for college is no small feat in an age when college costs are higher than ever and starting life with a college degree has never been more important. According to the Census Bureau, people with a bachelor's degree will earn, on average, nearly twice as much as people with only a high-school diploma (up from one and a half times in 1975). Those with advanced degrees can expect to earn nearly three times as much as a typical high school graduate. And the gap keeps widening. Since 1990, the real (inflation-adjusted) median income of full-time workers has increased over 5 percent for those with a bachelor's degree and over 9 percent for those with advanced degrees but has remained stagnant for high school graduates.

These income statistics make it clear that a college education is one of the best risk-free investments you can make. At the same time, the investment itself keeps going up. According to the College Board, average college costs for the 2000-2001 school year were as shown in Table 8.1

Keep in mind that the average costs in this table are for 1 year of college for one child. They also do not take inflation into account. To estimate the cost of college when your kids are ready to attend, use the calculator at www.finaid.com. Enter today's cost of college plus an inflation factor, and the calculator will tell you how much it will cost to send one child to college for 4 years. For example, if you wanted to send your 8-year-old child to a 4-year private institution in

TABLE 8.1 Average College Costs (2000–2001)

	TUITION AND FEES	BOOKS AND SUPPLIES	ROOM AND BOARD	TRANSPORTATION AND OTHER EXPENSES	TOTAL
Four-year private institution	$16,332	$730	$6,209	$1,675	$24,946
Four-year public institution	$3,510	$704	$4,960	$2,164	$11,338
Four-year public institution (out-of-state tuition)	$9,020	$704	$4,960	$2,164	$16,848
Two-year private institution	$7,458	$661	$4,736	$1,824	$14,679
Two-year public institution (live at home)	$1,705	$663	N/A	N/A	$1,705

10 years, and if college costs continue to rise at a rate of 5 percent per year, the costs break down as follows:

Current 1-year costs:	$24,946.00
Tuition inflation rate:	5.00 percent
Years to enrollment:	10 years
First-year projected costs:	$40,634.41
Second-year projected costs:	$42,666.13
Third-year projected costs:	$44,799.43
Fourth-year projected costs:	$47,039.40
Total projected costs:	**$175,139.37**

Financial Aid

The College Board attempts to put the high cost of college in perspective by mentioning that financial aid is widely available. "A college education is still well within the grasp of all Americans," said College Board President Gaston Caperton when the latest figures were released. However, what is disturbing to a lot of parents and students is that most financial aid is now in the form of loans, not grants. In fact, loans now represent 59 percent of all aid, compared with just over 41 percent in 1980-1981. And what do we know about loans? One, they have to be paid back, and two, they carry interest charges. Who among us would want our children to start their careers deep in debt? In addition, if the cost of college is already high, imagine what it ends up costing when you factor in interest charges.

Nevertheless, if your child is older and you do not have much saved, you likely will need to rely on financial aid. In this case, you will need to understand the tricks of the trade for maximizing the amount of aid for which your family will qualify. For example, when colleges calculate the amount a family is expected to contribute to tuition, books, and living expenses, the parents' assets (not counting retirement plans or home equity) generally are calculated at 5.6 percent, whereas the child's assets are calculated at 35 percent. This would suggest that saving money in your child's name is a bad idea because it would reduce the amount of aid for which he or she would qualify. However, there are other reasons to save in the child's name, mainly to enable you to shift the investment income to the child so that it will be taxed at the child's low rate (subject to the "kiddie tax," discussed later). As you consider the savings programs discussed in this chapter, consider whether or not you will be applying for financial aid and keep those guidelines in mind. Start now brushing up on the arcane world of financial aid by visiting popular Web sites such as www.finaid.com and www.fafsa.ed.gov. Learning how financial aid works is an education in itself.

Tax Incentives for Education

The high cost of college hurts middle-income Americans the most. Low-income students generally qualify for need-based scholarships, whereas high-income families easily can afford the escalating costs. To help the people who need it the most, Congress has given parents and students several new tax incentives to help ease the burden of paying for college. Even some of these will not help middle-income people because of the low income requirements needed to take advantage of them. Be sure to pay attention to the income limits to determine which programs for which you are eligible. Some tax breaks are available to students (and/or their parents) who are already paying for college, whereas others are designed as savings vehicles for parents of younger children. We will look at each of these categories beginning with the most urgent: tax breaks for people who are currently paying for college.

Tax Breaks Available to Students and Parents Currently Paying for College

The following subsections discuss tax breaks for people currently paying for college.

STUDENT LOAN INTEREST DEDUCTION

If you are currently paying off student loans, you can deduct up to $2,500 in student loan interest without itemizing deductions. The deduction for 2001 is allowed for interest paid during the first 60 months of the payoff period.

Beginning in 2002, the 60-month requirement has been eliminated. To take the full deduction for 2001, your adjusted gross income (AGI) cannot exceed $40,000 if single or $60,000 if married filing jointly. If your AGI is between $40,000 and $55,000 if single or between $60,000 and $75,000 if married, you may deduct a portion of interest paid. If your AGI is over $55,000 (single) or $75,000 (joint), you may not claim the student loan interest deduction.

In 2002, the income eligibility requirements for the full deduction increase to $50,000 (single) and $100,000 (joint). If your income is between $50,000 and $65,000 (single) or between $100,000 and $130,000 (joint), you can take a partial deduction. After 2002, these phaseout ranges will be adjusted annually for inflation. In order to claim the deduction, all the following requirements must be met:

- If you are married, you must file a joint return (i.e., you cannot take the deduction if you are married filing separately).
- No one else can be claiming an exemption for you on his or her tax return.
- The loan must have been used to pay tuition and other *qualified higher education expenses* for yourself, your spouse, or someone who was your dependent when the loan was taken out.

Qualified higher education expenses are the total costs of attending an eligible educational institution, including graduate school. They include the costs of tuition and fees, room and board, books, supplies, and equipment. However, you must reduce these costs by the total amount paid for them with the following tax-free items (some of which will be covered later):

- Employer-provided educational assistance benefits.
- Tax-free withdrawals from an education IRA.
- U.S. savings bond interest used to pay qualified higher education expenses.
- Certain scholarships [see Internal Revenue Service (IRS) Publication 520, "Scholarships and Fellowships"].
- Veterans' educational assistance benefits.
- Any other nontaxable payments (other than gifts, bequests, or inheritances) received for educational expenses.
- The education expenses were incurred within a *reasonable period of time* before or after the loan was taken out. (Federal loan programs automatically meet this definition. For other loans, the IRS says that the reasonable period of time usually is determined "based on all the relevant facts and circumstances.")
- The person for whom the expenses were paid or incurred was an *eligible student.* (An eligible student is a student who was enrolled at least half-time in a program that leads to a degree, certificate, or other recognized educational credential.)

DEDUCTION FOR QUALIFIED HIGHER EDUCATION EXPENSES

Beginning in 2002, if your AGI is less than $65,000 (single) or $130,000 (joint), you can take an above-the-line deduction (meaning you do not have to itemize) for higher education expenses of up to $3,000 in 2002 and 2003 and up to $4,000 in 2004 and 2005. In 2004 and 2005, if your AGI does not exceed $80,000 (single) or $160,000 (joint), you can deduct up to $2,000. Qualified higher education expenses are defined in the same manner as for purposes of the Hope credit (see below). The deduction may not be claimed in a year that an education IRA distribution is taken; however, principal can be withdrawn from a 529 plan (described later) to pay tuition. This deduction will be eliminated in 2006 unless Congress enacts new legislation.

HOPE CREDIT

The Hope credit is available for students attending the first 2 years of college. They must be enrolled at least half-time in a program leading to a degree, certificate, or other recognized educational credential. Like any tax credit, the Hope credit is a direct reduction off your tax bill as opposed to a reduction in taxable income, which only reduces your tax bill partially. The Hope credit is the sum of (1) 100 percent of the first $1,000 of qualified tuition and related expenses paid for each eligible student and (2) 50 percent of the next $1,000, to a maximum of $1,500 per year *per eligible student*.

Qualified tuition and related expenses are somewhat narrowly defined for the purpose of claiming the Hope credit. They include tuition and fees *required for enrollment* or attendance at an eligible educational institution. Student-activity fees and fees for course-related books, supplies, and equipment are included *only* if the fees must be paid *to the institution* as a condition of enrollment or attendance. Living expenses, such as room and board, transportation, and student health fees do not qualify. In addition, you must reduce the qualified expenses by the amount of any tax-free scholarships and grants you may receive. In addition, you may not claim the Hope and lifetime-learning credit (described next) in the same year for the same child. (You may, however, take the Hope credit for one child and the lifetime-learning credit for another child.) In 2001, if you are taking tax-free withdrawals from an education IRA, you cannot claim the Hope credit unless you waive the tax-free treatment of the withdrawals. Beginning in 2002, you can claim the Hope credit and also take tax-free withdrawals from an education IRA or 529 plan (described later) as long as the credit and the tax-free withdrawals are not used for the same expenses.

To claim the full Hope credit, your AGI must be less than $40,000 (single) or $80,000 (joint). If your income is between $40,000 and $50,000 (single) or between $80,000 and $100,000 (joint), you may claim a partial credit. If your income is over $50,000 (single) or $100,000 (joint), you may not claim the Hope credit. Some parents who exceed the income limits have chosen to forego the $2,900 personal exemption for the child and let him or her file his or her own tax return so that he or she can claim the Hope credit. This strategy might save a few dollars in taxes depending on the parents' tax bracket and the child's own income. Keep in mind that the child may not claim more in credit than he or she owes in tax, so he or she will need to have at least $12,000 in taxable income in order to claim the full $1,500 credit. Incidentally, the student for whom the Hope credit is being claimed must not have a drug felony conviction on his or her record.

By February following the end of the tax year you should receive form 1098-T from the college indicating the amount of qualified education expenses you paid during the tax year. To claim the Hope credit, complete form 8863 and file it with your tax return. Enter the total credit on line 46 of form 1040.

LIFETIME-LEARNING CREDIT

Unlike the Hope credit, which is restricted to students pursuing a degree during the first 2 years of college, the lifetime-learning credit is available to *all* students enrolled in eligible educational institutions and can be taken an unlimited number of years. The student does not have to be pursuing a degree or be enrolled for a minimum number of credits. In addition, the felony drug conviction rule does not apply. However, while the Hope credit is per *student*, the lifetime-learning credit is per *family*. In 2001, the credit is equal to 20 percent of the first $5,000 of qualified tuition and related expenses paid during the tax year or a maximum of $1,000. Beginning in 2002, the 20 percent credit may be taken on the first $10,000 of education expenses, making the maximum credit $2,000. Other than these differences, the lifetime-learning credit is similar to the Hope credit: The definition of qualified education expenses is the same, as are the income eligibility requirements and the form used to claim the credit.

WITHDRAWALS FROM TRADITIONAL OR ROTH IRAS

As discussed in Chapter 7, if you are under age $59\frac{1}{2}$, you can take withdrawals from an IRA without penalty if the money is used for higher education expenses for yourself, your spouse, your children, or your grandchildren. When determining the amount of the withdrawal that is not subject to the 10 percent penalty, include qualified higher education expenses *not* covered by any tax-free scholarships or tax-free withdrawals from an education IRA. The definition of qualified higher education expenses is more liberal than it is for the Hope and lifetime-learning credits and includes tuition, fees, books, supplies, equipment, and even room and board if the student is at least a half-time student.

Keep in mind that although withdrawals are free from penalty, they are not free from *tax*, unless you are over age $59\frac{1}{2}$ and withdrawing from a Roth IRA that you have held 5 years (except for your contributions to a Roth IRA, which can be withdrawn tax-free at any time). Most financial planners discourage parents from taking IRA withdrawals to pay for their children's college mainly because they are going to need that money for their own retirement. However, students who work during high school and college can contribute to their own IRAs and earmark the tax-deferred savings for college expenses without worrying about early withdrawal penalties. Now that the education IRA (covered later) has been liberalized, this would seem to be a better option because withdrawals are tax-free as well as penalty-free. However, contributions cannot be made to an education IRA after the student turns 18 years of age. Roth IRAs are a very good savings vehicle for young people; if they do not use the money for college, they can use it to buy a first home or even let it ride for their own retirement.

EMPLOYER-PROVIDED EDUCATIONAL ASSISTANCE

If your employer offers educational assistance, you can accept up to $5,250 without being taxed on the income as long as it is used for tuition, fees, books, supplies, and equipment for undergraduate-level courses. The courses do not necessarily have to be work-related. This benefit was scheduled to expire at the end of 2001 but was reinstated by the Economic Growth and Tax Relief Reconciliation Act of 2001. At the same time that it was extended permanently, the benefit was expanded to include graduate-level courses beginning in 2002. You cannot use the tax-free educational expenses paid for by your employer as the basis for any other deduction or credit, including the Hope credit and the lifetime-learning credit.

Tax Incentives for Parents and Students Who Are Saving for College

The following subsections discuss tax incentives for people who are saving for college.

EDUCATION SAVINGS BONDS

If you cash in a U.S. savings bond to pay higher education expenses, you need not include the interest earned on the bond in your taxable income for the year. You will remember from Chapter 3 that the interest on U.S. savings bonds accrues each year but is not taxable until the bond is cashed in. With this tax break, you can cash in the bond and not be taxed on any of the interest as long as you pay at least that much in qualified higher education expenses. If the interest exceeds the expenses, you can exclude a portion of the interest.

Only Series EE bonds issued after January 1, 1990 and Series I bonds qualify for tax-free treatment. If your modified adjusted gross income (MAGI) is less than $55,750 (single) or $83,650 (joint), you can take the full exclusion. If your MAGI is between $55,750 and $70,750 (single) or between $83,650 and $113,650 (joint), you may take a partial exclusion. If your income is over $70,750 (single) or $113,650 (joint), or if you are married filing separately (regardless of income), you may not claim the exclusion at all. The bond must be issued either in your name (as the sole owner) or in your and your spouse's names (as co-owners). The child cannot be listed as an owner but can be listed as a payable-on-death beneficiary.

Qualified higher education expenses for the savings bond interest exclusion include tuition and fees required to enroll at an eligible educational institution but not room and board or the costs of courses involving sports, games, or hobbies that are not part of a degree program. The exclusion *may* be taken for contributions to a qualified state tuition program (529 plan) or an education IRA (covered later). When claiming the exclusion, the expenses must be reduced by other tax-free benefits such as scholarships, withdrawals from an education IRA, and any expenses used in figuring the Hope and lifetime-learning credits. If you are taking the deduction for student loan interest, you must add the amount back in to your AGI for the purpose of determining your MAGI.

You must use both the principal and interest from the bonds to pay qualified expenses in order to exclude the interest from your gross income. If the amount of eligible bonds you have cashed during the year exceeds the amount of qualified educational expenses paid during the year, the amount of excludable interest is reduced pro rata. For example, if bond proceeds were $10,000 ($8,000 principal and $2,000 interest) and the qualified educational expenses were $8,000, you could exclude 80 percent of the interest earned, which would equal $1,600 (0.8 × $2000).

To claim the exclusion, use form 8815 and attach it to your form 1040.

EDUCATION IRA

With a contribution limit of only $500 per year, education IRAs used to be too insignificant to do much good in saving for college. However, with the Economic Growth and Tax Relief Reconciliation Act of 2001, the education IRA has been revived as a useful college saving vehicle. Starting January 1, 2002, the contribution limit increases to $2,000 per year. Furthermore, the definition of qualified education expenses has been expanded to include elementary and secondary school expenses as well as college costs and includes such expenses as tuition, books, transportation, computers, and Internet access. The deadline for making each annual contribution has been extended from December 31 to April 15.

Each education IRA is set up in the name of a child, who is called the *beneficiary* on the account. Except in the case of special-needs children, the child must be under 18 years of age, and contributions may not be made after the child reaches age 18. Anyone who meets the income eligibility requirements (including the child himself or herself) may contribute to a child's education IRA, as long as the total contributions in 1 year do not exceed $2,000. Contributions are always nondeductible and do not affect any contributions you may be making to traditional or Roth IRAs. In order to make the full $2,000 contribution, your AGI must be less than $95,000 (single) or $190,000 (joint). You can make a partial contribution if your AGI is between $95,000 and $110,000 (single) or between $190,000 and $220,000 (joint). If your AGI is over $110,000 (single) or $220,000 (joint), you may not contribute to an education IRA. However, other members of the family can contribute to your child's education IRA. If your income is too high, you can always give the $2,000 to your sister (or other family member) and ask her to make the contribution to your child's account.

All withdrawals from an education IRA are tax-free as long as they are used for qualified education expenses. You can even take tax-free withdrawals the same year you claim the Hope or lifetime-learning credit as long as each tax benefit is used for different expenses. If in one year you withdraw more from an education IRA than you pay in education expenses, all or part of the withdrawal will be taxable. See IRS Publication 970, "Tax Benefits for Higher Education," for the formula to determine the taxable portion.

All the funds in an education IRA must be withdrawn by the time the beneficiary reaches age 30. If funds are left in the account after the beneficiary's education has been paid for, the account may be transferred to another family member and tax-free withdrawals made for that beneficiary's education. Any withdrawals not used for education will be taxable and in most cases subject to a 10 percent penalty. An exception to the 10 percent penalty may be made in the case of death or disability. If an education IRA is transferred to a surviving spouse or other family member as a result of the beneficiary's death, the education IRA retains its status, and the spouse or other family member can treat the education IRA as his or her own. There are no tax consequences as a result of the transfer.

You can set up an education IRA just as you would any other IRA: Contact a brokerage firm or mutual fund and fill out the required forms. You may then invest the funds as you wish, with all investment earnings building up tax-free. Please note that for financial aid purposes, education IRAs are presumed to be the assets of the child and therefore may reduce the amount of outside aid the student receives more than if the same assets were held in the parents' names.

If you open an education IRA when a child is first born and save $2,000 per year, the account will be worth nearly $75,000 when the child is ready to attend college, assuming that investment returns average 8 percent. If this will not be enough, or if you are getting a late start, consider opening a 529 plan.

Table 8.2 provides a summary of higher education tax benefits.

SECTION 529 STATE-SPONSORED SAVINGS PROGRAMS

Section 529 plans are growing in popularity and are expected to become as well known for college saving as 401(k) plans are for retirement saving. Authorized by Congress in 1996 and further liberalized in 2001, 529 plans (named after a section of the tax code) are sponsored by the states. Nearly all 50 states either have or are working on their version of a 529 plan. Since they are state-sponsored, the plans differ from state to state. You do not have to use your own state's plan, but there may be additional state tax benefits for doing so. Basically, a 529 plan works like an education IRA in that the savings grow tax-free and may be withdrawn tax-free starting in 2002 if used for education (withdrawals

TABLE 8.2 Summary of Tax Benefits for Higher Education

	MAXIMUM CREDIT/DEDUCTION	EXPENSES THAT QUALIFY	EDUCATION THAT QUALIFIES	SPECIAL CONDITIONS	INCOME LIMIT FOR FULL CREDIT/DEDUCTION	INCOME LIMIT FOR PARTIAL CREDIT/DEDUCTION
Student loan interest deduction	2001–$2,500 tax deduction, 2002–$2,500 tax deduction	Tuition and required enrollment fees, books, supplies, room and board transportation, and other necessary expenses	All undergraduate and graduate	Must be enrolled at least half-time in degree program $100,000 joint	2001–$40,000 single, $60,000 joint, 2002–$50,000 single, $130,000 joint	200–$55,000 single, $75,000 joint, 2002–$65,000 single,
Deduction for qualified higher education expenses	2001–N/A, 2002–$3,000 tax deduction	Tuition and required enrollment fees only	All undergraduate and graduate		2001–N/A, 2002–$65,000 single, $130,000 joint	N/A
Hope credit	2001–$1,500 tax credit per child, 2002–$1,500 tax credit per child	Tuition and required enrollment fees only	First 2 years of undergraduate	Can be claimed only for 2 years Must be enrolled at least half-time in degree program, no felony drug convictions	$40,000 single, $80,000 joint	$50,000 single, $100,000 joint
Lifetime learning credit	2001–$1,000 tax credit per family, 2002–$2,000 tax credit per family	Tuition and required enrollment fees only	All undergraduate and graduate		$40,000 single, $80,000 joint	$50,000 single, $100,000 joint

TABLE 8.2 *(Continued)*

	MAXIMUM CREDIT/ DEDUCTION	EXPENSES THAT QUALIFY	EDUCATION THAT QUALIFIES	SPECIAL CONDITIONS	INCOME LIMIT FOR FULL CREDIT/ DEDUCTION	INCOME LIMIT FOR PARTIAL CREDIT/ DEDUCTION
Education savings bonds	Interest is not taxed. Exclusion is equal to amount of higher education expenses.	Tuition and required enrollment fees, payments to education, IRAs, payments to state tuition programs	All undergraduate and graduate	Applies only to qualified series EE bonds issued after January 1, 1990, and series I bonds.	$55,750 single, $83,650 joint	$70,750 single, $113,650 joint
Education IRA	2001—$500 nondeductible contribution. Investment earnings are not taxed. 2002—$2,000 nondeductible contribution. Investment earnings are not taxed.	Tuition and required enrollment fees, books, supplies, equipment, room and board if at least a half-time student, payments to state tuition programs	All undergraduate and graduate, now includes elementary and secondary school expenses	Must withdraw assets at age 30	$95,000 single, $190,000 joint	$110,000 single, $220,000 joint
Employer's educational assistance program	Up to $5,250 in employer benefits not taxed	Tuition and required enrollment fees, books, supplies, equipment	2001—undergraduate only, 2002—all undergraduate and graduate		N/A	N/A

made in 2001 are taxed at the child's tax rate). The difference is that the contribution limits are much higher for 529 plans than for education IRAs and there are no income limits. Everyone may participate.

Section 529 plans are an outgrowth of prepaid tuition plans that have long been offered by individual colleges and universities. These plans allow parents of young children to lock in today's prices by depositing cash, either in a lump sum or in installments, so that when the child is ready to go to college, the tuition is all paid. The lack of flexibility in these programs has limited their popularity as parents have realized that their child may not want to go to the college they select and in fact may end up not going to college at all. In any case, the return on investment essentially equals the rate at which college costs are going up, an average of approximately 5 to 6 percent per year.

Today's section 529 plans come in two forms: prepaid tuition plans and savings plans. Some states offer both types of plans; others offer just one. The prepaid tuition plans sponsored by states are similar to the ones offered by individual colleges except that they allow the child to go to any state-run college or university and, in some cases, other states' universities as well. However, the return on investment is still equal to the inflation rate, which does not help if you are late getting started saving and want to earn more than 5 or 6 percent a year.

The 529 savings plans offer much more flexibility. The child can attend the college of his or her choice, and the savings can be invested in a variety of professionally managed portfolios. The typical 529 plan offers age-based portfolios that invest more aggressively in stocks when the child is young and gradually shift into bonds and money market funds as the child gets closer to college age. An important factor to weigh when choosing among 529 plans is the number and type of investment portfolios offered. Some plans offer limited choices, whereas others offer a broad range of professionally managed portfolios. You may not manage the portfolio yourself but must select one of the professionally managed portfolios offered by the plan. Some people see this as a drawback; others see it as a welcome relief from the burden of managing their children's college fund. Contributions to 529 plans are not deductible on your federal income tax return, although some states let you deduct all or part of your 529 contributions on your state tax return. Be sure to check out the tax benefits of your own state's plan before looking elsewhere, especially if you live in a high-income-tax state.

Contribution limits vary by state, but most plans allow you to contribute as much as $100,000; some plans even go as high as $250,000. The reason contribution limits vary is that the IRS has said that contributions should not exceed the amount that actually would be needed for college, and the states use different formulas for determining this amount. If you end up with money left over after your child has completed college, you can always name a new beneficiary

—another child in the family or even yourself (you always wanted to go back to school, didn't you?). If you take withdrawals that are not used for college, you will pay income tax plus a 10 percent penalty.

It is too soon to tell how 529 plans will be treated for financial aid eligibility. Before the law changed to allow tax-free withdrawals, the assets in the account were presumed to belong to the parents (with just 5.6 percent factored into the amount of college costs the family was expected to pay). Withdrawals taken from the plan to pay for college were presumed to be income to the child, half of which figured into the aid calculation. For example, if there was $25,000 in the plan and $5,000 was taken out to pay for 1 year of college, 5.6 percent of the remaining $20,000, or $1,120, would be figured into the parents' share of costs, whereas half the $5,000 withdrawal, or $2,500, would be included in the student's share. However, with withdrawals becoming tax-free as of January 1, 2002, this formula may change. It also may be expected that as 529 plans grow in popularity and hold a significant portion of a family's assets, they will figure more prominently in the calculations for financial aid eligibility.

Table 8.3 lists the 529 plans that were in effect in the summer of 2001. If you do not see your state's plan listed, it means it has not been finalized yet. For the latest information, visit www.savingforcollege.com. When evaluating 529 plans, you will need to consider (1) the tax savings available through your home state's plan, (2) the range of investment choices, (3) the expertise of the portfolio managers, and (4) annual fees. As with any prospective investment, consider the overall net after-tax return, taking into account all relevant factors.

WHICH PLAN IS BEST?

Of the three plans offering tax incentives for saving for college—education savings bonds, the education IRA, and the 529 plan—only two are really in the running for your serious college saving. The interest rate on savings bonds is so low that most investors would rather choose a plan with more flexibility and greater investment potential. Thus the question comes down to the education IRA and the 529 plan. Of these, which is the better choice? Actually, you may now contribute to both an education IRA and a 529 plan in the same year, so it is not absolutely necessary to make a choice. However, if you have a limited amount to contribute and want to keep life simple by having only one plan, you may wish to choose one over the other.

First, let us emphasize that both the education IRA and the 529 plan offer compelling ways to save for college. The investment earnings compound tax-free and withdrawals, if used for education expenses, may be taken tax-free. This is a better deal even than retirement accounts, whose earnings ultimately are taxable (except for the Roth IRA). You can hardly go wrong with either of these plans. If you have college-bound children, we urge you to start saving now, regardless

TABLE 8.3 529 Plans in Effect in Summer 2001

STATE	PLAN NAME	INVESTMENT MANAGER	INVESTMENT LIMIT*	STATE TAX DEDUCTION	WEB SITE/ TELEPHONE
Alaska	University of Alaska College Savings Plan	T. Rowe Price	$250,000 (balance)	No state tax	www.troweprice.com/college 800-369-3641
Arizona	Arizona Family College Savings Program	Securities Management & Research/College Savings Bank	$168,000 (contribution)	No	www.smrinvest.com 888-667-3239
Arkansas	GIFT College Investing Plan	Mercury Funds (Merrill Lynch)	$175,000 (balance)	No	www.thegiftplan.com 877-442-6553
California	Golden State ScholarShare College Savings Trust	TIAA-CREF	$165,886 (balance) (varies with age of beneficiary)	No	www.scholarshare.com 877-728-4338
Colorado	Scholars Choice College Savings Program	Salomon Smith Barney	$150,000 (contribution)	Full	www.scholars-choice.com 888-572-4652
Connecticut	The Connecticut Higher Education Trust Program	TIAA-CREF	$235,000 (balance)	No	www.aboutchet.com 888-799-2438
Delaware	Delaware College Investment Plan	Fidelity	$131,480 (balance)	No	www.fidelity.com/delaware 800-544-1655
Idaho	Idaho College Savings Program	TIAA-CREF	$235,000 (balance)	Partial	www.idsaves.com 8 66-433-2533
Illinois	Bright Start College Savings Program	Salomon Smith Barney	$160,000 (balance)	No	www.brightstartsavings.com 877-432-7444

TABLE 8.3 *(Continued)*

STATE	PLAN NAME	INVESTMENT MANAGER	INVESTMENT LIMIT*	STATE TAX DEDUCTION	WEB SITE/ TELEPHONE
Indiana	Indiana Family College Savings Plan	Bank One	$114,548	No	www.incollegesave.com 888-814-6800
Iowa	College Savings Iowa	State/Agency & Vanguard	$140,221 (balance)	Partial	www.collegesavingsiowa.com 888-672-9116
Kansas	Learning Quest Education Savings Program	American Century	$127,000 (contribution)	Partial	www.learningquestsavings.com 800-579-2203
Kentucky	Kentucky Education Savings Plan Trust	TIAA-CREF	$235,000 (balance)	No	www.kentuckytrust.org 877-598-7878
Louisiana	Student Tuition Assistance and Revenue Trust Saving program	State/Agency	$157,040 (contribution)	Partial	www.osfa.state.la.us 800-259-5626
Maine	NextGen College Investing Plan	Merrill Lynch	$225,000 (balance)	No	www.nextgenplan.com 877-463-9843
Massachusetts	U. Fund College Investing Plan	Fidelity	$171,125 (balance)	No	www.fidelity.com/ufund 800-544-2776
Michigan	Michigan Education Savings Program	TIAA-CREF	$125,000 (balance)	Partial	www.misaves.com 877-861-6377
Mississippi	Mississippi Affordable College Savings Program	TIAA-CREF	$235,000 (balance)	Partial	www.collegesavingsms.com 800-486-3670
Missouri	Missouri Saving for Tuition (MO$T) Program	TIAA-CREF	$235,000 (balance)	Partial	www.missourimost.org 888-414-6678

(continues)

TABLE 8.3 *(Continued)*

STATE	PLAN NAME	INVESTMENT MANAGER	INVESTMENT LIMIT*	STATE TAX DEDUCTION	WEB SITE/ TELEPHONE
Montana	Montana Family Education Savings Program	College Savings Bank	$168,000 (contribution)	Partial	www.montana.collegesavings.com 800-888-2723
Nebraska	College Savings Plan of Nebraska	Union Bank & Trust Co.	$165,000 (balance)	Partial	www.PlanForCollegeNow.com 888-993-3746
New Hampshire	The UNIQUE College Investing Plan	Fidelity	$166,600 (balance)	No state tax	www.fidelity.com/unique 800-544-1722
New Jersey	New Jersey Better Educational Savings Trust (NUBEST)	State/Agency	$150,000 (balance)	No	www.hesaa.org/njbest 877-465-2378
New Mexico	The Education Plan's College Savings Program	Schoolhouse Capital (State Street Global Advisors)	$202,225 (contribution)	Full	www.theeducationplan.com 877-337-5268
New York	New York College Choice Tuition Savings Program	TIAA-CREF	$100,000 (contribution) (varies with age of beneficiary)	Partial	www.nysaves.com 877-697-2837
North Carolina	College Vision Fund	State/Agency	$187,500 (contribution) (higher for out-of-state schools)	No	www.collegevisionfund.org 800-600-3453
Ohio	CollegeAdvantageSavings Plan Variable Investment Option	Putnam	$229,000 (balance)	Partial	www.collegeadvantage.com 800-233-6734

TABLE 8.3 *(Continued)*

STATE	PLAN NAME	INVESTMENT MANAGER	INVESTMENT LIMIT*	STATE TAX DEDUCTION	WEB SITE/ TELEPHONE
Oklahoma	Oklahoma College Savings Plan	TIAA-CREF (balance)	$235,000	No	www.ok4saving.org 877-654-7284
Oregon	Oregon College Savings Plan	Strong	$150,000 (balance)	Partial	www.OregonCollegeSavings.com 866-772-8464
Rhode Island	CollegeBoundFund	Alliance Capital	$246,023 (balance)	No	www.collegeboundfund.com 888-324-5057
Tennessee	BEST Savings Plan	TIAA-CREF	$100,000 (contribution)	No state tax	www.tnbest.org 888-486-2378
Utah	Utah Educational Savings Plan	State/Agency & Vanguard	$90,630 (contribution) (higher for out-of-state schools)	Partial	www.uesp.org 800-418-2551
Vermont	Vermont Higher Education Savings Plan	TIAA-CREF	$100,000 (contribution)	No	www.vsac.org 800-637-5860
Virginia	Virginia Education Savings Trust	State/Agency	$100,000 (contribution)	Partial	www.vpep.state.va.us 888-567-0540
Wisconsin	EdVest Wisconsin	State/Agency & Strong	$246,000 (balance)	Partial	www.edvest.state.wi.us 888-338-3789
Wyoming	College Achievement Plan	Merrill Lynch	$220,000 (balance)	No state tax	www.collegeachievementplan.com 877-529-2655

* Limits based on total contribution or account balance.

of their ages, because the earlier you start, the less you have to set aside. For example, to save up the full cost of a 4-year private university, assuming that college costs rise by 5 percent per year and investments earn 8 percent per year, you would need to set aside $535 per month if you start saving when the child is first born. If you wait until he or she is 5 years old, the saving requirement goes up to $737, and if you wait until he or she is 10, it jumps to $1,179. These numbers are not meant to scare you or to discourage you if you have not started saving yet but merely to encourage you to perhaps forego some of your everyday indulgences and start saving for college. Now let us look at the differences between the two plans.

Income Limits

If your income is over $95,000 (single) or $190,000 (joint), you cannot contribute the full $2,000 (in 2002) to an education IRA. However, as noted earlier, you can always give the money to a family member to contribute to your child's education IRA. (Considering how easy it is to get around the income restrictions, it is surprising that they are even there.)

Contribution Limits

The maximum annual contribution to an education IRA is $2,000 regardless of how many aunts, uncles, and cousins are contributing to the account. $2,000 a year will go only so far in saving for a child's education. If you plan to save more than this, you will need to go for the 529 plan.

Age Limits

You cannot add to an education IRA after the child reaches age 18. If you want to keep saving for graduate school or other continued education, you will need to do it through a 529 plan. In addition, education IRAs must be emptied by the time the beneficiary reaches age 30. There are no age restrictions on 529 plans.

Definition of Education Expenses

The education IRA now includes elementary and secondary school expenses in its definition of expenses qualifying for tax-free withdrawals. If you want to use the money prior to college, the education IRA is your only option. Otherwise, if used for post-secondary school education, the definition of qualified expenses is the same for the education IRA and the 529 plan. The IRS defines these expenses as tuition, fees, books, supplies, and equipment required for enrollment or attendance at an *eligible educational institution*, including reasonable costs for room and board for a student who attends school at least half-time. Room and board are considered reasonable if they are not more than either the school's posted room and board charges or $2,500 per year for students living off-campus and not at home. An eligible educational institution is any college, university, vocational school, or other post-secondary school educational institution eligible to participate in a student aid program administered by the Department of Education.

Investment Flexibility

With the education IRA, you have complete control over how the assets are invested, but with a 529 plan, you must choose one of the plan's professionally managed portfolios. You can change 529 plans if you do not like how the assets are being managed, but it is more trouble than simply selling one mutual fund and buying another within an education IRA. Of course, if you want to invest in individual securities, you may do so only in an education IRA.

Other Ways to Save

It is only recently that education IRAs and 529 plans have become such attractive college saving vehicles. Before this, parents found other ways to save. These methods still hold some appeal.

CUSTODIAL ACCOUNT IN THE CHILD'S NAME

Putting assets in a child's name so that the investment income will be taxed at a lower rate has long been a popular college-saving strategy. The idea here is to take the $25,000 or $50,000 that you have earmarked for your child's education and put it into an account held in trust for the child. As trustee on the account, you would direct the investments, but the income would be taxable to the child (subject to the "kiddie tax" discussed below). When the child reaches the age of majority (18 or 21 or 25 years depending on state law), the assets become the property of the child. At that point you no longer have legal control over the assets.

One advantage of these Uniform Gifts to Minors Act (UGMA) or Uniform Transfer to Minors Act (UTMA) accounts is that you do not have to use the money for education. As long as the expenditures benefit the child, the money can be used for cars, summer camp, or music lessons. One caveat: The assets in a UGMA or UTMA account may not be used to pay for normal parental support obligations, such as clothes or food.

The big disadvantage of UGMA and UTMA accounts (and it is a huge one) is that the money becomes the property of the child at what most of us would consider a very early age. At this point the child can do anything he or she wants with the account, including withdraw all the money and give it away to friends. Some parents choose to focus on the positive rather than the negative, using the UGMA account as an opportunity to teach their kids about financial responsibility. Periodic planning sessions at the kitchen table beginning when the child is in junior high school will help instill the importance of going to college and teach the child the financial realities of becoming an educated citizen. After all, if your child is responsible enough to go off to college at age 18, would it not be nice to think that you have raised him or her well enough to handle his or her own money at that age?

One important thing to understand about UGMA or UTMA accounts is the so-called kiddie tax. To keep parents from putting all their assets in their children's names in order to avoid paying income tax on the investment earnings, the Tax Reform Act of 1986 established rules limiting the amount of investment income a child can earn. In 2001, a child under age 14 can earn $750 in investment income without paying any tax (the income is sheltered by the standard deduction). The next $750 is taxed at the child's tax rate, presumably 10 percent (or 8 percent for assets held longer than 5 years). All unearned income over $1,500 received by a child under age 14 is taxed at the parents' highest marginal tax rate. Once the child reaches age 14 the "kiddie tax" no longer applies: From then on, all income is taxed at the child's tax rate. Note that the "kiddie tax" applies to *unearned* income. If your under-14 child works (in violation of child labor laws?), all wages are taxed at the child's tax rate.

CRUMMEY TRUST

If you like the idea of shifting tax liability to your child but dread the thought of all those assets falling into your child's hands at age 18, 21, or 25, you can set up a Crummey trust and legally control the assets for a longer period of time. A Crummey trust must be set up by an attorney and costs about $1,000 in legal fees. The investment income gets taxed at the child's rate and is subject to the "kiddie tax." In this regard, it is like a custodial account. However, you can specify conditions for disbursement. Thus, if your child ends up not going to college, for example, you can stipulate that assets be distributed at age 35 (or whatever age you specify) or on meeting a certain condition (such as starting a business).

SAVE IN YOUR OWN NAME

Some parents prefer to simply save money in their own names and earmark it for college. The disadvantage to saving in your own name is that you miss out on the tax breaks available with the other programs described in this chapter. However, by following some of the tax-saving guidelines in this book, such as deferring capital gains taxes by holding stocks long term, you may be able to minimize taxes anyway. The obvious advantage to keeping the assets in your own name is that you can do what you want with the money. If college plans fall through or you decide you would rather have a fancy boat than an educated child, the decision is yours to make. You also can give the assets to your child later on, if you want. For example, if you hold appreciated stock that you have been earmarking for college, rather than selling the stock in your own account and paying 20 percent capital gains tax, give the stock to your child. He or she can sell it in his or her account and pay capital gains tax at the 10 or 8 percent rate. Another good strategy is to keep assets in your own name until your child reaches age 14; at this point, you can transfer them to the child's account, and the investment income will not be subject to the "kiddie tax."

HIRE YOUR CHILD

If you operate a business as a sole proprietorship or a husband-and-wife partnership, you can hire your child under age 18 and not have to pay Social Security or Medicare taxes. The child can earn up to $4,550 and have it all sheltered from tax by the standard deduction. If he or she contributes $2,000 to a deductible IRA, he or she can earn up to $6,550 without owing any tax. In addition, you get a business deduction for money that will (hopefully) be used to pay college expenses. Once the child reaches age 18, you will have to pay Social Security and Medicare taxes, so you will need to consider whether or not it is worth it to keep him or her on the payroll. The downside to hiring your child is that you must follow tax-reporting requirements such as issuing W-2s and be prepared to prove to the IRS that your child has a legitimate job and is not being overpaid. A dentist was nailed recently by the IRS for "hiring" his 8- and 10-year-old children as laboratory workers and paying them a "salary" that exactly matched the amount he was paying in child support.

Tips on Paying for College

Following are some tips on paying for college.

Educate Yourself First

As tax incentives increase and financial aid becomes available to nearly everyone, the cost of college keeps going higher and higher. Unless you are among the very rich, you cannot ignore the many rules and regulations that let you take advantage of tax breaks and low-interest loans and scholarships for students. If you are just starting to look into this, you will be amazed by the complexity of the whole college financing system. However, the only way to be sure you are taking advantage of every available break is to stay on top of the rules. Use the information in this chapter to build on your knowledge, and keep in mind that income limits and other nuances of the programs are changing constantly.

Claim All the Credits You are Entitled to

This advice may seem obvious, but it can be easy to overlook some of the credits and deductions to which you may be entitled. For example, the $3,000 deduction for higher education expenses is brand new and does not even start until 2002; if you were not staying on top of the latest tax laws by reading this book, you could easily miss it. Do not forget: There is room for creativity here. If your AGI is too high to take advantage of certain valuable credits, see if there is anything you can do to bring it under the limit, such as deferring income to next year or making a hefty contribution to a retirement plan. It is only by knowing the rules and understanding your own personal situation that you can maximize tax benefits in all areas (not just college).

Get Advice

If staying on top of all the tax and financial aid rules is too time-consuming for you, consult a professional who is well versed in this area. Be careful of "consultants" who are selling products or who charge for information that is easily obtained for free. However, if you can find an advisor who will charge a few hundred dollars to save you thousands in taxes or direct college costs, you will have made yourself a wise investment.

Do Not Ignore Your Own Retirement

We touched on this earlier but feel the need to mention it again. If you wait until your kids are through college to start saving for your own retirement, you will never make it. There is a reason why the retirement chapter came before the college chapter in this book. Retirement plans should be put in place first because retirement is a much larger goal. Moreover, the outside resources available to you once you get there are limited. (Do you trust Social Security to be there when you need it and to provide all the income you will need?) College, on the other hand, offers a variety of money-saving options. In addition to getting scholarships and loans, students can save money by attending community college for the first 2 years or taking periodic breaks so that they can work and earn enough money for the next year's tuition. Some parents feel that involving their child in the college financing process builds character and a better appreciation for the education.

Family Financial Planning

So far in this chapter we have focused on meeting the needs of college-bound children. However, family financial planning extends beyond saving for college. We have not even talked about grandparents yet, but they should be brought into the picture too. Whether they are in a position to help pay for part of your children's college expenses or are in need of help themselves, it is important to consider the entire family when doing investment and tax planning. In addition, there are all the complications of marriage and divorce, children and stepchildren, cousins who ask for loans, uncles who give money with strings, and the very big subject of death—commonly and euphemistically referred to as *estate planning*.

We will start our discussion there because estate planning drives many of the decisions made during life. A detailed discussion of estate planning is beyond the scope of this book, but we will cover the basics enough to understand the rules concerning gifts because income shifting among family members is a popular strategy for reducing taxes on investment income. Earlier in the chapter we noted that if your income is too high to contribute to an education IRA, you can give the $2,000 to your sister to contribute to your child's account. This may seem like a rather shifty strategy (after all, if Congress had wanted you to contribute to the child's education IRA, it would not have imposed any income limits), but it is a perfectly legal maneuver. You can give any person as much as $10,000 a year without any income, gift, or estate tax consequences. There is no income tax to the recipient because you already paid income tax on that money when you first earned it. There is no gift or estate tax due because of a simple and straightforward rule that says you can give away up to $10,000 a year to as many people as you want without any gift or estate tax. You and your spouse can each do this, so together you can give away up to $20,000 to anyone you want with no tax consequences whatsoever. Even if you were to give away more than $10,000, neither you nor the recipient would have to pay gift taxes right away. For amounts over $10,000, the gift applies against your *exemption equivalent*, or the amount you may leave other people, either in life or at death, without paying any estate tax.

The estate tax is on a slippery slope right now, having been altered significantly by the Economic Growth and Tax Relief Reconciliation Act of 2001. In a nutshell, the exemption equivalent will be going up in the years ahead, meaning that you can leave more to your heirs without paying estate tax. Over the same period, the estate tax rates will be coming down, so if your estate is worth more than the exemption equivalent, the excess will be taxed at a lower rate. Then in 2010 the estate tax is eliminated—but for 1 year only. In 2011 it is scheduled to be reinstated—not because Congress necessarily wanted it to but because lawmakers are prohibited from taking budgetary action more than 10 years out. It is very likely that the estate planning rules will be changed again before 2010, and there is a good chance that the repeal for that 1 year will be reversed. (Otherwise we could see a spike in the death rate among rich people in 2010 and lots of suspicious-looking heirs walking around.)

The bottom line is that all these changes make it very hard to plan. Before, you never knew when you were going to die, but you could pretty much count on present law being in effect whenever that happened. Now, you not only do not know when you will die but you also have no idea what laws will be in effect when you do. Still, without making this too complicated, there are some guidelines you can follow.

Exemption Equivalent

The most important concept to grasp is the exemption equivalent. Again, this is the amount you can leave behind without any of it being subject to gift or estate tax. The reason we talk about gift and estate tax as if it is one tax is that in a way it is. Most people think of the estate tax as the tax imposed on the value of their estate at death. A better way to think of it is as the tax imposed on assets transferred to other people *during life and at death*. Whatever is not given away during life obviously will be given away at death. And all of it will be considered when calculating the estate tax. For example, let us say that in 2002 you give your sister $100,000. In 2003, you die, leaving an estate worth $1,500,000. To keep this simple, let us say that you are not married and that the $1,500,000 was distributed according to your will to various friends and relatives. Counting the $100,000 you gave to your sister during your life and the $1,500,000 you gave to everyone else at your death, the total amount transferred is $1,600,000. In 2003, the exemption equivalent will be $1,000,000. This means that the estate tax will be calculated on $600,000 ($1,600,000 − $1,000,000).

The thing to understand about gifts is that gifts of $10,000 and under can chip away at your estate (in a good way) and ultimately reduce the amount of estate tax owed. In the preceding example, if you had started several years ago giving away $10,000 a year to all your friends and relatives, your estate might be under the $1,000,000 exemption equivalent by the time you died, and there would be no estate tax due at all. This is the basic idea behind $10,000 gifting strategies, which you and/or your parents may want to employ, whether to help the kids with college or simply to reduce the amount of estate tax paid by members of the family. (Technically, the estate tax is paid by the estate, but since it cuts into the amount eventually distributed to heirs, it is as if it is coming out of their pocket.) Table 8.4 shows the exemption equivalent and top estate tax rate for 2001 to 2010.

Now that it is all clear that the exemption equivalent applies to both lifetime gifts and bequests after death, we must explain a new provision of the tax bill that complicates things a bit. Previously, the exemption equivalent for gifts made during life (not counting gifts of $10,000 and under) and bequests made at death was the same. Thus, in determining if estate tax was due, your executor would simply add up all your over-$10,000 gifts made during your lifetime plus the amount transferred to heirs at death and subtract the exemption equivalent in

TABLE 8.4 Exemption Equivalent and Top Estate Tax Rate (2001–2011)

YEAR	EXEMPTION	TOP TAX RATE
2001	$675,000	55%
2002	$1,000,000	50%
2003	$1,000,000	49%
2004	$1,500,000	48%
2005	$2,000,000	47%
2006	$2,000,000	46%
2007	$2,000,000	45%
2008	$2,000,000	45%
2009	$3,500,000	45%
2010	Estate tax repealed	0%
2011	$1,000,000	55%

effect for that year ($675,000 in 2001). Under the new rules, the exemption equivalent on gifts is capped at $1,000,000, whereas the exemption equivalent on bequests at death makes up the balance of the increasing exemption equivalent shown in the table. Furthermore, the gift tax stays in effect (subject to the $1,000,000 exemption) even during the 1 year the estate tax is repealed. You can work with this. Just do not give away more than $1,000,000 during your life—not counting all the little $10,000 gifts, of course.

When you give a gift of more than $10,000, you have to file a gift tax return using form 709. If you and your spouse are jointly gifting $20,000 to one individual, the gift will not be taxable under the annual exclusion, but you have to file a gift tax return (you can use form 709A) and include "the consenting spouse's signature." The gift tax return is filed by April 15 following the year of the gift; if you get an extension for filing your regular income tax, the extension also applies to the gift tax return. As noted earlier, you do not have to pay the tax at the time you file the return. Save copies of your gift tax returns so that your executor will be able to accurately calculate the estate and gift tax due when tying up your final affairs.

Exceptions

Following are exceptions to the gift and estate tax.

UNLIMITED MARITAL DEDUCTION

One key exception to the exemption equivalent is that you can give your spouse any amount (in life or at death) without it being taxed. Thus, in the preceding example, if you were married and left $1,500,000 to your spouse, there would be no estate tax due because your only taxable gift was the $100,000 to your sister, and that was well under the exemption equivalent. When your spouse dies, the estate tax will come due—unless your spouse remarries and leaves everything to the new spouse (much to the chagrin of your children, to be sure). A popular estate-planning strategy is what is called a *bypass trust* or *marital trust* that would allow you to leave, say, $1,000,000 to your spouse (the amount of the exemption equivalent in 2002) and the remaining $500,000 to other heirs. Since the $500,000 left to other heirs is under the exemption equivalent, it will not be taxed. When your spouse dies, he or she can leave the $1,000,000 without it being taxed (assuming that he or she has been spending all of the investment income and the account has not grown in value). With the exemption equivalent changing practically year by year, attorneys are having to revise trust documents to replace language that says "$675,000" (the exemption equivalent for 2001) with "the current exemption equivalent."

PAYMENTS FOR COLLEGE AND MEDICAL BILLS

Another exception to the $10,000 limit on tax-free gifts relates to direct payments to colleges and health care providers. There are no limits on these transfers. Thus, if your parents, say, were interested in reducing the size of their estate and also wanted to help out with their grandchildren's college, they could write checks to the college and not worry about staying under the $10,000 limit per recipient per year. In addition, it is worth noting that 529 plans have a special provision that allows a donor to contribute $50,000 at one time and have it apply to the next 5 years worth of $10,000 gifts. The advantage is that the lump sum of money can be invested immediately and start growing tax-free for the child's benefit while future growth is removed from the parents' estate. The disadvantage is that if the donor dies within the 5-year period, the remaining amount (say, the $30,000 if he or she dies in the second year) will apply against the exemption equivalent and may result in tax. However, it seems to us that if the donor did *not* give away the $50,000, it would still be in his or her estate when he or she died, so taxwise, he or she is no worse off for having made the gift.

Income-Shifting Strategies

The idea behind income-shifting strategies is that the family is an economic and social unit and that moving money around within the unit can lower the rate at which certain kinds of income is taxed. Years ago, when the highest marginal tax rate was 70 percent and high-income taxpayers were being very creative in their quest for tax relief, income-shifting strategies took forms that could only be called abusive—high-income professionals putting a chunk of their salary in their children's names, for example. Since then, the IRS has cracked down on schemes that were clearly designed to evade taxes by imposing laws that prohibit massive shifts of income to lower-bracket family members. The prohibition against shifting earned income to family members and imposition of the "kiddie tax" are two of the most significant rules discouraging major income-shifting strategies. There are still a few strategies left, but generally they cannot be expected to save huge amounts in taxes and often are not worth the trouble.

GIFTS OF STOCK

One of the most common income-shifting strategies is to give appreciated stock instead of cash to a lower-bracket family member. Why should you pay capital gains taxes at 20 percent when your child or low-income parent can sell the stock in his or her account and pay the tax at the 10 or 8 percent rate? Be aware that it must be a legitimate gift, which means it is subject to gift tax rules if over $10,000. Also, the recipient must have control over the use of the proceeds. You cannot transfer the stock just to make the sale and then take the proceeds back again. This strategy works best when you are supporting a low-bracket family member anyway and are simply giving them stock instead of cash. By the way, this may seem obvious but it bears mentioning: Do not give stock on which you have a *loss* to a family member in a lower bracket. The loss will not be worth as much to him or her, and you will be giving up the right to take the tax deduction when the stock is sold.

One other caveat you should keep in mind: If you gift appreciated stock during your lifetime, the recipient assumes your cost basis and holding period, but if you wait until after you die to give it away, the recipient receives a step-up in basis. Let us say that you hold 1,000 shares of stock XYZ that, after several stock splits, has an adjusted cost basis of $5 per share. Today it is selling for $50. If you give the stock to your son today (a $50,000 gift), and if he sells it right away, he will report a capital gain of $45,000 ($45 × 1,000). If the gain is taxed at the 8 percent rate, the tax will be $3,600 ($45,000 × 0.08). However, if you die today and your son inherits the stock, his basis will be $50 per share. If he sells it right away, his gain will be zero and the tax will be zero. Incidentally, with the repeal(?) of the estate tax in 2010, this step-up in basis has been eliminated (for just the 1 year the repeal is in effect), except for assets of $1.3 million (plus $3 million left to a spouse), whose basis may be stepped up at the discretion of the executor. IRA assets, by the way, never enjoy a step-up in basis because they operate under different rules for taxation of withdrawals.

HELP WITH IRA CONTRIBUTIONS

If your children and/or parents are eligible to contribute to an IRA—that is, they have earned income—but do not have enough cash to make the contribution, consider giving them the money to do so. In most cases a Roth IRA makes sense, although you will have to weigh the value of the tax deduction at their low bracket (deductible IRA) against the promise of tax-free income in the future (Roth IRA). If your parents are over age 70½, the only kind of IRA to which they can contribute is a Roth IRA. If you figure that the whole idea here is to keep money within the family rather than sending chunks of it to the U.S. Treasury, giving money to family members for the purpose of deferring taxes on investment earnings makes a lot of sense.

LOANS TO FAMILY MEMBERS

You can lend money to a family member at zero or low interest as long as you follow certain rules. If you do not follow the rules, the amount you should have charged in interest but did not will be taxable to you even though you never received it, and the foregone interest will be considered a gift from you, applying against your exemption equivalent. Here are the rules: If the loan is under $10,000, you do not have to worry about any of this. You also do not have to worry if the loan is under $100,000 and the borrower's net investment income (not earned income) for the year is $1,000 or less. Presumably, any family member who needs to borrow money would not have enough assets to generate more than $1,000 in investment income, so you should be clear on this. You can always lend money to a family member (or anyone else) at market rates without worrying about rules designed to keep people on the up and up about loans that are really gifts. Get help with this to make sure you are charging the correct amount and are documenting the loan properly. Incidentally, if you make a bona fide loan to a family member who does not pay it back, you may be able to write off the loss.

FAMILY TRUSTS

Sophisticated estate-planning strategies that enable wealthy families to avoid estate taxes are beyond the scope of this book. However, it is worth mentioning that irrevocable trusts—where you give up complete control of the assets and cannot ever take them back again—may save income taxes and estate taxes (but not gift taxes). By turning the assets over to a trust, you remove them from your estate, and the trust, not you, pays income tax on the investment income. Needless to say, you will want to make sure that you will not ever need the money before transferring assets to an irrevocable trust. You also will need the advice of an attorney and/or an accountant before making such a move. Revocable trusts—the kind that can be revoked and the assets taken back—are considered incomplete gifts and therefore offer no income tax or estate tax benefits. The main advantage to a revocable trust established during your lifetime is to ease the transfer of assets after your death by avoiding the delays, publicity, and administrative expense of probate. You will need an attorney to implement any kind of trust, so make that sure you get good professional advice that takes into account your entire financial and family situation.

LIFE INSURANCE

Cash-value life insurance offers tax-free buildup of interest income, and the proceeds are not taxable to beneficiaries. For these reasons, life insurance can be a good tool for family financial planning. Of course, you must consider the investment merits of the policy, including fees and interest paid on the cash-value buildup as well as the value of the life insurance itself in protecting family members. To shelter life insurance from estate tax, you must not have ownership rights in the policy. This means you must assign to another person the right to change beneficiaries, the right to surrender or cancel the policy, the right to assign it to another person, and the right to borrow against it. If you retain any of these ownership rights, or if you assign them within 3 years preceding your death, the policy will be included in your estate.

There has been some question as to whether you can continue to pay the premiums on a policy that you have assigned to another person, essentially treating the premiums as gifts to that person. For example, you take out a policy on your life and give it to your daughter, who is named as beneficiary. You pay the premiums to keep the policy in force. In the past the IRS has contested this arrangement, but now it agrees to follow court decisions that allow the policy to remain outside the insured's estate. However, if you are nervous about this, you can set up a life insurance trust and fund it with enough money to pay the premiums. The trust would be the owner of the policy, and as long as you set up more than 3 years before your death, the policy would not be included in your estate.

As you can see, income-shifting strategies involve tradeoffs that you must weigh before making a decision. None of the choices are cut and dried because there are so many factors to take into consideration—not just financial matters but personal matters such as whether or not you really want income-producing assets to be transferred irrevocably to another member of the family. In many cases the tax savings are not worth the side effects. In other cases they accomplish both tax savings and important family goals. When it comes to tricky, tax-saving maneuvers, tread carefully, and do not hesitate to get professional advice.

Family Events

Major life events, such as the birth of a child or death of a spouse, carry such intense emotional drama that it somehow seems sacrilegious to taint the joy or gravity of the occasion by talking about money and taxes. However, this is what financial planners do, and in the end, you love us for it. As planners always say, the four big occasions—births, deaths, marriages, and divorces—require a whole new look at family finances. Sometimes all that is required is changing a beneficiary designation or adding a new name to a will. Other times a family's entire financial life is ripped apart and requires numerous decisions at a time when the affected people are not very well versed in the laws and may not be emotionally equipped to think clearly.

Following are some of the tax and financial considerations that go with each of these major life events. Keep them in mind for when/if you are the lucky/sorrowful person experiencing them. We will consider them in the order in which they usually occur.

Marriage

If young lovers had any idea of the many laws they were subjecting themselves to by entering into the institution of marriage, they may think long and hard before tying the knot. Many of these laws are favorable, to be sure. They offer certain protections to spouses that people in other committed relationships do not have, such as the right to inherit the assets in a partner's retirement plan. However, rights usually imply an equal number of responsibilities, such as being on the hook for a partner's debts. Many of the laws governing marriage are state laws and obviously too numerous to list here. However, we can cover a few of the tax and financial-planning implications of marriage.

TAX PLANNING

If you have not set the date yet, consider whether you want to get married this year or next. For tax purposes, your marital status on the last day of the year determines your filing status for the whole year. Thus whether you get married on December 31 or January 1 can make a big difference in the amount of tax you will pay. The so-called marriage penalty was addressed in the Economic Growth and Tax Relief Reconciliation Act of 2001, but the long-sought-after relief phases in over several years. Chances are that if you calculate the tax both ways, you will find that filing separate returns as two single individuals would result in less tax than if both of you filed jointly. This is even more likely to be the case if you are blending families and one or both of you are currently filing as head of household. However, you should do the calculations for yourself. You probably will not want to defer the wedding indefinitely to save taxes, but if you can save a few hundred dollars (maybe thousands, if you both have high incomes) by postponing the wedding into the next tax year, you can take a longer honeymoon. Table 8.5 shows the phase-in of increases in the standard deduction for married couples filing joint returns.

FINANCIAL PLANNING

The decision to keep assets separate or throw them all into the same pot is one of the first financial issues you will face as a married couple. You will approach the decision quite differently depending on whether you are a young, dewy-eyed couple starting out with more love than money or two mature individuals who have spent a lifetime building assets and familial connections. It generally makes sense for young couples to combine finances because they will be approaching major financial events such as buying a house and raising children as a couple. Older people who are remarrying may want to keep most of their assets separate so that they can arrange to have them transferred to children from a previous marriage at their death if this is what they want to do. A prenuptial agreement also may be a wise move not just to protect the spouse with the most assets but also to protect a spouse who is coming into a marriage with little money and who may be giving up career income to raise children or join a spouse

TABLE 8.5   Phase-In of Increase in Standard Deduction for Married Couples Filing Joint Returns

CALENDAR YEAR	STANDARD DEDUCTION FOR JOINT RETURNS AS A PERCENTAGE OF THE STANDARD DEDUCTION FOR SINGLE RETURNS
2005	174%
2006	184%
2007	187%
2008	190%
2009 and later	200%

in retirement. A consultation with an attorney or financial planner may be a smart thing to do before wedding plans are finalized.

Birth of a Child

We will not tell you what the Department of Agriculture has figured that it costs to raise a child from birth through high school because it may discourage you from ever having a family. (Okay, it is $165,630 for middle-income families, not counting summer camp or music lessons. You can visit www.usda.gov for the latest figures or remain blissfully ignorant of the high cost of raising kids.) However, whether you consider the tax and financial implications of having a child before you throw the birth control pills away or wait until after the pregnancy test shows positive, there are lots of things you need to know.

TAX PLANNING

Try to have the child before the end of the year, if possible. This will give you the $2,900 personal exemption (in 2001), saving you $783 in taxes if you are in the 27 percent tax bracket. As part of your childbirth preparation, study up on the tax breaks for families with children. These include

- *Child tax credit*. Remember that a tax credit is a direct reduction off your tax bill and is far more valuable than a tax deduction. In 2001, the child tax credit for children under age 17 is $600. The credit will be going up in future years (see Table 8.6). Your AGI must be less than $110,000 if married filing jointly or $75,000 if single.

- *Dependent-care credit*. If you hire someone to care for your children while you work, you may be eligible for the dependent-care credit. If your AGI is over $28,000, you may take a credit of 20 percent of up to $2,400 in expenses for one child or $4,800 for two or more, for a maximum credit of $480 for one child or $960 for two or more. In 2002, the maximum expenses on which the credit may be taken goes up to $3,000 for one child or $6,000 for two or more.

- *Adoption credit*. In 2001, a tax credit of up to $5,000 may be available to cover the costs of adopting a child if your AGI is less than $115,000 (joint)

TABLE 8.6 Child Tax Credit

CALENDAR YEAR	CREDIT AMOUNT PER CHILD
2001–2004	$600
2005–2008	$700
2009	$800
2010	$1,000

or $75,000 (single). In 2002, the adoption credit goes up to $10,000 and the income limits rise to $150,000 for all.

FINANCIAL PLANNING

In between feedings and diaper changes, consider your child's future. Start a college savings plan. Get some life insurance on both you and your spouse to cover the child through college. Make sure that you have adequate health insurance. Execute a will, even if you have no assets right now, so that you can name a guardian for your child. Get the grandparents involved. If they have a lot of assets in IRAs, it may be wise to name the grandchildren as beneficiaries for all or part of the accounts to stretch out the distributions and have the income taxed at lower rates. If you and/or your parents have done an estate plan, make sure that you all update it with the birth of each child.

Divorce

Of all the major life events, divorce is possibly the most threatening financially because you are never prepared for it. In addition, the adversarial relationship that often exists between divorcing spouses inhibits the kind of cooperation that results in smooth planning and maximum benefits for the whole family. The best advice we can give divorcing couples is to take your time, try to put your animosity on hold while you look at what is best for everyone concerned, and consider meeting with a mediator who understands the tax laws and can help you work out a viable plan that is fair to all.

TAX PLANNING

Divorce requires a shift from married filing jointly to filing status of single or head of household. When you choose to make this shift is often a key part of divorce planning. If you are legally divorced on the last day of the year, you may not file a joint return, so choose your divorce date carefully. If you have children, there are some very complicated rules about which parent can claim the exemption. See IRS Publication 501, "Exemptions, Standard Deduction and Filing Information." Be aware that alimony is tax-deductible to the payer and taxable to the recipient, whereas child support is the opposite; however, there are strict rules prohibiting the classification of child support as alimony. Distributions from retirement plans may be taken without penalty prior to age $59\frac{1}{2}$ if they are part of a qualified domestic relations order (QDRO). And finally, be aware of the *after-tax* value of assets (i.e., what you would net if they were sold) when splitting up property. These are just a few of the tax ramifications of divorce. Do not try to remember them all. Get help.

FINANCIAL PLANNING

Long-term financial planning is usually low on the list of priorities for divorcing couples, who tend to be more concerned about property settlements and how they will pay the bills once the household has been split in two. Of course, you will need to take care of the short-term needs of the family. However, do not let longer-term financial goals such as retirement and college planning get derailed. Review all your financial dealings, and update insurance policies, wills, and beneficiary designations to reflect your new status.

Death of a Spouse

It can be said that all marriages will come to an end—through death if not divorce. The good thing about death (if you can say such a thing) is that you can plan for it. This is what estate planning is all about, after all. However, estate planning tends to focus on the legalities of transferring assets at death without paying much attention to how the surviving spouse will carry on following the death of the first spouse. One of the most worthwhile planning activities a couple can engage in is to sit down and contemplate what would happen if either of them died.

TAX PLANNING

One exception to the marital-status-on-the-last-day-of-the-year rule is that if your spouse dies during the year, you may file a joint return for that year even though technically you are a single individual on the last day of the year (as long as you did not remarry, of course). If you have dependent children, you may file as a qualifying widow(er) with dependent child for 2 years following the year of the death of your spouse and be eligible for more tax breaks than if you filed as single or head of household. Without your spouse's income, you may fall into a lower tax bracket. If previously you had been ineligible for certain tax breaks due to a too-high AGI, you may want to take another look at them to see which deductions and credits you may be eligible for now.

FINANCIAL PLANNING

Young couples need to worry about how the surviving spouse and children would carry on. Life insurance should be purchased for any spouse whose income is essential to the family. In the case of a stay-at-home parent, enough insurance should be purchased to provide for child care and housekeeping services. For older couples who are living off their assets, life insurance is not as important because the investment income would continue. However, you should think about any income you are currently depending on that would stop with the death of a spouse, such as Social Security or corporate pension, and purchase enough insurance to replace it.

CHAPTER 9

Managing Taxes All Year Long

All it takes is one big tax surprise to get you thinking about taxes all year long. Whether you do your taxes yourself or have them prepared by an accountant, the news that you owe *way* more than you thought you would is unpleasant at best and financially devastating at worst. It is not so much the tax that hurts—after all, if you owe a lot of tax, it means that you made a lot of money—but the fact that you were not prepared for it. When it comes to most large expenditures in our lives—vacations, college, major home improvements—we have an opportunity to plan ahead and either save the money ahead of time or arrange financing. However, taxes can hit us like a brick. Assuming that we get right on it as soon as our 1099s come in at the end of January, we still have only a couple of months to raise the money and pay by April 15. Lucky for us, the Internal Revenue Service (IRS) now accepts credit cards, but this means paying a 2.5-percent fee plus interest charges if we cannot pay the credit card balance right away—not exactly prudent financial management. And this is on top of any penalties the IRS might charge for underpaying our taxes during the year.

Investors have a bigger challenge than most people with year-round tax management because you never know at the beginning of the year how your investments will perform. It is easier to estimate salary and other predictable income and either have the proper amount withheld from your paycheck or make quarterly estimated tax payments. However, when you do not even know which securities you will be buying during the year, much less how much income they will generate, you have some tricky tax planning to do. This chapter will give you some ideas for dealing with these uncertainties.

Throughout this book we have been trying to familiarize you with form 1040. It is really not as intimidating as it looks, with all its fine print and references to items that do not concern you (farm income?). If you do your taxes yourself, you are already familiar with this form and have a good sense about how income is reported (more on this in Chapter 10) and how the various deductions reduce your income for the purpose of determining how much tax you owe. However, if you have an accountant prepare your taxes, the only part of the form you may be familiar with is the line that says "Sign here." Otherwise, you probably rely on your accountant to give you the bottom-line news about how much you owe or—if you are lucky—how much of a refund you will get.

Even if you have an accountant prepare your taxes, it is very important that you have a fundamental understanding of how taxes work so that you can do things throughout the year to minimize them. By the time you sit down with your accountant, the tax year is over. While there still may be a few things you can do between January and April to reduce your tax bill (such as contribute to some retirement plans), for the most part, tax preparation involves reporting what *already happened*. If you are to have any hope of changing the outcome of the story, you must be aware of tax events *as they are transpiring* so that you can do offsetting transactions or at least set aside enough money so that you will be prepared to write a check to the government for the tax on all that income you earned.

Tax-Planning Worksheet

To simplify the tax-planning process without straying too far from form 1040, we have created a tax-planning worksheet (located at the end of this chapter) that eliminates the fine print and allows you to focus on income and deductions that apply to *you*, not some farmer in the Midwest (unless, of course, you *are* a farmer in the Midwest). Unlike the form 1040, you will fill out this worksheet at the *beginning* of the tax year—in pencil—and update it throughout the year as your tax situation changes. We cannot tell you how often you should update your tax-planning worksheet because it all depends on your investment activity during the year. If nothing unexpected happens—that is, your bonds keep paying the interest you expect and you do not sell any stocks for a capital gain or loss—you can let the worksheet ride as long as it reflects an accurate estimate for the year. However, if your mutual fund pays a larger-than-expected dividend or you close out a stock position, enter your changes on the worksheet. At the same time, figure out how you will deal with the tax—either by setting funds aside or by making an estimated tax payment (more on this later).

How To Use the Tax-Planning Worksheet

Keep in mind that this is just a worksheet. It is not your final tax report, so if you want to round off the numbers and guess at certain items, this is okay. In fact, the purpose of the worksheet is to allow you to make assumptions early in the year and then firm them up as the year goes along. Any kind of estimate—even a wrong one—is better than being totally in the dark until after the tax year is over. So sharpen your pencil and take a stab at the following items. It may help to have a copy of your latest tax return handy to use as a baseline from which you can make adjustments for this year's numbers.

Income

Start your annual tax planning by estimating your income from all sources.

EARNED INCOME

Earned income includes wages, salary, bonuses, commission income, and tips —all the income you receive from your job. If you are self-employed, enter your business income from schedule C. If you work for an employer and your salary is reduced by contributions to a 401(k) or other retirement plan, enter the amount *after* the contribution; that is, if your salary is $50,000 and you contribute $4,000 to a retirement plan, enter your earned income as $46,000. However, do not subtract amounts withheld for taxes (we will be calculating the tax later). In this section you will be listing all the taxable income related to your work.

Compared with investment income, this is the easy part of the worksheet because you usually have a pretty good idea at the beginning of the year what your earned income will be for the rest of the year. The exception, of course, is if you are self-employed or if commissions or bonuses comprise a substantial part of your income. In this case, you will have to take a guess and revise your estimate as you go along. You probably are used to doing this anyway on a more informal basis. By using the worksheet, you can make the adjustments on paper and factor in the other tax items in order to estimate your total tax bill.

INTEREST

If you expect to receive interest income during the year, use the interest worksheet to estimate the amount you expect to receive. Enter the amount you have on deposit in bank accounts, savings accounts, certificates of deposit, money market funds, credit union accounts, and any other interest-bearing accounts. If the amount is expected to vary—say, you have $30,000 on deposit now but plan to spend $10,000 for a vacation this summer—estimate the average amount you expect to have in savings over the entire year. Also estimate the interest rate for the year. Since short-term rates do not change very much, you probably are safe in using the current rate, but keep an eye on rates throughout the year. To estimate your total interest for the year, multiply the total average amount on deposit by the interest rate.

In the second section, list any taxable bonds you own and the amount of interest you expect to receive during the year. Do not include tax-exempt municipal bonds in this section. If you own municipal bonds *and* receive Social Security benefits, complete the third section for use later in calculating the taxable portion of your Social Security benefits.

DIVIDENDS

If you own dividend-paying stocks or mutual funds, use the dividend worksheet to estimate the amount of dividend income you expect to receive during the year. Although companies often raise their dividends, it is usually not by very much, so the current dividend can serve as your estimate. Simply enter the amount of shares you own and the annual dividend per share, and multiply the two to estimate your dividend income for the year for each position you hold. If you do not plan to hold the stock for the entire year, you can make the adjustment now by assuming that you will receive, say, just one or two quarterly dividends. If you are not sure how long you will hold the stock, you can estimate the dividend income as if you plan to hold it for the entire year and make the adjustment if you sell it.

Mutual fund dividends are slightly more variable than dividends on stocks, but you can estimate them by calling the fund to ask what the current yield is or go to www.morningstar.com. If you have owned the fund awhile and have noticed that the dividend tends to be quite stable, you can use that amount. Do not include capital gains distributions on the dividend worksheet. As you will see when we get to Chapter 10 on the nuts and bolts of reporting, these worksheets will be corresponding to the appropriate tax schedules to make your life (or your accountant's life) easier when the time comes to substitute these penciled estimates with the final numbers.

CAPITAL GAINS (OR LOSSES)

If you are an active investor, this is the part that undoubtedly gives you the most trouble and creates the most surprises at tax time. Unless you are careful about logging your trades and keeping track of gains and losses, you could be totally in the dark about the tax impact of your investment activity until you finally sit down (in January? April?) and tally everything up. However, you do have an edge over mutual fund investors in the tax-awareness department because you control the purchases and sales that determine your capital gains income. All you have to do is vow to log your trades throughout the year and stay on top of where you stand. Mutual fund investors generally have no idea how much capital gains income they will earn until the check (or mutual fund statement) hits the mailbox near the end of the year.

If you buy individual securities, the capital gain/loss worksheet is pretty straightforward. We recommend that you enter the name of the security, date purchased, and total cost at the time you enter the buy order, leaving the other columns blank until you close out the position. This will allow you to see at a glance which positions are still open so that you can remind yourself to check their status and perhaps take losses while they are still short term (one year or less) or wait until after the one-year anniversary to sell for the long-term gain. You also can use the information to match up gains and losses throughout the year and take the appropriate action, such as realizing short-term gains if you already have short-term losses (or vice versa). Since these worksheets are designed for a single tax year, the first thing you will need to do is carry forward positions purchased in previous years. As you close out positions, enter the date of sale, proceeds, and amount of gain or loss. Place a checkmark in the short- or long-term column and carry the information down to the summary so that you will have an ongoing record of your short- and long-term gains and losses. Also be sure to indicate in the summary any losses you are carrying forward from previous years. Keep these losses in mind as you are making your investment decisions throughout the year and try to use them up as quickly as possible.

If you invest in mutual funds, you can try several methods for estimating your capital gains income. First, keep an eye on the markets so that you will have some idea of how the stocks and/or bonds in the portfolio are doing. This, of course, does not tell you if the portfolio manager will be realizing those gains or losses, but at least it gives you an idea of the direction in which your investments are going. Next, consider calling the fund periodically to ask about capital gains that have been realized this year. As noted in Chapter 4, mutual funds tend to accumulate capital gains all throughout the year and pay one big distribution near the end of the year. By keeping an eye on fund activity, you can more accurately estimate your taxable income for the year.

Where these worksheets get tricky is in separating short-term gains from long-term capital gains. On form 1040, all capital gains income is lumped together and reported on line 13. This total amount is then used to determine your adjusted gross income (AGI)—the estimate of which is another key part of tax planning. However, when it comes to calculating the tax on capital gains, your net short-term gains are treated as ordinary income, whereas your net long-term gains are taxed at a maximum rate of 20 percent (or 10 percent if you are in the 15-percent tax bracket or lower). Thus you will need to treat your capital gains income differently depending on which type of tax planning you are doing. If you are estimating your total income for the purpose of determining your AGI —a very important number for determining deduction phaseouts and eligibility for certain tax credits and strategies (such as Roth IRA contributions or conversions)—you will want to add together your short- and long-term gains and enter the total where indicated on the worksheet. However, if you are attempting to estimate your total tax, you will want to separate short-term gains from long-term gains so that you can calculate the tax at the different rates. More will be said on this in a moment. For now, just enter your capital gains or losses on the worksheet. If you are entering a loss, put the number in parentheses, and subtract it from the rest of your income.

IRA DISTRIBUTIONS

If you take taxable IRA distributions during the year, whether under the required minimum distribution rules or not, enter the amount on the tax-planning worksheet. If the distribution is subject to the 10-percent premature distribution penalty because you are under age 59½ and do not qualify for any of the exceptions noted in Chapter 7, indicate this on the form and be sure to factor it into your total tax bill when you add everything up at the end. Obviously, tax-free Roth IRA distributions do not need to be included.

OTHER INCOME

In order to make this book comprehensible to investors who prefer to get their information here rather than slogging through the tax code, we must necessarily omit detailed information on situations that affect only a small number of people (such as those Midwest farmers whose efforts we certainly do appreciate but who can keep schedule F to themselves). If you receive taxable income from any source not discussed so far, except for Social Security benefits (which we will be covering later), enter it here. This includes alimony, the taxable portion of pension or annuity income, rental income, royalties, and any other types of taxable income.

Adjustments to Income

Unless you are self-employed or eligible to deduct your IRA contribution, there is a good chance you will not have any adjustments to income, in which case your AGI will be the same as your total income. As you can see from the worksheet, these adjustments are very specific and relate to certain key items, such as the student loan interest deduction or alimony paid. If you contribute to a traditional IRA and are eligible to deduct the contribution (see Chapter 7), be sure to enter the amount of your contribution here. Add up all your adjustments to income and subtract from your total income to determine your AGI. Remember this number because it is an important part of tax planning. Moreover, as your income changes throughout the year and you erase your wrong guesses and replace them with more accurate numbers, be sure to update your AGI estimate as well.

Deductions and Exemptions

As you can see from the worksheet, deductions and exemptions come *after* you have calculated your AGI. The bad news is that no matter how much you would like to reduce your AGI so that you can take advantage of certain benefits and strategies, there is nothing you can do in the deduction department to make this happen. The only thing you can do is earn less income or qualify for one of the adjustments listed in that section. The good news is that we have not gotten to your final taxable income yet. Before we calculate the tax, there still may be some things you can do to reduce your final tax bill.

DEDUCTIONS

The first step is to be aware of the standard deduction for your filing status. If the total of all your deductions does not equal the standard deduction, you can simply enter the standard deduction on your tax-planning worksheet. However, if you have a lot of mortgage interest expense, state income tax expense, or property tax expense (the most common deductions), use the deduction worksheet to estimate your actual expenses and enter the total on the tax-planning worksheet.

The first part of the worksheet will help you find your standard deduction. If your situation is rather straightforward—you are under age 65, not blind, and not being claimed as an exemption on someone else's tax return—use the first table. Otherwise, refer to the appropriate table for your situation. If you are pretty sure that you will be using the standard deduction, you need not bother with the deduction worksheet and can simply enter your standard deduction on your tax-planning worksheet. However, do look over the deduction worksheet and your last year's tax return to be sure you are not missing anything. If you pay state income tax and own real estate, there is a good chance that your itemized deductions will exceed the standard deduction.

Use the remaining parts of the worksheet to estimate your deductible expenses for the year. If your financial situation is similar to last year's—you are living in the same house and expect to give similar amounts to charity—you can refer to last year's schedule A for this year's estimate (understanding that the amounts will be slightly different, of course). If you are planning a major transaction that will affect your deductions, such as buying or refinancing a house, you can use this form to estimate your deductions, prorating the amount based on when you expect to complete the transaction.

> **NOTE**
>
> If your AGI is over $137,300 ($68,650 for married filing separately) in 2002, your deductions are subject to phaseout rules. Keep this in the back of your mind for now. The worksheet for the 3-percent reduction is covered later.

Medical and Dental Expenses

Only unreimbursed medical expenses and health insurance premiums that exceed 7.5 percent of your AGI are deductible. Thus, unless you have high health insurance premiums and/or incur major medical expenses during the year, you probably will not qualify for this deduction. On the worksheet, multiply your AGI by 7.5 percent and enter the amount. This serves as your bogey. If you expect your family to be in good health and do not plan to pay this much in medical expenses, you need not bother filling out the medical expense section of the deduction worksheet and can just assume that you will be out of luck on this one. (Actually, think of it as being *in* luck.) If your situation changes, you can always update the worksheet. By the way, deductible medical expenses are not subject to the 3-percent reduction of itemized deductions that occurs if your AGI is over $137,300.

State and Local Income Tax and Property Tax

State income taxes are deductible on your federal tax return. We have necessarily omitted details on state taxes because this book is written for a national audience. However, if you pay state income tax, pull out last year's tax return and base this year's estimate on that. And be sure to factor in your state income tax bracket on future investment decisions. If you pay local or foreign income taxes, estimate them as well. In addition, if you own a home or other real estate, estimate the property taxes you will pay this year. Unfortunately, these are the only taxes that are deductible on your federal income tax return. If you shop, you also may pay sales tax; if you smoke, you also pay cigarette taxes; if you drive, you also pay driver's license taxes; if you hunt or fish, you pay license fees. However, these taxes are not deductible.

NOTE

If you think that you may be subject to the alternative minimum tax (AMT), you will need to think about tax planning in an entirely different light. State income taxes and some of the other usual deductions are not deductible under the AMT. Please see Chapter 11 for more information on the AMT.

When estimating deductible taxes, only include those amounts which actually will be paid during the tax year. It can get a little tricky when you pay part of your 2002 state income tax in 2003, for example, but you are only allowed to deduct taxes actually paid during the tax year. This can be an advantage if you are looking to increase your deductions; a popular strategy is to prepay your state income taxes by, say, writing the check in December 2002 for taxes owed in April 2003. You may or may not decide to do this. In any case, you can enter your best estimate of the amount of state and local income taxes and real estate taxes you expect to pay this year.

Interest Expense

Only two kinds of interest expense are tax deductible: home mortgage interest and investment interest. Keep in mind that if your home mortgage is being amortized, the amount that goes toward interest decreases little by little and the amount that goes toward principal increases, as explained in Chapter 5. If you assume that this year's home mortgage interest deduction will be the same as last year's, you may overestimate this deduction. Check with your lender or use the calculator at www.timevalue.com to estimate the amount of interest you will pay this year.

Investment interest may be difficult to estimate if you are an active trader and use margin throughout the year. The only advice we can give is to do the best you can. Pay attention to your brokerage statements, and enter your investment interest onto the deduction worksheet as you progress throughout the year. It actually would not be a bad idea *not* to factor this deduction into your estimates; qualifying for a deduction you did not think you were entitled to can only be good news. Remember the two key things about deducting investment interest: You cannot deduct more than you receive in investment income, and you may not deduct interest on a loan used to buy tax-exempt securities. Also, you may only deduct interest actually paid during the tax year.

Gifts to Charity

You may deduct donations to religious, charitable, educational, and other philanthropic organizations approved by the IRS to receive deductible contributions. Your donation may be in the form of cash or property. If you give property, such as shares of stock, the value of the gift is considered to be the fair market value of the property on the day you make the gift (not your cost). In fact, giving appreciated stock to charity is a popular way to avoid capital gains tax and receive a hefty tax deduction at the same time. However, there are special rules concerning gifts of appreciated property; more will be said about this in Chapter 10. You may not deduct services or volunteer time. If you are able to estimate your charitable contributions now, go ahead and do so. Practically speaking, many people wait until the end of the year to decide how much they want to give to charity. And again, it never hurts to underestimate your deductions.

Casualty and Theft Losses

Now here is a paradoxical category on the worksheet. If you could estimate casualty and theft losses in advance, would you not do all you could to avoid them? Think positively and leave this section blank. Only fill in if something bad happens during the year.

Job Expenses and Other Miscellaneous Deductions

You may be able to deduct certain job expenses and other miscellaneous expenses such as tax-preparation fees. Most of these expenses may only be deducted if they exceed 2 percent of your AGI, and only the part that exceeds the 2 percent is deductible. A detailed discussion of job and other miscellaneous deductions is beyond the scope of this book, but you can refer to J. K. Lasser's *Your Income Tax 2002* (Wiley, 2002) for more information. For tax-estimation purposes, you may want to leave this part blank anyway. The intense search for tax deductions usually takes place at the end of the year. Until then, be conservative in your estimates. The main purpose of these tax-planning worksheets is to help you estimate your taxable *income* and to consider deductions only insofar as they will give you some reasonable guess as to your tax bracket and final tax bill.

Three-Percent Reduction in Itemized Deductions

If you itemize deductions and your AGI is over $137,300 ($68,650 for married filing separately) in 2002, you must reduce your deductions according to the formula on the 3-percent reduction worksheet. Practically speaking, this is not likely to make a huge difference in your estimate of your taxable income, especially since you are not even sure yet what your total deductions will be. If you feel comfortable with ballpark estimates, you probably can skip this task and wait until you prepare your tax return to let your computer or accountant do it.

Personal Exemptions

This is the easiest part of the worksheet. Just multiply your total number of exemptions, including yourself and your spouse, by $3,000 (for 2002). This is the amount you get to take off your taxable income just for being alive—unless you are subject to the AMT, in which case you might as well be dead (just kidding). (See Chapter 11.)

Tax on Social Security Benefits

If you are not receiving Social Security benefits, you can skip this part and go on to the next section. If you are receiving Social Security, you probably are aware already that part of your benefits may be taxable. If you paid taxes on your Social Security benefits last year and expect your other income to be about the same this year, you can use the number on line 20b of last year's 1040 for your tax-planning worksheet. If you want to be more precise, or if this is the first full year you will be receiving benefits, you can use the Social Security worksheets to estimate the taxable portion of your benefits. The most important thing for investors to understand about the tax on Social Security benefits is that tax-exempt interest is entered into the formula, even though the interest itself is not taxable.

Taxable Income

Now that you have entered all your income, adjustments to income, and deductions and exemptions onto the tax-planning worksheet, subtract the total of your deductions and exemptions from your AGI, and there you have it: your taxable income. This is the number that, once finalized, will go on line 39 of your form 1040 and determine your final tax bill. Knowing this number in advance will enable you to look up your tax in the tax tables so that you can arrange to have the proper amount of tax withheld from your paycheck or make more accurate quarterly estimated tax payments (see Table 9.1). It also will allow you to look up your tax bracket, etch it in your memory, and use it for every investment and tax-planning decision you make. If any part of your taxable income is composed of long-term capital gains, be sure to separate out that part and calculate the tax at the 20-percent rate (or 10 percent if you are in the 15-percent tax bracket or lower). And remember that completing this tax-planning worksheet at the beginning of the year is only part of the process. You must update it throughout the year as your tax situation changes.

TABLE 9.1 2002 Tax Rate Schedule

TAXABLE INCOME ($)	BASE AMOUNT OF TAX ($)	+	RATE ON EXCESS (%) (ALSO CALLED MARGINAL TAX RATE)	OF THE AMOUNT OVER ($)
Single				
0 to 6,000	0	+	10.0	0
6,000 to 27,950	600.00	+	15.0	6,000
27,050 to 67,700	3,892.50	+	27.0	27,950
67,700 to 141,250	14,625.00	+	30.0	67,700
141,250 to 307,050	36,690.00	+	35.0	141,250
Over 307,050	94,720.00	+	38.6	307,050
Head of Household				
0 to 10,000	0	+	10.0	0
10,000 to 37,450	1,000.00	+	15.0	10,000
37,450 to 96,700	5,117.50	+	27.0	37,450
96,700 to 156,600	21,115.00	+	30.0	96,700
156,600 to 307,050	39,085.00	+	35.0	156,600
Over 307,050	91,742.50	+	38.6	307,050
Married Filing Jointly and Qualifying Widow(er)s				
0 to 12,000	0	+	10.0	0
12,000 to 46,700	1,200.00	+	15.0	12,000
46,700 to 112,850	6,405.00	+	27.0	46,700
112,850 to 171,950	24,265.50	+	30.0	112,850
171,950 to 307,050	41,995.50	+	35.0	171,950
Over 307,050	89,280.50	+	38.6	307,050
Married Filing Separately				
0 to 6,000	0	+	10.0	0
6,000 to 23,350	600.00	+	15.0	6,000
23,350 to 56,425	3,202.50	+	27.0	23,350
56,425 to 85,975	12,132.75	+	30.0	56,425
85,975 to 153,525	20,997.75	+	35.0	85,975
Over 153,525	44,640.25	+	38.6	153,525

Making Estimated Tax Payments

As much as we would all like to postpone paying taxes as long as possible in order to have use of the money, the IRS prefers that we pay taxes on our income as soon as we earn it. Actually, *prefers* is probably too mild a word here. There are definite rules about how much tax we must pay in during the tax year, and if we pay too little and have to come up with too large a chunk in April, we might get slapped with a penalty.

If all your taxable income is from your job, you do not need to worry about making estimated tax payments. Just make sure that your employer withholds from your paycheck at least 90 percent of this year's tax liability or, if you are not sure what this is yet, at least 100 percent of last year's tax liability (110 percent if your AGI is over $150,000). Use your 2001 tax return as a guide to your withholding for 2002: If, when you file your taxes in April, you have to send a check, or if you will be getting a large refund, arrange to have your withholding raised or lowered accordingly. IRS Publication 919, "How Do I Adjust My Tax Withholding?" is an excellent guide for estimating your tax and filling out the W-4 that tells your employer how much to withhold. Be sure to do a quick check sometime in the fall, comparing your estimated tax liability and your latest pay stub to see if you are on track to have the proper amount withheld.

If Your Income Will Be Higher This Year

If you earn a significant amount of taxable income that is not subject to tax with-holding—this includes investment income—you must make quarterly estimated tax payments on April 15, June 15, September 15, and January 15. Self-employed individuals already do this because their taxes are not withheld by an employer. However, if you are accustomed to having your taxes withheld and are new to investing, you will need to become familiar with the rules for making estimated tax payments.

There are two reasons for making quarterly estimated tax payments on investment income as it is earned during the year: First, it reduces the likelihood that you will have to pay a penalty for underpayment of taxes, and second, it spares you the anxiety of having to come up with a large sum of money in April. The general rule for avoiding penalties is to make sure you pay—through withholding and/or estimated tax payments—at least 90 percent of this year's tax liability. However, you will avoid penalties if you pay in at least 100 percent of *last year's* tax liability (or 110 percent if your AGI is over $150,000)—another reason for using the tax-planning worksheet and keeping your eye on your AGI.

Some people like to make estimated tax payments even when they are not required to in order to avoid the anxiety of having to come up with a large lump sum on April 15. If you are worried about being on the hook for an extraordinary amount of tax, you may want to send in the check now and get it out of the way —especially if you might be tempted to spend it. On the other hand, there are

Example

Your 2001 tax liability was $15,000, all of it paid through withholding. You arrange to have the same amount withheld in 2002. Your AGI is under $150,000. In June 2002 you realize a $40,000 long-term capital gain. Even though you will owe an additional $8,000 in long-term capital gains tax, you need not pay the tax now because your 2002 withholding will equal 100 percent of your 2001 tax liability.

Example

We will use the same facts as above except that your AGI is over $150,000 and your 2001 tax bill was $32,000. Your $40,000 gain realized in June will bring your 2002 tax bill up to $40,000 ($32,000 + $8,000). To avoid penalties, your withholding and/or estimated tax payments must equal 110 percent of last year's tax bill, or $35,200.

two reasons why you may not want to do this. First, if you have other stock positions, you may have losses later in the year that can offset some of these gains. If you are too hasty in paying the IRS, you will be giving up use of the money until you get your refund (however, you can always send in part of the tax due). And second, you probably can make better use of the money during the time it will be in your possession. Using the preceding example, if you set aside the $8,000 in a money market fund at 3.5 percent for 9½ months, you will be $222 richer next April 15. It is *not* recommended that you invest your tax reserves back into the stock market. Then you really will be subject to April 15 anxiety. If there is any chance that you will succumb to the temptation to spend or to speculate with your tax reserves, write a check to the IRS now and be done with it.

If Your Income Will Be Lower This Year

As noted earlier, you will always be safe from penalties if you pay in at least 100 percent of last year's tax bill (110 percent if your AGI over $150,000). This works fine if you expect your income to be higher this year. All you have to do is pay in the required amount and keep an eye on your investment activity during the year so that you can set aside enough funds to pay the additional tax in April. However, what if you expect your income to be *lower* this year? In this case, paying in 100 percent of last year's tax bill would result in an overpayment and tie up use of the funds until you get your tax refund—something you probably can ill afford if your income is substantially lower this year. Here you will want to go with the rule that requires you to pay in 90 percent of this year's tax liability. It requires a little more effort because you will have to estimate your tax liability carefully in advance and keep an eye on your income and your tax payments all throughout the year to make sure that you pay in just enough but not too much.

To stay safe from penalties without overpaying your taxes:

- If you expect an *increase* in income and your AGI is $150,000 or less, make sure that you pay in at least 100 percent of last year's tax liability through withholding and/or quarterly estimated tax payments. If your AGI is *more than* $150,000, make sure you pay in at least 110 percent of last year's tax liability.

- If you expect your income to stay the same or go down, make sure that you pay in at least 90 percent of this year's tax liability.

Tips on Making Estimated Tax Payments

Use form 1040-ES. Form 1040-ES is a simple form on which you state your name, address, Social Security number, and the amount you are paying. You do not have to explain how you arrived at your estimate; the purpose of the form is really just to make sure that your account gets credited properly. Once the IRS identifies you as someone who makes quarterly estimated tax payments, it will send you preprinted forms that you can use for future payments.

Pay attention to payment dates. The official due dates for estimated taxes are April 15, June 15, September 15, and January 15. If any of these days fall on a weekend, the deadline is the following Monday. Like your tax return, the check does not have to arrive by the deadline but merely needs to be postmarked by that date. If you plan to file and pay your taxes by January 31, you can skip the January 15 quarterly deadline. (Many investors are not able to do this because 1099s generally do not arrive until the end of January.) Keep in mind that the April 15 deadline for the first quarter's estimate coincides with the tax-filing deadline for your previous year's taxes. If you are getting a refund, you can apply it to this year's taxes and make up any difference with a separate check.

Understand the penalty. Although the word *penalty* sounds ominous, the actual penalty for underpaying your taxes is simply an interest charge on the amount underpaid. At the time of this writing, the IRS interest rate is 7 percent. If you are short on funds, it is not a bad loan. The IRS will calculate the penalty for you, so you do not even need to send it in with your tax return on April 15. You will receive a bill from the IRS a few weeks later. The one exception to letting the IRS figure your penalty is if your income is not distributed equally throughout the year—say, you realize a large capital gain in December and that is why your April, June, and September estimated payments were too little. In this case you will want to complete form 2210, which allows you to reduce the penalty by accounting for the fact that your income was earned unevenly throughout the year. *Warning:* This is complicated without tax software or an accountant's expertise.

Tips for Managing Taxes All Year Long

As you have no doubt gathered from reading this book, tax-savvy investors tend to be *proactive* rather than *reactive* in their approach to taxes. You have to be. You cannot wait until the year is over to see where you stand because, unlike your earned income, investment income can be widely variable. You must prepare yourself for the consequences of your investment activity well in advance of April 15. In addition, investing is all about rate of return—and the amount that ends up in your pocket is all that counts. You may not have much choice about how your earned income will be taxed, but you do have a choice about how your investment income will be taxed. Hence you must stay on top of your investment activity and incorporate tax consequences into every decision.

Following is a summary of tax pointers discussed in this book in order of importance.

Contribute to Retirement Plans

The most valuable tax tip in this book is to max out contributions to retirement accounts. If you have a choice about when to contribute—say, you are a self-employed individual contributing to a Keogh plan or you are contributing to IRAs —do it early in the year. Early contributions have that much more time to grow, and if you are simply transferring the funds from a taxable account, it is better to get them under the tax-sheltered umbrella as soon as possible. Otherwise, you will just have more taxable income to report. If you are contributing to a 401(k) or 403(b) plan, review your contribution amount at the beginning of each year and increase it if possible.

Consider Converting to a Roth IRA

If you have a traditional or rollover IRA and your AGI is less than $100,000, consider converting to a Roth IRA. You will have to pay income tax on the amount converted at the time of the conversion, but thereafter the assets will grow tax-free. There are no required minimum distributions at age 70½, and you can pass the assets to your heirs income-tax-free. Roth conversions are ideal for people who expect to be in a high tax bracket when they retire and/or who have many years ahead of them for the assets to grow. However, before converting a traditional IRA to a Roth IRA, you will need to weigh the current tax liability against the future tax benefits before making a decision.

Manage Capital Gains and Losses

Taxes usually take a back seat when you are deciding whether to keep or sell capital assets such as stocks, bonds, and mutual fund shares. And this is as it should be. However, the realization that a particular transaction will create a huge tax liability may cause you to rethink the strategy. And this is also as it should be. Likewise, the realization that a particular transaction could save you a lot in taxes may prompt you to do something you otherwise might not have done strictly for investment reasons—and the result might be exactly what you want. In all investing, taxes add another dimension to the usual investment considerations. While taxes rarely should drive investment decisions, they must necessarily play a part. The following tax strategies are desirable, assuming they jibe with your investment goals:

- *Defer gains by not selling.* No sale, no transaction to report, no tax. It is as simple as that.

- *Make gains long term.* Hold profitable stocks one year and a day to qualify for favorable long-term capital gains treatment.

- *Make losses short term.* Sell unprofitable stocks before you have held them over one year.

- *Match gains and losses—carefully.* If you have short-term gains, take short-term losses to offset them. If you have long-term gains, isolate them in a tax year when you do not have losses in order to take advantage of the lower tax rate. If you have sizable losses, take sizable gains, even if they are long term; otherwise, you will have to carry your losses forward, and chances are they eventually will be absorbed by long-term gains anyway.

- *Identify securities.* If you are selling part of a larger position, identify the securities that will give you the most favorable tax results. If selling for a gain, identify your high-basis securities. If selling for a loss, choose your low-basis shares.

- *Do bond swaps.* These are much easier to do than stock swaps because you can retain the character of your investment without violating wash sale rules.

Minimize Ordinary Income

Look at your tax-planning worksheet. Is there a lot of taxable interest and dividend income? If you are in the 30-percent tax bracket or higher, consider transforming some or all of that income to tax-free or tax-deferred income. If you own taxable bonds, consider switching to tax-free municipal bonds (calculate the yield differential for your tax bracket; see Chapter 3). If your short-term money is in a taxable account, consider switching to a tax-free money market fund. If you own mutual funds that are paying hefty dividends, consider owning a similar fund within a tax-deferred annuity. Sometimes advisors recommend converting ordinary income to capital gains, but this involves making a different kind of investment—a riskier one. If you like the way your portfolio is positioned, you can switch to more tax-favored investments within the stock/bond allocations without changing its overall character.

Manage Your Mutual Funds

Start paying attention to the tax efficiency of mutual funds. If your mutual funds are not very tax efficient, consider switching to funds that are. Also, time your purchases and sales to minimize taxes. Call the fund to find out the date and amount of the annual capital gains distributions, and consider selling before that date. Likewise, never buy a fund just before the distribution. When selling or exchanging part of your mutual fund holdings, consider the four methods of basis calculation (see Chapter 4), and use the method with the most favorable tax result. Do this *before* you sell the shares!

Keep Track of Investment Expenses

You may be surprised by the many costs you incur in the process of earning investment returns. If you itemize deductions and spend more than 2 percent of your AGI on these expenses, you can deduct the part that exceeds the 2 percent of AGI. Consider everything you spend money on that helps you invest: professional fees paid to an accountant for tax planning advice; fees paid to brokers or money managers for investment advice; books, magazines, and seminars; IRA and Keogh fees (if you write a separate check rather than having the fees taken out of account assets); computer software; and payments to clerical or office workers who help you manage your investments. Keep in mind that you may not deduct expenses associated with tax-exempt securities, so if your portfolio includes municipal bonds, you will need to separate out expenses related to that part of your portfolio.

Shift Assets to Family Members

If your income is too high to take advantage of certain deductions and credits, consider having your kids file their own tax returns. You will have to do some serious number crunching to determine if a full deduction (or credit) at the child's low bracket is worth more than a partial deduction at your high bracket, so tread carefully here. Also, do not forget about giving appreciated stock to family members you are supporting so that they can pay the capital gains tax at their low rate. If $10,000-per-year gifts are part of your estate plan, make the gifts early in the year so that the appreciation will be taxed at the receiver's tax rate, not yours.

Start Planning Next Year Before This Year Is Over

It is always good to have a handle on two years worth of income and tax estimates. In this way, you can employ favorable year-end strategies. For example, if you know that your income will be higher this year than next, you can take steps to defer income into next year and accelerate deductions into this year by postponing year-end bonuses or waiting until after the new year to bill clients while prepaying state income taxes and making two years worth of charitable contributions in December. Conversely, if you know that next year's income will be higher than this year's, you can do the opposite: accelerate income and defer deductions. However, you also must be aware of the deduction phaseouts and whether or not you might be subject to the alternative minimum tax (see Chapter 11). In fact, planning for two tax years at a time can help you avoid the AMT for at least one of those years.

Watch Effective Dates of Tax Law Changes

The Economic Growth and Tax Relief Reconciliation Act of 2001 calls for the gradual phasing in of certain items. Each year going forward, there will be slightly different rules concerning income limits, retirement plan contribution limits, and many other items. In addition, Congress is likely to tweak the rules here and there to fix certain items that were passed in haste. Without making yourself crazy trying to memorize the next 10 years worth of tax rules, just understand that the rules will be changing in the years ahead and that you will need to stay on top of them. One change that is clear is that everyone's tax brackets will be going down in the years ahead. Thus, even if your income stays the same, your deductions will be worth less, and the yield differential between taxable and tax-free securities may narrow. You will need to reevaluate all your investment strategies in light of your new tax bracket.

Keep the Right Records

The adage you use when cleaning out your refrigerator—"when it doubt throw it out"—does not apply to tax record keeping. This does not mean that you need to keep every pay stub and utility bill for as long as you live, but it does mean keeping certain records for a definite period of time. The main record-keeping rule for investors is this: Keep all records relating to investments for at least six years after the *due date* of the tax return on which you reported the sale of the investment. Obviously, this means keeping the records for as long as you *own* the investment so that you can calculate your cost basis when the time comes to report the sale. However, since the IRS has three years after that to audit you and another three years after that to scrutinize your records if it suspects that you did not report all your income, you will want to have proof of all your investment activity during the entire *six-year* period—beginning with the *due date* of your return. The due date of your 2001 return is April 15, 2002 unless you get an extension to August 15, 2002 or October 15, 2002. So keep documentation relating to transactions reported on your 2001 tax return until April, August, or October of 2008.

WHICH RECORDS SHOULD YOU KEEP?

Keep all 1099s that come in the mail in January. In fact, as soon as each 1099 arrives, verify against your brokerage statements and your own records that the amount is correct. Mistakes do happen, and the reason financial institutions are required to send 1099s soon after the close of the year is to give you an opportunity to correct mistakes. The IRS will be receiving copies of the same 1099s and will be looking for those numbers on your tax return. Also keep all brokerage statements, mutual fund statements, and other statements verifying income. Most people are used to keeping records of deductible expenses, but the IRS is more concerned about the underreporting of income. Be prepared to prove that you have reported all the income you received. You need not keep confirmation slips if the information is summarized on a brokerage or mutual fund statement.

Remember that home improvements allow you to increase your cost basis in your house. Do not count on having all your gains excluded under the $250,000/$500,000 capital gains exclusion on home sales; you never know what might happen to real estate values in the future. If housing prices skyrocket, you will wish you had all those Home Depot receipts that prove how much money you put into the remodeling of your kitchen. If you own rental property, keep all records relating to repairs and maintenance.

Keep copies of tax returns indefinitely. There is no statute of limitations for failure to file. Also, tax returns contain valuable information that may come in handy later, such as nondeductible IRA contributions or rolled over gains on previous home sales that you will need for adjusting the basis in your present home. Other than investment-related records, keep anything that will help you justify the information on your tax return in case of audit: proof of all your income (wages, interest, dividends, and so on) and receipts and canceled checks for all deductible expenses. Donations to charity in excess of $250 must be supported by a receipt from the charity.

Avoid an Audit

Pay attention to those 1099s and make sure that you report all your income. Claim all the tax deductions to which you are entitled, but do be aware that certain deductions, such as the home office deduction and contributions to charity that seem high in relation to your income, raise a flag. A very small percentage of tax returns is ever audited, so most likely you will be safe. Many audits, in fact, are handled by mail and deal with a specific item on your return. All you have to do is produce the required documentation, and you are done with it. If you do get called for a full audit, come prepared with organized records and a willingness to cooperate. Do not volunteer information about a part of your return that is not being questioned, but do answer all questions firmly and truthfully. Despite what you have heard or read, most IRS agents are reasonable and willing to work with you—as long as you reciprocate. However, if the thought of facing the IRS has you breaking out in a cold sweat, find a professional to represent you. A CPA, enrolled agent, or attorney can represent you before the IRS, and you do not even need to be there.

Find a Tax Advisor

Until the entire U.S. Tax Code is overhauled (something under consideration, believe it or not), taxes will remain one of the most complicated areas of our financial lives. And the more successful we become, the more complicated they get. Tax-preparation software is great for filling out tax returns and providing some level of guidance, but for sophisticated tax-planning advice, there is nothing like a professional who understands your financial situation and knows how to apply some of the more arcane tax laws to reduce your tax bill. You can look at the hiring of a tax professional in simple investment terms: If you stand to save more in taxes than the advisor charges in fees, you have a good deal. Do not forget to factor the value of your time into the equation. Keep in mind that tax professionals come with varying levels of expertise, ranging from simple tax preparers in a booth at the mall to tax attorneys with a sophisticated knowledge of the law and a unique ability to analyze it. As an investor, you probably want someone who can do more than fill out tax forms after the year is over but rather will take a more proactive approach and guide you throughout the tax year. If your situation is complicated by the alternative minimum tax (AMT), stock options, or trader status (see Chapters 11 to 13), be sure to find an advisor with expertise in these areas.

Tax Planning Worksheets

Estimated income and deductions for tax year 20_____

FILING STATUS _____

NUMBER OF DEPENDENTS (including self and spouse) _____

INCOME

Earned Income _____

Taxable Interest (see Interest Worksheet) _____

Dividends (see Dividend Worksheet) _____

Capital Gain (or Loss) (see Capital Gain/Loss Worksheet)

Net Short-Term Gain (Loss) _____

Net Long-Term Gain (Loss) _____

Total Capital Gains (or Losses) _____

IRA Distributions _____

Subject to 10% penalty? ___Yes ___No

Other Income (alimony, farm income, pension income, royalties, etc.) _____

Social Security income subject to tax (see Social Security Worksheets) _____

TOTAL INCOME _____

ADJUSTMENTS TO INCOME

IRA Deduction _____

One-Half of Self-Employment Tax (if filing
Schedule C) _____

Self-Employed Health Insurance Deduction _____

Self-Employed Contributions to Qualified Plans _____

Other Deductions (Student loan interest deduction,
medical savings account deduction, moving expenses,
penalty on early withdrawal of savings, alimony paid) _____

TOTAL ADJUSTMENTS _____

ADJUSTED GROSS INCOME—AGI
(subtract Total Adjustments from Total Income) _____

DEDUCTIONS AND EXEMPTIONS

    Itemized Deductions (see Deduction Worksheet)   _____

    Less 3% reduction if applicable (see 3% Reduction Worksheet)   _____

    Total Itemized Deduction or Standard Deduction   _____

    Personal Exemptions (see Personal Exemption Worksheet)   _____

      TOTAL DEDUCTIONS AND EXEMPTIONS   _____

TAXABLE INCOME
(subtract Total Deductions and Exemptions from AGI)   _____

Note: If any part of this number is composed of long-term capital gains (see above) separate out that part and calculate the tax at 20% (or 10% if your tax bracket is 15% or lower).

TOTAL TAX (see Table 9.1: 2002 Tax Rate Table)   _____

MARGINAL TAX RATE   _____

Interest Worksheet

Bank, savings, and money market accounts

Name of Bank or Financial Institution	Amount on Deposit ($) (If amount is expected to vary throughout the year, estimate the average amount.)	Interest Rate (%)	Expected Annual Interest ($)
			Total $

Taxable Bonds

Name of Issuer	Face Amount	Interest Rate (%)	Annual Interest ($)
			Total $

Total Taxable Interest $_____

Tax-Exempt Bonds (use if receiving Social Security benefits)

Name of Issuer	Face Amount	Interest Rate (%)	Annual Interest ($)
			Total $

Total Tax-Free Interest $_____

Dividend Worksheet

Stocks

Name of Company	No. Shares Owned	Annual Dividend Per Share ($)	Expected Dividend ($) (No. shares × annual dividend)
			Total $

Mutual Funds

Name of Fund	Amount Invested ($)	Annual Yield (%) (Do not include capital gains income.)	Expected Dividend ($) (Amount invested × annual yield)
			Total $

Capital Gain/Loss Worksheet

Stocks, Bonds, Mutual Fund Shares

Name of Security	Date Acquired (mo., day, yr.)	Total Cost ($)	Date Sold (mo., day, yr.)	Sales Proceeds ($)	Gain or Loss (Subtract total cost from sales proceeds.)	Short-Term (X)	Long-Term (X)

Mutual Fund Capital Gains Distributions

Name of Fund	Capital Gains Distribution	Short-Term (X)	Long-Term (X)

Summary—Short-Term Gains/Losses

Short-Term Loss Carry Forward from Previous year	$
Security	Amount of Short-Term Gain or Loss
	Total $

Summary—Long-Term Gains/Losses

Long-Term Loss Carry Forward from Previous year	$
Security	Amount of Long-Term Gain or Loss
	Total $

Deduction Worksheet

Standard Deductions for 2002

Standard Deduction Chart for Most People

Single	$ 4,700
Married filing joint return or Qualifying widow(er) with dependent child	7,850
Head of Household	6,900
Married filing separate return	3,925

Additional standard deductions if 65 or older and blind:

1. Unmarried: To the $4,700 standard deduction from the table, add $1,150 if 65 or older and/or $1,150 if blind ($2,300 if both 65 or older and blind).

2. Married: To the $7,850 from the table add $900 if 65 or older and/or $900 if blind ($1,800 if both 65 or older and blind).

Standard deduction for dependents (if someone else can claim an exemption for you): The lesser of:

1. The basic standard deduction for single taxpayers ($4,700), or

2. The greater of:

   a. $750, or

   b. The dependent's earned income plus $250

Medical and Dental Expenses

Only unreimbursed medical expenses and health insurance premiums that exceed 7.5% of AGI are deductible.

Multiply AGI by 7.5% and enter here: $_____

List health insurance premiums and medical and dental expenditures. Do not include expenses reimbursed by insurance.

Nature of Expenditure	Amount
	Total $

State and Local Income Taxes and Property Taxes

State Income Tax $_____

Local Income Tax $_____

Property Tax $_____

Other Real Estate Taxes $_____

Interest Expense

Home mortgage interest $_____

Investment interest $_____

Gifts to Charity

Name of Charity	Amount of Gift
	Total Gifts ($)

Casualty and Theft Losses

Type of Loss	Amount of Loss
	Total Losses ($)

Job Expenses and Other Miscellaneous Deductions

Multiply your AGI by 2% (.02) and enter here: $_____

Expense	Amount
	Total $

Worksheet for 3% Reduction

Use if your AGI is over:

$137,300 (if single)

$206,000 (if married filing jointly or qualifying widow[er])

$171,650 (if head of household)

$103,000 (if single filing separately)

1. Enter your 2002 AGI $_____

2. Enter threshold amount for your filing status   _____

3. Sutract Line 2 from Line 1.   _____

4. Multiply the amount on Line 3 by 3%.   _____

5. Enter total itemized deductions.   _____

6. Enter the amount for medical and dental expenses, investment interest, casualty or theft losses, and gambling losses. These deductions are not subject to the reduction.   _____

7. Subtract Line 6 from Line 5.*   _____

8. Multiply the amount on Line 7 by 80% (.80).   _____

9. Enter the smaller of Line 4 and Line 8. This is the disallowed amount.   _____

10. Subtract Line 9 from Line 5. This is the net amount of itemized deductions you may claim on Schedule A   _____

*If the amount on Line 7 is zero, the reduction does not apply.   _____

Personal Exemption Worksheet

Enter total number of exemptions from top of Tax Planning Worksheet. _____

Multiply this number times $3,000 _____

Enter total on Personal Exemption line of Tax Planning Worksheet _____

Social Security Worksheet

To determine taxable portion of Social Security benefits

SS Worksheet I: Personal Benefits Data

Estimated benefit for the year	50% of benefit	85% of benefit

SS Worksheet II: Figuring Your Provisional Income

1. Enter taxable income listed under Income section of Tax Planning Worksheet: _____

2. Enter total tax-free income from Interest Worksheet. _____

3. Add Lines 1 and 2. _____

4. Enter total Adjustments to Income from the Tax Planning Worksheet (if any): _____

5. Subtract Line 4 from Line 3. _____

6. Enter 50% of SS benefit from above: _____

7. Add Lines 5 and 6. This is your provisional income. _____

Social Security benefits are taxable if:

You are filing as single, head of household, or qualifying widow(er) with dependent child and your provisional income is over $25,000.

You are married filing a joint return and your provisional income is over $32,000.

If your provisional income exceeds these amounts, go on to SS Worksheet III, Figuring Taxable Benefits.

SS Worksheet III: Figuring Taxable Benefits

1. Enter your provisional income from Line 7 of Worksheet II. _____

2. Enter $25,000 if single, head of household or qualifying widow(er) or $32,000 if married filing jointly. _____

3. Subtract Line 2 from Line 1. _____

4. Enter 50% of Line 3. _____

5. Enter 50% of your SS benefit from SS Worksheet I.   _____

6. Enter $34,000 (single) or $44,000 (joint).   _____

7. Subtract Line 6 from Line 1. If zero or less, enter 0 and go to Line 13.
   Otherwise, go on to Line 8.   _____

8. Enter $4,500 (single) or $6,000 (joint).   _____

9. Enter the smallest of Line 4, Line 5, or Line 8.   _____

10. Multiply Line 7 by 85% (.85).   _____

11. Add Lines 9 and 10.   _____

12. Enter 85% of your SS benefit from SS Worksheet I.   _____

13. Taxable Social Security benefit. If Line 7 is zero, enter on Line 13 the
    smaller of Line 4 or line 5. If Line 7 is more than zero, enter the smaller
    of Line 11 or Line 12. This is the taxable part of your benefits.
    Enter this amount on the Tax Planning Worksheet.   _____

CHAPTER 10

The Nuts and Bolts of Reporting

When you strip away the fine print and focus only on the tax rules that apply to you, filing your tax return does not have to be that complicated. After all, your employer and the financial service firms where you have your investments tell you how much income you have to report. All you have to do is transfer the numbers shown on your W-2s and 1099s to form 1040. For your deductions, just gather up your receipts and enter the amounts on the appropriate lines of the form. Then take out your calculator and do some simple arithmetic, refer to the tax tables to see how much tax you owe, sign the form, and mail it in. What could be easier?

Well, okay, maybe it is not quite this simple. If it were, all the nation's CPAs would have to find something else to do for a living, and you would not have to spend a whole weekend in the spring getting your tax stuff together. However, if you approach tax filing as a natural extension of the tax *planning* you do all year long, it really does become much easier. When you think about taxes all the time, you are more inclined to do the little things throughout the year that eventually will make tax filing easy, like logging your stock trades and writing down your tax-deductible expenditures as you make them. Remember, you do not have to submit your trade confirmations and receipts with your tax return. You only need to produce them if you are audited. Make a habit of logging all your tax information in one place and stashing the little pieces of paper away for safekeeping in the unlikely event that you are audited. When the time comes to file your return, you can simply take out your logbook and transfer the numbers to the proper Internal Revenue Service (IRS) forms. A personal finance software package such as Quicken or Microsoft Money can make the tax-planning and tax-filing process a breeze because it allows you to flag tax items as you enter them. When the time comes to prepare your taxes, you can print out reports for each category and either take them to your accountant or enter them on the forms yourself. If you use a compatible tax-preparation software package, you can even have the numbers transferred directly to your tax return.

Although accountants and tax-preparation software packages make tax filing much easier than if you had to do it all by hand with pencil, paper, and abacus, it is important not to lose sight of the fundamental process. Thus in this chapter we will be going over the forms and what numbers to put where. Please understand that our goal is to simplify the process and make it more understandable, not to clutter your mind with details you do not need to know, so if you encounter a section that does not apply to you, feel free to skip over it.

Overview of Tax Forms

The IRS has created hundreds of forms for use in filing taxes. You will be glad to know that most of them do not apply to you. The main forms investors need are described below and reproduced in Appendix I.

Form 1040

Form 1040 is the mother of all tax forms—it is the place where all the other numbers from all the other forms are added up and summarized. It is amazing to think that your entire tax life can fit onto two simple pages, but it is true. Of course, if you read the fine print, you will see additional instructions such as "Attach Schedule B" or "see page 27." This is where you find out that this tax-filing business is a little more complicated than you thought (or that we are trying to make it seem).

Form 1040A is the simplified version of form 1040. You can use it if your taxable income is less than $50,000 and you do not itemize deductions. You may not use it if you are self-employed.

Form 1040EZ is the "EZ-est" tax form of all. You can use it if your taxable income is less than $50,000, you are not itemizing deductions, and you are either single or married and not claiming any dependents. Your taxable interest must not exceed $400. We assume that if you are reading this book, your financial situation is too complex for form 1040EZ. However, if your children worked and earned more than $4,550 in 2001 and you are claiming them as dependents (which you can do if they are under age 19 or under age 24 and a student), 1040EZ is the form for them.

Tax Schedules

In addition to form 1040, you also may file one of the following schedules.

SCHEDULE A: IF YOU ITEMIZE DEDUCTIONS

Schedule A allows you to list all your deductions, such as state income tax, home mortgage interest, and gifts to charity. Only use schedule A if you do not take the standard deduction. Transfer the total to line 36 of form 1040.

SCHEDULE B: IF YOU RECEIVE MORE THAN $400 IN INTEREST AND/OR DIVIDENDS

Shortly after the end of the year, you will receive form 1099-INT and/or form 1099-DIV. These forms are issued by the financial institutions where you have your accounts and state how much taxable interest or dividends you received during the year. The IRS also gets copies of these forms. If the total is more than $400, list the payers and enter the amounts on schedule B (or schedule 1 if filing form 1040A) and transfer the total to line 9 of form 1040.

SCHEDULE C: IF YOU ARE SELF-EMPLOYED OR OWN A SMALL BUSINESS

Schedule C is for business owners and self-employed individuals. It is where you report your gross income for the year, as well as all your business expenses. You also will use schedule C to list your investment expenses if you qualify as a trader (see Chapter 13). Transfer your total net business income to line 12 of form 1040.

SCHEDULE D: IF YOU SELL STOCKS, BONDS, OR MUTUAL FUND SHARES

Schedule D is where you report capital gains and losses. Only use this form if you sell a capital asset such as a stock, bond, or mutual fund shares during the year. After the end of the year, you will receive form 1099-B showing your sales proceeds. We remind you that the IRS also receives a copy of this form. On schedule D you list the name of the security, the date you acquired it, the date you sold it, the sales price, your cost basis, and the net gain or loss. Part I is for short-term capital gains and losses; part II is for long-term gains and losses. If you have more than four transactions for each part, put the overflow on schedule D-1, which is the continuation sheet for schedule D. In part III you net out your gains and losses; part IV shows you how to compute the tax.

SCHEDULE E: IF YOU RECEIVE REAL ESTATE RENTAL INCOME

If you own property for investment and receive rental income, schedule E is where you report the income and also deduct expenses such as maintenance and repairs. If you own units in a real estate limited partnership, you will receive form K-1 at the end of the year showing the amount to be reported on schedule E.

Additional Forms

You also may need to file other forms with your tax return. For example, if you make nondeductible IRA contributions, you will need to file form 8606; if you cashed in savings bonds used for higher education expenses, you will file form 8815. The more complicated your return is, the more forms and schedules you will file. However, the instructions are pretty clear. If you are doing your taxes by hand, you will be referred to the proper form. For example, if you are taking any of the education tax credits such as the Hope credit or the lifetime-learning credit, line 46 of form 1040 tells you to attach form 8863. You can download tax forms from www.irs.gov or obtain them from your local IRS office. Some libraries and post offices also have tax forms. If you are using a tax software package to do your taxes, the program will automatically include the proper forms and schedules. If you have an accountant prepare your taxes, you can depend on him or her to have the proper form and to fill it out for you.

The remainder of this chapter provides the nuts and bolts of reporting for the various investments and strategies we have talked about in this book.

Interest and Dividend Income

Following are the nuts and bolts of reporting interest and dividend income.

Reporting Interest Income

Form 1099-INT is the official statement of interest earned during the year. It is completed by financial institutions and bond issuers, and a copy is sent to both you and the IRS. If you have questions or doubts about its accuracy, be sure to notify the issuer right away so that corrections can be made.

If you receive less than $400 in interest income, you can report it directly on line 8a of form 1040. If you receive more than $400 in taxable interest, list each payer on schedule B, and transfer the total to line 8a. If you receive tax-exempt interest, enter it on line 8b of form 1040. The main reason for entering tax-exempt interest is for the purpose of figuring the tax on Social Security benefits; if this situation does not apply to you, you must still enter the amount, but it will not be taxed.

PENALTIES ON EARLY WITHDRAWALS

If you are penalized for making an early withdrawal from a certificate of deposit, you may lose part of your interest or principal. You must report the full amount of interest credited to your account, but you may deduct the amount of the penalty on line 30 of form 1040.

ACCRUED INTEREST ON BONDS

When you buy bonds between interest payment dates, your form 1099-INT will include interest you paid to the seller at the time you bought the bond. This amount is taxable to the seller, not you. Be sure to subtract the amount of accrued interest on your tax return so that you are not taxed on it. Enter the full amount of interest on line 1 of schedule B along with your other interest income. Underneath the subtotal write "Accrued interest," and enter the amount you are subtracting.

BUYING BONDS AT A PREMIUM

Bond premium is the extra amount over the face amount that you pay when bond prices increase due to falling interest rates. For example, if you pay $1,200 for a bond with a $1,000 face amount, the $200 is the bond premium. You can amortize the premium on a taxable bond by deducting it over the life of the bond. Amortizing is usually advantageous because it helps offset the taxable interest income each year. When you amortize the premium, you reduce your basis each year by the amount amortized. Then, if you redeem the bond at par, you have neither a gain nor a loss. If you do not amortize the premium, your basis will remain the same as your cost. If you redeem the bond at par or sell it for less than you paid, you will realize a capital loss.

To amortize bond premium, report the full interest from the bond on line 1 of schedule B along with your other interest income. On a separate line, subtract the amortized premium from a subtotal of all the interest. Label the subtraction "ABP adjustment." This interest-offset rule applies to all taxable bonds acquired at a premium after 1987.

You may not claim a deduction for a premium paid on a tax-exempt bond; however, you must still decrease your basis by the premium.

BUYING BONDS AT A DISCOUNT

There are two types of bond discounts: original-issue discount (OID) and market discount. OID arises when a bond is originally issued at a price less than its face amount. Market discount arises when a bond is selling for less than par on the secondary market because interest rates have risen since the bond was issued. Each of these discounts is treated differently for tax purposes.

OID is the difference between the face amount (redemption price at maturity) and the issue price. For example, a $1,000 bond that is issued at $600 has an OID of $400 ($1,000 − $600). All obligations that pay no interest before maturity, such as zero-coupon bonds, are considered to be issued at a discount. Generally, part of the OID must be reported as interest income each year you hold the bond, whether or not you actually receive any payment from the bond issuer. This is also true for certificates of deposit, time deposits, and similar savings arrangements with a term of more than one year, provided payment of interest is deferred until maturity. OID is reported to you on form 1099-OID. If you pay a premium for an OID bond, the OID may be reduced by the amount of the premium. Include the full amount of the OID on schedule B along with your other interest income. Under the subtotal write "OID adjustment," and subtract the amount of the premium. Your basis for the obligation is increased by the taxable OID for purposes of figuring gain on a sale or redemption. OID rules do not apply to obligations with a term of 1 year or less, tax-exempt obligations (except for certain stripped tax-exempts), or U.S. savings bonds.

Market discount arises where the price of a bond declines below its face amount as a result of an increase in interest rates. When you realize a profit on a market-discount bond, the portion of the profit equal to the accrued discount must be reported as ordinary interest income rather than as a capital gain. There are two methods for figuring the accrued market discount. The basic method, called the *ratable-accrual method*, is figured by dividing the market discount by the number of days in the period from the date you bought the bond until the date of maturity. This daily amount is then multiplied by the number of days you held the bond to determine your accrued market discount. The other method is the *constant-yield method* used in IRS Publication 1212 to compute taxable OID. Rather than report market discount in the year you sell the bond, you may elect, in the year you acquire the bond, to report market discount each year as interest income. You may use either the ratable-accrual method or the constant-yield method.

BUYING SHORT-TERM OBLIGATIONS AT A DISCOUNT

Short-term obligations maturing in one year or less from date of issue may be purchased at a discount. This discount is reported on form 1099-INT and is considered interest income in the year the obligation is paid. For example, if you pay $9,800 for a $10,000 Treasury bill that matures in January 2003, you will report $200 in interest on your 2003 tax return.

INTEREST ON TREASURY SECURITIES

Interest on securities issued by the federal government is taxable on your federal return but is not taxable by state or local governments. Interest income from Treasury securities is reported in box 3 of form 1099-INT. You will report this on schedule B (or directly on form 1040 if less than $400). You will not report it on your state tax return.

INTEREST ON U.S. SAVINGS BONDS

The increase in redemption value of Series EE and Series I bonds is taxable as interest, but you do not have to report it until you redeem the bond. In other words, you may defer the interest income until the year in which you cash the bond or the bond finally matures. You do not have to make a special election on your tax return to defer the interest. You simply postpone reporting the interest until you redeem the bond.

TAX-FREE INTEREST ON STATE AND LOCAL GOVERNMENT OBLIGATIONS

Tax-exempt interest is reported on schedule B or, if less than $400, directly on line 8b of form 1040. If a tax-exempt bond is originally issued at a discount, the gain attributable to the OID at sale or maturity is not taxable. However, if you buy a tax-exempt bond at a market discount and later sell it for more than you paid, your profit is taxable as a capital gain.

Reporting Dividend Income

Form 1099-DIV is used for reporting corporate dividends as well as mutual fund distributions. How you report this income will depend on which box it is reported in.

ORDINARY DIVIDENDS

Ordinary dividends from stocks and real estate investment trusts (REITs) are reported in box 1 of form 1099-DIV. Report this income on line 9 of form 1040. If it is more than $400, also complete schedule B.

MUTUAL FUND DISTRIBUTIONS

Ordinary dividends and short-term capital gain distributions are reported in box 1 of form 1099-DIV. As with other dividends, report this income on line 9 of form 1040. If it is more than $400, also complete schedule B.

Long-term capital gain distributions from mutual funds are reported in box 2a of form 1099-DIV or on a substitute statement. You must report this income on schedule D unless all three of the following apply: (1) the only amounts you have to report on schedule D are capital gain distributions from box 2a of form 1099-DIV (that is, you have no other stock or bond sales to report), (2) none of the 1099-DIVs have an entry in box 2a (28-percent rate gain), box 2c (unrecaptured section 1250 gain), or box 2d (section 1202 gain), and (3) if you are filing form 4952 (relating to investment interest expense deduction), the amount on line 4e is zero. If all three of these conditions apply, you may enter your capital gains distributions on line 13 of form 1040 or line 10 of form 1040A. Be sure you use the capital gains tax worksheet in the IRS instructions to figure your tax.

Return of capital distributions are reported in box 3 of form 1099-DIV. This income is not taxable. However, it is used to reduce your basis in your shares. If your basis already has been reduced to zero, additional nontaxable distributions must be reported as either long- or short-term capital gains on schedule D, depending on how long you held the shares.

Exempt-interest dividends are not reported via 1099 but rather on a separate statement used for informational purposes only. Report exempt-interest dividends on line 8b of form 1040 along with your other tax-exempt interest.

Undistributed capital gains are reported on form 2439, box 1a. In the unusual event that you receive undistributed capital gains, report them on line 11 of schedule D. To get a tax credit for the tax paid by the fund, enter the tax on line 64 of form 1040. Increase the basis of your mutual fund shares by the excess of the undistributed gains included on schedule D over the tax credit claimed on line 64 of form 1040.

Claiming the Investment Interest Expense Deduction

If you are itemizing deductions and paid interest expense on margin loans or other loans whose proceeds were used to invest in non-tax-exempt securities, use form 4952 to claim the deduction. As you will see when completing the form, you may not deduct more investment interest than you receive in investment income. Any overflow may be carried over to next year.

Reporting Capital Gains and Losses

Capital gains and losses are reported on schedule D. If you sold stocks, bonds, or other investment property through a broker, the sale is reported to you and to the IRS on form 1099-B. You will enter this amount in column (d). Your cost basis goes in column (e). To determine your gain or loss, subtract column (e) from column (d). On your statement, the broker will indicate whether gross proceeds or gross proceeds minus commissions and option premiums were reported to the IRS. If the gross proceeds were reported, enter that amount as the sales price in column (d) and add any commissions or option premiums to cost basis in column (e). If only the net proceeds were reported, enter that amount as the sales price in column (d) of schedule D and do not include commissions or option premiums in column (e).

You may report many different types of transactions on schedule D: sales of securities, sales of mutual fund shares, and sales of personal residences where part of the gain does not qualify for the $250,000/$500,000 capital gains tax exclusion.

Stock Sales

On schedule D you must identify shares of stock you sold. This identification consists of number of shares, company name, date acquired, and cost. As discussed in Chapter 2, if you are selling part of your holdings, the IRS will presume that you are selling the first shares acquired (FIFO method of identification). If you wish to sell a different lot of securities, you will need to make the identification at the time you place the sell order and receive written confirmation from your broker. In column (a) of schedule D, enter the number of shares and name of company. In columns (b) and (c), enter the acquisition date and sale date, respectively. For the purpose of determining your holding period, the period starts on the day *after* your purchase order is executed and ends *on* the date your sale order is executed, even if delivery and payment are not made until several days after the trading dates. Your holding period is considered long term if the security is owned *more than* one year (that is, you bought on January 3, 2002 and sold on January 4, 2003). If the holding period is *one year or less*, it is considered short term (you bought on January 3, 2002 and sold on January 3, 2003). Short-term capital gains and losses go in part I of schedule D; long-term gains and losses go in part II.

In column (e) you enter your cost or other basis. Usually, this is the price you paid including commissions. If you received the stock by gift, your cost basis and acquisition date are the same as the donor's. If you received the stock by inheritance, your cost basis is the fair market value of the stock on the day the decedent died (or six months later if that election is made by the executor). The holding period for inherited stocks is always long term, regardless of how long you or the decedent actually held them. If you have received stock dividends or additional shares as a result of stock splits, your basis is adjusted as discussed in Chapter 2.

Bond Sales

If you sell bonds for more or less than you paid, the capital gain or loss is reported on schedule D. As with stocks, enter your sales proceeds in column (d), your cost or other basis in column (e), and the gain or loss in column (f). Be sure to adjust your basis for any accrued interest or any premium or discount you are amortizing, as discussed earlier in this chapter.

Mutual Fund Sales

If you sell or redeem mutual fund shares (including switching to a different fund within the same fund family), you must report the sale on schedule D. The mutual fund will send you form 1099-B reporting your proceeds. This amount goes in column (d). You fill in the other columns giving the number of shares and name of fund (column a), date acquired (column b), date sold (column c), cost or other basis (column e), and gain or loss (column f). As discussed in Chapter 4, there are four ways to identify mutual fund shares when selling: first in, first out (FIFO), specific identification, single average-cost method, and double average-cost method. Specific identification gives you the most flexibility in structuring your gains and losses, but you must make the identification at the time you sell the shares. If you do not do this, you must use one of the other three methods. As with stocks, your holding period begins the day after you bought the shares and ends on the day the shares were sold. Your holding period is long term if it is at least one year and a day.

Real Estate Sales

Capital gains reporting for real estate will depend on whether it is your personal residence or income property.

PRINCIPAL RESIDENCE

The sale of your principal residence is reported on schedule D only if the gain is not fully covered by the $250,000/$500,000 capital gain exclusion for principal residences. If the sales price exceeds $250,000 (single) or $500,000 (joint), the settlement agent will report the sale to the IRS (and to you) on form 1099-S unless you provide written certification that your gain is fully excluded under the rules. To report a gain that is not fully excluded, enter your sales proceeds in column (d) of schedule D. In column (e), report your adjusted basis in the property. This is the amount you paid, plus purchase expenses such as title insurance and recording fees, and improvements made to the property over the time you owned it. If you rolled over a gain from a previous sale, you must decrease your basis by the amount of the deferred gain. Subtract your basis (column e) from your sales proceeds (column d) to determine your net gain. If you meet the tests for the $250,000/$500,000 capital gain exclusion—that is, you have owned and occupied the home for two of the five years preceding sale—but the gain exceeds these amounts, enter the full amount of the gain on schedule D, and on a separate line enter the excludable portion ($250,000 or $500,000) as a loss. Label the excludable amount as "Section 121 exclusion." If you are selling your principal residence at a loss, you may not deduct the loss and therefore need not report the sale. However, if you convert the house from personal use to rental use, you may claim a loss on the sale. In this case, your basis is the lower of (1) your adjusted basis for the house at the time of conversion or (2) the fair market value at the time of conversion. Add to this amount the cost of capital improvements made after the conversion, and subtract depreciation and casualty-loss deductions claimed after the conversion. To deduct a loss, you must be able to show that this basis exceeds the sales price.

RENTAL PROPERTY

If you own rental property and qualify for the exception to the passive-activity loss limitation that allows you to take a $25,000 deduction against other income (that is, your AGI is less than $100,000, as discussed in Chapter 5), you must report your income and expenses on schedule E. You also may have to file form 8582 unless you meet the following tests: (1) your only passive activities are rental real estate activities, (2) you have no credits related to passive activities, (3) you actively participated in the rental real estate operations, (4) your total losses from the rental real estate activities are $25,000 or less ($12,500 or less if married filing separately and you lived apart from your spouse all year), (5) your modified adjusted gross income is $100,000 or less ($50,000 or less if married filing separately and you lived apart from your spouse all year), and (6) you do not own any interest in a rental real estate activity as a limited partner or beneficiary of a trust or estate.

Tax Reporting Associated with Retirement Accounts

One of the great benefits of doing all your investing in retirement accounts is that you do not have to report any of the investment income as it is earned. You will not receive any 1099s and need not worry about reporting stock, bond, or mutual fund sales on schedule D. However, your contributions and distributions may require special reporting procedures.

Contributions

If your contributions are all made to a 401(k) or 403(b) plan through your employer, they are not reported on your personal tax return; the contribution amount is simply excluded from your reportable income. The financial institutions where you have your individual retirement account (IRA) will report your contributions to the IRS on form 5498, but you only need to report them on your tax return if you are claiming a tax deduction. If you are making a fully or partially deductible IRA contribution, enter the amount on line 23 of form 1040. If any part of your IRA contribution is nondeductible, you must also file form 8606 to establish the amount of after-tax money in your IRA. Be sure to save copies of this form so that you will not be taxed again on this money when you take it out. If you convert a traditional IRA to a Roth IRA, you also must file form 8606. Your regular annual contributions to a Roth IRA do not need to be reported on your tax return. If you are self-employed and making a contribution to one of the qualified plans described in Chapter 7, enter the amount on line 29 of form 1040.

Distributions

If you take distributions from any kind of retirement account, the amount is reported to the IRS (and to you) on form 1099-R. Box 1 shows the total amount of the distribution without taking any withholding into account. Box 2a shows the taxable amount. If you are paying tax on the entire distribution (as opposed to rolling it over), report this income on line 15b if the distribution is from an IRA or line 16b if from a pension or annuity (or lines 11b and 12b, respectively, if you file form 1040A). Box 4 shows the amount of federal income tax withheld. Be sure to include this amount under "Payments" on line 58 of form 1040 (line 36 of form 1040A) so that you will get credit for it.

PAYING THE 10 PERCENT PREMATURE DISTRIBUTION PENALTY

Box 7 of form 1099-R features a code that tells the IRS whether or not it should be looking for a premature distribution penalty on your tax return. If your IRA or pension distribution is subject to the 10 percent premature distribution penalty because you are under age 59 $\frac{1}{2}$ and either are not rolling it over or do not qualify for one of the penalty exceptions, enter the amount of the penalty on line 54 of form 1040. If you are subject to the penalty but box 7 does not feature code 1, you also must file form 5329.

REPORTING A ROLLOVER

If you arranged to have your distribution directly rolled over to an IRA or another employer's plan, box 7 will feature code G or H, respectively. If box 7 features code H, meaning that the amount was transferred directly to another employer's plan, you need not report anything on your tax return, either the distribution or the rollover. If box 7 features code G (direct transfer to an IRA rollover account), or if you took receipt of the distribution and rolled all or part of it to an IRA within 60 days, enter the full, taxable amount of the distribution on line 15a if it is from an IRA or line 16a if from a pension or annuity, subtract the amount you are rolling over and enter the taxable amount, if any, on line 15b or 16b, and write "Rollover" next to it. If you are rolling over the entire amount, enter zero on line 15b or 16b; do not leave it blank.

CLAIMING AN EXCEPTION TO THE PREMATURE DISTRIBUTION PENALTY

If box 7 features code 1, this means that you are under age 59½, and the payer has no reason to believe that you are exempt from the 10-percent premature distribution penalty. This does not mean that you cannot claim an exemption for medical payments or one of the other exceptions discussed in Chapter 7; it just means that you have to file form 5329 to claim the exemption. The instructions for form 5329 explain how to do this. If the trustee knows that you are exempt from the 10 percent penalty due to disability, it will enter code 3 in box 7; if you are taking distributions as a beneficiary following the IRA holder's death, it will enter code 4. In these cases you need not file form 5329.

IF YOU ARE OVER AGE 59½

If you are over age 59½, box 7 will feature code 7. In this case the IRS will not be looking for a penalty, but it will be looking for the distribution amount to be included with your taxable income. If you are rolling over all or part of the distribution, follow the instructions above.

COMPANY STOCK

If you received a qualifying lump-sum distribution that includes securities of your employer's company, the total net unrealized appreciation is shown in box 6 of form 1099-R. This amount is not taxed until you sell the securities. At that time the sale is reported on schedule D.

SPECIAL RULES FOR PEOPLE BORN BEFORE 1936

If you were born before 1936, special rules apply if you receive a qualified lump-sum distribution. The definition of a qualified lump-sum distribution is one that meets both of these tests: (1) you received within a single taxable year your entire balance from the employer's qualified plan (or plans, if more than one), and (2) the distribution was paid because (a) you are over 59½, *or* (b) you are an employee who separated from service, *or* (c) you are self-employed and became disabled, *or* (d) you are the beneficiary of a deceased employee. If you were born before 1936 and your lump-sum distribution meets these tests, you may choose to figure your tax using the 10-year averaging method. If you participated in the plan before 1974, you may elect to apply a 20-percent rate to the pre-1974 part of the lump-sum distribution if 20 percent is lower than the averaging rate. The capital gain portion of the distribution is shown in box 3 of form 1099-R. However, averaging and capital gain treatment are not allowed if any of the following are true: (1) you rolled over any part of the lump-sum distribution to an IRA or an employer qualified plan, (2) you received the distribution during the first five years that you participated in the plan, (3) you previously received a distribution from the plan that you rolled over tax-free to an IRA or another qualified employer plan, (4) you elected 10- or 5-year averaging or capital gains treatment for any other lump-sum distribution after 1986. If you are the beneficiary of a deceased plan participant, the participant's age, not yours, determines your right to claim averaging, and the five-year participation rule dos not apply.

DISTRIBUTIONS FROM PRIVATE ANNUITY CONTRACTS

Distributions from private annuity contracts are also reported on form 1099-R. The taxable amount is shown in box 2a, and this is the amount you should report on line 16b of form 1040. If you are under age 59½, the distribution may be subject to the 10-percent premature distribution penalty unless you are disabled or the distribution is part of a series of substantially equal payments, made at least annually over your life expectancy, or made over the joint life expectancies of you and a beneficiary. If either of these exceptions applies, file form 5329 to claim the exemption.

PARTIALLY TAX-FREE IRA DISTRIBUTIONS

If you ever in your life made a nondeductible contribution to a traditional IRA, you must follow a complicated set of rules to determine the tax-free portion of each distribution. As you know, your after-tax money will come out tax-free, whereas the rest of the money in the account—the investment earnings plus any deductible contributions that you made over the years—will be taxable. When you take a distribution, you cannot just claim that you are taking it from the after-tax pot. Instead, you have to file form 8606 and show the calculations that determine the ratio of after-tax to before-tax money in the account. Your IRA custodian will not indicate on form 1099-R whether any part of a distribution is a tax-free return of basis allocable to nondeductible contributions. It is up to you to keep records that show the nondeductible contributions you have made. IRS instructions require you to keep copies of all form 8606s on which nondeductible contributions have been designated, as well as copies of (1) your tax returns for years you made nondeductible contributions to traditional IRAs, (2) form 5498 showing all IRA contributions and the value of your IRAs for each year you received a distribution, and (3) form 1099-R showing IRA distributions. According to the IRS, you should keep such records until you have withdrawn all IRA funds. To calculate the tax-free portion of an IRA distribution, add up all your nondeductible contributions made over the years and divide that number by your total IRA balance at the end of the year in which the distribution is made. Include the distribution in the total. This is the percentage of the distribution that is not taxable. For example, let us say that you have made a total of $6,000 in nondeductible contributions to IRAs. In November 2002, you take a distribution of $10,000. On December 31, 2002, the total value of all of your IRAs is $60,000. Add in the $10,000 distribution for a total of $70,000. Divide your $6,000 in nondeductible contributions by the $70,000 total value to get a ratio of 8.57 percent. To determine the tax-free portion of the distribution, multiply $10,000 by 0.0857. In this example, $857 of the distribution would be tax-free, so you would report the balance, $9,143, as a taxable IRA distribution on line 15b of form 1040.

IF YOU ARE OVER AGE 70½

Once you turn 70½, you are required to start taking minimum annual distributions from your IRA, as discussed in Chapter 7. To calculate the required amount for each year, take the total of your IRA accounts as of December 31 of the preceding year and divide by your life expectancy as indicated in the IRS table. This is the amount you must take out by December 31 and report on line 15b of form 1040. If you do not take the required amount, you must pay a 50 percent penalty on the underwithdrawal. This penalty is reported on form 5329, and the amount is entered on line 54 of form 1040. In some cases the IRS will waive the penalty if it was due to reasonable error and steps have been taken to correct it. Send your statement of explanation along with form 5329, and pay the penalty. If the IRS grants your request for waiver, you will receive a refund. Incidentally, you are not allowed to contribute to traditional IRAs after the age of 70½ (contributions to Roth IRAs are allowed at any age). If you make what is called an *excess contribution* to an IRA and do not correct it by your filing due date including extensions, the penalty is 6 percent. Report this penalty on form 5329, and transfer the amount to line 54 of form 1040. The earnings on the excess contribution must be reported as income for the year the contribution was made.

DISTRIBUTIONS FROM ROTH IRAS

Report distributions from Roth IRAs on form 8606. Distributions from Roth IRAs are applied in the following order: (1) Roth IRA contributions (these amounts represent a return of your basis and are not taxable), (2) amounts converted from traditional IRAs to Roth IRAs (these amounts also represent a return of basis and are not taxable), and (3) earnings. If your distribution does not exceed the total of your contributions, none of it will be taxable; however, you must enter the amount on form 8606 and file it with your tax return. If any part of your distribution comes from earnings, the calculations will show up on form 8606, and this taxable amount is transferred to line 15b of form 1040.

CONVERTING A TRADITIONAL IRA TO A ROTH IRA

If your adjusted gross income (AGI) is $100,000 or less, you may convert a traditional IRA to a Roth IRA by paying the tax and either having the account moved to a different trustee or having your current trustee retitle the account as a Roth IRA. If you are age 70½ or older, the amount of your minimum required distribution for the year in which you make the conversion may not be converted; instead, you must take the distribution and pay the tax on it and convert the rest (or part of the account if you do not wish to convert it all). The tax for a Roth conversion is reported on form 8606, and the amount is transferred to line 15b of form 1040. If you convert a traditional IRA to a Roth IRA and later change your mind, you can recharacterize the IRA back to a traditional IRA. One reason for doing this is if you learn that you are not eligible to make the conversion because your AGI exceeded $100,000. Another reason to recharacterize a Roth IRA conversion is if the account has declined in value and you would rather convert to a Roth IRA at a time when you will pay less tax. By recharacterizing a converted Roth IRA back to a traditional IRA, you have a second chance to do the conversion. However, you may not convert it back to a Roth IRA in the same calendar year that you do the recharacterization. Use form 8606 for all these maneuvers.

Tax Reporting Associated with College and Family Planning

Following are the nuts and bolts of reporting for the various education tax incentives.

Student Loan Interest Deduction

If you are taking the student loan interest deduction, enter the amount of interest you paid on student loans (up to $2,500 in 2001) on line 24 of form 1040 or line 17 of form 1040A. Please note that you may not take this deduction if you are being claimed as a dependent on someone else's tax return. See Chapter 8 for more information on the student loan interest deduction.

Hope and Lifetime-Learning Credits

To claim the Hope and/or lifetime-learning credit, complete form 8863 and enter the total amount of credit on line 46 of form 1040 or line 29 of form 1040A.

Education IRAs

Contributions to education IRAs are nondeductible and therefore are not reported on form 1040. Distributions are reported on form 8606. If total distributions for a tax year do not exceed the qualified higher education expenses, they are entirely tax-free. Any distributions that exceed expenses are taxable and reported on line 15b of form 1040 or line 11b of form 1040A. A beneficiary may waive tax-free treatment of education IRA distributions in order to qualify for the Hope or lifetime-learning credit. If a waiver is not made and tax-free treatment for any part of the distribution is claimed, no Hope credit or lifetime-learning credit may be claimed for that year.

Traditional or Roth IRA Withdrawals Used for Higher Education

IRA withdrawals used for qualified higher education expenses are not subject to the 10-percent premature distribution penalty. However, they are subject to tax, unless they meet the rules for tax-free withdrawals from a Roth IRA. As with any IRA distribution, report the amount on line 15 of form 1040 or line 11 of form 1040A. If you are under age 59½ and claiming the exception to the distribution premature distribution penalty, complete form 5329 and file it with your tax return as noted in the section on IRA distributions above.

Interest Exclusion for Series EE and Series I Savings Bonds

If you are claiming the interest exclusion for Series EE savings bonds issued after 1989 or Series I savings bonds as discussed in Chapter 8, complete form 8815 and file it with your tax return. The amount of the exclusion varies with the amount of educational expenses you pay and your modified adjusted gross income (MAGI) in the year of redemption. On form 8815, educational expenses must be reduced by the amount of any nontaxable scholarship or fellowship grants, tax-free distributions from a section 529 plan, educational expenses taken into account when figuring a Hope or lifetime-learning credit, and tax-free distributions from an education IRA. If savings bonds are redeemed and the proceeds contributed to a section 529 plan or education IRA, the transfer is treated as an education expense eligible for the exclusion. If the redemption amount exceeds the amount of educational expenses (after any required reduction), the excludable amount is based on the ratio of expenses to redemption amount.

Gift-Tax Reporting

As noted in Chapter 8, you may give away up to $10,000 per recipient per year ($20,000 for joint gifts) without any gift-tax consequences. These gifts need not be reported. However, if you give away more than $10,000 to any individual other than your spouse in one year (not including tuition or medical payments), you must file a gift-tax return. Form 709 is used to report gifts of more than $10,000. If the gift is $20,000 or less and is a joint gift, you may be able to use a short form, form 709-A, rather than form 709 to report the gifts. See the form instructions. Even when form 709 is filed, the gift-tax liability computed on the form may be offset by the applicable credit applied to gift taxes as well as estate taxes. For example, in 2001, you and your spouse each have an applicable credit of $220,550 that exempts up to $675,000 in lifetime or at-death transfers. In 2002, the exemption equivalent is $1,000,000.

"Kiddie Tax" Reporting

If you have a child under age 14 who earned more than $1,500 in investment income in 2001, the amount over $1,500 is taxed at your (the parent's) tax rate.

Please note that the "kiddie tax" applies only to investment income such as interest, dividends, and profits from the sale of property, not wages or self-employment income. Form 8615 is used to report the child's income and compute the tax, which is reported on the child's personal income tax return. You can elect on form 8814 to report the child's investment income on your own return, provided the child received only interest and dividend income. However, this election generally is not advisable because it would cause your AGI to increase and may adversely affect your right to claim various deductions. As you will see when you complete the form, you will need to enter your taxable income so that the tax on earnings over $1,500 can be computed at your tax rate. If you are unable to file your return by April 15, you can file the child's return based on an estimate of the tax and file an amended return later.

Estimated Tax

If you earn income that is not subject to withholding, you may have to pay estimated tax according to the rules discussed in Chapter 9. The form used to pay estimated tax is form 1040-ES. This is a series of four vouchers, one for each of the quarterly estimated payment dates: April 15, June 15, September 15, and January 15. Simply enter your name, address, Social Security number, and payment amount and send it in with your check. You also should write your Social Security number and "2002 Form 1040-ES" on your check.

Change of Address

If you move, notify the IRS of your new address using form 8822.

Installment Agreement Request

If you cannot pay your tax and wish to set up an installment agreement, enter your request on form 9465. If the amount owed is less than $10,000, your request will be granted automatically. Interest will be charged on the unpaid balance, and a $43 processing fee will be charged when your request is approved.

Special Situations/ Advanced Tax Rules

CHAPTER 11

Alternative Minimum Tax

There is a parallel universe in the tax world. It is called the alternative minimum tax (AMT) and often has the word *dreaded* in front of it, as in "the 'dreaded' alternative minimum tax." Until recently, normal people—that is, non-rich people who do not go overboard on tax deductions—did not have to worry about the AMT. However, when it was first created back in 1969, it was not indexed to inflation. Thus, as salaries have crept up along with the cost of living, more people now are considered to have high incomes, and their seemingly normal deductions are considered excessive. This combination of high income and high deductions is what triggers the AMT because it looks like you are a rich person trying to avoid paying your fair share of tax. This is, after all, why the AMT was created—to prevent wealthy people from claiming so many tax deductions that they paid little or no tax. To make sure that they pay some tax, the AMT takes away many of the usual tax deductions and applies a flat tax rate to all income (as opposed to the usual progressive schedule that taxes some income at 10 percent, some at 15 percent, and so on).

Theoretically, everyone is supposed to calculate their tax both ways and pay whichever amount is higher. For the majority of taxpayers, this would be a waste of time, so very few people do it. Accountants and tax software packages are alert to the AMT and know which items are likely to trigger it, so if you use either of these to prepare your taxes, you can be fairly certain that the AMT will be considered for you and you will be given the good or bad news accordingly. If you do your taxes manually, you should be aware of the AMT, and if your income is high and your deductions are many, be prepared to enter this parallel universe where nothing is as it seems and tax deductions you think would lower your tax no longer do you any good.

Estimating Your Chances of Having to Pay the AMT and Planning Accordingly

There is no simple rule of thumb that tells you whether or not you are subject to the AMT because it is based on a combination of your income and deductions. However, if your income is more than $75,000 and you have large write-offs for personal exemptions (you always knew having all those kids would get you into trouble), state income taxes, interest on home equity loans not used to buy or improve your home, and other miscellaneous deductions, you could be a candidate for the AMT. If you exercised incentive stock options (more on this in Chapter 12), you may be subject to the AMT for that reason alone.

To determine whether or not you will pay the AMT, you must add up all the so-called preference items on your regular tax return. If they exceed the exemption amount for your income and filing status—welcome to the AMT. You really need to prepare your regular taxes first so that you can refer to your 1040 for the exact amounts you are claiming. However, there is a big catch 22 when it comes to year-end tax planning. Certain classic strategies that are used to reduce regular taxes—such as deferring income and accelerating deductions—can be disadvantageous if you are subject to the AMT. Thus, if you wait until the tax year is over to see if you are subject to the AMT, you could find that you did the exact wrong things at the end of the year in an effort to reduce your taxes.

For example, if you paid your 2002 state income tax before December 31 in order to deduct it on your 2001 return and then find out that you are subject to the AMT in 2001, you not only will have paid the tax earlier than you needed to but you also will have lost that deduction for 2002 if it turns out that you will be going back to paying regular tax in 2002. Thus it is crucial for tax-planning purposes to find out before the end of the year if you are a candidate for the AMT. If so, you can put off paying some of those otherwise deductible expenses in the hope of being able to claim them as deductions next year. On the income side, it makes sense to accelerate income if you are subject to the AMT because all income is taxed at either the 26- or 28-percent rate. If you go back to paying regular tax next year, you will likely be in the 30-percent bracket or higher.

A popular AMT tax-planning strategy—assuming that you cannot avoid it entirely—is to alternate years. In the year you must pay the AMT, you accelerate income by taking prepayments of salary or bonus, taking retirement distributions, or realizing short-term capital gains; this additional income will be taxed at either the 26- or 28-percent rate instead of the higher rate it would be subject to if you took it next year when you will be in the 30-percent bracket or higher. At the same time, you can postpone expenses that are not deductible under the AMT, such as medical expenses and state income tax, saving them for the following year when you will be paying regular tax. These maneuvers are obviously very tricky but worth it.

Calculating the AMT

Since the AMT was designed originally for people who took exotic write-offs for such things as mining costs and intangible drilling expenses, the form used to figure the AMT can be quite intimidating. Even the instructions that go with the form are not very clear, often referring to sections of the tax code but not explaining those sections in the instructions. For example, it tells you to add in any interest expense that was "paid or accrued on indebtedness attributable to property held for investment within the meaning of section 163(d)(5)," but it does not tell you what that is. Unless you have the complete tax code sitting on your desk, you likely will need help calculating the AMT, whether you get it from your friendly accountant or your efficient tax software package. Of course, it might be said safely that if you do not know what something means, it probably does not apply to you. The AMT is mostly about adding back in deductions that you took on your regular tax return, so if you encounter deductions on the AMT form that you do not understand, you probably did not take them in the first place.

Form 6251 (located in Appendix II) is used to calculate the AMT. In part I you add up all the *adjustments and preferences* that you are claiming on your regular tax return. In part II you calculate your AMT income by *adding* those adjustments and preferences back in to your income as found on line 37 of form 1040. (Note that in getting to line 37 of form 1040 you deducted a number of items from your gross income; now you are adding them back in. The number on line 37 is your taxable income *before* subtracting the $2,900 for each personal exemption; this essentially means that you forfeit the personal exemption under the AMT.) In part III you subtract the AMT exemption amount for your income and filing status. In part IV you adjust for long-term capital gains taxes from schedule D using the worksheet provided. When you get to the bottom of form 6251, you will compare your regular tax as shown on line 40 of form 1040 with the AMT tax that you just calculated and pay whichever amount is higher. If your regular tax is higher, you can tear up form 6251 and forget you ever had to go through this exercise. If the AMT is higher, you attach form 6251 to form 1040 and take out your checkbook.

Adjustments and Preferences for AMT

Part I of form 6251 lists a total of 28 tax-preference items that are added back into your income if you are subject to the AMT. Most of these do not apply to most people, so we will not cover them here (refer to form 6251 for the complete list). The most common tax-preference items are the following.

STANDARD DEDUCTION OR ITEMIZED DEDUCTIONS

If you took the standard deduction, you must add it back in to your income by listing it in part I under "Adjustments and preferences of form 6251." If you itemized deductions, you must add some, but not all, of those deductions back to your income.

MEDICAL EXPENSES

Under the AMT, you can deduct only those medical expenses which exceed 10 percent of your AGI. Thus, if you claimed a deduction for medical expenses that exceeded 7.5 percent of AGI on your regular tax return, and if your medical expenses did not exceed 10 percent of your AGI, you will have to add that deduction back in. If your medical expenses did exceed 10 percent of your AGI, you may deduct the part that exceeds 10 percent. Form 6251 shows you how to do this.

TAXES

State income taxes and property taxes, as noted on line 9 of schedule A, must be added back in. You can still deduct taxes paid for business or rental purposes.

INTEREST

If you took out a home equity loan and used the proceeds for some purpose other than to buy, build, or improve your home, the interest is not deductible under the AMT. You must add it back to your income on form 6251. Home mortgage interest is still deductible under the AMT. Investment interest expense claimed on form 4952 is still deductible, but you have to fill out a new form 4952 and tweak it according to AMT rules. This is where you will need either the tax code or a smart accountant.

MISCELLANEOUS ITEMIZED DEDUCTIONS

If you took a deduction for job expenses and other miscellaneous deductions that exceeded 2 percent of your AGI, the amount entered on line 26 of schedule A must be added back in.

INCENTIVE STOCK OPTIONS

For the regular tax, no income is recognized when an incentive stock option (ISO) is exercised—that is, when you buy the stock at the option price but do not sell it. However, for the AMT tax, the mere exercise of ISOs—even if you continue to hold the stock—creates a taxable event. You must add to your AMT income the difference between the option price (the price you paid) and the fair market value of the stock on the day you exercised. The silver lining here is that your basis in the stock is increased by the amount of the adjustment for AMT purposes, so when you sell, your gain (assuming you have one) will be lower than if you had to pay tax on the difference between the option price and sales price. If you sell the stock in the same year that you exercise the ISO, the tax treatment under the regular tax and the AMT is the same. No AMT adjustment is required.

PRIVATE-ACTIVITY BONDS

If you receive tax-exempt interest from private-activity bonds issued after August 7, 1986, the interest is not taxable under the regular tax, but it is a preference item under the AMT. This means that you must add it to your income on form 6251.

SPECIAL SITUATIONS

A number of other deductions must be added in for the AMT that you probably never deducted in the first place: mining exploration and development costs, depletion allowances, intangible drilling costs, and the like. If you claimed any of these deductions, you probably have a sharp accountant who will help you figure the AMT, and thus we can spare readers the details of these unusual situations.

AMT Income

In order not to add insult to injury, form 6251 does allow you to reduce your AMT income by any phaseouts you were subject to under the regular tax if you itemized deductions and your AGI is over $132,950. After all, it cannot exactly take away your deductions and then make you pay tax on the amount you were not entitled to deduct under the regular tax.

Exemption Amount

Once you have calculated your AMT income by adding back in the various adjustments and preference items in part I and subtracted the phaseout amount in part II, in part III you refer to the instructions to determine your exemption amount. This exemption amount is subtracted from your AMT income in the manner of a standard deduction. If you are single or head of household and your AMT income is $112,500 or less, your exemption amount in 2001 is $35,750. If you are married filing jointly and your AMT income is $150,000 or less, your exemption amount is $49,000. If you are married filing separately and your AMT income is $75,000 or less, your exemption amount is $24,500. If your AMT income is more than $247,500 if single or head of household, $330,000 if married filing jointly, or $165,000 if married filing separately, there is no exemption amount for you. If your AMT income is between these amounts—$112,500 to $247,000 (single or head of household), $150,000 to $330,000 (married filing jointly), or $75,000 to $165,000 (married filing separately)—you must complete the worksheet on page 7 of form 6251 instructions to determine your exemption amount.

The last thing to do in part III before determining your tax is to make an adjustment for long-term capital gains taxes. The worksheet in part IV of form 6251 will show you how to do this.

Figuring the AMT

If your AMT income after the exemption amount and adjustment for capital gains tax is $175,000 or less ($87,500 or less if married filing separately), multiply it by 26 percent. Otherwise, multiply it by 28 percent and subtract $3,500 ($1,750 if married filing separately). This is your AMT. Now compare this amount with your regular tax as shown on line 40 of form 1040. If the AMT is higher, enter the amount on line 41 and attach form 6251 to your tax return.

AMT Credit

Under a very few limited circumstances, you may be able to claim an AMT credit that gets you back, next year and in future years, some of that extra tax you paid under the AMT. The most common circumstance is if you exercised stock options and got hit with the AMT in one year and the very next year went back to paying regular tax. The credit you are allowed to take in any one year cannot exceed the difference between your regular tax and the AMT, which means that you must fill out form 6251 in order to find out what your AMT would be (and you obviously cannot claim it if you are subject to the AMT again). Use form 8801 (located in Appendix II), and follow the instructions.

AMT Relief Ahead?

Nearly everyone recognizes that the AMT has become overly burdensome on middle-income taxpayers and no longer serves the purpose for which it was intended. Congress threw it a bone with the Economic Growth and Tax Relief Reconciliation Act of 2001 by increasing the AMT exemption by $2,000 for singles and $4,000 for couples for tax years 2001 through 2004. However, after 2004, the exemptions go back to the previous amounts, and the bigger problem—lack of indexing—remains. In the years ahead, more and more people will be subject to the AMT as their salaries move into AMT range and have higher deductions resulting from increased state income tax and other items that go along with earning more income. Indeed, many of the tax breaks bestowed by the Economic Growth and Tax Relief Reconciliation Act of 2001 will be unavailable to people subject to the AMT. So far the word out of Washington is that revamping the AMT is not a priority because only the tax professionals are howling; individual taxpayers do not seem to recognize the problem and therefore are not writing their congressional representatives to get it fixed. However, the sorry state of the AMT is beginning to gain national attention, so stay tuned.

CHAPTER 12

Stock Options

You know all those warnings we have been issuing throughout this book about how tax considerations should not override investment considerations? This goes double—triple—for this chapter. Stock options have very specific tax rules associated with them. They also require alert decision making. Unlike some investments that can be bought, held, and nearly forgotten about, stock options come with certain rights and responsibilities that you must take advantage of (or not) within a specific time period. Too often people focus on the tax rules without realizing that in most cases the amount of money they will end up with is largely determined by the price of the stock. It is easy to say that if you exercise an option and hold the stock one year and a day, your gain will be taxed at 20 percent instead of 30 percent or whatever your tax bracket is if you were to sell right away. What is not so easy to say is whether you will even have a gain or, if you do, how much of one you will have. Saving 7 or 15 percentage points —the difference between the long-term capital gain rate and your highest marginal tax rate—is nothing when you are dealing with a stock that is moving up and down by 50, 80, or even 90 percent over a year's time.

One reason that people tend to focus on the taxes is that the rules are right there in black and white. Because the future price of a stock can never be known, the tendency is to focus on what you do know and make assumptions about the rest. Most people assume that the stock price will be higher in the future; some people even go so far as to estimate the percentage gain, perhaps 50 or 80 percent, and base their decisions on that scenario. Hardly anyone assumes that the stock price will be lower.

One reason for this is that people are dealing with their own company's stock. They believe in the company. Through their jobs, they are contributing personally to the company's success. Of course, they would like to think that the stock price will be higher in the future and understandably cannot be very objective when analyzing the prospects of this particular stock. However, when a person has his or her whole livelihood plus the vast majority of his or her net worth tied up in one company, it makes financial planners cringe. Is this stock really so much better than all the other stocks out there that you are willing to bet your whole financial future on it? Shouldn't you think about diversifying even a little bit?

With these caveats out of the way, we will get back to the subject at hand, which is to familiarize you with the tax implications of receiving, holding, and exercising stock options. Please remember to keep the tax angle in perspective and understand that your return largely will depend on the future value of the stock. And this is a matter of speculation and judgment, not black-and-white rules.

What Are Stock Options?

In Chapter 2 we talked about option contracts that trade on the Chicago Board Options Exchange. The stock options we will be covering in this chapter are different, but the fundamental principle is the same: An option gives you the right to buy the underlying stock at a specific price by a specific date. Usually there is a bargain element involved: If the stock is trading at, say, $10, your employer might grant you an option to buy the stock at $5. (Options are usually spoken of in plural, as in *1,000 options*. Each option gives you the right to buy one share of stock.) There are three events associated with stock options: (1) you *receive* the options, (2) you *exercise* the options—this means that you buy the stock at the option price, and (3) you *sell* the stock. The tax consequences associated with these events depend on which type of option you are dealing with.

Options come in two varieties: *nonqualified stock options* and *incentive stock options*. The tax treatment differs for each type of option, so be sure that you know which type of option you have when understanding the tax implications discussed in this chapter.

Nonqualified Options

Nonqualified options (NQSOs) are the most common type of stock option. They are generally issued to employees of profitable public companies and may be considered an important part of your compensation package. Recalling the three events associated with stock options, here are the tax implications for nonqualified options:

1. Receive the options—no taxable event

Example

On January 5, 2002, you receive options to buy 1,000 shares of XYZ at $5 per share. You stash the options away and report nothing on your tax return.

2. Exercise the options and buy the stock—taxable event. Report as ordinary income the difference between the exercise price and fair market value on the day of exercise.

Example

On February 10, 2003, you exercise the options and buy 1,000 shares of XYZ at $5 per share, investing a total of $5,000. On this date the stock is trading at $15 per share. On your 2003 tax return you report $10,000 in ordinary income. This is the difference between the exercise price ($5) and fair market value of the stock ($15) on the day of exercise multiplied times 1,000 shares. Assuming a tax bracket of 27 percent, you will pay ordinary income tax of $2,700. Your basis in the stock is now fair market value on the date of exercise, or $15,000.

3. Sell the stock—taxable event. Report long- or short-term gain or loss. Your holding period begins the day after you bought the stock, as with any other stock purchase. Your basis is fair market value on the date of exercise.

Example

On February 11, 2004, you sell the 1,000 shares of XYZ for $27 per share, netting proceeds of $27,000. On your 2004 tax return you will report the sale on schedule D. Your long-term gain is $12,000 ($27,000 − $15,000). You pay long-term capital gains tax of $2,400 ($12,000 × 20 percent).

To keep these events straight, it may help to understand how the Internal Revenue service (IRS) views this process. When you first receive the options, you really have not gotten anything yet because the value of options lies in their *potential*. When you exercise the options, you are realizing this potential by obtaining stock worth more than the exercise price. To the IRS, this "bonus" is considered compensation, and this is why it is taxed as ordinary income. After this, your investment in the stock is just like any other, no different than if you had paid cash for the shares on the open market. You are not taxed on any gain (or loss) until you sell. Your holding period begins the day after you buy the stock, and long-term gains are taxed at a maximum of 20 percent (or 18 percent if you hold the stock five years).

In view of these circumstances, it can be tempting to exercise your options as early as possible so that you will pay less ordinary income tax. For example, if you had exercised when the stock was trading at $7, you would pay ordinary income tax on just $2,000 (the difference between the $5 option price and the $7 market price). This would establish your basis at $7,000, and the rest of the appreciation, from $7 to $27, would be taxable at long-term capital gains rates.

On the other hand, what if the stock goes the other way? What if your options go *under water*—that is, the stock is trading at less than the option price? Let us say that the stock goes to $4. If you had exercised when the stock was at $7, you would have paid ordinary income tax on $2,000, yet you would be holding a losing position. If you sell the stock at $4, for tax purposes you will realize a loss of $3,000 ($7,000 − $4,000). (Your actual out-of-pocket loss will be $1,000 because you paid $5 for the stock plus the ordinary income tax you already paid on the $2,000). While there is some tax consolation in claiming a $3,000 loss, especially if it is short term, the fact remains that you have a loss. If you had not exercised the options, you would not be out anything at all. Indeed, the beauty of options lies in the fact that they give you a choice—an option, if you will. You do not have to exercise. Often it is better to wait until you are forced to exercise (either just before expiration or you leave the company) or you think the stock has reached its peak and then immediately turn around and sell the stock. Granted, you are giving up the right to pay tax at long-term capital gains rates, but at least you know you will have income to pay taxes *on*. Also, a lot of people choose to simultaneously exercise and sell for one very practical reason: You do not have to come up with the cash to exercise. Most brokerage firms offer "cashless" exercise programs that essentially lend you the money to exercise and then subtract the exercise cost from the sales proceeds.

If you do exercise and decide to hold the stock, look at your position as the IRS does: as if you had purchased the stock on the open market for cash. Do you like the stock and want to keep holding it? Does it fit with the rest of your portfolio and constitute a sound investment? Then hang onto the stock. However, do not keep it just so that you can pay tax at long-term capital gains rates because the difference between 20 and 30 percent (or whatever your tax bracket is) just is not that great, especially when you are dealing with a volatile stock.

Incentive Stock Options

Incentive stock options (ISOs) are not as common as nonqualified stock options. They are limited in number and usually reserved for executives and other important people at a company. They offer more favorable tax treatment but are not without their traps. The main difference between ISOs and NQSOs is that if you meet the holding-period requirements—that is, you hold the stock at least one year after the exercise date and two years after the grant date (the date you received the options)—all your gain qualifies for long-term capital gains treatment, and no tax is due until you sell the shares (except for a possible AMT snag, which we will get to in a minute). If you do not meet these holding-period requirements, you have what is called a *disqualifying disposition*, which means that you forfeit the favorable long-term capital gains treatment on the spread between the exercise price and fair market value on the date of exercise. In other words, under a disqualifying disposition, your ISOs are taxed as if they were NQSOs.

The AMT snag comes into play in the year you exercise your ISOs. The spread between the exercise price and fair market value on the date of exercise is considered a preference item for the AMT. If this amount in itself is large enough to trigger the AMT, or if you are subject to the AMT for other reasons, you will pay tax at AMT rates of 26 or 28 percent. If you sell the stock the same calendar year, you can avoid the AMT tax, but of course this means that you will fail to meet the one-year holding period requirement for long-term capital gains treatment.

Now let us look at the three events associated with options and how tax treatment differs for ISOs. These examples assume that the holding requirements are met and that it is not a disqualifying disposition.

EVENT 1 Receive the options—no taxable event. In this respect, ISOs are like NQSOs.

EVENT 1 Example 1

On January 5, 2002, you receive options to buy 1,000 shares of stock XYZ at $5 per share. You stash the options away and report nothing on your tax return.

EVENT 2 Exercise the options and buy the stock—no taxable event under the *regular* tax system. If the spread between the exercise price and fair market value on the date of exercise is large enough to trigger the AMT, or if you are otherwise subject to the AMT, the amount will be taxable at the AMT rate of 26 or 28 percent.

EVENT 2 Example 1

On February 10, 2003, you exercise incentive stock options and buy 1,000 shares of XYZ at $5 per share, investing a total of $5,000. On this date, the stock is trading at $15 per share. Since you are not subject to the AMT, there is nothing to report on your tax return.

EVENT 2 Example 2

Instead of receiving 1,000 incentive stock options, you received 100,000 options. On February 10, 2003, when the stock was trading at $15, you exercised your options and bought 100,000 shares of stock at $5. On your 2003 tax return, you will report a $1,000,000 ($15 − $5 × 100,000) preference item and pay AMT tax of 28 percent, or $280,000.

EVENT 3 Sell the stock—taxable event. Report the sale on schedule D. As with any stock sale, your gain is the difference between the sales proceeds and your basis (the amount you paid for the stock at exercise). Since you held the stock more than one year, your gain is taxed at a maximum of 20 percent (or 18 percent if you held the stock five years). If you paid the AMT in the year of exercise, you have a different basis for AMT purposes: Your AMT basis is increased by the amount of the adjustment.

EVENT 3 Example 1

Going back to our 1,000-share example, on February 10, 2003, you exercise ISOs and buy 1,000 shares of XYZ at $5 per share. On February 11, 2004, you sell the 1,000 shares of XYZ for $27 per share, netting proceeds of $27,000. On your 2004 tax return you will report the sale on schedule D. Your long-term gain is $22,000 ($27,000 − $5,000). You pay long-term capital gains tax of $4,400 ($22,000 × 0.20).

EVENT 3 Example 2

Using the 100,000-share example where you paid the AMT in the year you exercised, on February 11, 2004, you sell the 100,000 shares of XYZ for $27 per share, netting proceeds of $2,700,000. If you are again subject to the AMT (it is likely you will be with this size gain), your gain is the difference between the sales price ($2,700,000) and your AMT basis ($1,500,000), or $1,200,000.

The best outcome you can hope for with ISOs is that you will escape the AMT on exercise and the stock will rise into the stratosphere, giving you huge gains, all taxable at a mere 20 percent (you may have to carefully schedule your exercise and sale dates to avoid the AMT). Sometimes it does not work out this way. The worst scenario is when you exercise the options and pay the AMT and then the stock tanks. In this case you have a loss on your investment *and* you had to pay the dreaded AMT. You can get some or all of the AMT back in future years through the AMT credit, but this is small consolation when you are sitting on a big loss and cursing yourself for exercising when you did not really have to. The reason people like to exercise ISOs early is to minimize the AMT bite. As with NQSOs, the sooner you exercise (assuming that the stock is steadily rising), the smaller will be the spread between the exercise price and fair market value on the date you exercise. For example, if your exercise price is $5 and you exercise when the stock is trading at $7 instead of $20, your AMT preference amount is $2 ($\times$ the number of shares), not $15. This amount may even be low enough to escape the AMT and would be even more reason to exercise early. However, once you exercise, you have real dollars tied up in the stock, and your money is now subject to risk. Until you exercise, you get to ride the fortunes of the company without putting any of your own money at risk. Be wary of moves that offer the best tax consequences under the best market conditions but are disastrous if the stock goes the other way. In other words, maintain a healthy dose of pessimism as you analyze the investment potential of the stock in question.

If you do find yourself in the dreaded situation of having triggered the AMT after which the stock immediately tanked, you can get out of it by selling the stock before the end of the year. Yes, it will be a disqualifying disposition, which means you will be forfeiting the right to pay tax at long-term capital gains rates. However, if you have no capital gain, this obviously is not worth very much. Even if you do have a gain (for example, the stock is trading higher than your exercise price but lower than fair market value on the date of exercise), the ordinary income tax may be less than the AMT tax. For example, let us say that you have 1,000 options with an exercise price of $5. On the date of exercise, the stock is trading at $80. The $75,000 spread ($80 − $5 × 1,000) is an AMT preference item taxed at a 28-percent rate, or $21,000. Now let us say that the stock falls to $25 in December. If you sell then, you will pay ordinary income tax on the spread between the exercise price ($5) and the sales price ($25), or $20,000. At the 38.6-percent tax bracket, the tax amounts to $7,720—far less than the $21,000 in AMT tax you would have had to pay if you had kept the stock. Selling the stock before the end of the year will undo the AMT and reduce your tax bill —and may even give you a short-term capital loss. The only reason you might not do this is if you are in love with the stock and hoping against hope that it will turn around. Forget it. It probably will not. And besides, you can always buy it back after 30 days if you love it that much. (Do not buy it sooner than this or the sale may be disallowed under the wash sale rule.)

Understand Your Options

It could be said that the tax aspects of options are relatively minor compared with all the other things you must pay attention to when you are granted stock options. You must first understand what kind of options you have, nonqualified or incentive. You must know when the options become yours—that is, when you gain the right to exercise them. You must know the option price and also be aware of the current trading price so that you can estimate the value of the options at any given time. And most important, you must know when the options will expire. Almost worse than exercising an option and watching the stock tank is letting in-the-money options expire because you overlooked the expiration date or did not realize that if you left the company the options would expire. Read your option paperwork and fully understand this valuable form of compensation.

CHAPTER 13

Qualifying as a Trader

Are you so active and successful at stock trading that you consider it your business? If so, you may be able to qualify as a trader and write off many more of your investment expenses than you could as an investor. Frankly, most active investors do not qualify as traders. You have to really trade a *lot*, and although trading probably does not have to be your sole occupation, it should take up quite a bit of your time and be a consistent enough activity that it may be considered an ongoing business.

If you do qualify as a trader, you get to deduct on schedule C (located in Appendix III) the full expenses associated with running the business. These may include computers, software, office furniture, telephone lines, Internet service, fax machines, research services, assistants' salaries, office rent (or home office deduction), and more. As a trader, you are not subject to the 2-percent floor for schedule A deductions that allows ordinary investors to write off only those expenses which exceed 2 percent of their AGI. This means that you do not have to itemize deductions in order to write off your business expenses and they are not subject to phaseouts if your AGI is over $132,950. Also, your interest expense write-off is not limited to the amount of investment income you receive, as it is for ordinary investors. Furthermore, if you make the mark-to-market election (described later), you can write off more than $3,000 in losses against ordinary income and are not subject to the wash sale rule.

Do you have to show a profit? Well, at some point you should. The general rule for distinguishing a real business from a hobby business is that you should show a profit three out of five years. If you are generally making money at the business but have a couple of off years, the Internal Revenue Service (IRS) will not have a problem with your writing off more than the business earns in those bad years (as long as you meet the other tests for qualifying as a trader). However, it is probably not a good idea to go into the stock trading business for a year, during which you outfit your office and write off $24,000 worth of equipment and then exit the "business" after losing money.

IRS Rules for Traders

The IRS says that you are a *trader in securities* if you are engaged in the *business* of buying and selling securities in your own account. To be engaged in business as a trader in securities

- You must seek to profit from daily market movements in the prices of securities and not from dividends, interest, or capital appreciation.
- Your activity must be substantial.
- You must carry on the activity with continuity and regularity.

Then the IRS goes on to cite the facts and circumstances that determine if your activity is a business—but without putting any definition on those circumstances. We can surmise from court cases what the IRS is looking for but cannot point you to any IRS publications that tell you exactly what you have to do to qualify as a trader. In the instructions for schedule D, the following factors are listed as being meaningful:

- Typical holding periods for securities bought and sold. (We gather that they must be short. How short? Maybe a day, maybe a week. Definitely not months; that would make you an investor.)
- The frequency and dollar amount of your trades during the year. (Lots of trades, lots of dollars. How many? You probably should be entering several trades every day. The frequency of trading is probably more meaningful than the dollar amount invested.)
- The extent to which you pursue the activity to produce income for a livelihood. (Ideally, this should be your full-time occupation.)
- The amount of time you devote to the activity. (A few hours a week will not cut it. Is 10 hours enough? Probably not. How about 20? Maybe, as long as you enter lots of trades. Thirty hours a week probably would be enough to convince the IRS that you are serious about this.)

What if you do both trading and investing? In other words, you have some stocks that you buy to hold and others that you buy to trade? The IRS says that you can split these activities and write off the expenses associated with trading on schedule C and the expenses associated with investing (that is, those which exceed 2 percent of your AGI) on schedule A. Be sure to keep separate records and use different brokerage accounts for each activity.

Reporting Income and Expenses

With any other business, you would report both income and expenses on schedule C and carry over your net profit (or loss) to line 12 of form 1040. However, the securities trading business is unlike any other when it comes to reporting. Here, you report your stock trades on schedule D (if you are not making the mark-to-market election), incorporating commissions into your cost basis and net proceeds just as you would if you were an ordinary investor. You enter your business expenses on schedule C. Since the IRS tends to get nervous when it sees business expenses and no income on schedule C, it is a good idea to attach a statement to your tax return explaining that you are a securities trader and that your income is reported on schedule D. You do not have to pay self-employment tax on the income, even though as a securities trader you are considered self-employed. This is another one of the unusual—and beneficial—aspects of tax reporting for securities traders.

When reporting your stock trades on schedule D, the process is the same as for investors, except that you obviously will have many more pages of the schedule D continuation sheet. Unless you make the mark-to-market election, your excess trading losses are limited to $3,000 against ordinary income and you are subject to the wash sale rule, which disallows losses on securities repurchased within 30 days before or after sale. You will not need to worry about calculating the long-term capital gains tax because presumably you will not have any long-term gains. You are a *trader*, remember.

When reporting your business expenses on schedule C, you can list such expenses as margin interest, utilities, seminars, research services, and other expenses you incur in the process of conducting business. Please see IRS Publication 535 for a complete discussion of business expenses and how to report them on schedule C. In addition to your ordinary and recurring business expenses, you can deduct up to $24,000 in one year for capital equipment such as computers and office equipment used more than 50 percent of the time for your securities trading business. You also can take the home office deduction as long as you use the space regularly and exclusively for trading and the deduction does not throw you into a net loss position. Use form 8829 to claim the home office deduction.

Mark-to-Market Traders

If you choose to become a *mark-to-market trader,* you get additional tax benefits. For one, you are not subject to the wash sale rule, so you can buy and sell with abandon, writing off losses on securities you may decide to buy back 15 minutes later. For another, your losses are not limited to $3,000. However, there is extra paperwork involved in this election—and you may need professional tax help to set it up. Please note that you do not have to make the mark-to-market election to qualify as a trader, but it does offer some juicy tax breaks.

With the mark-to-market election, you book all your gains and losses on the last business day of the year as if you had sold everything and wiped the slate clean. Then you start over again on the first business day of the following year with all new cost bases for the securities you pretended to sell. Your gains are not eligible for long-term capital gains treatment, but as noted earlier, this is an unlikely proposition for traders anyway. You must make the mark-to-market election for the 2002 tax year by the time you file your 2001 tax return, normally April 15, 2002. If you request an extension, include the mark-to-market election with your extension request; do not wait until you file your tax return. Please see IRS Revenue Procedure 99-17 in Internal Revenue Bulletin 99-7 for details on how to make the mark-to-market election. When you file your tax return for the first full year as a mark-to-market trader, you have to file form 3115 to request a change in accounting method. This is a complicated form and not easy to fill out. Get some tax help with this. And finally, as a mark-to-market trader, you do not report your gains and losses on schedule D but rather on part II of form 4797, Sales of Business Property.

IRS Forms for Individuals

Form
1040A

Department of the Treasury—Internal Revenue Service

U.S. Individual Income Tax Return   (99)   **2001**   IRS Use Only—Do not write or staple in this space.

OMB No. 1545-0085

Label
(See page 20.)

L
A
B
E
L

H
E
R
E

| Your first name and initial | Last name | Your social security number |

| If a joint return, spouse's first name and initial | Last name | Spouse's social security number |

| Home address (number and street). If you have a P.O. box, see page 21. | Apt. no. | ▲ **Important!** ▲ |

| City, town or post office, state, and ZIP code. If you have a foreign address, see page 21. | | You **must** enter your SSN(s) above. |

Use the IRS label.

Otherwise, please print or type.

Presidential Election Campaign
(See page 21.)

▶ **Note.** Checking "Yes" will not change your tax or reduce your refund.
Do you, or your spouse if filing a joint return, want $3 to go to this fund? . . . ▶

You ☐ Yes ☐ No   Spouse ☐ Yes ☐ No

Filing status

Check only one box.

1 ☐ Single
2 ☐ Married filing joint return (even if only one had income)
3 ☐ Married filing separate return. Enter spouse's social security number above and full name here. ▶ _____
4 ☐ Head of household (with qualifying person). (See page 22.) If the qualifying person is a child but not your dependent, enter this child's name here. ▶ _____
5 ☐ Qualifying widow(er) with dependent child (year spouse died ▶). (See page 23.)

Exemptions

If more than seven dependents, see page 23.

6a ☐ **Yourself.** If your parent (or someone else) can claim you as a dependent on his or her tax return, **do not** check box 6a.

b ☐ **Spouse**

c Dependents:

(1) First name Last name	(2) Dependent's social security number	(3) Dependent's relationship to you	(4) ✓if qualifying child for child tax credit (see page 24)
	:		☐
	:		☐
	:		☐
	:		☐
	:		☐
	:		☐
	:		☐

No. of boxes checked on 6a and 6b ____

No. of your children on 6c who:
• lived with you ____
• did not live with you due to divorce or separation (see page 25) ____

Dependents on 6c not entered above ____

Add numbers entered on lines above ____

d Total number of exemptions claimed.

Income

Attach Form(s) W-2 here. Also attach Form(s) 1099-R if tax was withheld.

If you did not get a W-2, see page 26.

Enclose, but do not attach, any payment.

7 Wages, salaries, tips, etc. Attach Form(s) W-2. .... | 7 |

8a **Taxable** interest. Attach Schedule 1 if required. .... | 8a |
b **Tax-exempt** interest. **Do not** include on line 8a. | 8b |

9 Ordinary dividends. Attach Schedule 1 if required. .... | 9 |

10 Capital gain distributions (see page 26). .... | 10 |

11a Total IRA distributions. | 11a | **11b** Taxable amount (see page 26). | 11b |

12a Total pensions and annuities. | 12a | **12b** Taxable amount (see page 27). | 12b |

13 Unemployment compensation, qualified state tuition program earnings, and Alaska Permanent Fund dividends. | 13 |

14a Social security benefits. | 14a | **14b** Taxable amount (see page 29). | 14b |

15 Add lines 7 through 14b (far right column). This is your **total income.** ▶ | 15 |

Adjusted gross income

16 IRA deduction (see page 31). | 16 |
17 Student loan interest deduction (see page 31). | 17 |
18 Add lines 16 and 17. These are your **total adjustments.** | 18 |

19 Subtract line 18 from line 15. This is your **adjusted gross income.** ▶ | 19 |

For Disclosure, Privacy Act, and Paperwork Reduction Act Notice, see page 55.   Cat. No. 11327A   Form **1040A** (2001)

FORM 1040A

Form 1040A (2001)   Page **2**

Tax, credits, and payments	20	Enter the amount from line 19 (adjusted gross income).		20	

	21a	Check if: ☐ **You** were 65 or older ☐ Blind ☐ **Spouse** was 65 or older ☐ Blind ⎱ Enter number of boxes checked ▶ 21a ☐			

Standard Deduction for—

• People who checked any box on line 21a or 21b **or** who can be claimed as a dependent, see page 33.

• All others:
Single, $4,550

Head of household, $6,650

Married filing jointly or Qualifying widow(er), $7,600

Married filing separately, $3,800

	b	If you are married filing separately and your spouse itemizes deductions, see page 33 and check here . . . . ▶ 21b ☐		
	22	Enter your **standard deduction** (see left margin).		22
	23	Subtract line 22 from line 20. If line 22 is more than line 20, enter -0-.		23
	24	Multiply $2,900 by the total number of exemptions claimed on line 6d.		24
	25	Subtract line 24 from line 23. If line 24 is more than line 23, enter -0-. This is your **taxable income.** ▶		25
	26	**Tax,** including any alternative minimum tax (see page 34).		26
	27	Credit for child and dependent care expenses. Attach Schedule 2.	27	
	28	Credit for the elderly or the disabled. Attach Schedule 3.	28	
	29	Education credits. Attach Form 8863.	29	
	30	Child tax credit (see page 37).	30	
	31	Adoption credit. Attach Form 8839.	31	
	32	Rate reduction credit. See the worksheet on page xx.	32	
	33	Add lines 27 through 32. These are your **total credits.**		33
	34	Subtract line 33 from line 26. If line 33 is more than line 26, enter -0-.		34
	35	Advance earned income credit payments from Form(s) W-2.		35
	36	Add lines 34 and 35. This is your **total tax.** ▶		36
	37	Federal income tax withheld from Forms W-2 and 1099.	37	
	38	2001 estimated tax payments and amount applied from 2000 return.	38	

If you have a qualifying child, attach Schedule EIC.

	39a	**Earned income credit (EIC).**	39a	
	b	Nontaxable earned income. 39b		
	40	Additional child tax credit. Attach Form 8812.	40	
	41	Add lines 37, 38, 39a, and 40. These are your **total payments.** ▶		41

Refund	42	If line 41 is more than line 36, subtract line 36 from line 41. This is the amount you **overpaid.**		42

Direct deposit? See page 48 and fill in 43b, 43c, and 43d.

	43a	Amount of line 42 you want **refunded to you.** ▶		43a
	▶ b	Routing number ☐☐☐☐☐☐☐☐☐ ▶ **c** Type: ☐ Checking ☐ Savings		
	▶ d	Account number ☐☐☐☐☐☐☐☐☐☐☐☐☐☐☐☐☐		
	44	Amount of line 42 you want **applied to your 2002 estimated tax.**	44	

Amount you owe	45	**Amount you owe.** Subtract line 41 from line 36. For details on how to pay, see page 49. ▶		45
	46	Estimated tax penalty (see page 49).	46	

Third party designee	Do you want to allow another person to discuss this return with the IRS (see page 52)? ☐ **Yes.** Complete the following. ☐ **No**

Designee's name ▶   Phone no. ▶ (   )   Personal identification number (PIN) ▶ ☐☐☐☐☐

Sign here

Under penalties of perjury, I declare that I have examined this return and accompanying schedules and statements, and to the best of my knowledge and belief, they are true, correct, and accurately list all amounts and sources of income I received during the tax year. Declaration of preparer (other than the taxpayer) is based on all information of which the preparer has any knowledge.

Joint return? See page 21.

Keep a copy for your records.

Your signature	Date	Your occupation	Daytime phone number ( )
Spouse's signature. If a joint return, **both** must sign.	Date	Spouse's occupation	

Paid preparer's use only

Preparer's signature ▶	Date	Check if self-employed ☐	Preparer's SSN or PTIN
Firm's name (or yours if self-employed), address, and ZIP code ▶		EIN	
		Phone no. ( )	

Form **1040A** (2001)

FORM 1040A *(Continued)*

Department of the Treasury—Internal Revenue Service

Form
1040EZ

**Income Tax Return for Single and
Joint Filers With No Dependents** (99) **2001**

OMB No. 1545-0675

Label

(See page 12.)
**Use the IRS
label.**
Otherwise,
please print
or type.

L
A
B
E
L

H
E
R
E

Your first name and initial | Last name

Your social security number

If a joint return, spouse's first name and initial | Last name

Spouse's social security number

Home address (number and street). If you have a P.O. box, see page 21. | Apt. no.

▲ **Important!** ▲
You **must** enter your
SSN(s) above.

City, town or post office, state, and ZIP code. If you have a foreign address, see page 21.

**Presidential
Election
Campaign**
(page 12)

Note. Checking "Yes" will not change your tax or reduce your refund.
Do you, or spouse if a joint return, want $3 to go to this fund? . . . . ▶

| | You | Spouse |
| | ☐ Yes ☐ No | ☐ Yes ☐ No |

Income

**Attach
Form(s) W-2
here.**
Enclose, but
do not attach,
any payment.

Note. You
must check
Yes or No.

1 Total wages, salaries, and tips. This should be shown in box 1 of your W-2
   form(s). Attach your W-2 form(s). | 1

2 Taxable interest. If the total is over $400, you cannot use Form 1040EZ. | 2

3 Unemployment compensation, qualified state tuition program earnings, and
   Alaska Permanent Fund dividends (see page 14). | 3

4 Add lines 1, 2, and 3. This is your **adjusted gross income.** | 4

5 Can your parents (or someone else) claim you on their return?
   Yes. Enter amount from ☐ worksheet on back.   **No.** If **single,** enter 7,450.00.
   If **married,** enter 13,400.00.
   See back for explanation. | 5

6 Subtract line 5 from line 4. If line 5 is larger than line 4, enter 0.
   This is your **taxable income.** ▶ | 6

**Credits,
payments,
and tax**

7 Rate reduction credit. See the worksheet on page 14. | 7

8 Enter your Federal income tax withheld from box 2 of your W-2 form(s). | 8

9a **Earned income credit (EIC).** See page 15. | 9a

 b Nontaxable earned income.   9b

10 Add lines 7, 8, and 9a. These are your **total credits and payments.** ▶ | 10

11 **Tax.** Use the amount on **line 6 above** to find your tax in the tax table on pages
    24–28 of the booklet. Then, enter the tax from the table on this line. | 11

Refund

Have it directly
deposited! See page
20 and fill in 12b,
12c, and 12d.

12a If line 10 is larger than line 11, subtract line 11 from line 10. This is your **refund.** ▶ | 12a

 b Routing number

 c Type: ☐ Checking ☐ Savings

 d Account number

**Amount
you owe**

13 If line 11 is larger than line 10, subtract line 10 from line 11. This is
    the **amount you owe.** See page 21 for details on how to pay. ▶ | 13

**Third party
designee**

Do you want to allow another person to discuss this return with the IRS (see page 8)? ☐ **Yes.** Complete the following. ☐ **No**

Designee's
name ▶   Phone
no. ▶ (   )   Personal identification
number (PIN)

**Sign
here**

Joint return?
See page 21.

Keep a copy
for your
records.

Under penalties of perjury, I declare that I have examined this return, and to the best of my knowledge and belief, it is true, correct, and
accurately lists all amounts and sources of income I received during the tax year. Declaration of preparer (other than the taxpayer) is based
on all information of which the preparer has any knowledge.

Your signature | Date | Your occupation | Daytime phone number

Spouse's signature. If a joint return, **both** must sign. | Date | Spouse's occupation

**Paid
preparer's
use only**

Preparer's
signature ▶   Date   Check if
self-employed ☐   Preparer's SSN or PTIN

Firm's name (or
yours if self-employed),
address, and ZIP code ▶   EIN
Phone no. (   )

For Disclosure, Privacy Act, and Paperwork Reduction Act Notice, see page 23.   Cat. No. 11329W   Form **1040EZ** (2001)

FORM 1040EZ

SCHEDULES A&B	**Schedule A—Itemized Deductions**	OMB No. 1545-0074
(Form 1040)	(Schedule B is on back)	**2001**
Department of the Treasury Internal Revenue Service (99)	► **Attach to Form 1040.** ► **See Instructions for Schedules A and B (Form 1040).**	Attachment Sequence No. **07**

Name(s) shown on Form 1040

Your social security number

Medical and Dental Expenses		**Caution.** Do not include expenses reimbursed or paid by others.		
	1	Medical and dental expenses (see page A-2)	1	
	2	Enter amount from Form 1040, line 34 .	2			
	3	Multiply line 2 above by 7.5% (.075)	3	
	4	Subtract line 3 from line 1. If line 3 is more than line 1, enter -0-		4
Taxes You Paid (See page A-2.)	5	State and local income taxes	5	
	6	Real estate taxes (see page A-2)	6	
	7	Personal property taxes	7	
	8	Other taxes. List type and amount ►	8	
	9	Add lines 5 through 8		9
Interest You Paid (See page A-3.) **Note.** Personal interest is not deductible.	10	Home mortgage interest and points reported to you on Form 1098	10	
	11	Home mortgage interest not reported to you on Form 1098. If paid to the person from whom you bought the home, see page A-3 and show that person's name, identifying no., and address ► ------------------------------------ ------------------------------------	11	
	12	Points not reported to you on Form 1098. See page A-3 for special rules	12	
	13	Investment interest. Attach Form 4952 if required. (See page A-3.)	13	
	14	Add lines 10 through 13		14
Gifts to Charity If you made a gift and got a benefit for it, see page A-4.	15	Gifts by cash or check. If you made any gift of $250 or more, see page A-4	15	
	16	Other than by cash or check. If any gift of $250 or more, see page A-4. You **must** attach Form 8283 if over $500	16	
	17	Carryover from prior year	17	
	18	Add lines 15 through 17		18
Casualty and Theft Losses	19	Casualty or theft loss(es). Attach Form 4684. (See page A-5.)		19
Job Expenses and Most Other Miscellaneous Deductions (See page A-5 for expenses to deduct here.)	20	Unreimbursed employee expenses—job travel, union dues, job education, etc. You **must** attach Form 2106 or 2106-EZ if required. (See page A-5.) ► .... ------------------------------------	20	
	21	Tax preparation fees	21	
	22	Other expenses—investment, safe deposit box, etc. List type and amount ►	22	
	23	Add lines 20 through 22	23	
	24	Enter amount from Form 1040, line 34 .	24			
	25	Multiply line 24 above by 2% (.02)	25	
	26	Subtract line 25 from line 23. If line 25 is more than line 23, enter -0- . . .		26
Other Miscellaneous Deductions	27	Other—from list on page A-6. List type and amount ► .... ------------------------------------		27
Total Itemized Deductions	28	Is Form 1040, line 34, over $132,950 (over $66,475 if married filing separately)? ☐ **No.** Your deduction is not limited. Add the amounts in the far right column for lines 4 through 27. Also, enter this amount on Form 1040, line 36. ☐ **Yes.** Your deduction may be limited. See page A-6 for the amount to enter.	►	28

For Paperwork Reduction Act Notice, see Form 1040 instructions.   Cat. No. 11330X   Schedule A (Form 1040) 2001

FORM 1040, Schedule A

Schedules A&B (Form 1040) 2001

OMB No. 1545-0074   Page **2**

Name(s) shown on Form 1040. Do not enter name and social security number if shown on other side.

Your social security number

Schedule B—Interest and Ordinary Dividends

Attachment
Sequence No. **08**

		Amount	
Part I **Interest** (See page B-1 and the instructions for Form 1040, line 8a.) **Note.** If you received a Form 1099-INT, Form 1099-OID, or substitute statement from a brokerage firm, list the firm's name as the payer and enter the total interest shown on that form.	**1** List name of payer. If any interest is from a seller-financed mortgage and the buyer used the property as a personal residence, see page B-1 and list this interest first. Also, show that buyer's social security number and address ▶		
	2 Add the amounts on line 1	**2**	
	3 Excludable interest on series EE and I U.S. savings bonds issued after 1989 from Form 8815, line 14. You **must** attach Form 8815	**3**	
	4 Subtract line 3 from line 2. Enter the result here and on Form 1040, line 8a ▶	**4**	
	Note. If line 4 is over $400, you must complete Part III.		

		Amount	
Part II **Ordinary** **Dividends** (See page B-1 and the instructions for Form 1040, line 9.) **Note.** If you received a Form 1099-DIV or substitute statement from a brokerage firm, list the firm's name as the payer and enter the ordinary dividends shown on that form.	**5** List name of payer. Include only ordinary dividends. If you received any capital gain distributions, see the instructions for Form 1040, line 13 ▶		
	6 Add the amounts on line 5. Enter the total here and on Form 1040, line 9 . ▶	**6**	
	Note. If line 6 is over $400, you must complete Part III.		

		Yes	No
Part III **Foreign** **Accounts** **and Trusts** (See page B-2.)	You must complete this part if you **(a)** had over $400 of taxable interest or ordinary dividends; **(b)** had a foreign account; or **(c)** received a distribution from, or were a grantor of, or a transferor to, a foreign trust.		
	7a At any time during 2001, did you have an interest in or a signature or other authority over a financial account in a foreign country, such as a bank account, securities account, or other financial account? See page B-2 for exceptions and filing requirements for Form TD F 90-22.1		
	b If "Yes," enter the name of the foreign country ▶		
	8 During 2001, did you receive a distribution from, or were you the grantor of, or transferor to, a foreign trust? If "Yes," you may have to file Form 3520. See page B-2		

For Paperwork Reduction Act Notice, see Form 1040 instructions.

Schedule B (Form 1040) 2001

FORM 1040, Schedule B

Schedule 1 Department of the Treasury—Internal Revenue Service
(Form 1040A) **Interest and Ordinary Dividends
for Form 1040A Filers** (99)   **2001**   OMB No. 1545-0085

Name(s) shown on Form 1040A | Your social security number

Part I

Interest

(See page 62 and the instructions for Form 1040A, line 8a.)

Note. If you received a Form 1099-INT, Form 1099-OID, or substitute statement from a brokerage firm, enter the firm's name and the total interest shown on that form.

1 List name of payer. If any interest is from a seller-financed mortgage and the buyer used the property as a personal residence, see page 62 and list this interest first. Also, show that buyer's social security number and address.   Amount

1		

2 Add the amounts on line 1. | 2 | |
3 Excludable interest on series EE and I U.S. savings bonds issued after 1989 from Form 8815, line 14. You **must** attach Form 8815. | 3 | |
4 Subtract line 3 from line 2. Enter the result here and on Form 1040A, line 8a. | 4 | |

Part II

Ordinary dividends

(See page 62 and the instructions for Form 1040A, line 9.)

Note. If you received a Form 1099-DIV or substitute statement from a brokerage firm, enter the firm's name and the ordinary dividends shown on that form.

5 List name of payer. Include only ordinary dividends. If you received any capital gain distributions, see the instructions for Form 1040A, line 10.   Amount

5		

6 Add the amounts on line 5. Enter the total here and on Form 1040A, line 9. | 6 | |

For Paperwork Reduction Act Notice, see Form 1040A instructions.   Cat. No. 12075R   Schedule 1 (Form 1040A) 2001

FORM 1040A, Schedule 1

SCHEDULE D
(Form 1040)

Department of the Treasury
Internal Revenue Service (99)

Capital Gains and Losses

► Attach to Form 1040.   ► See Instructions for Schedule D (Form 1040).

► Use Schedule D-1 to list additional transactions for lines 1 and 8.

OMB No. 1545-0074

2001

Attachment
Sequence No. **12**

Name(s) shown on Form 1040

Your social security number

Part I   Short-Term Capital Gains and Losses—Assets Held One Year or Less

(a) Description of property (Example: 100 sh. XYZ Co.)	(b) Date acquired (Mo., day, yr.)	(c) Date sold (Mo., day, yr.)	(d) Sales price (see page D-5 of the instructions)	(e) Cost or other basis (see page D-5 of the instructions)	(f) Gain or (loss) Subtract (e) from (d)	
1						

2 Enter your short-term totals, if any, from Schedule D-1, line 2 . . . . | **2** | | | |

3 Total short-term sales price amounts. Add lines 1 and 2 in column (d) . . . . . | **3** | | | |

4 Short-term gain from Form 6252 and short-term gain or (loss) from Forms 4684, 6781, and 8824 . . . . | **4** | |

5 Net short-term gain or (loss) from partnerships, S corporations, estates, and trusts from Schedule(s) K-1 . . . . | **5** | |

6 Short-term capital loss carryover. Enter the amount, if any, from line 8 of your 2000 Capital Loss Carryover Worksheet . . . . | **6** | ( ) |

7 **Net short-term capital gain or (loss).** Combine lines 1 through 6 in column (f). | **7** | |

Part II   Long-Term Capital Gains and Losses—Assets Held More Than One Year

(a) Description of property (Example: 100 sh. XYZ Co.)	(b) Date acquired (Mo., day, yr.)	(c) Date sold (Mo., day, yr.)	(d) Sales price (see page D-5 of the instructions)	(e) Cost or other basis (see page D-5 of the instructions)	(f) Gain or (loss) Subtract (e) from (d)	(g) 28% rate gain or (loss) * (see instr. below)
8						

9 Enter your long-term totals, if any, from Schedule D-1, line 9 . . . . | **9** | | | | |

10 Total long-term sales price amounts. Add lines 8 and 9 in column (d) . . . . . | **10** | | | | |

11 Gain from Form 4797, Part I; long-term gain from Forms 2439 and 6252; and long-term gain or (loss) from Forms 4684, 6781, and 8824 . . . . | **11** | | |

12 Net long-term gain or (loss) from partnerships, S corporations, estates, and trusts from Schedule(s) K-1. . . . . | **12** | | |

13 Capital gain distributions. See page D-1 of the instructions . . . . | **13** | | |

14 Long-term capital loss carryover. Enter in both columns (f) and (g) the amount, if any, from line 13 of your 2000 Capital Loss Carryover Worksheet . . . . . . | **14** | ( ) | ( ) |

15 Combine lines 8 through 14 in column (g) . . . . | **15** | | |

16 **Net long-term capital gain or (loss).** Combine lines 8 through 14 in column (f) **Next:** Go to Part III on the back. | **16** | | |

*28% rate gain or loss includes **all** "collectibles gains and losses" (as defined on page D-5 of the instructions) and up to 50% of the eligible gain on qualified small business stock (see page D-4 of the instructions).

For Paperwork Reduction Act Notice, see Form 1040 instructions.   Cat. No. 11338H   Schedule D (Form 1040) 2001

FORM 1040, Schedule D

Schedule D (Form 1040) 2001   Page **2**

Part III   Taxable Gain or Deductible Loss

17 Combine lines 7 and 16 and enter the result. If a loss, go to line 18. If a gain, enter the gain on Form 1040, line 13, and complete Form 1040 through line 39 . . . .   **17**

     Next: • If both lines 16 and 17 are gains **and** Form 1040, line 39, is more than zero, complete Part IV below.
          • Otherwise, skip the rest of Schedule D and complete Form 1040.

18 If line 17 is a loss, enter the **smaller** of that loss or ($3,000) (or, if married filing separately, ($1,500)) here and on Form 1040, line 13. Then complete Form 1040 through line 37 . . . .   **18** (   )

     Next: • If the loss on line 17 is more than the loss on line 18 **or** if Form 1040, line 37, is less than zero, skip **Part IV** below and complete the **Capital Loss Carryover Worksheet** on page D-6 of the instructions before completing the rest of Form 1040.
          • Otherwise, skip **Part IV** below and complete the rest of Form 1040.

Part IV   Tax Computation Using Maximum Capital Gains Rates

19 Enter your unrecaptured section 1250 gain, if any, from line 17 of the worksheet on page D-7 of the instructions **19**

     If line 15 or line 19 is more than zero, see the instructions for line 40 on page D-8 of the instructions. Otherwise, go to line 20.

20 Enter your taxable income from Form 1040, line 39 . . . . .   **20**

21 Enter the **smaller** of line 16 or line 17 . .   **21**

22 If you are deducting investment interest expense on Form 4952, enter the amount from Form 4952, line 4e. Otherwise, enter -0-   **22**

23 Subtract line 22 from line 21. If zero or less, enter -0- **23**

24 Subtract line 23 from line 20. If zero or less, enter -0- **24**

25 Figure the tax on the amount on line 24. Use the Tax Table or Tax Rate Schedules, whichever applies   **25**

26 Enter the **smaller** of:
     • The amount on line 20 **or**
     • $45,200 if married filing jointly or qualifying widow(er);
       $27,050 if single;
       $36,250 if head of household; or   . . .   **26**
       $22,600 if married filing separately

     If line 26 is greater than line 24, go to line 27. Otherwise, skip lines 27 through 33 and go to line 34.

27 Enter the amount from line 24 . . . .   **27**

28 Subtract line 27 from line 26. If zero or less, enter -0- and go to line 34   **28**

29 Enter your qualified 5-year gain, if any, from line 5 of the worksheet on page D-8 . .   **29**

30 Enter the **smaller** of line 28 or line 29 . . . .   **30**

31 Multiply line 30 by 8% (.08) **31**

32 Subtract line 30 from line 28 . . . .   **32**

33 Multiply line 32 by 10% (.10) **33**

     If the amounts on lines 23 and 28 are the same, skip lines 34 through 37 and go to line 38.

34 Enter the **smaller** of line 20 or line 23 . . . .   **34**

35 Enter the amount from line 28 (if line 28 is blank, enter -0-) . . .   **35**

36 Subtract line 35 from line 34 . . . .   **36**

37 Multiply line 36 by 20% (.20) **37**

38 Add lines 25, 31, 33, and 37 . . . .   **38**

39 Figure the tax on the amount on line 20. Use the Tax Table or Tax Rate Schedules, whichever applies   **39**

40 **Tax on all taxable income (including capital gains). Enter the smaller** of line 38 or line 39 here and on Form 1040, line 40 . . . .   **40**

✺

Schedule D (Form 1040) 2001

FORM 1040, Schedule D *(Continued)*

SCHEDULE D-1
(Form 1040)

Department of the Treasury
Internal Revenue Service (99)

Continuation Sheet for Schedule D
(Form 1040)

▶ See instructions for Schedule D (Form 1040).
▶ Attach to Schedule D to list additional transactions for lines 1 and 8.

OMB No. 1545-0074

2001

Attachment
Sequence No. **12A**

Name(s) shown on Form 1040

Your social security number

| Part I | Short-Term Capital Gains and Losses—Assets Held One Year or Less |

(a) Description of property (Example: 100 sh. XYZ Co.)	(b) Date acquired (Mo., day, yr.)	(c) Date sold (Mo., day, yr.)	(d) Sales price (see page D-5 of the instructions)	(e) Cost or other basis (see page D-5 of the instructions)	(f) Gain or (loss). Subtract (e) from (d)	
1						
2 Totals. Combine columns (d) and (f). Enter here and on Schedule D, line 2 . . . . ▶ 2						

For Paperwork Reduction Act Notice, see Form 1040 instructions.

Cat. No. 10424K

Schedule D-1 (Form 1040) 2001

FORM 1040, Schedule D-1

Name(s) shown on Form 1040. Do not enter name and social security number if shown on other side. | Your social security number

Part II   Long-Term Capital Gains and Losses—Assets Held More Than One Year

(a) Description of property (Example: 100 sh. XYZ Co.)	(b) Date acquired (Mo., day, yr.)	(c) Date sold (Mo., day, yr.)	(d) Sales price (see page D-5 of the instructions)	(e) Cost or other basis (see page D-5 of the instructions)	(f) Gain or (loss). Subtract (e) from (d)	(g) 28% rate gain or (loss) * (see instr. below)
8						
9 **Totals.** Combine columns (d), (f), and (g). Enter here and on Schedule D, line 9 . . . . . . ▶ **9**						

*28% rate gain or loss includes all "collectibles gains and losses" (as defined on page D-5 of the instructions) and up to 50% of the eligible gain on qualified small business stock (see page D-4 of the instructions).

FORM 1040, Schedule D-1 *(Continued)*

SCHEDULE E
(Form 1040)

Department of the Treasury
Internal Revenue Service (99)

Supplemental Income and Loss
(From rental real estate, royalties, partnerships,
S corporations, estates, trusts, REMICs, etc.)

► **Attach to Form 1040 or Form 1041.** ► **See Instructions for Schedule E (Form 1040).**

OMB No. 1545-0074

2001

Attachment
Sequence No. **13**

Name(s) shown on return

Your social security number

Part I	**Income or Loss From Rental Real Estate and Royalties**	**Note.** If you are in the business of renting personal property, use **Schedule C or C-EZ** (see page E-1). Report farm rental income or loss from **Form 4835** on page 2, line 39.

1	Show the kind and location of each **rental real estate property:**		2	For each rental real estate property listed on line 1, did you or your family use it during the tax year for personal purposes for more than the greater of:		Yes	No
A	....			• 14 days **or**	A		
B	....			• 10% of the total days rented at fair rental value?	B		
C	....			(See page E-1.)	C		

Income:

			Properties			Totals
			A	B	C	(Add columns A, B, and C.)
3	Rents received	**3**				**3**
4	Royalties received	**4**				**4**

Expenses:

5	Advertising	**5**				
6	Auto and travel (see page E-2) .	**6**				
7	Cleaning and maintenance . . .	**7**				
8	Commissions	**8**				
9	Insurance	**9**				
10	Legal and other professional fees	**10**				
11	Management fees	**11**				
12	Mortgage interest paid to banks, etc. (see page E-2)	**12**				**12**
13	Other interest	**13**				
14	Repairs	**14**				
15	Supplies	**15**				
16	Taxes	**16**				
17	Utilities	**17**				
18	Other (list) ►	**18**				
19	Add lines 5 through 18	**19**				**19**
20	Depreciation expense or depletion (see page E-3)	**20**				**20**
21	Total expenses. Add lines 19 and 20	**21**				
22	Income or (loss) from rental real estate or royalty properties. Subtract line 21 from line 3 (rents) or line 4 (royalties). If the result is a (loss), see page E-3 to find out if you must file **Form 6198** . . .	**22**				
23	Deductible rental real estate loss. **Caution.** Your rental real estate loss on line 22 may be limited. See page E-3 to find out if you must file **Form 8582**. Real estate professionals must complete line 42 on page 2	**23**	( )	( )	( )	
24	**Income.** Add positive amounts shown on line 22. **Do not** include any losses				**24**	
25	**Losses.** Add royalty losses from line 22 and rental real estate losses from line 23. Enter total losses here				**25**	( )
26	**Total rental real estate and royalty income or (loss).** Combine lines 24 and 25. Enter the result here. If Parts II, III, IV, and line 39 on page 2 do not apply to you, also enter this amount on Form 1040, line 17. Otherwise, include this amount in the total on line 40 on page 2				**26**	

For Paperwork Reduction Act Notice, see Form 1040 instructions. Cat. No. 11344L Schedule E (Form 1040) 2001

FORM 1040, Schedule E

Schedule E (Form 1040) 2001   Attachment Sequence No. **13**   Page **2**

Name(s) shown on return. Do not enter name and social security number if shown on other side.	Your social security number

Note. If you report amounts from farming or fishing on Schedule E, you must enter your gross income from those activities on line 41 below. Real estate professionals must complete line 42 below.

Part II — Income or Loss From Partnerships and S Corporations

Note. If you report a loss from an at-risk activity, you **must** check either column (e) or (f) on line 27 to describe your investment in the activity. See page E-5. If you check column (f), you must attach **Form 6198**.

27	(a) Name	(b) Enter **P** for partnership; **S** for S corporation	(c) Check if foreign partnership	(d) Employer identification number	Investment At Risk? (e) All is at risk	(f) Some is not at risk
A						
B						
C						
D						
E						

	Passive Income and Loss		Nonpassive Income and Loss		
	(g) Passive loss allowed (attach **Form 8582** if required)	(h) Passive income from **Schedule K-1**	(i) Nonpassive loss from **Schedule K-1**	(j) Section 179 expense deduction from **Form 4562**	(k) Nonpassive income from **Schedule K-1**
A					
B					
C					
D					
E					
28a Totals					
b Totals					

29 Add columns (h) and (k) of line 28a **29**

30 Add columns (g), (i), and (j) of line 28b . . . .   **30** (   )

31 Total partnership and S corporation income or (loss). Combine lines 29 and 30. Enter the result here and include in the total on line 40 below **31**

Part III — Income or Loss From Estates and Trusts

32	(a) Name	(b) Employer identification number
A		
B		

	Passive Income and Loss		Nonpassive Income and Loss	
	(c) Passive deduction or loss allowed (attach **Form 8582** if required)	(d) Passive income from **Schedule K-1**	(e) Deduction or loss from **Schedule K-1**	(f) Other income from **Schedule K-1**
A				
B				
33a Totals				
b Totals				

34 Add columns (d) and (f) of line 33a **34**

35 Add columns (c) and (e) of line 33b . . . .   **35** (   )

36 Total estate and trust income or (loss). Combine lines 34 and 35. Enter the result here and include in the total on line 40 below **36**

Part IV — Income or Loss From Real Estate Mortgage Investment Conduits (REMICs)—Residual Holder

37	(a) Name	(b) Employer identification number	(c) Excess inclusion from **Schedules Q**, line 2c (see page E-6)	(d) Taxable income (net loss) from **Schedules Q**, line 1b	(e) Income from **Schedules Q**, line 3b

38 Combine columns (d) and (e) only. Enter the result here and include in the total on line 40 below   **38**

Part V — Summary

39 Net farm rental income or (loss) from **Form 4835**. Also, complete line 41 below **39**

40 **Total** income or (loss). Combine lines 26, 31, 36, 38, and 39. Enter the result here and on Form 1040, line 17 ▶   **40**

41 **Reconciliation of Farming and Fishing Income.** Enter your **gross** farming and fishing income reported on Form 4835, line 7; Schedule K-1 (Form 1065), line 15b; Schedule K-1 (Form 1120S), line 23; and Schedule K-1 (Form 1041), line 14 (see page E-6) **41**

42 **Reconciliation for Real Estate Professionals.** If you were a real estate professional (see page E-4), enter the net income or (loss) you reported anywhere on Form 1040 from all rental real estate activities in which you materially participated under the passive activity loss rules . . .   **42**

⊛   Schedule E (Form 1040) 2001

FORM 1040, Schedule E *(Continued)*

☐ CORRECTED (if checked)

PAYER'S name, street address, city, state, ZIP code, and telephone no.	Payer's RTN (optional)	OMB No. 1545-0112	
		20**01** Form **1099-INT**	**Interest Income**
PAYER'S Federal identification number · RECIPIENT'S identification number	1 Interest income not included in box 3 $		**Copy B** **For Recipient**
RECIPIENT'S name	2 Early withdrawal penalty $	3 Interest on U.S. Savings Bonds and Treas. obligations $	This is important tax information and is being furnished to the Internal Revenue
Street address (including apt. no.)	4 Federal income tax withheld $	5 Investment expenses $	Service. If you are required to file a return, a negligence penalty or
City, state, and ZIP code	6 Foreign tax paid	7 Foreign country or U.S. possession	other sanction may be imposed on you if this income is taxable and
Account number (optional)	$		the IRS determines that it has not been reported.

Form **1099-INT** (Keep for your records.) Department of the Treasury - Internal Revenue Service

☐ CORRECTED (if checked)

PAYER'S name, street address, city, state, ZIP code, and telephone no.	1 Ordinary dividends $	OMB No. 1545-0110	
	2a Total capital gain distr. $	20**01**	**Dividends and Distributions**
	2b 28% rate gain $	Form **1099-DIV**	
PAYER'S Federal identification number · RECIPIENT'S identification number	2c Qualified 5-year gain $	2d Unrecap. sec. 1250 gain $	**Copy B** **For Recipient**
RECIPIENT'S name	2e Section 1202 gain $	3 Nontaxable distributions $	This is important tax information and is being furnished to the Internal Revenue
Street address (including apt. no.)	4 Federal income tax withheld $	5 Investment expenses $	Service. If you are required to file a return, a negligence penalty or
City, state, and ZIP code	6 Foreign tax paid $	7 Foreign country or U.S. possession	other sanction may be imposed on you if this income is taxable and
Account number (optional)	8 Cash liquidation distr. $	9 Noncash liquidation distr. $	the IRS determines that it has not been reported.

Form **1099-DIV** (Keep for your records.) Department of the Treasury - Internal Revenue Service

☐ CORRECTED (if checked)

PAYER'S name, street address, city, state, ZIP code, and telephone no.	1 Original issue discount for 2001* $	OMB No. 1545-0117	
	2 Other periodic interest $	20**01** Form **1099-OID**	**Original Issue Discount**
PAYER'S Federal identification number · RECIPIENT'S identification number	3 Early withdrawal penalty $	4 Federal income tax withheld $	**Copy B** **For Recipient**
RECIPIENT'S name	5 Description		This is important tax information and is being furnished to the Internal Revenue Service. If you are
Street address (including apt. no.)	6 Original issue discount on U.S. Treasury obligations*		required to file a return, a negligence penalty or other
City, state, and ZIP code	7 Investment expenses $		sanction may be imposed on you if this income is taxable and
Account number (optional)	* This may not be the correct figure to report on your income tax return. See instructions on the back.		the IRS determines that it has not been reported.

Form **1099-OID** (Keep for your records.) Department of the Treasury - Internal Revenue Service

FORMS 1099-INT, 1099-DIV, and 1099-OID

Form **4952**	**Investment Interest Expense Deduction**	OMB No. 1545-0191
Department of the Treasury Internal Revenue Service (99)	▶ **Attach to your tax return.**	**2001** Attachment Sequence No. **72**

Name(s) shown on return	Identifying number

Part I   Total Investment Interest Expense

1	Investment interest expense paid or accrued in 2001. See instructions	**1**
2	Disallowed investment interest expense from 2000 Form 4952, line 7	**2**
3	**Total investment interest expense.** Add lines 1 and 2	**3**

Part II   Net Investment Income

4a	Gross income from property held for investment (excluding any net gain from the disposition of property held for investment)	**4a**	
b	Net gain from the disposition of property held for investment . . .	**4b**	
c	Net capital gain from the disposition of property held for investment	**4c**	
d	Subtract line 4c from line 4b. If zero or less, enter -0-	**4d**	
e	Enter the amount from line 4c that you elect to include in investment income. Do not enter more than the amount on line 4b. See instructions . . . . ▶	**4e**	
f	Investment income. Add lines 4a, 4d, and 4e. See instructions	**4f**	
5	Investment expenses. See instructions	**5**	
6	**Net investment income.** Subtract line 5 from line 4f. If zero or less, enter -0-	**6**	

Part III   Investment Interest Expense Deduction

7	Disallowed investment interest expense to be carried forward to 2002. Subtract line 6 from line 3. If zero or less, enter -0-	**7**
8	**Investment interest expense deduction.** Enter the **smaller** of line 3 or 6. See instructions .	**8**

Section references are to the Internal Revenue Code unless otherwise noted.

General Instructions

Purpose of Form

Use Form 4952 to figure the amount of investment interest expense you can deduct for 2001 and the amount you can carry forward to future years. Your investment interest expense deduction is limited to your net investment income.

For additional information, see **Pub. 550,** Investment Income and Expenses.

Who Must File

If you are an individual, estate, or a trust and you claim a deduction for investment interest expense, you must complete Form 4952 and attach it to your tax return unless **all** of the following apply.

● Your investment interest expense is not more than your investment income from interest and ordinary dividends.

● You have no other deductible investment expenses.

● You have no disallowed investment interest expense from 2000.

Allocation of Interest Expense Under Temporary Regulations Section 1.163-8T

If you paid or accrued interest on a loan and used the loan proceeds for more than one purpose, you may have to allocate the interest. This is necessary because different rules apply to investment interest, personal interest, trade or business interest, home mortgage interest, and passive activity interest. See **Pub. 535,** Business Expenses.

Specific Instructions

Part I—Total Investment Interest Expense

Line 1

Enter the investment interest expense paid or accrued during the tax year, regardless of when you incurred the indebtedness. **Investment interest expense** is interest paid or accrued on a loan or part of a loan that is allocable to property held for investment (as defined on page 2).

Include investment interest expense reported to you on Schedule K-1 from a partnership or an S corporation. Include

amortization of bond premium on taxable bonds purchased after October 22, 1986, but before January 1, 1988, unless you elected to offset amortizable bond premium against the interest payments on the bond. A taxable bond is a bond on which the interest is includible in gross income.

Investment interest expense **does not** include any of the following:

● Home mortgage interest.

● Interest expense that is properly allocable to a passive activity. Generally, a passive activity is any business activity in which you **do not** materially participate and any rental activity. See the separate instructions for **Form 8582,** Passive Activity Loss Limitations, for details.

● Any interest expense that is capitalized, such as construction interest subject to section 263A.

● Interest expense related to tax-exempt interest income under section 265.

● Interest expense, disallowed under section 264, on indebtedness with respect to life insurance, endowment, or annuity contracts issued after June 8, 1997, even if the proceeds were used to purchase any property held for investment.

For Paperwork Reduction Act Notice, see back.   Cat. No. 13177Y   Form **4952** (2001)

FORM 4952

☐ CORRECTED (if checked)

FILER'S name, street address, city, state, ZIP code, and telephone no.	**1** Date of closing	OMB No. 1545-0997	
	2 Gross proceeds $	**2001** Form **1099-S**	**Proceeds From Real Estate Transactions**

FILER'S Federal identification number	TRANSFEROR'S identification number	**3** Address or legal description	**Copy B**
TRANSFEROR'S name			**For Transferor** This is important tax information and is being furnished to the Internal Revenue Service. If you are required to file a return, a negligence penalty or other sanction may be imposed on you if this item is required to be reported and the IRS determines that it has not been reported.
Street address (including apt. no.)			
City, state, and ZIP code		**4** Transferor received or will receive property or services as part of the consideration (if checked) . . . ▶ ☐	
Account number (optional)		**5** Buyer's part of real estate tax $	

Form **1099-S**   (Keep for your records.)   Department of the Treasury - Internal Revenue Service

---

☐ CORRECTED (if checked)

TRUSTEE'S or ISSUER'S name, street address, city, state, and ZIP code	**1** IRA contributions (other than amounts in boxes 2, 3, 4, and 8–11) $	OMB No. 1545-0747	
	2 Rollover contributions $	**2001** Form **5498**	**IRA Contribution Information**

TRUSTEE'S or ISSUER'S Federal identification no.	PARTICIPANT'S social security number	**3** Roth conversion amount $	**4** Recharacterized contributions $	**Copy B**
PARTICIPANT'S name		**5** Fair market value of account $	**6** Life insurance cost included in box 1 $	**For Participant**
Street address (including apt. no.)		**7** IRA ☐ SEP ☐ SIMPLE ☐ Roth IRA ☐ Ed IRA ☐		This information is being furnished to the Internal Revenue Service.
City, state, and ZIP code		**8** SEP contributions $	**9** SIMPLE contributions $	
Account number (optional)		**10** Roth IRA contributions $	**11** Ed IRA contributions $	

Form **5498**   (Keep for your records.)   Department of the Treasury - Internal Revenue Service

FORMS 1099-S and 5498

Form **8606**	**Nondeductible IRAs and Coverdell ESAs**	OMB No. 1545-1007
Department of the Treasury Internal Revenue Service (99)	▶ See separate instructions. ▶ Attach to Form 1040, Form 1040A, or Form 1040NR.	**2001** Attachment Sequence No. **48**

Name. If married, file a separate form for each spouse required to file Form 8606. See page 3 of the instructions. | **Your social security number**

Fill in Your Address Only if You Are Filing This Form by Itself and Not With Your Tax Return ▷

Home address (number and street, or P.O. box if mail is not delivered to your home) | Apt. no.

City, town or post office, state, and ZIP code

Part I | **Nondeductible Contributions to Traditional IRAs and Distributions From Traditional, SEP, and SIMPLE IRAs**

Complete Part I only if:
- You made nondeductible contributions to a traditional IRA for 2001,
- You took distributions from a traditional, SEP, or SIMPLE IRA in 2001 (other than a rollover, conversion, recharacterization, or return of certain contributions) **and** you made nondeductible contributions to a traditional IRA in 2001 or an earlier year, **or**
- You converted part, but not all, of your traditional, SEP, and SIMPLE IRAs to Roth IRAs in 2001 (excluding any portion you recharacterized) **and** you made nondeductible contributions to a traditional IRA in 2001 or an earlier year.

1   Enter your nondeductible contributions to traditional IRAs for 2001, including those made for 2001 from January 1, 2002, through April 15, 2002 (see page 3 of the instructions) **1**

2   Enter your total basis in traditional IRAs for 2000 and earlier years (see page 3 of the instructions)   **2**

3   Add lines 1 and 2   . . . .   **3**

> **In 2001, did you take a distribution from traditional, SEP, or SIMPLE IRAs or make a Roth IRA conversion?**   **No** ──▶ Enter the amount from line 3 on line 14. Do not complete the rest of Part I.
>
>   **Yes** ──▶ Go to line 4.

4   Enter those contributions included on line 1 that were made from January 1, 2002, through April 15, 2002   **4**

5   Subtract line 4 from line 3   . . . .   **5**

6   Enter the value of **all** your traditional, SEP, and SIMPLE IRAs as of December 31, 2001, plus any outstanding rollovers (see page 4 of the instructions) **6**

7   Enter your distributions from traditional, SEP, and SIMPLE IRAs in 2001. **Do not** include rollovers, conversions to a Roth IRA, certain returned contributions, or recharacterizations of traditional or SEP IRA contributions (see page 4 of the instructions) **7**

8   Enter the net amount you converted from traditional, SEP, and SIMPLE IRAs to Roth IRAs in 2001. **Do not** include any portion of an amount converted that you later recharacterized (see page 4 of the instructions). Also enter this amount on line 16   . . . .   **8**

9   Add lines 6, 7, and 8   . . . . . .   **9**

10   Divide line 5 by line 9. Enter the result as a decimal rounded to at least 3 places. If the result is 1.0 or more, enter 1.0   . . . . . .   **10**   ×   .

11   Multiply line 8 by line 10. This is the nontaxable portion of the amount you converted to Roth IRAs. Also enter this amount on line 17   . .   **11**

12   Multiply line 7 by line 10. This is the nontaxable portion of your distributions that you did not convert to a Roth IRA **12**

13   Add lines 11 and 12. This is the nontaxable portion of all your distributions **13**

14   Subtract line 13 from line 3. This is **your total basis in traditional IRAs for 2001 and earlier years** **14**

15   **Taxable distributions from traditional, SEP, and SIMPLE IRAs.** Subtract line 12 from line 7. Also include this amount on Form 1040, line 15b; Form 1040A, line 11b; or Form 1040NR, line 16b . .   **15**

> **Note:** *You may be subject to an additional 10% tax on the amount on line 15 if you were under age 59½ at the time of the distribution (see page 4 of the instructions).*

For Paperwork Reduction Act Notice, see page 8 of the instructions.   Cat. No. 63966F   Form **8606** (2001)

FORM 8606

Form 8606 (2001)   Page **2**

Part II Conversions From Traditional, SEP, or SIMPLE IRAs to Roth IRAs

Complete Part II if you converted part or all of your traditional, SEP, and SIMPLE IRAs to a Roth IRA in 2001 (excluding any portion you recharacterized).

Caution: *If your modified adjusted gross income is over $100,000 **or** you are married filing separately and you lived with your spouse at any time in 2001, you **cannot** convert any amount from traditional, SEP, or SIMPLE IRAs to Roth IRAs for 2001. If you erroneously made a conversion, you must recharacterize (correct) it (see page 3 of the instructions).*

16	Enter the net amount you converted from traditional, SEP, and SIMPLE IRAs to Roth IRAs in 2001. **Do not** include any portion that you later recharacterized back to traditional, SEP, or SIMPLE IRAs in 2001 or 2002. If you completed Part I, enter the amount from line 8. Otherwise, see page 6 of the instructions	**16**
17	Enter your basis in the amount on line 16. If you completed Part I, enter the amount from line 11. Otherwise, see page 6 of the instructions	**17**
18	**Taxable amount of Roth IRA conversions.** Subtract line 17 from line 16. Also include this amount on Form 1040, line 15b; Form 1040A, line 11b; or Form 1040NR, line 16b	**18**

Part III Distributions From Roth IRAs

Complete Part III only if you took a distribution from a Roth IRA in 2001 (other than a rollover, recharacterization, or return of certain contributions—see page 6 of the instructions).

19	Enter your total distributions from Roth IRAs in 2001. **Do not** include rollovers, recharacterizations of Roth IRA conversions or contributions, or certain returned contributions (see page 6) . . .	**19**
20	Enter your basis in Roth IRA contributions (see page 6 of the instructions)	**20**
21	Subtract line 20 from line 19 (see **Note** below). If zero or less, enter -0- and skip lines 22 and 23 .	**21**
22	Enter your basis in Roth IRA conversions (see page 7 of the instructions)	**22**
23	Subtract line 22 from line 21. If zero or less, enter -0-	**23**

If you made a Roth IRA conversion in 1998 and are reporting the taxable portion over 4 years, go to line 24. Otherwise, skip lines 24 through 26 and go to line 27.

24	Enter the amount from your 1998 Form 8606, line 17	**24**	
25	Enter the sum of the amounts, if any, on your: 1998 Form 8606, line 22; 1999 Form 8606, line 21; and 2000 Form 8606, line 21. . . .	**25**	
26	Subtract line 25 from line 24. If zero or less, enter -0-		**26**
27	**Taxable distributions from Roth IRAs.** Add lines 23 and 26. Also include this amount on Form 1040, line 15b; Form 1040A, line 11b; or Form 1040NR, line 16b		**27**

Note: *You may be subject to an additional tax on Form 5329 of up to 10% of the amount on line 21 if you were under age 59½ at the time of the distribution (see page 7 of the instructions).*

Part IV Distributions From Coverdell Education Savings Accounts (ESAs)

Complete Part IV only if you took a distribution from a Coverdell ESA in 2001, other than a rollover or returned excess contributions (see page 7 of the instructions).

28	Enter your total distributions from Coverdell ESAs in 2001. **Do not** include rollovers or returned excess contributions	**28**
29	Do you elect to waive the exclusion from income for Coverdell ESA distributions? If you check "No" and exclude from income any portion of your Coverdell ESA distributions, no one may claim a Hope or lifetime learning credit for your 2001 qualified higher education expenses.	**29**

    ☐ **Yes.** Enter -0-.
    ☐ **No.** Enter your qualified higher education expenses for 2001.

30   **Taxable amount.** Is line 28 equal to or less than line 29?

    ☐ **Yes.** Enter -0-. None of your Coverdell ESA distributions are taxable for 2001. Keep a copy of this form to figure your basis in future years (see page 7 of the instructions).

    ☐ **No.** See the worksheet on page 7 of the instructions for the amount to enter. Also include this amount in the total on Form 1040, line 15b; Form 1040A, line 11b; or Form 1040NR, line 16b. If you checked "No" on line 29, see page 8 of the instructions to find out if you owe an additional 10% tax on Form 5329.   **30**

Sign Here Only if You Are Filing This Form by Itself and Not With Your Tax Return

Under penalties of perjury, I declare that I have examined this form, including accompanying attachments, and to the best of my knowledge and belief, it is true, correct, and complete.

▶ _____ ▶ _____
    Your signature   Date

Form **8606** (2001)

FORM 8606 *(Continued)*

☐ CORRECTED (if checked)

PAYER'S name, street address, city, state, and ZIP code		**1** Gross distribution $	OMB No. 1545-0119 2̶0̶01 Form **1099-R**	**Distributions From Pensions, Annuities, Retirement or Profit-Sharing Plans, IRAs, Insurance Contracts, etc.**
		2a Taxable amount $		
		2b Taxable amount not determined ☐	Total distribution ☐	**Copy B**
PAYER'S Federal identification number	RECIPIENT'S identification number	**3** Capital gain (included in box 2a) $	**4** Federal income tax withheld $	**Report this income on your Federal tax return. If this form shows Federal income**
RECIPIENT'S name		**5** Employee contributions or insurance premiums $	**6** Net unrealized appreciation in employer's securities $	**tax withheld in box 4, attach this copy to your return.**
Street address (including apt. no.)		**7** Distribution code	IRA/ SEP/ SIMPLE ☐	**8** Other $ ___ %	This information is being furnished to the Internal
City, state, and ZIP code		**9a** Your percentage of total distribution ___ %	**9b** Total employee contributions $	Revenue Service.
Account number (optional)		**10** State tax withheld $ $	**11** State/Payer's state no.	**12** State distribution $ $
		13 Local tax withheld $ $	**14** Name of locality	**15** Local distribution $ $

Form **1099-R**　　　　　　　　　　　　　　　　Department of the Treasury - Internal Revenue Service

FORM 1099-R

Form **5329**	**Additional Taxes on Qualified Plans (Including IRAs) and Other Tax-Favored Accounts**	OMB No. 1545-0203 **2001**
Department of the Treasury Internal Revenue Service	► Attach to Form 1040. ► See separate instructions.	Attachment Sequence No. **29**

Name of individual subject to additional tax. If married filing jointly, see page 2 of the instructions. | Your social security number

Fill in Your Address Only If You Are Filing This Form by Itself and Not With Your Tax Return	Home address (number and street), or P.O. box if mail is not delivered to your home	Apt. no.
	City, town or post office, state, and ZIP code	If this is an amended return, check here ► ☐

If you **only** owe the 10% tax on early distributions and distribution code 1 is correctly shown on Form 1099-R, you may be able to report this tax directly on Form 1040, line 55, without filing Form 5329. See the instructions for Form 1040, line 55.

Part I **Tax on Early Distributions**

Complete this part if a taxable distribution was made from your qualified retirement plan, including an IRA, or modified endowment contract before you reached age 59½. If you received a Form 1099-R that incorrectly indicates an early distribution or you received a Roth IRA distribution, you also may have to complete this part. See page 2 of the instructions.

Note: *You must include the taxable amount of the distribution on Form 1040, line 15b or 16b.*

1	Early distributions included in gross income. For Roth IRA distributions, see page 2 of the instructions	**1**		
2	Early distributions not subject to additional tax. Enter the appropriate exception number from page 2 of the instructions: _____	**2**		
3	Amount subject to additional tax. Subtract line 2 from line 1	**3**		
4	**Tax due.** Enter 10% (.10) of line 3. Also include this amount on Form 1040, line 55	**4**		
	Caution: *If any part of the amount on line 3 was a distribution from a SIMPLE IRA, you may have to include 25% of that amount on line 4 instead of 10% (see page 3).*			

Part II **Tax on Certain Taxable Distributions From Coverdell Education Savings Accounts (ESAs)**

Complete this part if you had a taxable amount on Form 8606, line 30.

Note: *You must include the taxable amount of the distribution on Form 1040, line 15b.*

5	Taxable distributions from your Coverdell ESAs, from Form 8606, line 30	**5**		
6	Taxable distributions not subject to additional tax (see page 3)	**6**		
7	Amount subject to additional tax. Subtract line 6 from line 5	**7**		
8	**Tax due.** Enter 10% (.10) of line 7. Also include this amount on Form 1040, line 55	**8**		

Part III **Tax on Excess Contributions to Traditional IRAs**

Complete this part if you contributed more to your traditional IRAs for 2001 than is allowable or you had an excess contribution on line 16 of your 2000 Form 5329.

9	Enter your excess contributions from line 16 of your 2000 Form 5329. If zero, go to line 15 . .	**9**		
10	If your traditional IRA contributions for 2001 are less than your maximum allowable contribution, see page 3. Otherwise, enter -0- .	**10**		
11	Taxable 2001 distributions from your traditional IRAs	**11**		
12	2001 withdrawals of prior year excess contributions included on line 9 (see page 3)	**12**		
13	Add lines 10, 11, and 12	**13**		
14	Prior year excess contributions. Subtract line 13 from line 9. If zero or less, enter -0-	**14**		
15	Excess contributions for 2001 (see page 3). Do not include this amount on Form 1040, line 23 .	**15**		
16	Total excess contributions. Add lines 14 and 15	**16**		
17	**Tax due.** Enter 6% (.06) of the **smaller** of line 16 **or** the value of your traditional IRAs on December 31, 2001 (including contributions for 2001 made in 2002). Also include this amount on Form 1040, line 55 . .	**17**		

For Paperwork Reduction Act Notice, see page 4 of separate instructions.   Cat. No. 13329Q   Form **5329** (2001)

FORM 5329

Form 5329 (2001)   Page **2**

| **Part IV** | **Tax on Excess Contributions to Roth IRAs** |

Complete this part if you contributed more to your Roth IRAs for 2001 than is allowable or you had an excess contribution on line 24 of your 2000 Form 5329.

18	Enter your excess contributions from line 24 of your 2000 Form 5329. If zero, go to line 23 . .	18	
19	If your Roth IRA contributions for 2001 are less than your maximum allowable contribution, see page 3. Otherwise, enter -0-	19		
20	2001 distributions from your Roth IRAs (see page 3)	20		
21	Add lines 19 and 20	21	
22	Prior year excess contributions. Subtract line 21 from line 18. If zero or less, enter -0- . . .	22	
23	Excess contributions for 2001 (see page 3)	23	
24	Total excess contributions. Add lines 22 and 23	24	
25	**Tax due.** Enter 6% (.06) of the **smaller** of line 24 **or** the value of your Roth IRAs on December 31, 2001 (including contributions for 2001 made in 2002). Also include this amount on Form 1040, line 55 . . .	25	

| **Part V** | **Tax on Excess Contributions to Coverdell ESAs** |

Complete this part if the contributions to your Coverdell ESAs in 2001 were more than is allowable or you had an excess contribution on line 32 of your 2000 Form 5329.

26	Enter the excess contributions from line 32 of your 2000 Form 5329. If zero, go to line 31 . .	26	
27	If the contributions to your Coverdell ESAs in 2001 were less than the maximum allowable contribution, see page 3. Otherwise, enter -0- . .	27		
28	2001 distributions from your Coverdell ESAs, from Form 8606, line 28	28		
29	Add lines 27 and 28	29	
30	Prior year excess contributions. Subtract line 29 from line 26. If zero or less, enter -0- . . .	30	
31	Excess contributions for 2001 (see page 4)	31	
32	Total excess contributions. Add lines 30 and 31	32	
33	**Tax due.** Enter 6% (.06) of the **smaller** of line 32 **or** the value of your Coverdell ESAs on December 31, 2001. Also include this amount on Form 1040, line 55	33	

| **Part VI** | **Tax on Excess Contributions to Archer MSAs** |

Complete this part if you or your employer contributed more to your Archer MSAs in 2001 than is allowable or you had an excess contribution on line 40 of your 2000 Form 5329.

34	Enter the excess contributions from line 40 of your 2000 Form 5329. If zero, go to line 39 . .	34	
35	If the contributions to your Archer MSAs for 2001 are less than the maximum allowable contribution, see page 4. Otherwise, enter -0-	35		
36	Taxable 2001 distributions from your Archer MSAs, from Form 8853, line 10	36		
37	Add lines 35 and 36	37	
38	Prior year excess contributions. Subtract line 37 from line 34. If zero or less, enter -0- . . .	38	
39	Excess contributions for 2001 (see page 4). Do not include this amount on Form 1040, line 25	39	
40	Total excess contributions. Add lines 38 and 39	40	
41	**Tax due.** Enter 6% (.06) of the **smaller** of line 40 **or** the value of your Archer MSAs on December 31, 2001. Also include this amount on Form 1040, line 55	41	

| **Part VII** | **Tax on Excess Accumulation in Qualified Retirement Plans** |

Complete this part if you did not receive the minimum required distribution from your qualified retirement plan, including an IRA.

42	Minimum required distribution (see page 4)	42	
43	Amount actually distributed to you	43	
44	Subtract line 43 from line 42. If zero or less, enter -0-	44	
45	**Tax due.** Enter 50% (.50) of line 44. Also include this amount on Form 1040, line 55	45	

Signature. Complete **only** if you are filing this form by itself and not with your tax return.

| **Please Sign Here** | Under penalties of perjury, I declare that I have examined this form, including accompanying schedules and statements, and to the best of my knowledge and belief, it is true, correct, and complete. Declaration of preparer (other than taxpayer) is based on all information of which preparer has any knowledge. |
| | ▶ Your signature | ▶ Date |

Paid Preparer's Use Only	Preparer's signature ▶		Date	Check if self-employed ☐	Preparer's SSN or PTIN
	Firm's name (or yours if self-employed), address, and ZIP code			EIN	
				Phone no. ( )	

⊛   Form **5329** (2001)

FORM 5329 *(Continued)*

Form **4972**

Department of the Treasury
Internal Revenue Service (99)

Tax on Lump-Sum Distributions

(From Qualified Plans of Participants Born Before 1936)

▶ Attach to Form 1040 or Form 1041.

OMB No. 1545-0193

2001

Attachment
Sequence No. **28**

Name of recipient of distribution

Identifying number

Part I	Complete this part to see if you can use Form 4972

			Yes	No
1	Was this a distribution of a plan participant's entire balance (excluding deductible voluntary employee contributions and certain forfeited amounts) from all of an employer's qualified plans of one kind (pension, profit-sharing, or stock bonus)? If "No," **do not** use this form	**1**		
2	Did you roll over any part of the distribution? If "Yes," **do not** use this form	**2**		
3	Was this distribution paid to you as a beneficiary of a plan participant who was born before 1936? . . .	**3**		
4	Were you **(a)** a plan participant who received this distribution, **(b)** born before 1936, **and (c)** a participant in the plan for at least 5 years before the year of the distribution?	**4**		
	If you answered "No" to both questions 3 **and** 4, **do not** use this form.			
5a	Did you use Form 4972 after 1986 for a previous distribution from your own plan? If "Yes," **do not** use this form for a 2001 distribution from your own plan	**5a**		
b	If you are receiving this distribution as a beneficiary of a plan participant who died, did you use Form 4972 for a previous distribution received for that participant after 1986? If "Yes," **do not** use the form for this distribution	**5b**		

Part II	Complete this part to choose the 20% capital gain election (see instructions)

6	Capital gain part from Form 1099-R, box 3 . . . . ▶	**6**	
7	Multiply line 6 by 20% (.20) . . . . ▶	**7**	
	If you also choose to use Part III, go to line 8. Otherwise, include the amount from line 7 in the total on Form 1040, line 40, or Form 1041, Schedule G, line 1b, whichever applies.		

Part III	Complete this part to choose the 10-year tax option (see instructions)

8	Ordinary income from Form 1099-R, box 2a minus box 3. If you did not complete Part II, enter the taxable amount from Form 1099-R, box 2a.	**8**	
9	Death benefit exclusion for a beneficiary of a plan participant who died before August 21, 1996	**9**	
10	Total taxable amount. Subtract line 9 from line 8	**10**	
11	Current actuarial value of annuity from Form 1099-R, box 8. If none, enter -0-	**11**	
12	Adjusted total taxable amount. Add lines 10 and 11. If this amount is $70,000 or more, **skip** lines 13 through 16, enter this amount on line 17, and go to line 18	**12**	
13	Multiply line 12 by 50% (.50), but **do not** enter more than $10,000 . **13**		
14	Subtract $20,000 from line 12. If line 12 is $20,000 or less, enter -0- **14**		
15	Multiply line 14 by 20% (.20) **15**		
16	Minimum distribution allowance. Subtract line 15 from line 13	**16**	
17	Subtract line 16 from line 12	**17**	
18	Federal estate tax attributable to lump-sum distribution	**18**	
19	Subtract line 18 from line 17. If line 11 is zero, **skip** lines 20 through 22 and go to line 23 . .	**19**	
20	Divide line 11 by line 12 and enter the result as a decimal (rounded to at least three places). . . . . **20** .		
21	Multiply line 16 by the decimal on line 20 . . . . **21**		
22	Subtract line 21 from line 11 . . . . **22**		
23	Multiply line 19 by 10% (.10)	**23**	
24	Tax on amount on line 23. Use the Tax Rate Schedule in the instructions	**24**	
25	Multiply line 24 by ten (10). If line 11 is zero, **skip** lines 26 through 28, enter this amount on line 29, and go to line 30	**25**	
26	Multiply line 22 by 10% (.10) **26**		
27	Tax on amount on line 26. Use the Tax Rate Schedule in the instructions **27**		
28	Multiply line 27 by ten (10) . . . . ▶	**28**	
29	Subtract line 28 from line 25. (Multiple recipients, see instructions.) . . . . ▶	**29**	
30	**Tax on lump-sum distribution.** Add lines 7 and 29. Also include this amount in the total on Form 1040, line 40, or Form 1041, Schedule G, line 1b, whichever applies . . . . . . ▶	**30**	

For Paperwork Reduction Act Notice, see instructions.

Cat. No. 13187U

Form **4972** (2001)

FORM 4972

□ CORRECTED (if checked)

RECIPIENT'S/LENDER'S name, address, and telephone number		OMB No. 1545-1576 20**01** Form **1098-E**	**Student Loan Interest Statement**
RECIPIENT'S Federal identification no.	BORROWER'S social security number	**1** Student loan interest received by lender $	**Copy B** **For Borrower**
BORROWER'S name			This is important tax information and is being furnished to the Internal Revenue Service. If you are required to file a return, a negligence penalty or other sanction may be imposed on you if the IRS determines that an underpayment of tax results because you overstated a deduction for student loan interest.
Street address (including apt. no.)			
City, state, and ZIP code			
Account number (optional)		**2** Box 1 includes loan origination fees and/or capitalized interest (if checked) . . . . . □	

Form **1098-E**   (Keep for your records.)   Department of the Treasury - Internal Revenue Service

□ CORRECTED (if checked)

PAYER'S name, street address, city, state, ZIP code, and telephone no.		**1** Unemployment compensation $	OMB No. 1545-0120 20**01**	**Certain Government and Qualified State Tuition Program Payments**
		2 State or local income tax refunds, credits, or offsets $	Form **1099-G**	
PAYER'S Federal identification number	RECIPIENT'S identification number	**3** Box 2 amount is for tax year	**4** Federal income tax withheld $	**Copy B** **For Recipient**
RECIPIENT'S name		**5** Qualified state tuition program earnings $	**6** Taxable grants $	This is important tax information and is being furnished to the Internal Revenue Service. If you are required to file a return, a negligence penalty or other sanction may be imposed on you if this income is taxable and the IRS determines that it has not been reported.
Street address (including apt. no.)		**7** Agriculture payments $	**8** The amount in box 2 applies to income from a trade or business ► □	
City, state, and ZIP code				
Account number (optional)				

Form **1099-G**   (Keep for your records.)   Department of the Treasury - Internal Revenue Service

FORMS 1098-E and 1099-G

Form **8815**

Department of the Treasury
Internal Revenue Service (99)

**Exclusion of Interest From Series EE and I
U.S. Savings Bonds Issued After 1989**
(For Filers With Qualified Higher Education Expenses)
▶ Attach to Form 1040 or Form 1040A.

OMB No. 1545-1173

2001

Attachment
Sequence No. **57**

Name(s) shown on return

Your social security number

1	**(a)** Name of person (you, your spouse, or your dependent) who was enrolled at or attended an eligible educational institution	**(b)** Name and address of eligible educational institution

If you need more space, attach a statement.

2	Enter the total qualified higher education expenses you paid in 2001 for the person(s) listed in column (a) of line 1. See the instructions to find out which expenses qualify	**2**
3	Enter the total of any nontaxable educational benefits (such as nontaxable scholarship or fellowship grants) received for 2001 for the person(s) listed in column (a) of line 1. See the instructions	**3**
4	Subtract line 3 from line 2. If zero or less, **stop.** You **cannot** take the exclusion	**4**
5	Enter the total proceeds (principal and interest) from all series EE and I U.S. savings bonds issued after 1989 that you **cashed during 2001**	**5**
6	Enter the interest included on line 5. See instructions	**6**
7	If line 4 is equal to or more than line 5, enter "1.000." If line 4 is less than line 5, divide line 4 by line 5. Enter the result as a decimal (rounded to at least three places)	**7**	× .
8	Multiply line 6 by line 7	**8**
9	Enter your modified adjusted gross income. See instructions . . . **Note:** *If line 9 is $70,750 or more if single or head of household, or $113,650 or more if married filing jointly or qualifying widow(er),* **stop.** *You* **cannot** *take the exclusion.*	**9**
10	Enter: $55,750 if single or head of household; $83,650 if married filing jointly or qualifying widow(er)	**10**
11	Subtract line 10 from line 9. If zero or less, skip line 12, enter -0- on line 13, and go to line 14	**11**
12	Divide line 11 by: $15,000 if single or head of household; $30,000 if married filing jointly or qualifying widow(er). Enter the result as a decimal (rounded to at least three places)	**12**	× .
13	Multiply line 8 by line 12	**13**
14	**Excludable savings bond interest.** Subtract line 13 from line 8. Enter the result here and on Schedule B (Form 1040), line 3, or Schedule 1 (Form 1040A), line 3, whichever applies . . ▶	**14**

General Instructions

Section references are to the Internal Revenue Code.

Purpose of Form

If you cashed series EE or I U.S. savings bonds in 2001 that were issued after 1989, you may be able to exclude from your income part or all of the interest on those bonds. Use this form to figure the amount of any interest you may exclude.

Who May Take the Exclusion

You may take the exclusion if **all four** of the following apply.

1. You cashed qualified U.S. savings bonds in 2001 that were issued after 1989.

2. You paid qualified higher education expenses in 2001 for yourself, your spouse, or your dependents.

3. Your filing status is any status **except** married filing separately.

4. Your modified AGI (adjusted gross income) is less than: $70,750 if single or head of household; $113,650 if married filing jointly or qualifying widow(er). See the instructions for line 9 to figure your modified AGI.

U.S. Savings Bonds That Qualify for Exclusion

To qualify for the exclusion, the bonds must be series EE or I U.S. savings bonds issued after 1989 in your name, or, if you are married, they may be issued in your name and your spouse's name. Also, you must have been age 24 or older before the bonds were issued. A bond bought by a parent and issued in the name of his or her child under age 24 does not qualify for the exclusion by the parent or child.

Recordkeeping Requirements

Keep the following records to verify interest you exclude.

● Bills, receipts, canceled checks, or other documents showing you paid qualified higher education expenses in 2001.

● A written record of each post-1989 series EE or I bond that you cash. Your record must include the serial number, issue date, face value, and total redemption proceeds (principal and interest) of each bond. You may use **Form 8818**, Optional Form To Record Redemption of Series EE and I U.S. Savings Bonds Issued After 1989.

For Paperwork Reduction Act Notice, see back of form.

Cat. No. 10822S

Form **8815** (2001)

FORM 8815

Form **8863**	**Education Credits** **(Hope and Lifetime Learning Credits)**	OMB No. 1545-1618
Department of the Treasury Internal Revenue Service	▶ See instructions on pages 2 and 3. ▶ Attach to Form 1040 or Form 1040A.	**2001** Attachment Sequence No. **50**
Name(s) shown on return		Your social security number

Part I   Hope Credit. Caution: *The Hope credit may be claimed for no more than **2** tax years for the **same** student.*

1

(a) Student's name (as shown on page 1 of your tax return) First, Last	(b) Student's social security number (as shown on page 1 of your tax return)	(c) Qualified expenses (but **do not** enter more than $2,000 for each student). See instructions	(d) Enter the **smaller** of the amount in column (c) or $1,000	(e) Subtract column (d) from column (c)	(f) Enter one-half of the amount in column (e)
....					
....					
....					

2   Add the amounts in columns (d) and (f)   . . . . .   **2**   ///////////////

3   Tentative Hope credit. Add the amounts on line 2, columns (d) and (f)   . . . . . . ▶   **3**

Part II   Lifetime Learning Credit

4

	(a) Student's name (as shown on page 1 of your tax return) First Last	(b) Student's social security number (as shown on page 1 of your tax return)	(c) Qualified expenses. See instructions
Caution: *You cannot take the Hope credit and the lifetime learning credit for the same student.*			

5   Add the amounts on line 4, column (c), and enter the total **5**
6   Enter the **smaller** of line 5 or $5,000   . . . .   **6**

7   Tentative lifetime learning credit. Multiply line 6 by 20% (.20)   . . . . ▶   **7**

Part III   Allowable Education Credits

8   Tentative education credits. Add lines 3 and 7 . . . .   **8**
9   Enter: $100,000 if married filing jointly; $50,000 if single, head of household, or qualifying widow(er) **9**
10   Enter the amount from Form 1040, line 34 (or Form 1040A, line 20)*   **10**
11   Subtract line 10 from line 9. If line 10 is equal to or more than line 9, **stop;** you cannot take any education credits **11**
12   Enter: $20,000 if married filing jointly; $10,000 if single, head of household, or qualifying widow(er) **12**
13   If line 11 is equal to or more than line 12, enter the amount from line 8 on line 14 and go to line 15. If line 11 is less than line 12, divide line 11 by line 12. Enter the result as a decimal (rounded to at least three places) . . . .   **13**   ✕ .

14   Multiply line 8 by line 13 . . . . ▶   **14**
15   Enter the amount from Form 1040, line 42 (or Form 1040A, line 26) **15**
16   Enter the total, if any, of your credits from Form 1040, lines 43 through 45 (or from Form 1040A, lines 27 and 28) **16**
17   Subtract line 16 from line 15. If line 16 is equal to or more than line 15, **stop;** you cannot take any education credits **17**
18   **Education credits.** Enter the **smaller** of line 14 or line 17 here and on Form 1040, line 46 (or Form 1040A, line 29)   . . . . ▶   **18**

*See Pub. 970 for the amount to enter if you are filing Form 2555, 2555-EZ, or 4563 or you are excluding income from Puerto Rico.

For Paperwork Reduction Act Notice, see page 4.   Cat. No. 25379M   Form **8863** (2001)

FORM 8863

Form **709**		**United States Gift (and Generation-Skipping Transfer) Tax Return**		OMB No. 1545-0020	
		(Section 6019 of the Internal Revenue Code) (For gifts made during calendar year 2001)		**2001**	
Department of the Treasury Internal Revenue Service		▶ **See separate instructions.**			

Part 1—General Information

						Yes	No
1	Donor's first name and middle initial		2 Donor's last name		3 **Donor's social security number**		
4	Address (number, street, and apartment number)				5 Legal residence (domicile) (county and state)		
6	City, state, and ZIP code				7 Citizenship		

		Yes	No
8	If the donor died during the year, check here ▶ ☐ and enter date of death................... , ...		
9	If you received an extension of time to file this Form 709, check here ▶ ☐ and attach the Form 4868, 2688, 2350, or extension letter .		
10	Enter the total number of separate donees listed on Schedule A—count each person only once. ▶		
11a	Have you (the donor) previously filed a Form 709 (or 709-A) for any other year? If the answer is "No," do not complete line 11b .		
11b	If the answer to line 11a is "Yes," has your address changed since you last filed Form 709 (or 709-A)?		
12	Gifts by husband or wife to third parties.—Do you consent to have the gifts (including generation-skipping transfers) made by you and by your spouse to third parties during the calendar year considered as made one-half by each of you? (See instructions.) (If the answer is "Yes," the following information must be furnished and your spouse must sign the consent shown below. **If the answer is "No," skip lines 13–18 and go to Schedule A.**)		
13	Name of consenting spouse	14 SSN	
15	Were you married to one another during the entire calendar year? (see instructions)		
16	If the answer to 15 is "No," check whether ☐ married ☐ divorced or ☐ widowed, and give date (see instructions) ▶		
17	Will a gift tax return for this calendar year be filed by your spouse?		
18	**Consent of Spouse**—I consent to have the gifts (and generation-skipping transfers) made by me and by my spouse to third parties during the calendar year considered as made one-half by each of us. We are both aware of the joint and several liability for tax created by the execution of this consent.		

Consenting spouse's signature ▶   Date ▶

Part 2—Tax Computation

1	Enter the amount from Schedule A, Part 3, line 15	1		
2	Enter the amount from Schedule B, line 3	2		
3	Total taxable gifts (add lines 1 and 2)	3		
4	Tax computed on amount on line 3 (see Table for Computing Tax in separate instructions). . .	4		
5	Tax computed on amount on line 2 (see Table for Computing Tax in separate instructions). . .	5		
6	Balance (subtract line 5 from line 4)	6		
7	Maximum unified credit (nonresident aliens, see instructions)	7	220,550	00
8	Enter the unified credit against tax allowable for all prior periods (from Sch. B, line 1, col. C) . .	8		
9	Balance (subtract line 8 from line 7)	9		
10	Enter 20% (.20) of the amount allowed as a specific exemption for gifts made after September 8, 1976, and before January 1, 1977 (see instructions)	10		
11	Balance (subtract line 10 from line 9)	11		
12	Unified credit (enter the smaller of line 6 or line 11)	12		
13	Credit for foreign gift taxes (see instructions)	13		
14	Total credits (add lines 12 and 13)	14		
15	Balance (subtract line 14 from line 6) (do not enter less than zero)	15		
16	Generation-skipping transfer taxes (from Schedule C, Part 3, col. H, Total)	16		
17	Total tax (add lines 15 and 16)	17		
18	Gift and generation-skipping transfer taxes prepaid with extension of time to file	18		
19	If line 18 is less than line 17, enter **balance due** (see instructions)	19		
20	If line 18 is greater than line 17, enter **amount to be refunded**	20		

(left margin: Attach check or money order here.)

Sign Here

Under penalties of perjury, I declare that I have examined this return, including any accompanying schedules and statements, and to the best of my knowledge and belief, it is true, correct, and complete. Declaration of preparer (other than donor) is based on all information of which preparer has any knowledge.

▶ Signature of donor	Date

Paid Preparer's Use Only	Preparer's signature ▶	Date	Check if self-employed ▶ ☐
	Firm's name (or yours if self-employed), address, and ZIP code ▶	Phone no. ▶ ( )	

For Disclosure, Privacy Act, and Paperwork Reduction Act Notice, see page 11 of the separate instructions for this form.   Cat. No. 16783M   Form **709** (2001)

FORM 709

Form 709 (2001)   Page **2**

SCHEDULE A	**Computation of Taxable Gifts** (Including Transfers in Trust)

A   Does the value of any item listed on Schedule A reflect any valuation discount? If the answer is "Yes," see instructions   . .Yes ☐   No ☐

B   ☐ ◄ Check here if you elect under section 529(c)(2)(B) to treat any transfers made this year to a qualified state tuition program as made ratably over a 5-year period beginning this year. See instructions. Attach explanation.

Part 1—Gifts Subject Only to Gift Tax. *Gifts less political organization, medical, and educational exclusions—see instructions*

A Item number	B • Donee's name and address • Relationship to donor (if any) • Description of gift • If the gift was made by means of a trust, enter trust's EIN and attach a description or copy of the trust instrument (see instructions) • If the gift was of securities, give CUSIP number	C Donor's adjusted basis of gift	D Date of gift	E Value at date of gift
1				

Total of Part 1 (add amounts from Part 1, column E) . . . . ►

Part 2—Gifts That are Direct Skips and are Subject to Both Gift Tax and Generation-Skipping Transfer Tax. You must list the gifts in chronological order. *Gifts less political organization, medical, and educational exclusions—see instructions. (Also list here direct skips that are subject only to the GST tax at this time as the result of the termination of an "estate tax inclusion period." See instructions.)*

A Item number	B • Donee's name and address • Relationship to donor (if any) • Description of gift • If the gift was made by means of a trust, enter trust's EIN and attach a description or copy of the trust instrument (see instructions) • If the gift was of securities, give CUSIP number	C Donor's adjusted basis of gift	D Date of gift	E Value at date of gift
1				

Total of Part 2 (add amounts from Part 2, column E) . . . . ►

Part 3—Taxable Gift Reconciliation

1	Total value of gifts of donor (add totals from column E of Parts 1 and 2)	**1**	
2	One-half of items .... attributable to spouse (see instructions)	**2**	
3	Balance (subtract line 2 from line 1)	**3**	
4	Gifts of spouse to be included (from Schedule A, Part 3, line 2 of spouse's return—see instructions) . .	**4**	
	If any of the gifts included on this line are also subject to the generation-skipping transfer tax, check here ► ☐ and enter those gifts also on Schedule C, Part 1.		
5	Total gifts (add lines 3 and 4)	**5**	
6	Total annual exclusions for gifts listed on Schedule A (including line 4, above) (see instructions) . . .	**6**	
7	Total included amount of gifts (subtract line 6 from line 5)	**7**	

Deductions (see instructions)

8	Gifts of interests to spouse for which a marital deduction will be claimed, based on items .... of Schedule A	**8**		
9	Exclusions attributable to gifts on line 8	**9**		
10	Marital deduction—subtract line 9 from line 8	**10**		
11	Charitable deduction, based on items ....less exclusions . .	**11**		
12	Total deductions—add lines 10 and 11		**12**	
13	Subtract line 12 from line 7		**13**	
14	Generation-skipping transfer taxes payable with this Form 709 (from Schedule C, Part 3, col. H, Total) .		**14**	
15	Taxable gifts (add lines 13 and 14). Enter here and on line 1 of the Tax Computation on page 1 . . .		**15**	

(If more space is needed, attach additional sheets of same size.)   Form **709** (2001)

FORM 709, Schedule A

Form 709 (2001)   Page **3**

| SCHEDULE A | Computation of Taxable Gifts *(continued)* |

16 Terminable Interest (QTIP) Marital Deduction. (See instructions for line 8 of Schedule A.)

If a trust (or other property) meets the requirements of qualified terminable interest property under section 2523(f), and

  a. The trust (or other property) is listed on Schedule A, and

  b. The value of the trust (or other property) is entered in whole or in part as a deduction on line 8, Part 3 of Schedule A,

then the donor shall be deemed to have made an election to have such trust (or other property) treated as qualified terminable interest property under section 2523(f).

    If less than the entire value of the trust (or other property) that the donor has included in Part 1 of Schedule A is entered as a deduction on line 8, the donor shall be considered to have made an election only as to a fraction of the trust (or other property). The numerator of this fraction is equal to the amount of the trust (or other property) deducted on line 10 of Part 3, Schedule A. The denominator is equal to the total value of the trust (or other property) listed in Part 1 of Schedule A.

    If you make the QTIP election (see instructions for line 8 of Schedule A), the terminable interest property involved will be included in your spouse's gross estate upon his or her death (section 2044). If your spouse disposes (by gift or otherwise) of all or part of the qualifying life income interest, he or she will be considered to have made a transfer of the entire property that is subject to the gift tax (see Transfer of Certain Life Estates on page 4 of the instructions).

17 Election Out of QTIP Treatment of Annuities

☐ ◄ Check here if you elect under section 2523(f)(6) **NOT** to treat as qualified terminable interest property any joint and survivor annuities that are reported on Schedule A and would otherwise be treated as qualified terminable interest property under section 2523(f). (See instructions.) Enter the item numbers (from Schedule A) for the annuities for which you are making this election ►

| SCHEDULE B | Gifts From Prior Periods |

If you answered "Yes" on line 11a of page 1, Part 1, see the instructions for completing Schedule B. If you answered "No," skip to the Tax Computation on page 1 (or Schedule C, if applicable).

A Calendar year or calendar quarter (see instructions)	B Internal Revenue office where prior return was filed	C Amount of unified credit against gift tax for periods after December 31, 1976	D Amount of specific exemption for prior periods ending before January 1, 1977	E Amount of taxable gifts

1	Totals for prior periods (without adjustment for reduced specific exemption) **1**				
2	Amount, if any, by which total specific exemption, line 1, column D, is more than $30,000 . . . . . **2**				
3	Total amount of taxable gifts for prior periods (add amount, column E, line 1, and amount, if any, on line 2). (Enter here and on line 2 of the Tax Computation on page 1.) **3**				

(If more space is needed, attach additional sheets of same size.)   Form **709** (2001)

FORM 709, Schedule A *(Continued)*

Form 709 (2001)   Page **4**

| SCHEDULE C | Computation of Generation-Skipping Transfer Tax |

Note: *Inter vivos direct skips that are completely excluded by the GST exemption must still be fully reported (including value and exemptions claimed) on Schedule C.*

Part 1—Generation-Skipping Transfers

A Item No. (from Schedule A, Part 2, col. A)	B Value (from Schedule A, Part 2, col. E)	C Split Gifts (enter ½ of col. B) (see instructions)	D Subtract col. C from col. B	E Nontaxable portion of transfer	F Net Transfer (subtract col. E from col. D)
1					
2					
3					
4					
5					
6					

If you elected gift splitting and your spouse was required to file a separate Form 709 (see the instructions for "Split Gifts"), you must enter all of the gifts shown on Schedule A, Part 2, of your spouse's Form 709 here.	Split gifts from spouse's Form 709 (enter item number)	Value included from spouse's Form 709	Nontaxable portion of transfer	Net transfer (subtract col. E from col. D)
In column C, enter the item number of each gift in the order it appears in column A of your spouse's Schedule A, Part 2. We have preprinted the prefix "S-" to distinguish your spouse's item numbers from your own when you complete column A of Schedule C, Part 3. In column D, for each gift, enter the amount reported in column C, Schedule C, Part 1, of your spouse's Form 709.	S- S- S- S- S- S- S- S-			

Part 2—GST Exemption Reconciliation (Section 2631) and Section 2652(a)(3) Election

Check box ▶ ☐ if you are making a section 2652(a)(3) (special QTIP) election (see instructions)

Enter the item numbers (from Schedule A) of the gifts for which you are making this election ▶ ....

1	Maximum allowable exemption (see instructions)	**1**	
2	Total exemption used for periods before filing this return	**2**	
3	Exemption available for this return (subtract line 2 from line 1)	**3**	
4	Exemption claimed on this return (from Part 3, col. C total, below)	**4**	
5	Exemption allocated to transfers not shown on Part 3, below. **You must attach a Notice of Allocation.** (See instructions.)	**5**	
6	Add lines 4 and 5	**6**	
7	Exemption available for future transfers (subtract line 6 from line 3)	**7**	

Part 3—Tax Computation

A Item No. (from Schedule C, Part 1)	B Net transfer (from Schedule C, Part 1, col. F)	C GST Exemption Allocated	D Divide col. C by col. B	E Inclusion Ratio (subtract col. D from 1.000)	F Maximum Estate Tax Rate	G Applicable Rate (multiply col. E by col. F)	H Generation-Skipping Transfer Tax (multiply col. B by col. G)
1					55% (.55)		
2					55% (.55)		
3					55% (.55)		
4					55% (.55)		
5					55% (.55)		
6					55% (.55)		
					55% (.55)		
					55% (.55)		
					55% (.55)		

| Total exemption claimed. Enter here and on line 4, Part 2, above. May not exceed line 3, Part 2, above . . . . . | | **Total generation-skipping transfer tax.** Enter here, on line 14 of Schedule A, Part 3, and on line 16 of the Tax Computation on page 1 . . . . | |

(If more space is needed, attach additional sheets of same size.)   ⊕   Form **709** (2001)

FORM 709, Schedule C

Form **709-A**
(Rev. November 2000)
Department of the Treasury
Internal Revenue Service

United States Short Form Gift Tax Return

OMB No. 1545-0021

Calendar year 20.........

1 Donor's first name and middle initial	2 Donor's last name	3 Donor's social security number

4 Address (number, street, and apartment number)	5 Legal residence (domicile)

6 City, state, and ZIP code	7 Citizenship

8 Did you file any gift tax returns for prior periods? . . . . ☐ Yes ☐ No

If "Yes," state when and where earlier returns were filed ▶

9 Name of consenting spouse	10 Consenting spouse's social security number

Note: *Do not use this form to report gifts of closely held stock, partnership interests, fractional interests in real estate, or gifts for which the value has been reduced to reflect a valuation discount. Instead, use Form 709.*

List of Gifts

(a) Donee's name and address and description of gift	(b) Donor's adjusted basis of gift	(c) Date of gift	(d) Value at date of gift

Consent

I consent to have the gifts made by my spouse to third parties during the calendar year considered as made one-half by each of us.

Consenting
spouse's signature ▶   Date ▶

Sign Here

Under penalties of perjury, I declare that I have examined this return, and to the best of my knowledge and belief, it is true, correct, and complete. Declaration of preparer (other than donor) is based on all information of which preparer has any knowledge.

▶ Signature of donor   Date

Paid Preparer's Use Only

Preparer's signature ▶	Date	Check if self-employed ▶ ☐
Firm's name (or yours if self-employed), address, and ZIP code ▶		Phone no. ▶ ( )

For Disclosure, Privacy Act, and Paperwork Reduction Act Notice, see the instructions.   Cat. No. 10171G   Form **709-A** (Rev. 11-2000)

FORM 709-A

Form **8615**

Department of the Treasury
Internal Revenue Service (99)

**Tax for Children Under Age 14
Who Have Investment Income of More Than $1,400**

▶ Attach only to the child's Form 1040, Form 1040A, or Form 1040NR.
▶ See separate instructions.

OMB No. 1545-0998

2000

Attachment
Sequence No. **33**

Child's name shown on return

Child's social security number

Before you begin: If the child, the parent, or any of the parent's other children under age 14 received capital gains (including capital gain distributions) or farm income, see **Pub. 929**, Tax Rules for Children and Dependents. It explains how to figure the child's tax using the **Capital Gain Tax Worksheet** in the Form 1040 or Form 1040A instructions or Schedule D or J (Form 1040).

A Parent's name (first, initial, and last). **Caution:** See instructions before completing.

B Parent's social security number

C Parent's filing status (check one):

☐ Single ☐ Married filing jointly ☐ Married filing separately ☐ Head of household ☐ Qualifying widow(er)

Part I	Child's Net Investment Income		
1	Enter the child's investment income, such as taxable interest, ordinary dividends, and capital gain distributions. See instructions. If this amount is $1,400 or less, **stop;** do not file this form.	**1**	
2	If the child **did not** itemize deductions on **Schedule A** (Form 1040 or Form 1040NR), enter $1,400. If the child **did** itemize deductions, see instructions	**2**	
3	Subtract line 2 from line 1. If the result is zero or less, **stop;** do not complete the rest of this form but **do** attach it to the child's return	**3**	
4	Enter the child's **taxable income** from Form 1040, line 39; Form 1040A, line 25; or Form 1040NR, line 38	**4**	
5	Enter the **smaller** of line 3 or line 4	**5**	

Part II	Tentative Tax Based on the Tax Rate of the Parent Listed on Line A		
6	Enter the parent's **taxable income** from Form 1040, line 39; Form 1040A, line 25; Form 1040EZ, line 6; TeleFile Tax Record, line K; Form 1040NR, line 38; or Form 1040NR-EZ, line 14. If less than zero, enter -0-	**6**	
	Note: If the total of lines 4 and 6 above is not more than $43,850, lines 7 through 16 may not have to be completed. For details, see the instructions for line 6.		
7	Enter the total net investment income, if any, from Forms 8615, line 5, of **all other** children of the parent identified above. **Do not** include the amount from line 5 above	**7**	
8	Add lines 5, 6, and 7	**8**	
9	Enter the tax on line 8 based on the **parent's** filing status. See instructions. If the **Capital Gain Tax Worksheet** or **Schedule D** or **J** (Form 1040) is used to figure the tax, check here ▶ ☐	**9**	
10	Enter the parent's tax from Form 1040, line 40; Form 1040A, line 26, minus any alternative minimum tax; Form 1040EZ, line 10; TeleFile Tax Record, line K; Form 1040NR, line 39; or Form 1040NR-EZ, line 15. If any tax is from **Form 4972** or **8814**, see instructions. If the **Capital Gain Tax Worksheet** or **Schedule D** or **J** (Form 1040) was used to figure the tax, check here ▶ ☐	**10**	
11	Subtract line 10 from line 9 and enter the result. If line 7 is blank, also enter this amount on line 13 and go to **Part III**	**11**	
12a	Add lines 5 and 7	12a	
b	Divide line 5 by line 12a. Enter the result as a decimal (rounded to at least three places)	**12b**	× .
13	Multiply line 11 by line 12b	**13**	

Part III	Child's Tax—If lines 4 and 5 above are the same, enter -0- on line 15 and go to line 16.		
14	Subtract line 5 from line 4 .	14	
15	Enter the tax on line 14 based on the **child's** filing status. See instructions. If the **Capital Gain Tax Worksheet** or **Schedule D** or **J** (Form 1040) is used to figure the tax, check here ▶ ☐	**15**	
16	Add lines 13 and 15	**16**	
17	Enter the tax on line 4 based on the **child's** filing status. See instructions. If the **Capital Gain Tax Worksheet** or **Schedule D** or **J** (Form 1040) is used to figure the tax, check here ▶ ☐	**17**	
18	Enter the **larger** of line 16 or line 17 here and on Form 1040, line 40; Form 1040A, line 26; or Form 1040NR, line 39	**18**	

For Paperwork Reduction Act Notice, see page 2 of the instructions.

Cat. No. 64113U

Form **8615** (2000)

FORM 8615

Note: At time of printing, the 2001 form was not available.

Form **8814**

Department of the Treasury
Internal Revenue Service (99)

**Parents' Election To Report
Child's Interest and Dividends**
► See instructions below and on back.
► Attach to parents' Form 1040 or Form 1040NR.

OMB No. 1545-1128

2001

Attachment
Sequence No. **40**

Name(s) shown on your return | Your social security number

Caution: *The Federal income tax on your child's income, including capital gain distributions, may be less if you file a separate tax return for the child instead of making this election. This is because you cannot take certain tax benefits that your child could take on his or her own return. For details, see* **Tax Benefits You May Not Take** *on the back.*

A Child's name (first, initial, and last) | **B** Child's social security number

C If more than one Form 8814 is attached, check here . . . . ► ☐

Part I Child's Interest and Dividends To Report on Your Return

1a Enter your child's **taxable** interest. If this amount is different from the amounts shown on the child's Forms 1099-INT and 1099-OID, see the instructions . . . . | **1a**

b Enter your child's **tax-exempt** interest. **Do not** include this amount on line 1a . . . . | **1b**

2 Enter your child's ordinary dividends, including any Alaska Permanent Fund dividends. If your child received any ordinary dividends as a nominee, see the instructions . . . . | **2**

3 Enter your child's capital gain distributions. If your child received any capital gain distributions as a nominee, see the instructions . . . . | **3**

4 Add lines 1a, 2, and 3. If the total is $1,500 or less, skip lines 5 and 6 and go to line 7. If the total is $7,500 or more, **do not** file this form. Your child **must** file his or her own return to report the income . . . . | **4**

5 Base amount . . . . | **5** | 1,500 | 00

6 Subtract line 5 from line 4. If you checked the box on line C above or if you entered an amount on line 3, see the instructions. Also, include this amount in the total on Form 1040, line 21, or Form 1040NR, line 21. In the space next to line 21, enter "Form 8814" and show the amount. Go to line 7 below . . . . ► | **6**

Part II Tax on the First $1,500 of Child's Interest and Dividends

7 Amount not taxed . . . . | **7** | 750 | 00

8 Subtract line 7 from line 4. If the result is zero or less, enter -0- . . . . | **8**

9 **Tax.** Is the amount on line 8 less than $750?
☐ **No.** Enter $75 here and see the **Note** below.
☐ **Yes.** Multiply line 8 by 10% (.10). Enter the result here and see the **Note** below. | **9**

Note: *If you checked the box on line C above, see the instructions. Otherwise, include the amount from line 9 in the tax you enter on Form 1040, line 40, or Form 1040NR, line 39. Be sure to check box* **a** *on Form 1040, line 40, or Form 1040NR, line 39.*

General Instructions

Purpose of Form. Use this form if you elect to report your child's income on your return. If you do, your child will not have to file a return. You can make this election if your child meets **all** of the following conditions.

● Was under age 14 on January 1, 2002.

● Is required to file a 2001 return.

● Had income only from interest and dividends, including Alaska Permanent Fund dividends.

● Had gross income for 2001 that was less than $7,500.

● Had no estimated tax payments for 2001 (including any overpayment of tax from his or her 2000 return applied to 2001 estimated tax).

● Had no Federal income tax withheld from his or her income.

You must also qualify. See **Parents Who Qualify To Make the Election** below.

How To Make the Election. To make the election, complete and attach Form(s) 8814 to your tax return and file your return by the due date (including extensions). A separate Form 8814 must be filed for **each** child whose income you choose to report.

Parents Who Qualify To Make the Election. You qualify to make this election if you file Form 1040 or Form 1040NR and **any** of the following apply.

● You are filing a joint return for 2001 with the child's other parent.

● You and the child's other parent were married to each other but file separate

returns for 2001 **and** you had the **higher** taxable income. If you do not know if you had the higher taxable income, see **Pub. 929**, Tax Rules for Children and Dependents.

● You were unmarried, treated as unmarried for Federal income tax purposes, or separated from the child's other parent by a divorce or separate maintenance decree. You must have had custody of your child for most of the year (you were the custodial parent). If you were the custodial parent and you remarried, you may make the election on a joint return with your new spouse. But if you and your new spouse do not file a joint return, you qualify to make the election only if you had **higher** taxable income than your new spouse.

(continued)

For Paperwork Reduction Act Notice, see back of form. | Cat. No. 10750J | Form **8814** (2001)

FORM 8814

Form **1040-ES**
Department of the Treasury
Internal Revenue Service

2001 Payment Voucher **4**

OMB No. 1545-0087

File only if you are making a payment of estimated tax by check or money order. Mail this voucher with your check or money order payable to the **"United States Treasury."** Write your social security number and "2001 Form 1040-ES" on your check or money order. Do not send cash. Enclose, but do not staple or attach, your payment with this voucher.

Calendar year—Due Jan. 15, 2002

Amount of estimated tax you are paying by check or money order. | $

Type or print			
Your first name and initial		Your last name	Your social security number
If joint payment, complete for spouse			
Spouse's first name and initial		Spouse's last name	Spouse's social security number
Address (number, street, and apt. no.)			
City, state, and ZIP code (If a foreign address, enter city, province or state, postal code, and country.)			

For Privacy Act and Paperwork Reduction Act Notice, see instructions on page 5.

Form **1040-ES**
Department of the Treasury
Internal Revenue Service

2001 Payment Voucher **3**

OMB No. 1545-0087

File only if you are making a payment of estimated tax by check or money order. Mail this voucher with your check or money order payable to the **"United States Treasury."** Write your social security number and "2001 Form 1040-ES" on your check or money order. Do not send cash. Enclose, but do not staple or attach, your payment with this voucher.

Calendar year—Due Sept. 17, 2001

Amount of estimated tax you are paying by check or money order. | $

Type or print			
Your first name and initial		Your last name	Your social security number
If joint payment, complete for spouse			
Spouse's first name and initial		Spouse's last name	Spouse's social security number
Address (number, street, and apt. no.)			
City, state, and ZIP code (If a foreign address, enter city, province or state, postal code, and country.)			

For Privacy Act and Paperwork Reduction Act Notice, see instructions on page 5.

Tear off here

Form **1040-ES**
Department of the Treasury
Internal Revenue Service

2001 Payment Voucher **2**

OMB No. 1545-0087

File only if you are making a payment of estimated tax by check or money order. Mail this voucher with your check or money order payable to the **"United States Treasury."** Write your social security number and "2001 Form 1040-ES" on your check or money order. Do not send cash. Enclose, but do not staple or attach, your payment with this voucher.

Calendar year—Due June 15, 2001

Amount of estimated tax you are paying by check or money order. | $

Type or print			
Your first name and initial		Your last name	Your social security number
If joint payment, complete for spouse			
Spouse's first name and initial		Spouse's last name	Spouse's social security number
Address (number, street, and apt. no.)			
City, state, and ZIP code (If a foreign address, enter city, province or state, postal code, and country.)			

For Privacy Act and Paperwork Reduction Act Notice, see instructions on page 5.

Tear off here

Form **1040-ES**
Department of the Treasury
Internal Revenue Service

2001 Payment Voucher **1**

OMB No. 1545-0087

File only if you are making a payment of estimated tax by check or money order. Mail this voucher with your check or money order payable to the **"United States Treasury."** Write your social security number and "2001 Form 1040-ES" on your check or money order. Do not send cash. Enclose, but do not staple or attach, your payment with this voucher.

Calendar year—Due April 16, 2001

Amount of estimated tax you are paying by check or money order. | $

Type or print			
Your first name and initial		Your last name	Your social security number
If joint payment, complete for spouse			
Spouse's first name and initial		Spouse's last name	Spouse's social security number
Address (number, street, and apt. no.)			
City, state, and ZIP code (If a foreign address, enter city, province or state, postal code, and country.)			

For Privacy Act and Paperwork Reduction Act Notice, see instructions on page 5.

Page 7

FORM 1040-ES, Payment Vouchers

Form **8822**	**Change of Address**	OMB No. 1545-1163

(Rev. Oct. 2000)
Department of the Treasury
Internal Revenue Service

▶ Please type or print.

▶ See instructions on back.   ▶ Do not attach this form to your return.

Part I   **Complete This Part To Change Your Home Mailing Address**

Check **all** boxes this change affects:

1 ☐ Individual income tax returns (Forms 1040, 1040A, 1040EZ, TeleFile, 1040NR, etc.)

     ▶ If your last return was a joint return and you are now establishing a residence separate
from the spouse with whom you filed that return, check here . . . . ▶ ☐

2 ☐ Gift, estate, or generation-skipping transfer tax returns (Forms 706, 709, etc.)

     ▶ For Forms 706 and 706-NA, enter the decedent's name and social security number below.

     ▶ Decedent's name   ▶ Social security number

3a Your name (first name, initial, and last name)	**3b** Your social security number

4a Spouse's name (first name, initial, and last name)	**4b** Spouse's social security number

5 Prior name(s). See instructions.

6a Old address (no., street, city or town, state, and ZIP code). If a P.O. box or foreign address, see instructions.	Apt. no.

6b Spouse's old address, if different from line 6a (no., street, city or town, state, and ZIP code). If a P.O. box or foreign address, see instructions.	Apt. no.

7 New address (no., street, city or town, state, and ZIP code). If a P.O. box or foreign address, see instructions.	Apt. no.

Part II   **Complete This Part To Change Your Business Mailing Address or Business Location**

Check **all** boxes this change affects:

8 ☐ Employment, excise, and other business returns (Forms 720, 940, 940-EZ, 941, 990, 1041, 1065, 1120, etc.)
9 ☐ Employee plan returns (Forms 5500 and 5500-EZ).
10 ☐ Business location

11a Business name	**11b** Employer identification number

12 Old mailing address (no., street, city or town, state, and ZIP code). If a P.O. box or foreign address, see instructions.	Room or suite no.

13 New mailing address (no., street, city or town, state, and ZIP code). If a P.O. box or foreign address, see instructions.	Room or suite no.

14 New business location (no., street, city or town, state, and ZIP code). If a foreign address, see instructions.	Room or suite no.

Part III   **Signature**

Daytime telephone number of person to contact (optional) ▶ ( )

Sign Here ▶

Your signature	Date	▶ If Part II completed, signature of owner, officer, or representative	Date
If joint return, spouse's signature	Date	▶ Title	

For Privacy Act and Paperwork Reduction Act Notice, see back of form.   Cat. No. 12081V   Form **8822** (Rev. 10-2000)

FORM 8822

Form **9465**
(Rev. November 2000)
Department of the Treasury
Internal Revenue Service (99)

Installment Agreement Request

▶ **If you are filing this form with your tax return, attach it to the front of the return. Otherwise, see instructions.**

OMB No. 1545-1350

Caution: *Do not file this form if you are currently making payments on an installment agreement. You must pay your other Federal tax liabilities in full or you will be in default on your agreement.*

1	Your first name and initial	Last name		Your social security number
	If a joint return, spouse's first name and initial	Last name		Spouse's social security number
	Your current address (number and street). If you have a P.O. box and no home delivery, enter your box number.			Apt. number
	City, town or post office, state, and ZIP code. If a foreign address, enter city, province or state, and country. Follow the country's practice for entering the postal code.			

2   If this address is new since you filed your last tax return, check here . . . . ▶ ☐

3	( )		4	( )		
	Your home phone number	Best time for us to call		Your work phone number	Ext.	Best time for us to call
5	Name of your bank or other financial institution:		6	Your employer's name:		
	Address			Address		
	City, state, and ZIP code			City, state, and ZIP code		

TIP *If you are filing this form in response to a notice, do not complete lines 7 through 9. Instead, attach the bottom section of the notice to this form and go to line 10.*

7   Enter the tax return for which you are making this request (for example, Form 1040) . . . . ▶ **7**

8   Enter the tax year for which you are making this request (for example, 2000) . . . . ▶ **8**

9   Enter the total amount you owe as shown on your tax return . . . . | **9** | |

10   Enter the amount of any payment you are making with your tax return (or notice). See instructions | **10** | |

11   Enter the amount you can pay each month. **Make your payments as large as possible to limit interest and penalty charges.** The charges will continue until you pay in full . . . . | **11** | |

12   Enter the date you want to make your payment each month. **Do not** enter a date later than the 28th. . ▶ **12**

13   If you want to make your payments by direct debit, see the instructions and fill in lines 13a, 13b, and 13c.

▶ a   Routing number ☐☐☐☐☐☐☐☐☐   ▶ c   Type: ☐ Checking   ☐ Savings

▶ b   Account number ☐☐☐☐☐☐☐☐☐☐☐☐☐☐☐☐☐

I authorize the U.S. Treasury and its designated Financial Agent to initiate a monthly ACH debit (electronic withdrawal) entry to the financial institution account indicated for payments of my Federal taxes owed, and the financial institution to debit the entry to this account. This authorization is to remain in full force and effect until I notify the U.S. Treasury Financial Agent to terminate the authorization. To revoke payment, I must contact the U.S. Treasury Financial Agent at **1-800-829-8815** no later than 7 business days prior to the payment (settlement) date. I also authorize the financial institutions involved in the processing of the electronic payments of taxes to receive confidential information necessary to answer inquiries and resolve issues related to the payments.

Your signature	Date	Spouse's signature. If a joint return, **both** must sign.	Date

FORM 9465

IRS Forms for the Alternative Minimum Tax

Form **6251**	**Alternative Minimum Tax—Individuals**	OMB No. 1545-0227
	▶ See separate instructions.	**2001**
Department of the Treasury Internal Revenue Service (99)	▶ Attach to Form 1040 or Form 1040NR.	Attachment Sequence No. **32**
Name(s) shown on Form 1040		Your social security number

Part I — Alternative Minimum Taxable Income

1	If you itemized deductions on Schedule A (Form 1040), go to line 2. Otherwise, enter your standard deduction from Form 1040, line 36, here and go to line 6	1
2	Medical and dental. Enter the **smaller** of Schedule A (Form 1040), line 4 **or** 2½% of Form 1040, line 34 .	2
3	Taxes. Enter the amount from Schedule A (Form 1040), line 9	3
4	Certain interest on a home mortgage **not** used to buy, build, or improve your home	4
5	Miscellaneous itemized deductions. Enter the amount from Schedule A (Form 1040), line 26	5
6	Refund of taxes. Enter any tax refund from Form 1040, line 10 or line 21	6 ( )
7	Investment interest. Enter difference between regular tax and AMT deduction	7
8	Post-1986 depreciation. Enter difference between regular tax and AMT depreciation	8
9	Adjusted gain or loss. Enter difference between AMT and regular tax gain or loss	9
10	Incentive stock options. Enter excess of AMT income over regular tax income	10
11	Passive activities. Enter difference between AMT and regular tax income or loss	11
12	Beneficiaries of estates and trusts. Enter the amount from Schedule K-1 (Form 1041), line 9	12
13	Tax-exempt interest income from private activity bonds issued after August 7, 1986	13

14 Other. Enter the amount, if any, for each item below and enter the total on line 14.

a Circulation expenditures .	i Mining costs	
b Depletion	j Patron's adjustment . .	
c Depreciation (pre-1987) . .	k Pollution control facilities .	
d Installment sales	l Research and experimental .	
e Intangible drilling costs . .	m Section 1202 exclusion . .	
f Large partnerships . . .	n Tax shelter farm activities .	
g Long-term contracts . . .	o Related adjustments . .	
h Loss limitations		14

15	Total adjustments and preferences. Combine lines 1 through 14	15
16	Enter the amount from Form 1040, line 37. If less than zero, enter as a (loss)	16
17	Enter as a positive amount any net operating loss deduction from Form 1040, line 21	17
18	If Form 1040, line 34, is over $132,950 (over $66,475 if married filing separately) and you itemized deductions, enter the amount, if any, from line 9 of the worksheet for Schedule A (Form 1040), line 28	18 ( )
19	Combine lines 15 through 18	19
20	Alternative tax net operating loss deduction (see page 6 of the instructions)	20
21	**Alternative minimum taxable income.** Subtract line 20 from line 19. (If married filing separately and line 21 is more than $173,000, see page 7 of the instructions.)	21

Part II — Alternative Minimum Tax

22 Exemption amount. (If this form is for a child under age 14, see page 7 of the instructions.)

IF your filing status is . . .	AND line 21 is not over . . .	THEN enter on line 22 . . .	
Single or head of household	$112,500	$35,750	22
Married filing jointly or qualifying widow(er) . .	150,000	49,000	
Married filing separately	75,000	24,500	

If line 21 is **over** the amount shown above for your filing status, see page 7 of the instructions.

23	Subtract line 22 from line 21. If zero or less, enter -0- here and on lines 26 and 28 and stop here . .	23
24	Go to Part III of Form 6251 to figure line 24 if you reported capital gain distributions directly on Form 1040, line 13, **or** you had a gain on both lines 16 and 17 of Schedule D (Form 1040) (as refigured for the AMT, if necessary). **All others:** If line 23 is $175,000 or less ($87,500 or less if married filing separately), multiply line 23 by 26% (.26). Otherwise, multiply line 23 by 28% (.28) and subtract $3,500 ($1,750 if married filing separately) from the result	24
25	Alternative minimum tax foreign tax credit (see page 7 of the instructions)	25
26	Tentative minimum tax. Subtract line 25 from line 24	26
27	Enter your tax from Form 1040, line 40 (minus any tax from Form 4972 and any foreign tax credit from Form 1040, line 43)	27
28	**Alternative minimum tax.** Subtract line 27 from line 26. If zero or less, enter -0-. Enter here and on Form 1040, line 41	28

For Paperwork Reduction Act Notice, see page 8 of the instructions.   Cat. No. 13600G   Form **6251** (2001)

FORM 6251

Form 6251 (2001) Page **2**

Part III	Line 24 Computation Using Maximum Capital Gains Rates

Caution: *If you* **did not** *complete Part IV of Schedule D (Form 1040), see page 8 of the instructions before you complete this part.*

29 Enter the amount from Form 6251, line 23 . . . . **29**

30 Enter the amount from Schedule D (Form 1040), line 23, or line 9 of the Schedule D Tax Worksheet on page D-9 of the instructions for Schedule D (Form 1040), whichever applies (as refigured for the AMT, if necessary) (see page 8 of the instructions) **30**

31 Enter the amount from Schedule D (Form 1040), line 19 (as refigured for the AMT, if necessary) (see page 8 of the instructions) **31**

32 Add lines 30 and 31 . . . . **32**

33 Enter the amount from Schedule D (Form 1040), line 23, or line 4 of the Schedule D Tax Worksheet on page D-9 of the instructions for Schedule D (Form 1040), whichever applies (as refigured for the AMT, if necessary) (see page 8 of the instructions) **33**

34 Enter the **smaller** of line 32 or line 33 . . . . **34**

35 Subtract line 34 from line 29. If zero or less, enter -0- **35**

36 If line 35 is $175,000 or less ($87,500 or less if married filing separately), multiply line 35 by 26% (.26). Otherwise, multiply line 35 by 28% (.28) and subtract $3,500 ($1,750 if married filing separately) from the result **36**

37 Enter the amount from Schedule D (Form 1040), line 28, or line 16 of the Schedule D Tax Worksheet on page D-9 of the instructions for Schedule D (Form 1040), whichever applies (as figured for the regular tax) (see page 8 of the instructions) **37**

38 Enter the **smallest** of line 29, line 30, or line 37. If zero, go to line 44 . . . **38**

39 Enter your qualified 5-year gain, if any, from Schedule D (Form 1040), line 29 (as refigured for the AMT, if necessary) (see page 8 of the instructions) **39**

40 Enter the **smaller** of line 38 or line 39 . . . . **40**

41 Multiply line 40 by 8% (.08) **41**

42 Subtract line 40 from line 38 . . . . **42**

43 Multiply line 42 by 10% (.10) **43**

44 Enter the **smaller** of line 29 or line 30 . . . . . **44**

45 Enter the amount from line 38 . . . . **45**

46 Subtract line 45 from line 44 . . . . **46**

47 Multiply line 46 by 20% (.20) **47**

If line 31 is zero or blank, skip lines 48 through 51 and go to line 52. Otherwise, go to line 48.

48 Enter the amount from line 29 . . . . **48**

49 Add lines 35, 38, and 46 . . . . **49**

50 Subtract line 49 from line 48 . . . . **50**

51 Multiply line 50 by 25% (.25) **51**

52 Add lines 36, 41, 43, 47, and 51 . . . . **52**

53 If line 29 is $175,000 or less ($87,500 or less if married filing separately), multiply line 29 by 26% (.26). Otherwise, multiply line 29 by 28% (.28) and subtract $3,500 ($1,750 if married filing separately) from the result **53**

54 Enter the **smaller** of line 52 or line 53 here and on line 24 . . . . **54**

Form **6251** (2001)

FORM 6251 *(Continued)*

Form **8801**	Credit For Prior Year Minimum Tax— Individuals, Estates, and Trusts	OMB No. 1545-1073
Department of the Treasury Internal Revenue Service (00)	▶ Attach to your tax return.	**2001** Attachment Sequence No. 74

Name(s) shown on return			Identifying number

Part I   Net Minimum Tax on Exclusion Items

1	Combine lines 16 through 18 of your 2000 Form 6251. Estates and trusts, see instructions . .	1	
2	Enter adjustments and preferences treated as exclusion items (see instructions)	2	
3	Minimum tax credit net operating loss deduction (see instructions)	3 (	)
4	Combine lines 1, 2, and 3. If zero or less, enter -0- here and on line 15 and go to Part II. If more than $165,000 and you were married filing separately for 2000, see instructions	4	
5	Enter: $45,000 if married filing jointly or qualifying widow(er) for 2000; $33,750 if single or head of household for 2000; or $22,500 if married filing separately for 2000. Estates and trusts, enter $22,500	5	
6	Enter: $150,000 if married filing jointly or qualifying widow(er) for 2000; $112,500 if single or head of household for 2000; or $75,000 if married filing separately for 2000. Estates and trusts, enter $75,000	6	
7	Subtract line 6 from line 4. If zero or less, enter -0- here and on line 8 and go to line 9 . . .	7	
8	Multiply line 7 by 25% (.25)	8	
9	Subtract line 8 from line 5. If zero or less, enter -0-. If this form is for a child under age 14, see instructions	9	
10	Subtract line 9 from line 4. If zero or less, enter -0- here and on line 15 and go to Part II. Form 1040NR filers, see instructions	10	
11	If for 2000 you reported capital gain distributions directly on Form 1040, line 13, **or** completed Schedule D (Form 1040 or 1041) and had an amount on line 25 or line 27 of Schedule D (Form 1040) (line 24 or line 26 of Schedule D (Form 1041)) or would have had an amount on either of those lines had you completed them, go to Part III of Form 8801 to figure the amount to enter on this line. **All others:** Multiply line 10 by 26% (.26) **if** line 10 is: $175,000 or less if single, head of household, married filing jointly, qualifying widow(er), or an estate or trust for 2000; or $87,500 or less if married filing separately for 2000. **Otherwise,** multiply line 10 by 28% (.28) and subtract from the result: $3,500 if single, head of household, married filing jointly, qualifying widow(er), or an estate or trust for 2000; or $1,750 if married filing separately for 2000	11	
12	Minimum tax foreign tax credit on exclusion items (see instructions)	12	
13	Tentative minimum tax on exclusion items. Subtract line 12 from line 11	13	
14	Enter the amount from your 2000 Form 6251, line 27, or Form 1041, Schedule I, line 38 . . .	14	
15	**Net minimum tax on exclusion items.** Subtract line 14 from line 13. If zero or less, enter -0-	15	

Part II   Minimum Tax Credit and Carryforward to 2002

16	Enter the amount from your 2000 Form 6251, line 28, or 2000 Form 1041, Schedule I, line 39	16	
17	Enter the amount from line 15 above	17	
18	Subtract line 17 from line 16. If less than zero, enter as a negative amount	18	
19	**2000 minimum tax credit carryforward.** Enter the amount from your 2000 Form 8801, line 26	19	
20	Enter the total of your 2000 unallowed nonconventional source fuel credit and 2000 unallowed qualified electric vehicle credit (see instructions)	20	
21	Combine lines 18, 19, and 20. If zero or less, **stop here** and see instructions	21	
22	Enter your 2001 regular income tax liability minus allowable credits (see instructions)	22	
23	Enter the amount from your 2001 Form 6251, line 26, or 2001 Form 1041, Schedule I, line 37 .	23	
24	Subtract line 23 from line 22. If zero or less, enter -0-	24	
25	**Minimum tax credit.** Enter the **smaller** of line 21 or line 24. Also enter this amount on your 2001 Form 1040, line 49; Form 1040NR, line 46; or Form 1041, Schedule G, line 2d	25	
26	**Minimum tax credit carryforward to 2002.** Subtract line 25 from line 21. Keep a record of this amount because you may use it in future years	26	

For Paperwork Reduction Act Notice, see page 4.	Cat. No. 10002S	Form **8801** (2001)

FORM 8801

Form 8801 (2001)   Page **2**

Part III   Line 11 Computation Using Maximum Capital Gains Rates

Caution: *If you did not complete Schedule D (Form 1040) for 2000 because you reported capital gain distributions directly on Form 1040, line 13, see the instructions before you complete this part. If you are an individual and you did not complete Part IV of your 2000 Schedule D (Form 1040), complete lines 20 through 27 of that Schedule D before completing this part. For an estate or trust that did not complete Part V of the 2000 Schedule D (Form 1041), complete lines 19 through 26 of that Schedule D before completing this part.*

27	Enter the amount from line 10	**27**
28	Enter the amount from your 2000 Schedule D (Form 1040), line 27 (or 2000 Schedule D (Form 1041), line 26)	**28**
29	Enter the amount from your 2000 Schedule D (Form 1040), line 25 (or 2000 Schedule D (Form 1041), line 24)	**29**
30	Add lines 28 and 29	**30**
31	Enter the amount from your 2000 Schedule D (Form 1040), line 22 (or 2000 Schedule D (Form 1041), line 21)	**31**
32	Enter the **smaller** of line 30 or line 31	**32**
33	Subtract line 32 from line 27. If zero or less, enter -0- . . . . ▶	**33**
34	Multiply line 33 by 26% (.26) **if** line 33 is: $175,000 or less if single, head of household, married filing jointly, qualifying widow(er), or an estate or trust for 2000; or $87,500 or less if married filing separately for 2000. **Otherwise,** multiply line 33 by 28% (.28) and subtract from the result: $3,500 if single, head of household, married filing jointly, qualifying widow(er), or an estate or trust for 2000; or $1,750 if married filing separately for 2000	**34**
35	Enter the amount from your 2000 Schedule D (Form 1040), line 36 (or 2000 Schedule D (Form 1041), line 35). If you did not complete Part IV of your 2000 Schedule D (Form 1040) (Part V of the 2000 Schedule D (Form 1041) for an estate or trust), enter -0-	**35**
36	Enter the **smallest** of line 27, line 28, or line 35 . . . . . . ▶	**36**
37	Multiply line 36 by 10% (.10)	**37**
38	Enter the **smaller** of line 27 or line 28	**38**
39	Enter the amount from line 36	**39**
40	Subtract line 39 from line 38 . . . . ▶	**40**
41	Multiply line 40 by 20% (.20)	**41**
	If line 29 is zero or blank, skip lines 42 through 45 and go to line 46.	
42	Enter the amount from line 27	**42**
43	Add lines 33, 36, and 40	**43**
44	Subtract line 43 from line 42	**44**
45	Multiply line 44 by 25% (.25)	**45**
46	Add lines 34, 37, 41, and 45	**46**
47	Multiply line 27 by 26% (.26) **if** line 27 is: $175,000 or less if single, head of household, married filing jointly, qualifying widow(er), or an estate or trust for 2000; or $87,500 or less if married filing separately for 2000. **Otherwise,** multiply line 27 by 28% (.28) and subtract from the result: $3,500 if single, head of household, married filing jointly, qualifying widow(er), or an estate or trust for 2000; or $1,750 if married filing separately for 2000	**47**
48	Enter the **smaller** of line 46 or line 47 here and on line 11	**48**

Form **8801** (2001)

FORM 8801 *(Continued)*

IRS Forms for Small Businesses

SCHEDULE C
(Form 1040)

Department of the Treasury
Internal Revenue Service   (99)

Profit or Loss From Business
(Sole Proprietorship)

▶ Partnerships, joint ventures, etc., must file Form 1065 or Form 1065-B.

▶ **Attach to Form 1040 or Form 1041.**   ▶ **See Instructions for Schedule C (Form 1040).**

OMB No. 1545-0074

2001

Attachment
Sequence No. **09**

Name of proprietor	Social security number (SSN)

A	Principal business or profession, including product or service (see page C-1 of the instructions)	B Enter code from pages C-7 & 8 ▶

C	Business name. If no separate business name, leave blank.	D Employer ID number (EIN), if any

E	Business address (including suite or room no.) ▶ ....
	City, town or post office, state, and ZIP code

F	Accounting method: **(1)** ☐ Cash **(2)** ☐ Accrual **(3)** ☐ Other (specify) ▶ ....
G	Did you "materially participate" in the operation of this business during 2001? If "No," see page C-2 for limit on losses . ☐ Yes ☐ No
H	If you started or acquired this business during 2001, check here . . . . ▶ ☐

Part I   Income

1	Gross receipts or sales. **Caution.** If this income was reported to you on Form W-2 and the "Statutory employee" box on that form was checked, see page C-2 and check here . . . . . . ▶ ☐	1	
2	Returns and allowances	2	
3	Subtract line 2 from line 1	3	
4	Cost of goods sold (from line 42 on page 2)	4	
5	**Gross profit.** Subtract line 4 from line 3	5	
6	Other income, including Federal and state gasoline or fuel tax credit or refund (see page C-2) . . .	6	
7	**Gross income.** Add lines 5 and 6 . . . . ▶	7	

Part II   Expenses. Enter expenses for business use of your home **only** on line 30.

8	Advertising	8			19	Pension and profit-sharing plans	19	
9	Bad debts from sales or services (see page C-3) . .	9			20	Rent or lease (see page C-4):		
					a	Vehicles, machinery, and equipment .	20a	
10	Car and truck expenses (see page C-3)	10			b	Other business property . . .	20b	
11	Commissions and fees . .	11			21	Repairs and maintenance . . .	21	
12	Depletion	12			22	Supplies (not included in Part III) .	22	
13	Depreciation and section 179 expense deduction (not included in Part III) (see page C-3) . .	13			23	Taxes and licenses	23	
					24	Travel, meals, and entertainment:		
14	Employee benefit programs (other than on line 19) . . .	14			a	Travel	24a	
					b	Meals and entertainment		
15	Insurance (other than health) .	15			c	Enter nondeduct- ible amount in- cluded on line 24b (see page C-5)		
16	Interest:							
a	Mortgage (paid to banks, etc.) .	16a			d	Subtract line 24c from line 24b	24d	
b	Other	16b			25	Utilities	25	
17	Legal and professional services	17			26	Wages (less employment credits) .	26	
18	Office expense	18			27	Other expenses (from line 48 on page 2)	27	

28	**Total expenses** before expenses for business use of home. Add lines 8 through 27 in columns . ▶	28	

29	Tentative profit (loss). Subtract line 28 from line 7	29	
30	Expenses for business use of your home. Attach **Form 8829**	30	
31	**Net profit or (loss).** Subtract line 30 from line 29.		
	• If a profit, enter on **Form 1040, line 12,** and **also** on **Schedule SE, line 2** (statutory employees, see page C-5). Estates and trusts, enter on Form 1041, line 3.	31	
	• If a loss, you **must** go to line 32.		

32	If you have a loss, check the box that describes your investment in this activity (see page C-5).	
	• If you checked 32a, enter the loss on **Form 1040, line 12,** and **also** on **Schedule SE, line 2** (statutory employees, see page C-5). Estates and trusts, enter on Form 1041, line 3.	32a ☐ All investment is at risk.
	• If you checked 32b, you **must** attach Form 6198.	32b ☐ Some investment is not at risk.

For Paperwork Reduction Act Notice, see Form 1040 instructions.   Cat. No. 11334P   Schedule C (Form 1040) 2001

FORM 1040, Schedule C

Schedule C (Form 1040) 2001
Page **2**

Part III	**Cost of Goods Sold** (see page C-6)

33 Method(s) used to value closing inventory: **a** ☐ Cost   **b** ☐ Lower of cost or market   **c** ☐ Other (attach explanation)

34 Was there any change in determining quantities, costs, or valuations between opening and closing inventory? If "Yes," attach explanation . . . . ☐ **Yes**   ☐ **No**

35	Inventory at beginning of year. If different from last year's closing inventory, attach explanation . .	35	
36	Purchases less cost of items withdrawn for personal use	36	
37	Cost of labor. Do not include any amounts paid to yourself	37	
38	Materials and supplies	38	
39	Other costs	39	
40	Add lines 35 through 39	40	
41	Inventory at end of year	41	
42	**Cost of goods sold.** Subtract line 41 from line 40. Enter the result here and on page 1, line 4 . .	42	

Part IV	**Information on Your Vehicle.** Complete this part **only** if you are claiming car or truck expenses on line 10 and are not required to file Form 4562 for this business. See the instructions for line 13 on page C-3 to find out if you must file.

43 When did you place your vehicle in service for business purposes? (month, day, year) ▶ .... / .... / ....

44 Of the total number of miles you drove your vehicle during 2001, enter the number of miles you used your vehicle for:

a Business .... **b** Commuting .... **c** Other ....

45 Do you (or your spouse) have another vehicle available for personal use? . . . . ☐ **Yes**   ☐ **No**

46 Was your vehicle available for use during off-duty hours? . . . . ☐ **Yes**   ☐ **No**

47a Do you have evidence to support your deduction? . . . . ☐ **Yes**   ☐ **No**

b If "Yes," is the evidence written? . . . . ☐ **Yes**   ☐ **No**

Part V	**Other Expenses.** List below business expenses not included on lines 8–26 or line 30.

....		
....		
....		
....		
....		
....		
....		
....		

48	**Total other expenses.** Enter here and on page 1, line 27	48	

Schedule C (Form 1040) 2001

✦

FORM 1040, Schedule C *(Continued)*

Form **8829**	**Expenses for Business Use of Your Home**	OMB No. 1545-1266
	▶ File only with Schedule C (Form 1040). Use a separate Form 8829 for each home you used for business during the year.	**2001**
Department of the Treasury Internal Revenue Service (99)	▶ See separate instructions.	Attachment Sequence No. **66**

Name(s) of proprietor(s) | | Your social security number

Part I   Part of Your Home Used for Business

1	Area used regularly and exclusively for business, regularly for day care, or for storage of inventory or product samples. See instructions	1	
2	Total area of home	2	
3	Divide line 1 by line 2. Enter the result as a percentage	3	%

- For day-care facilities not used exclusively for business, also complete lines 4–6.
- All others, skip lines 4–6 and enter the amount from line 3 on line 7.

4	Multiply days used for day care during year by hours used per day	4		hr.
5	Total hours available for use during the year (365 days × 24 hours). See instructions	5	8,760 hr.	
6	Divide line 4 by line 5. Enter the result as a decimal amount	6		
7	Business percentage. For day-care facilities not used exclusively for business, multiply line 6 by line 3 (enter the result as a percentage). All others, enter the amount from line 3 ▶	7		%

Part II   Figure Your Allowable Deduction

8	Enter the amount from Schedule C, line 29, **plus** any net gain or (loss) derived from the business use of your home and shown on Schedule D or Form 4797. If more than one place of business, see instructions		8	

See instructions for columns (a) and (b) before completing lines 9–20. | (a) Direct expenses | (b) Indirect expenses

9	Casualty losses. See instructions	9				
10	Deductible mortgage interest. See instructions	10				
11	Real estate taxes. See instructions	11				
12	Add lines 9, 10, and 11	12				
13	Multiply line 12, column (b) by line 7		13			
14	Add line 12, column (a) and line 13				14	
15	Subtract line 14 from line 8. If zero or less, enter -0-				15	
16	Excess mortgage interest. See instructions	16				
17	Insurance	17				
18	Repairs and maintenance	18				
19	Utilities	19				
20	Other expenses. See instructions	20				
21	Add lines 16 through 20	21				
22	Multiply line 21, column (b) by line 7		22			
23	Carryover of operating expenses from 2000 Form 8829, line 41		23			
24	Add line 21 in column (a), line 22, and line 23				24	
25	Allowable operating expenses. Enter the **smaller** of line 15 or line 24				25	
26	Limit on excess casualty losses and depreciation. Subtract line 25 from line 15				26	
27	Excess casualty losses. See instructions		27			
28	Depreciation of your home from Part III below		28			
29	Carryover of excess casualty losses and depreciation from 2000 Form 8829, line 42		29			
30	Add lines 27 through 29				30	
31	Allowable excess casualty losses and depreciation. Enter the **smaller** of line 26 or line 30				31	
32	Add lines 14, 25, and 31				32	
33	Casualty loss portion, if any, from lines 14 and 31. Carry amount to **Form 4684**, Section B				33	
34	Allowable expenses for business use of your home. Subtract line 33 from line 32. Enter here and on Schedule C, line 30. If your home was used for more than one business, see instructions ▶				34	

Part III   Depreciation of Your Home

35	Enter the **smaller** of your home's adjusted basis or its fair market value. See instructions	35	
36	Value of land included on line 35	36	
37	Basis of building. Subtract line 36 from line 35	37	
38	Business basis of building. Multiply line 37 by line 7	38	
39	Depreciation percentage. See instructions	39	%
40	Depreciation allowable. Multiply line 38 by line 39. Enter here and on line 28 above. See instructions	40	

Part IV   Carryover of Unallowed Expenses to 2002

41	Operating expenses. Subtract line 25 from line 24. If less than zero, enter -0-	41	
42	Excess casualty losses and depreciation. Subtract line 31 from line 30. If less than zero, enter -0-	42	

For Paperwork Reduction Act Notice, see page 4 of separate instructions.   Cat. No. 13232M   Form **8829** (2001)

✴

FORM 8829

Index

Content Development by Demetra Georgopoulos

DESIGNED TO REINFORCE ESSENTIAL READING SKILLS

GRADE 1

By completing this workbook your child will gain systematic practice in the following reading concepts:

a) Phonics

b) Rhyming Words

c) Following Written Directions

d) Reading Predictable Word Patterns

W9-BRM-253

Color Words

a. Use the color key to color the picture.

red	
purple	
green	
orange	
blue	
yellow	
brown	
black	

Beaver Books Publishing © 2005   Reading Series

Color the Picture

a. Say the name of the things you see in the picture. Follow the directions and color.

Directions:

1. Color the alligator green.
2. Color the small frog pink.
3. Color the owl brown.
4. Color the baby duck red.
5. Color the sun yellow.
6. Color the bear orange.

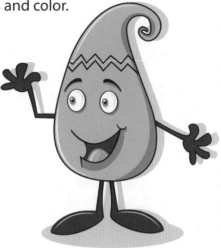

Do you see the cat?   It is on the mat.

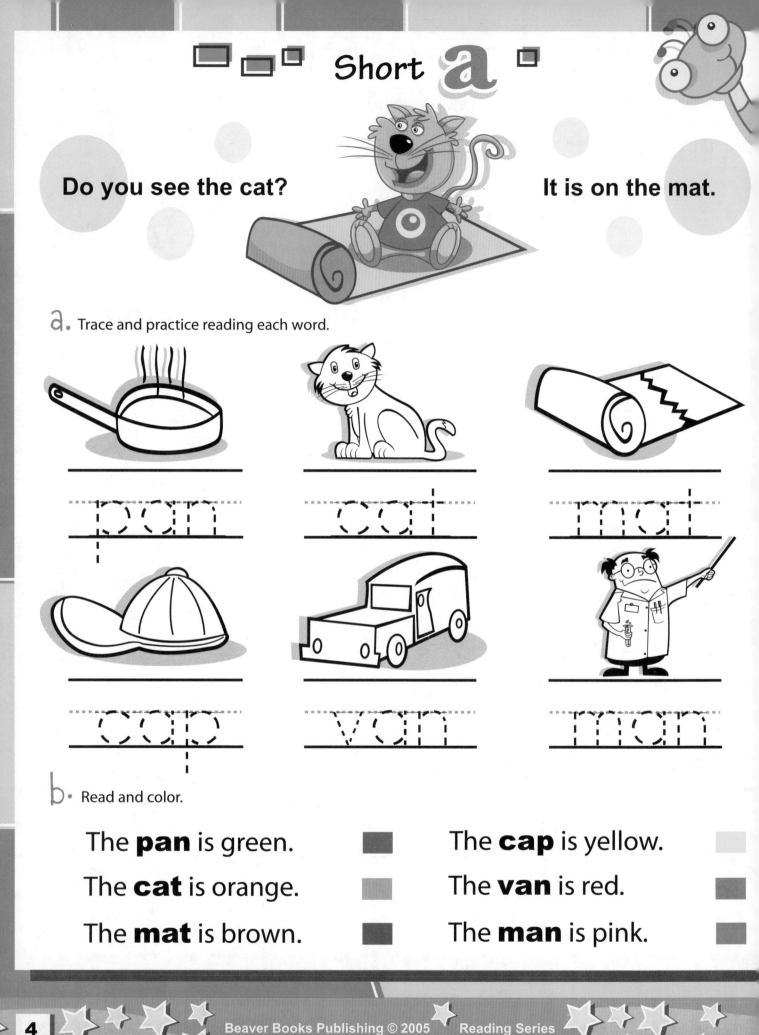

a. Trace and practice reading each word.

pan   cat   mat

cap   van   man

b. Read and color.

The **pan** is green.   The **cap** is yellow.

The **cat** is orange.   The **van** is red.

The **mat** is brown.   The **man** is pink.

Short  e

Do you see the egg?

It is in the nest.

a. Trace and practice reading each word.

jet

bed

egg

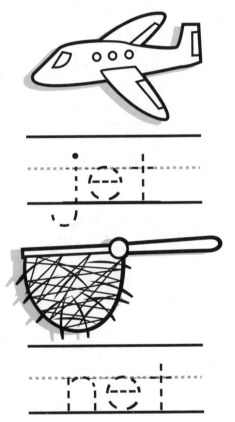

net

nest

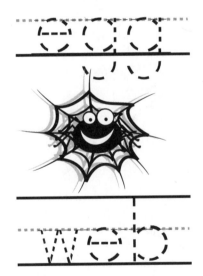

web

b. Read and color.

The **jet** is green. ▮

The **bed** is red. ▮

The **egg** is blue. ▮

The **net** is orange. ▮

The **nest** is brown. ▮

The **web** is black. ▮

Short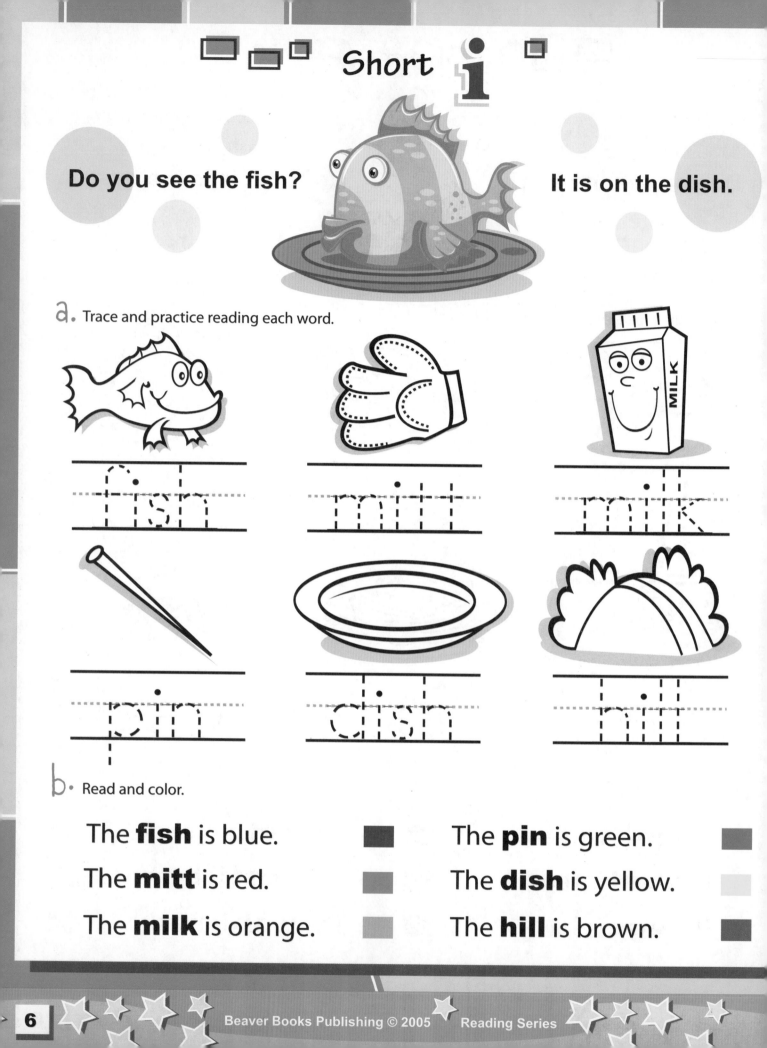

Do you see the fish?   **It is on the dish.**

a. Trace and practice reading each word.

fish   mitt   milk

pin   dish   hill

b. Read and color.

The **fish** is blue.

The **mitt** is red.

The **milk** is orange.

The **pin** is green.

The **dish** is yellow.

The **hill** is brown.

Short  o

Do you see the frog?

It is on the log.

a. Trace and practice reading each word.

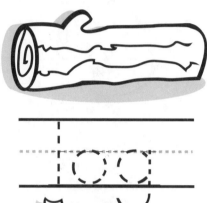

frog

log

sock

doll

dog

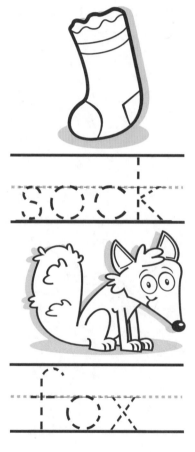

fox

b. Read and color.

The **frog** is green. ▮

The **log** is brown. ▮

The **sock** is orange. ▮

The **doll** is purple. ▮

The **dog** is black. ▮

The **fox** is red. ▮

Do you see the puppy? It is on the rug.

a. Trace and practice reading each word.

puppy bug jug

sun rug tub

b. Read and color.

The **puppy** is pink.

The **bug** is red.

The **jug** is blue.

The **sun** is yellow.

The **rug** is orange.

The **tub** is purple.

Coloring Fun

a. Follow the directions and color.

Use the color key to color the picture.

Color the words with a short **a** sound _____**red**_____ . ■

Color the words with a short **e** sound _____**blue**_____ . ■

Color the words with a short **i** sound _____**pink**_____ . ■

Color the words with a short **o** sound _____**yellow**_____ . □

Color the words with a short **u** sound _____**orange**_____ . ■

bus

hen

bed

jug

box

frog

pig

cat

lip

pan

Long Vowel A

When there is an e at the end of a word, it makes the vowel say it's name.

a. Trace and practice reading each word.

plane   plate   rake

vase   lake   gate

b. Read and color.

The **plane** is green.   The **vase** is red.

The **plate** is orange.   The **lake** is blue.

The **rake** is brown.   The **gate** is yellow.

Long Vowel E

When there is an **e** at the end of a word, it makes the vowel say it's name.

a. Trace and practice reading each word.

ear

tree

leaf

bee

seal

seed

b. Read and color.

The **ear** is pink.

The **tree** is brown.

The **leaf** is green.

The **bee** is yellow.

The **seal** is blue.

The **seed** is red.

Long Vowel I

> When there is an **e** at the end of a word, it makes the vowel say it's name.

a. Trace and practice reading each word.

vine

tie

pie

kite

fire

bike

b. Read and color.

The **vine** is brown. ■

The **tie** is purple. ■

The **pie** is orange. ■

The **kite** is yellow. ■

The **fire** is red. ■

The **bike** is pink. ■

Long Vowel O

When there is an **e** at the end of a word, it makes the vowel say it's name.

a. Trace and practice reading each word.

rose

rope

hose

nose

bone

robe

b. Read and color.

The **rose** is red.

The **rope** is yellow.

The **hose** is orange.

The **nose** is brown.

The **bone** is pink.

The **robe** is green.

Long Vowel U

When there is an **e** at the end of a word, it makes the vowel say it's name.

a. Trace and practice reading each word.

tube   lute   mule

cube   flute   tune

b. Read and color.

The **tube** is black.

The **lute** is yellow.

The **mule** is brown.

The **cube** is red.

The **flute** is blue.

The **tune** is green.

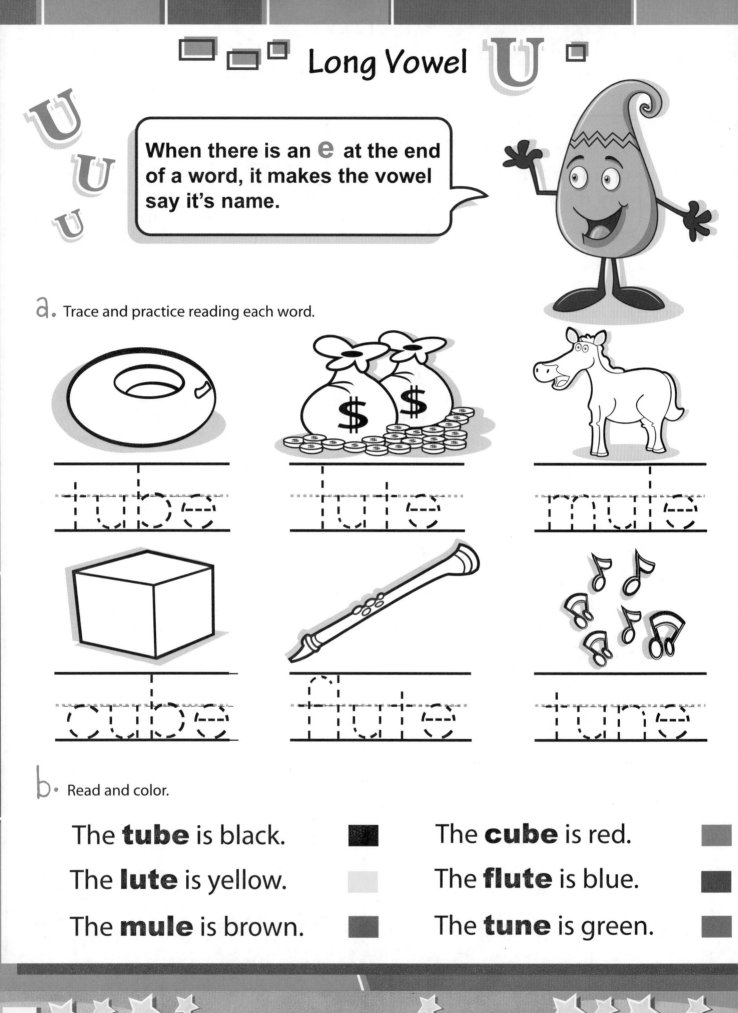

Coloring Fun

a. Follow the directions and color.

Use the color key to color the picture.

Color the words with a long **A** sound _____ . orange ▪

Color the words with a long **E** sound _____ . green ▪

Color the words with a long **I** sound _____ . yellow ▪

Color the words with a long **O** sound _____ . pink ▪

Color the words with a long **U** sound _____ . red ▪

Match the Blends

a. Say the name of each picture. Color the picture that has the same beginning blend.

clock

cat

club

glue

glove

goat

plant

plane

puppy

fly

fish

flag

blouse

bat

block

Beaver Books Publishing © 2005   Reading Series

Match the Blends

a. Say the name of each picture. Color the picture that has the same beginning blend.

truck

train

tub

dress

doll

drum

snail

snake

sun

fruit

frog

fish

star

stamp

sofa

a. Say the name of each picture. Circle the correct beginning digraph.

ch sh th   ch sh th   ch sh th

ch sh th   ch sh th   ch sh th

b. Read and color.

The **shark** is grey.

The **cheese** is yellow.

The **three** is blue.

The **thumb** is pink.

The **church** is red.

The **ship** is orange.

a. Say the name of each picture. Circle the correct ending digraph.

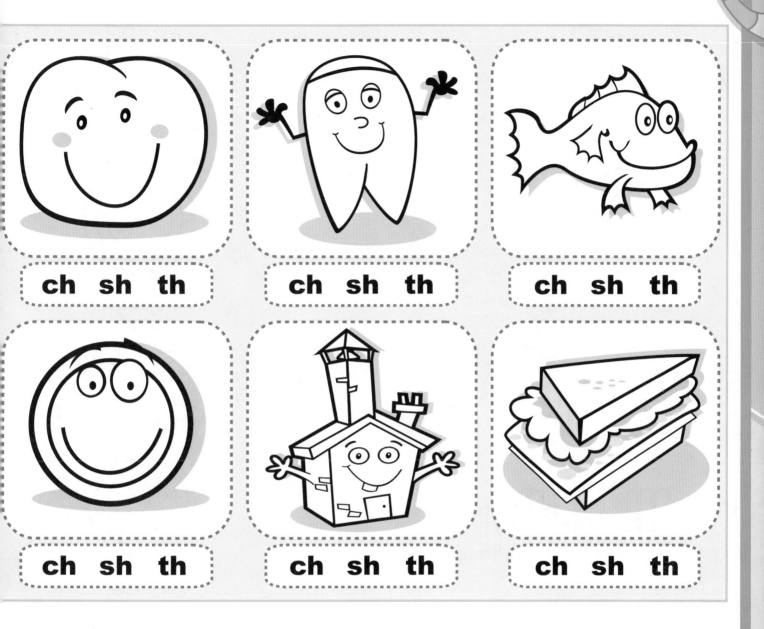

ch sh th   ch sh th   ch sh th

ch sh th   ch sh th   ch sh th

b. Read and color.

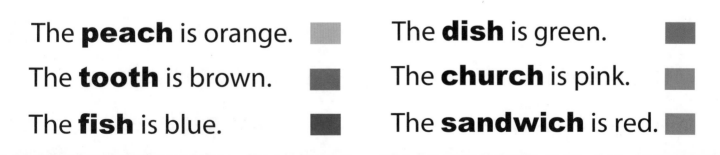

The **peach** is orange.   The **dish** is green.

The **tooth** is brown.   The **church** is pink.

The **fish** is blue.   The **sandwich** is red.

Rhyming Time

a. Draw lines to match the rhyming words.

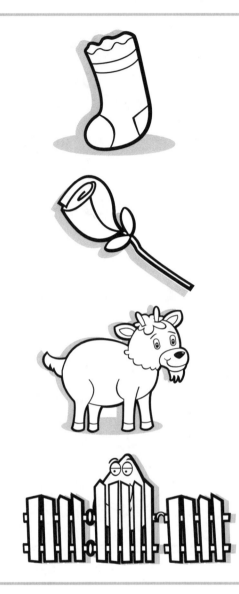

b. Read and color.

The **sock** is orange.	The **nose** is brown.
The **goat** is grey.	The **plate** is green.
The **rose** is pink.	The **boat** is yellow.
The **gate** is blue.	The **clock** is red.

Rhyming Time

a. Draw lines to match the rhyming words.

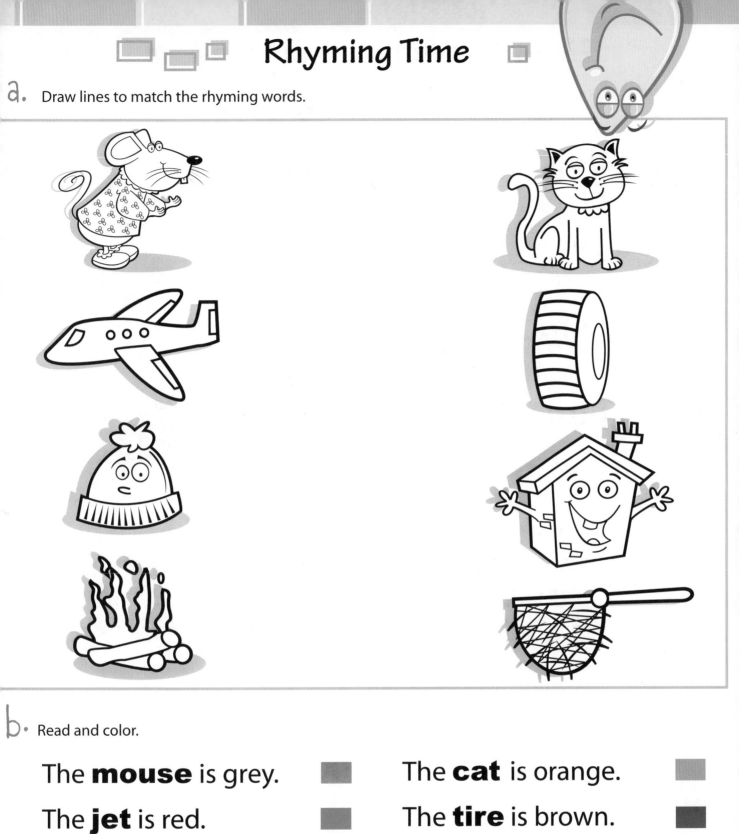

b. Read and color.

The **mouse** is grey.

The **jet** is red.

The **hat** is pink.

The **fire** is yellow.

The **cat** is orange.

The **tire** is brown.

The **house** is green.

The **net** is black.

a. Match the sentence to the correct picture.

I see a dog.

I see a cat.

I see a fish.

I see a bird.

b. What do you see? Draw your own picture.

I see a cat

Match Up

a. Circle the correct sentence that tells what the picture is about.

The cat is on the table. or **The cat is under the table.**

The dog is on the bed. or **The dog is under the bed.**

The fish is in the bowl. or **The fish is out of the bowl.**

Do you have a pet?

What makes your pet special?

Get Ready For Bed

a. Match the sentence to the correct picture. Draw a line to the correct picture.

I put on my pajamas.

I brush my teeth.

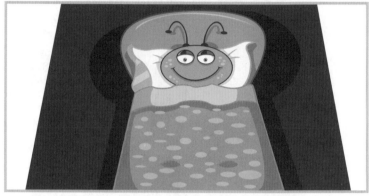

I go to sleep.

I read a story.

Beaver Books Publishing © 2005   Reading Series

Winter Time

Match the sentence to the correct picture. Draw a line to the correct picture.

**I put on my hat.
My hat is blue.**

**I put on my mittens.
My mittens are green.**

**I put on my snowsuit.
My snowsuit is red.**

Peanut Butter and Jam Sandwich

a. Read the recipe.

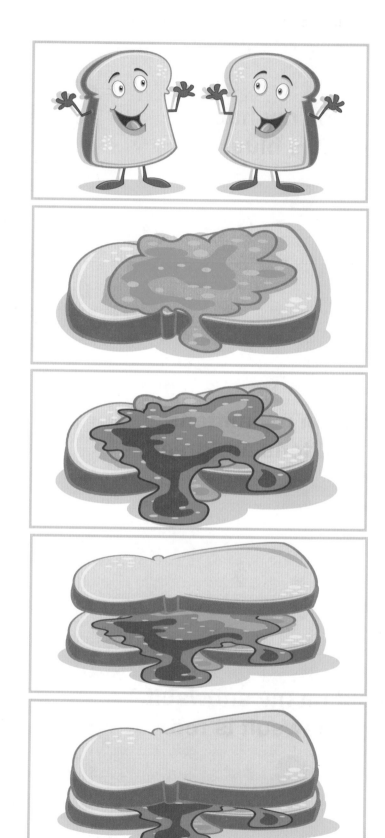

Get two pieces of bread.

Put some peanut butter on one piece of bread.

Put some jam on the peanut butter.

Put the other piece of bread on top.

Eat the peanut butter sandwich.

Sequencing Fun

Recipe reminder.

Help me remember how to make a peanut butter and jam sandwich!

Number the steps from one to five to show how to make a peanut butter and jam sandwich!

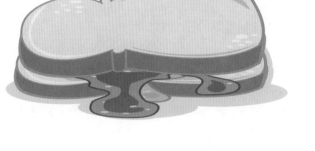

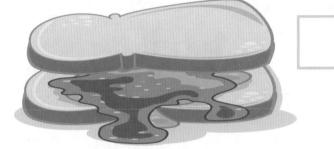

a. Match the sentence to the correct picture. Draw a line to the correct picture.

"I want to play ball",
said the dog.

"I want to play dolls",
said the cat.

"I want to play dressup",
said the fish.

Real or Make Believe?

a. Look at the pictures. Color the pictures that could be real.

This is a dog reading.

This is a bird eating a worm.

This is a talking tree.

What am I?

a. Match the correct description to each picture.

I am red.
I live in the ocean.

I am green.
I live in a pond.

I am yellow.
I live in the sky.

I am orange.
I live in a log.

Beaver Books Publishing © 2005   Reading Series

Following Directions

a. Follow the directions to complete the picture.

Directions:

1. Color the dinosaur green.
2. Color the small dinosaur blue.
3. Color the sun in the sky.
4. Draw three flowers.
5. Color the volcano red.
6. Draw two clouds.

a. Follow the directions to complete the picture.

Directions:

1. Color the big truck red.
2. Color the small car purple.
3. Draw a sun in the sky.
4. Draw three stick people.
5. Color the buildings orange.
6. Draw three clouds.

Color Word Search

a. Find the color words.

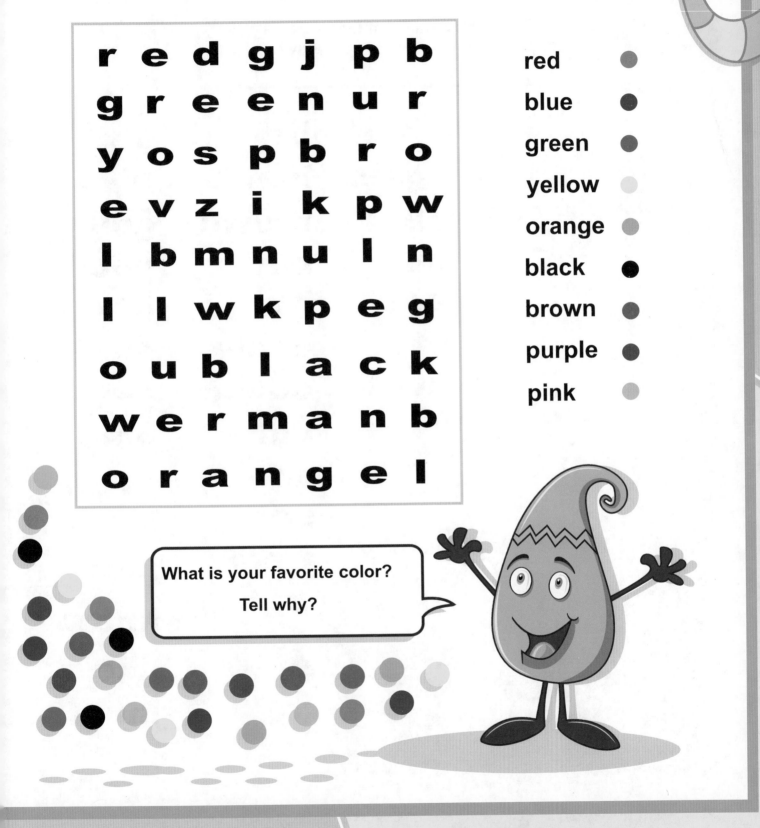

r	e	d	g	j	p	b
g	r	e	e	n	u	r
y	o	s	p	b	r	o
e	v	z	i	k	p	w
l	b	m	n	u	l	n
l	l	w	k	p	e	g
o	u	b	l	a	c	k
w	e	r	m	a	n	b
o	r	a	n	g	e	l

red ●
blue ●
green ●
yellow ●
orange ●
black ●
brown ●
purple ●
pink ●

What is your favorite color?

Tell why?

Everyday Words

a. Practice reading these word out loud.

How many of these words can you spell correctly?

after	be	get
again	black	give
all	brown	going
am	but	good
are	by	have
at	came	he
ate	could	her
	did	him
	do	I
	eat	into
	from	just
		know
		like
		must

Beaver Books Publishing © 2005   Reading Series

Everyday Words

a. Practice reading these word out loud.

new	soon	where
no	stop	when
now	take	white
on	that	who
our	them	will
out	then	with
play	there	yes
please	they	you
pretty	this	
ran	too	
red	under	
saw	want	
say	was	
she	well	
so	went	
some	what	

How many of these words can you spell correctly?